Roberto L. Quercetani

A WORLD HISTORY
OF LONG DISTANCE RUNNING

(1880-2002)
Track Events - Men and Women

SEP
Editrice

Lamine Diack
President, International Association of Athletics Federations
President, International Athletic Foundation

Foreword

The Foundation is once again proud to present
and support the work of the distinguished author,
historian and journalist, Roberto L. Quercetani.

Quercetani's latest work follows a logical
progression in the series of his numerous other
authoritative volumes on the history
of our sport, this time focussing on the
incredible story of long distance running
and some of the discipline's greatest champions.

And once again, Quercetani has managed
to transcend the times and distances
and performances, bringing a human touch
to these stories and details from the past.
In the process, he presents our sport and
its protagonists with the sensitivity and cultural
context they deserve, recognising that
our sport has also had a role in
shaping society in the last century.

In some ways, the long distance runner
symbolises the core values of our sport,
but also represents the basic dilemma
of the human condition.
The struggle, the sacrifice,
the enduring journey of the lone runner
constantly searching to improve and push
the limits of human capability; these challenges
were the same then as they are now.

On behalf of the entire Athletics Family,
I would like to salute my friend and colleague,
Roberto, for his newest achievement
and indelible contribution to the narrative
history of our sport.

Lamine Diack

ACKNOWLEDGEMENTS

We wish to thank the following authorities for their valuable contribution:

International Association of Athletics Federations (IAAF)
International Athletic Foundation (IAF)
Pierre Weiss
Robert J. Fasulo
"Track & Field News", Mountain View, CA
"Athletics International", Stanmore, Middx.
Alain Bouillé, Richard Hymans, Rooney Magnusson,
Giorgio Malisani, Ian R. Smith, Oscar Vecchi, Mel Watman

Text: Roberto L. Quercetani
Graphics: Diego Galbiati
Photolithography: Typecolor (Cassina de Pecchi - Milan)
Printing: Editoriale Ergon (Ronchi dei Legionari - Gorizia)
Produced by: SEP Editrice srl (Cassina de Pecchi - Milan)

Picture acknowledgements: All Sport Photographic (UK), Roberto L. Quercetani

PRINTED IN ITALY - July 2002

ISBN 88-87110-34-4

CONTENTS

MEN:

WOMEN:

INTRODUCTION

by Roberto L. Quercetani

The longest track events on the Olympic programme – 5000 and 10,000 metres – symbolize man's most beautiful challenge in terms of endurance-to-speed. Of course, challenging distance is tantamount to challenging fatigue: in this respect man's task has not changed much vis-à-vis the early days of modern athletics, except that contemporary training in its various forms and with the support of science applied to sport has been instrumental in pushing farther man's resistance to swift rhythms. Even so, endurance to suffering remains an unavoidable factor.

From a physiological viewpoint the 5000 and 10,000 metres belong to a very large extent to the aerobic sphere of running, which depends on oxygen intake, as opposed to anaerobic (without oxygen) running. Ken Doherty, a former U.S. decathlete and later an internationally known coach and author, gives in this respect the following percentages:

	Aerobic needs	Anaerobic needs
5000m	90 %	10 %
10,000m	95 %	5 %

The resulting situation is quite the opposite of what occurs in short distance events, which belong almost entirely to the anaerobic sphere. In the long races there is a stringent necessity to wisely distribute one's energies over the entire distance. Uniform pace would therefore appear to be a must. As in all ventures involving human beings, however, deviations from pure theory are quite common, more so in "hot" competitive races characterized by sudden bursts of speed, especially in the closing stage. This occurs, less frequently that's true, even in "cold" races, as are most if not all record attempts.

The purpose of this book is to retrace the history of the 5000 and 10,000 metres from the pioneer days of English distance runners - who used to run over the somewhat shorter 3 and 6 miles (= 4,828.04 m. and 9.656.07 m. respectively) – till present-day African marvels. Quite obviously, particular attention has been given to the "tenors" who towered above their contemporaries, from Alfred Shrubb of Great Britain all the way down to Haile Gebrselassie of Ethiopia. That is, to the men who made history for their competitive deeds and clock-wise as well. But I also tried to supply a connective tissue apt to do justice to many other runners who were also prominent at one time or another. Wherever possible, I tried to supply full details, such as intermediate times, for every record-breaking race as well as for other races in which major titles were at stake.

The map of long distance running has changed considerably, particularly in the past two decades. In the early days of modern athletics and throughout the first half of the 20th century most of the great distance runners came from the British Isles and Scandinavia, and chiefly from Finland. In later years several champion runners from other continents managed to enter the picture. Oceania, for example, was particularly prominent in the Sixties. Africa was a late comer, chiefly because of political and economic factors which have delayed its social development even in the domain of sport. But champions like Kipchoge Keino of Kenya eventually acted as trail blazers. This gave rise to what I chose to call "The African Wave", which really turned the tide. In recent years Europe has been gradually but inexorably outshone, as can be seen from the following table, which tells how the top 20 in World Year Lists were divided by continents at given intervals and in 2001.

5000 metres

Year	Africa	Europe	No.America	So.& Centr.America	Asia	Oceania
1920	-	16	4	-	-	-
1940	-	19	1	-	-	-
1960	1	16	1	-	-	2
1980	7	10	2	-	-	1
1990	7	11	2	-	-	-
2000	18	2	-	-	-	-
2001	18	2	-	-	-	-

10,000 metres

Year	Africa	Europe	No.America	So.&Centr.America	Asia	Oceania
1920	-	18	2	-	-	-
1940	-	19	-	1	-	-
1960	1	13	1	-	-	5
1980	4	9	2	-	3	2
1990	6	10	4	-	-	-
2000	17	2	1	-	-	-
2001	15	1	3	-	1	-

As if the above figures were not self-explanatory, one could remark that the two lone European entries for 5000 metres anno 2000 were Mohammed Mourhit of Belgium and Ismail Sghyr of France, both Moroccan at birth!

Several countries contribute to Africa's striking force: Kenya, Ethiopia, Morocco, Algeria, Burundi, Rwanda, Zimbabwe and South Africa. The lion's share belongs to Kenya, whose inexhaustible reservoir of distance talents reminds one of the equally strong impact little Finland used to have in this department in the years between the two World Wars. Observers from sundry countries of the globe - coaches, newspaper-men and even physiologists - have visited Kenya in recent years just to understand how a relatively small country of less than 30 million people, with few synthetic tracks, a limited number of qualified coaches and virtually no programme of sport medicine can produce so many outstanding talents in one of track's most popular departments. May I quote from the book "Kenya Track and Field" which was offered to the press at a recent edition of the World Championships: "Far from the laboratory and microscope, the origins of Kenyan success are found on the bare feet of Kenyan children who walk or run through the bush to school. Many make a second trip for lunch, totalling 10 to 15 kilometres a day. They run at an altitude of 1700 to 2700 metres in the lush mountain region of Western Kenya known as the Great Rift Valley". Ethiopia and Morocco may not have the same overflow of talent, yet they have exhibited topnotch performers on several occasions.

Men like Keino, Aouita and Gebrselassie have generated a strong spirit of emulation in their respective countries. With the medium of scholarships, mainly granted by U.S. colleges, or comparably advantageous situations offered by European clubs, many Africans have been able to use their athletic ability as a vehicle towards social and economic progress. Similar developments, even under partly different forms, may spring up in other parts of the world and thereby contribute to a further enlargement of the map of distance running.

Between 1912 - when the IAAF first introduced an official list of world records – and today, top performances have been bettered time and again. Here is a comparison of world records for the classic distance events as they were 90 years ago and as they are now, with the corresponding Kms./hour average speed: 5000 metres – 14:36.6 (20,533 Kms/ hr) and 12:39.36 (23,704 Kms/hr); 10,000 metres – 31:20.8 (19,140 Kms/hr) and 26:22.75 (22,745 Kms/hr). Of course I know that trying to compare champions and records from different epochs is an absurd game, considering how many factors have changed through the years. The running surfaces of our time are much faster than those on which Paavo Nurmi or even Emil Zátopek used to compete. Present-day training methods, largely studied through a scientific lens, cannot be compared with the empiric ones prevailing fifty or more years ago. Last but by no means least, international competition is far more intense now than it was at any previous time in the past. Economic incentives introduced in recent years have altered the philosophy of the sport in several ways. As a result of all this, it is advisable to value a champion only on the yardstick of his time. Even so, the above mentioned differences in record times and general standards as well, are so great that one can hardly escape the conclusion that the present generation of champion athletes is in all probability the strongest ever.

Women entered the picture of long distance running only two or three decades ago, at least in terms of international competition. I have tried to trace the history of their progress too. Races over 5000 and 10,000 metres were added to their programme just recently – for many years the prevailing distance event in their ranks was the 3000 metres. The advances of the distaff side in this department have been truly amazing: present-day world records for the classic distances (14:28.09 and 29:31.78) compare favourably, clock-wise at least, with some of the record marks made by the male sex in the first half of the 20th century. And nobody can say what the future is likely to bring.

Roberto L. Quercetani

NOTE:

All times are given as originally taken, i.e. with fractions of a second in halves, quarters, fifths, tenths or - in the era of automatic timing - hundredths. Kilometre fractions for world record races - unless otherwise specified - are for the leader at any given stage.

FROM PREHISTORY TO ALFRED SHRUBB, STANDARD-BEARER OF 20TH CENTURY GREATS

Intuition has it that long distance running had a choice role in the moving activities of man since time immemorial. Simply to go from one place to another, the whale of a distance apart, but also for the benefit of sheer amusement. Even nowadays we have living examples in this respect: in many African countries there are many boys who cover long distances on foot to go to school and come back. This form of "natural conditioning" may well be one of the reasons behind the so-called "African Wave" which has recently submerged runners from economically developed countries, where the use and abuse of modern means of transportation seems to have reduced the moving activity of man.

In the Olympic, Pythian, Isthmian and Nemean Games of the ancient Greeks the "dolichos" was the longest running event. At Olympia it was first included in the programme in 720 B.C. The race was won by Akanthos of Sparta. Tale has it that in 328 B.C. Ageas of Argos, winner of the "dolichos" at the Olympic Games during the morning hours, immediately after the event he set off and ran all day, arriving at Argos in the evening to announce his victory to fellow citizens. He was thus able to run approximately 110 kilometres in one day.

The length was 20 stades, i.e. 3,845.40 metres. In other venues the "dolichos" varied from 7 to 24 stades (1,346 to 4,614 metres). According to ancient writers, it was inspired by the performances of the "dromokerykes" or "hemerodromoi", professional messengers who carried dispatches over great distances, particularly during times of war.

There were no doubt outstanding distance runners even in more remote civilizations. For example, the Tarahumara Indians of Mexico were famous for their endurance feats.

The dawn of long distance running in modern times is usually identified with "Pedestrianism", which was practised in the British Isles from the 17th to the 19th century. It was a mixed type of activity described as "go as you please", in the sense that competitors were free to alternate running and walking. These were professional contests, mostly over long distances. A famous book, "Pedestrianism" by Walter Thom, published in 1813, is largely dedicated to the feats of Capt. Robert Barclay Allardyce, a celebrated pedestrian of the early 1800's. His fame was chiefly earned in 1809 when he walked a thousand miles in 1,000 hours on Newmarket Heath for a wager of 1,000 guineas. In the words of a knowledgeable observer, though, "such a feat was more a sleep-denying performance than an athletic one", as a quick calculation will confirm. Thom's book also contained ranking lists of notable performances of the 18th century and early 19th century. Among them is a 9:45 for 2 miles (3,218.69 m.) and 21:00 for 4 miles (6,437.40 m.) by Joseph Headley from Yorkshire in 1777 and a rather dubious 4:10 for one mile (1,609.35 m.) by John Todd, a Scotchman, on a course from Hyde Park Corner to the first milestone on the Uxbridge Road.

Deerfoot, the fleet-footed Indian

Most famous in the United States was Lewis Bennett, an Indian of the Seneca tribe, born on the Cattaraugus Reservation in Erie County, New York, "around 1830". This well-built athlete (1.79 m. / 73 kg.) became an attraction on both sides of the Atlantic. Known as "Deerfoot" for his smooth and fleet running style, he used to run in the traditional costume of his tribe, which endeared him to spectators, especially in England. Shrewd observers occasionally ventured the opinion that some of his opponents had been bribed to lose – a possibility that cannot be ruled out altogether, although it should be remembered that in those days a brave young man from the "New World" was likely to be regarded with a grain of jealousy by English traditionalists, probably overlooking the fact that the Seneca tribe had sided with the British Army during the American War of Independence. Bennett's most significant feat was a one-hour record of 18,589 metres, made in London in 1863 – an achievement that was to remain unsurpassed for 34 years among "pros" and for 41 years among amateurs. It is to be noted that the race was over 12 miles (19,312,20 m.). At the end of it "Deerfoot" "lost" by 1 yard to William Lang, who had a 100-yard start. The latter (born on 22 December 1838, 1.74 m. / 62 kg.) beat Bennett on other occasions and on 1 August 1863 at Manchester he ran 2 miles in 9:11 1/2, another record that was to stand for forty years. In this race Lang, an innkeeper known as the "Crow Catcher", had 1-mile fractions of 4:27 and 4:44 1/2. His most glorious day, however, was when he was matched against William Richards of Wales in a widely heralded 1-mile race at Manchester in 1865. The contest ended in a tie as both runners went home together in 4:17 1/4, a world record that stood among "pros" for 16 years. The two locked horns

again in a run-off seven days later and Lang won in 4:22.0.

Another great British runner of that period was John ("Jack") White, a tiny runner from Gateshead (born on 1 March 1838; 1.58 m./ 49 kg.), who on 11 May 1863 in London broke the half-hour barrier for 6 miles with 29:50.0 and went on to reach 10 miles in 52:14.0, beating Lang and "Deerfoot" among others. The latter retired at 3 miles. Lang was second at 6 miles in 29:50 1/5 but dropped out after 7 miles. Remarkable running on a narrow 260 yards (237.74 m.) cinder track. White ran at a steadily decreasing speed, as can be gathered from 1-mile splits: 4:40, 4:59, 4:57, 5:00, 5:04 and 5:10.

Throughout the 19th century professionals invariably outshone their amateur counterparts. But then these were different worlds thriving in different atmospheres. Generally , the "pros" had good economic incentives and .... looser rules too. Amateur athletics was born under strict rules and received the backing of influential personalities. In the long run, these factors turned the tide in its favour, namely in the latter part of the 19th century.

Noteworthy 2-mile performances were turned in by such excellent amateurs as William Slade, 9:42.0 in 1876, and William Snook, 9:33 2/5 in 1881. James Gibb, the man who introduced ping-pong in Great Britain, ran 3 miles in 14:46.0 and 6 miles in 32:07.0, both in 1877. James Warburton, known as "Choppy" for his short, irregular strides, was credited with 31:12 1/2 for 6 miles in 1879. But one had to wait a few more years to see an amateur finally capable of reaching and eventually surpassing in stature the best "pros". The man in question was a frail, willowy type, Walter Goodall George (born at Caine, Wiltshire, on 9 September 1858; 1.80 m. / 61 kg.). He practised cycling and football before laying all his eggs in the basket of athletics. Shortly before turning 20 he ran a mile, off 45 yards (41.14 m.), in 4:29.0. The following year, 1879, he won the mile in 4:26 1/5 and 4 miles in 20:51 4/5 at the English Championships, organized by the Amateur Athletic Club. In 1880 this meeting was held under the auspices of the Amateur Athletic Association and was the first in a long series which in the early decades of the 20th century was to develop into a major international event. George won no less than 10 titles at these Championships – at distances ranging from 880 yards to 10 miles. In 1884, his best year, he chalked up the following times, all of which were amateur bests:

1 mile, 4:18 2/5 at Birmingham on 21 June
2 miles, 9:17 2/5 at Stamford Bridge, London on 26 April (handicap race; halves of 4:32 4/5 and 4:44 3/5)
3 miles, 14:39.0 at Stamford Bridge on 17 May (handicap race; 1-mile fractions: 4:42 2/5, 4:55.0, 5:01 3/5)
6 miles, 30:21 1/2 at Stamford Bridge on 28 July (handicap race; 1-mile fractions: 4:45 3/5, 4:59 2/5, 5:07.0, 5:07 4/5, 5:08.0, 5:13.7)
10 miles, 51:20.0 at Stamford Bridge on 7 April (handicap race)
18,555 m. in 1 hour, at Stamford Bridge on 28 July (handicap race)
George was said to have run 10 miles in 49:29.0 in a training run.

His fame eventually caught the eye of American promoters and in 1882 he was invited to New York for three match races against Lon Myers, the only living man who was thought capable of holding his own against the Briton. This was the first chapter of a long feud which was to end in Australia in 1887, well after both had turned "pro". Out of nine clashes, the American won six and George three. It should be pointed out that their compass varied – Myers was able to do well from 100 yards to 1 mile, his strongest point being at 440 and 880 yards, whereas George's range went from 880 yards to 1-hour running. Therefore it was not easy to find a meeting point likely to suit both. Their clashes over a five-year period (1882-87) were at distances ranging from 880 yards to 1 mile. The George vs. Myers rivalry was in the opinion of many observers the highlight of athletics in the 19th century. George, a pharmacist by profession, was at times in financial difficulties during his amateur years. After he swept all before him on the British amateur scene, he turned his attention to the "other world", that of professionalism, where a Scotsman by the name of William Cummings reigned supreme. The

The mythical Deerfoot, a Seneca Indian who was the "Hero of two Worlds" in long distance running.

14

Walter George (GB), left, and Lon Myers (USA), two legendary figures in the latter part of the 19th century.

16

latter had been credited with 4:16 1/5 for the mile in 1881, and George badly wanted to meet him. In an attempt to preserve his amateur status, he applied to the AAA for permission to race Cummings on the following basis: half the gate money to be donated to an infirmary and the other half to be handed over to Cummings. But the AAA, as was to be expected, decided to turn down George's request, on the grounds that according to their rules an amateur could not compete with a professional. At that stage George decided to turn "pro". His most famous clashes with Cummings were over 1 mile. George won with 4:20 1/5 in 1885 and with 4:12 3/4 in 1886. The latter mark was to remain unsurpassed till 1915. The two locked horns on several other occasions. Notable among these was a 10 mile race at Stamford Bridge on 28 September 1885 in which Cummings bettered Bennett's record with 51:06 3/5, with George a distant second in 52:17.0.

Montague Shearman, the most famous athletics historian of the 19th century, described George as a man who in his training had a "semi-professional" approach. He was ahead of his time in this respect as he had a training run every day, the distance ranging from 300 yards to a mile. Although, as an apostle of moderation, he never ran all out, except perhaps in time trials which he used as pre-race tests. His chief aim was to preserve his physical well-being all along. He is viewed by some modern observers as a precursor of the "Fartlek" training methods, advocated by Gösta Holmér of Sweden in the early Forties of the 20th century. Be it as it may, he preserved his good health throughout the greater part of his career and long afterwards. He died at 85.

His Scottish rival William Jeffrey Cummings (born at Paisley on 10 June 1858) was a man of medium build (1.70 m. / 56 kg.) who embarked on an uncertain career as a "pro" when he was barely 18. He earned his early fame as a miler, but he was ultimately at his best over longer distances, as his above-mentioned victory over George in a 10-mile race aptly demonstrated.

No matter if George was the most gifted distance runner of his time, several others also deserve to be mentioned. Sidney Thomas, a pupil of Jack White, was credited with 14:24.0 for 3 miles (London, 3 June 1893) and 30:17 4/5 for 6 miles (London, 22 October 1892), both of which were still amateur bests at the end of the 19th century. Other outstanding athletes were James Kibblewhite, who won six AAA titles between 1889 and 1892 at distances ranging from 1 to 10 miles; and Fred Bacon, who as a "pro" crowned a great career with a new 1-hour record: 18,747 metres at Rochdale on 19 June 1897, thereby succeeding "Deerfoot" as record holder. As an amateur he had won 5 AAA titles in 1993-95, three of which at 1 mile. Just before the turn of the century, however, he lost his 1-hour record to Harry Watkins, who covered 18,878 metres stll at Rochdale on 16 September 1899. While enroute, Watkins reached 10 miles in 51:05 1/5, eclipsing Cummings' 14-year-old record.

At the turn of the century all best-on-record performances for the long distances were held by "pros". But, as previously related, there were men – like George, Bacon and others – who first blossomed in the amateur ranks and later reached their peak, clockwise at least, while in the "pro" ranks.

"Metric" continentals off to a slow start

The earliest attempts over 5000 and 10,000 metres date from the last decade of the 19th century. They were made by continental Europeans and were far below the standard achieved by the same time by British runners. For history's sake one should mention a couple of marks made by French amateurs: 9:18 1/5 for 3000 metres by Henri Deloge in Paris on 22 October 1899, enroute to a 4000 metre tape; and 16:29 1/5 for 5000 metres by Georges Touquet-Daunis at Lyons on 22 May 1899. The fastest 10,000 metre mark of the 19th century is generally credited to Walter George, actually an intermediate time of 31:40.0 taken at 6 1/4 miles (= 10,058 m.), enroute to a 12-miles tape (London, 28 July 1884).

The superiority of British distance runners was confirmed at the 1900 Olympics in

Paris. (At the inaugural edition of the Games – Athens 1896 – the longest track event was 1500 metres). This was in a team race over 5000 metres, run on a 500 m. circuit at Croix-Catelan. Great Britain and France were the only entrants. The former won and Charles Bennett was the fastest finisher in 15:29 1/5 – not 15:20.0 as given in most reference sources. His countryman John Rimmer was second in 15:35 1/2 and Henri Deloge of France third in 15:42.0. Bennett (born on 28 December 1870) was an engine driver and could point to 5 AAA titles at distances ranging from 1 to 10 miles.

Scandinavian distance runners, who were to play a major role in the early decades of the 20th century, happened to be just "round the corner" by the time of the Paris Olympics. The Finns introduced 5000 and 10,000 metres in their championship programme in 1909 and 1908 respectively. The Swedes had started earlier, with a championship race over 10,000 metres in 1896, but with mediocre marks.

Alf Shrubb, distance runner nonpareil

At the start of the 20th century a bright new star graced the tracks of Great Britain. The man in question was Alfred Shrubb (born at Slinfold, Sussex, on 12 December 1878).

Although not very impressive in physical build (1.69 m. / 54 kg.), he was endowed with great endurance. In his excellent book "History of British Athletics" Mel Watman evokes Shrubb's story in the following terms: "He could thank a stack of blazing straw for his introduction to athletics. One evening he heard the clanging of a firebell and together with a member of Horsham Blue Star Harriers who happened to be passing, he ran three miles to the scene of the fire. The athlete was impressed by the running of his companion – who was dressed in his working clothes and heavy boots – and persuaded him to join the local club". That was in 1898 and Shrubb's earliest honours date from 1901, when he won the first in a series of ten AAA titles – in a 10 mile race. Here is the detailed story of his victories in this meeting. They were to remain his greatest competitive achievements, because he never got a chance to compete in the Olympic Games.

1901: 1st in the 4 miles , 20:01 4/5 and in the 10 miles, 53:32.

1902: 1st in the 4 miles, 20:01 2/5 and in the 10 miles, 52:25 2/5.

1903: 1st in the mile, 4:24.0, in the 4 miles, 20:06, and in the 10 miles, 51:55 4/5

1904: 1st in the mile, 4:22.0, in the 4 miles, 19:56 4/5 and in the 10 miles, 54:30 2/5. (The AAA Championships were traditionally held in the first weekend of July, except for the 10 mile event, which was contested at an earlier date)

**Amenities vintage 1900:
an Olympian at 60, 100, 200 and .....quasi 5000 metres**

Among the many oddities supplied by the earliest editions of the Olympic Games here is one that certainly deserves a choice place. The British squad that won the 5000 metre team race in Paris (1900) consisted of four Britons and one Australian. The latter, 23-year-old Stanley Rowley, was actually ..... a sprinter. In his own business he did very well in those Games as he finished third in all sprint events: 60, 100 and 200 metres. Such was his devotion to sport that he also volunteered to help the British in the afore-mentioned 5000 metre team race as a "space-filler". Bill Mallon, the great Olympic historian, tells the story behind known stories. He says that Rowley was allowed to stop after running only seven laps of the 500-metre track (hence 3,500 metres) as he was hopelessly behind the other runners, who had all finished. Officials awarded him ten points for ... finishing in tenth place. But as a member of the winning team he was an Olympic victor, thereby reaping in that race more than he had actually achieved in the sprints. In his own country Rowley was known as an outstanding performer. He won Australasian titles in the sprints in 1897 (10.0 in the 100 y. and 22.4 in the 220 y.) and 1899 (9.9 and 22.2).

Shrubb had a deceptively short (5 ft. / 1.52 m.) stride and excelled on the track and in cross-country running. In the latter he won four English championship titles and led England to victory in the first two editions (1903 and '04) of the International Cross-Country Championships, a competition initially limited to England, Scotland, Wales and Ireland, which began to be worthy of its title in 1907, when France joined the parade. In later years more and more countries entered the picture and the event actually became a sort of world championship, a title officially recognised by the IAAF in 1973.

In 1903 Shrubb conquered two world amateur records: 9:11.0 (Ilford, 30 May) for 2 miles and 14:17 3/5 for 3 miles (London, 21 May). The latter was one of the earliest marks officially ratified by the IAAF in its first convention in 1913 . Shrubb had his golden year in 1904, when he set the following amateur records (listed in chronological order):

London, 12 May: 5 miles n 24:33 2/5
Glasgow, 11 June: 2 miles in 9:09 3/5, with the following half-mile fractions: 2:06, 2:21, 2:31 2/5 and 2:11 1/5. The 1-mile fractions (4:27 and 4:42 3/5) would suggest a clearly decelerating rhythm, but if we sum up the first and last 880 y. fractions we reach a surprising total of 4:17 1/5, only slightly worse than the British 1-mile record of the time, 4:16 4/5 by Joe Binks in the 1902 AAA Championhips.

Glasgow, 13 June: 4 miles in 19:23 2/5.
Abergavenny, 27 August: 3 miles in 14:17 1/5 (not submitted for approval).
Glasgow, 5 November: 11 3/4 miles in 60:32 1/5. Enroute he set the following records: 6 miles in 29:59 2/5, 7 miles in 35:04 3/5, 8 miles in 40:16.0, 9 miles in 45:27 3/5, 10 miles in 50:40 3/5, 11 miles in 56:23 2/5, 18,742 Km. in one hour. He was timed in 31:02 2/5 at 6 1/4 miles (=10,058.41 m.), which was tantamount to a new 10,000 metres record but was not ratified by the AAA, which simply ignored metric distances. The event was a "sealed" handicap, in which Shrubb's 13 opponents received starts ranging from 1 to 6 minutes. In this race, easily his greatest ever, Shrubb set off at a rather hot pace (first quarter in 64 4/5). One by one he caught all his opponents but obviously had to slow down gradually. His main target was George's 10-mile record (51:20.0), which he simply annihilated. When it was all over he was hoisted shoulder high from the track by enthusiastic spectators. As he later recalled, he was inspired during his long Odyssey by the skirl of bagpipes.

British milers from the first decade of the 20th century: E.L.Gay-Roberts leading from Alfred Shrubb and Joe Binks. Shrubb was the first great distance man of the century.

Successful and unsuccessful attempts

The date of Alfred Shrubb's most successful record attempts (5 November) has a distinct historical significance, even if not related to sport. It coincides with the celebration of Guy Fawkes Day, which recalls the famous Gunpowder Plot, the name given to a conspiracy for blowing up King James I and the British Parliament on 5 November 1605. Guy Fawkes was the central figure in the conspiracy, which was conceived as a reply to anti-Roman Catholic laws applied by the king. About 1 ton 12 cwt. of gunpowder concealed in a vault under the House of Lords was to act as the medium, but the attempt failed beforehand when one of the conspirators, through an anonymous letter, brought the plan to the knowledge of one of the would-be victims. Guy Fawkes, then 35, was arrested and finally executed in 1606. Ironically enough, Fawkes was the offspring of a Protestant couple but became a Catholic after his mother joined the Roman Catholic faith in connection with her second marriage. In Britain the anniversary of the discovery of the plot is still celebrated on Guy Fawkes' day (5 November) by fireworks and bonfires, and the carrying of "guys" through the streets.

Great Britain did not send a team to St.Louis for the 1904 Olympics and Shrubb was thus denied world-wide recognition, were it only in the eyes of casual posterity. The longest track event on the programme of the Games was the 1500 metres, which was won by John Lightbody of USA in 4:05 2/5, a new world record but certainly not comparable to the fastest times of British and American milers of those days. Lightbody, a versatile runner, had won the 800 metres in 1:56.0 two days earlier – all of this on a very poor track. In 1905 Shrubb went Down Under and spent several months touring Australasia. His non-stop involvement caught the eye of the AAA and in October of that year he was declared a professional. Shrubb continued to run as a "pro" for several years with remarkable success, even though he never again attained his peaks of 1904. A long time after that, namely in 1953, the AAA curiously reinstated him. He ran a road race when well in his eighties and passed away in Canada on 23 April 1964. In his book "Running and Cross-Country Running", published in 1908, he gave detailed information on his training in the 30-days period before his D-Day (Glasgow, 5 November 1904). He would usually have one and very often two sessions per day at distances ranging from 2 to 8 miles. In said period, however, he allowed himself 10 days of rest. His pace varied from "fairly slow" to "goodish". Shrubb had a habit of checking his net weight every day: in the period concerned it varied from 55.5 to 53.5 kilograms. As for his running strategy, he summarized it thus: "I made certain through training that I could stay the entire race in the lead". A seemingly simple recipe but one requiring great mental and physical strength. In 1908 he raced 10 miles against a relay team of 5 well-known American athletes each running 2 miles, and won in what was described as one of the most remarkable feats in track history. In the above-mentioned book Shrubb, ever the good patriot, also says: "The Briton has, I am convinced, a far greater stamina, as has been proved over and over again by our superiority in long distance races". Nowadays somebody could possibly air similar views about Kenyan or Ethiopian runners ....

Most of Shrubb's records withstood all assaults for a long time. His 6-mile mark was first to be bettered - in 1911. His 10-mile mark was the most durable as it was broken only in 1928. Surely his chief merit lay in assuring the coming-of-age of amateur runners vis-à-vis their "pro" colleagues. He was coached by Harry Andrews in the first two years of his career, and self-coached thereafter.

Low-profile competition in the Olympics

As previously mentioned, the longest track event at the 1904 Olympics in St.Louis was the 1500 metres. There was, however, a 4-

mile team race in which the fastest time was 21:17 4/5 by Arthur Newton of USA. A modest performance indeed, if compared with Alfred Shrubb's 19:56 4/5 at the AAA Championships earlier in the same year.

In 1906 Athens was given a chance to celebrate the tenth anniversary of the inaugural edition of the modern Olympics, held there in 1896. This was obviously a break of the 4-year interval adopted by the IOC, who accepted the change with some reluctance. In later years, however, official Olympic records degraded the 1906 festival to the rank of unofficial ("intercalated") Olympic Games. Be it as it may, the 1906 affair excelled its official predecessors in more than one way and I tend to agree with those who think that it may have helped save the Olympic movement, which was in desperate straits after the sloppy editions of 1900 and 1904.

The only long distance event of the 1906 Games was over 5 miles, with a strong field of 13 competitors. It was won by a qualified runner from England, Henry Hawtrey, who in the above-mentioned 1-mile race at the 1902 AAA Championhips had given Joe Binks, the eventual winner in British record time (4:16 4/5), a good race for his money, finishing only 2 yards behind. Hawtrey (born on 29 June 1882) won easily, leaving runner-up John Svanberg of Sweden 50 metres behind. Details:

Athens, 25 April 1906– 5 miles (8,046.75 m.): 1.Henry Hawtrey (GB) 26:11 4/5, 2.John Svanberg (Sweden) 26:19 2/5, 3.Edvard Dahl (Sweden) 26:26 1/5, 4.George Bonhag (USA), 5.Pericle Pagliani (Ita), 6.George Blake (Aus). John Daly (Ire) finished third a few centimetres ahead of Edvard Dahl but was disqualified for obstructing the Swede in the homestretch.

Two years later at the London Olympics the 5-mile race was again the only long distance event on the track programme. Easy winner was a Briton of German descent, Emil Voigt, a 26-year-old runner who a couple of weeks earlier had won the 4 miles at the AAA Championships in 19:47 2/5, a new meet record. Among his opponents in London was Charles Hefferon of South Africa, who ten days later was to finish second in the marathon race immortalized by the "case" of Italy's Dorando Pietri. Details:

London, 14 July 1908 – 5 miles (8,046.75 m.): 1.Emil Voigt (GB) 25:11 1/5, 2. Edward Owen (GB) 25:24.0, 3.John Svanberg (Swe) 25:37 1/5, 4.Charles Hefferon (SA) 25:44.0, 5.Archie Robertson (GB 26 :13.0, 6.Frederick Meadows (Can).

In these Games there was also a 3-mile team race which was won, predictably enough, by Great Britain. The fastest time, 14:39 3/5, was returned by Joe Deakin. This runner was 26 at the time, but was to remain at it for many more years, as related in the adjoining aside.

By that time other European countries were awakening to the fascinating game of long distance running. Sweden should be mentioned first. Johan ("John") Svanberg (born in Stockholm on 1 May 1881; 1.68 m. / 55 kg.) had a long and successful career, with a compass ranging from 1500 metres to the marathon. However, some of his Swedish records – e.g. 15:13.5 for 5000 metres and 31:30.9 for 10,000 metres, both in 1907 - were later removed from the record book when the track at Idrottsparken in Stockholm was found to be 90 cm. short. He ran the '10' in 32:18.4 under regular circumstances in 1908 but was ousted from the amateur ranks in 1909. He later emigrated to USA, where he had a career as a painter but also continued to run in the "pro" ranks with mixed fortunes, against the likes of Alfred Shrubb, Dorando Pietri, Johnny Hayes, Tom Longboat and Henri St.Yves. He probably achieved his most notable success in 1909, when he beat Hayes in a marathon at Chicago, thereby netting a purse of $7,500. Georg Peterson, also from Sweden, ran 10,000 metres in 31:30.0 at Halmstad on 5 June 1910. In this race the 27-year-old Swede was matched against a five-man relay team yet he won easily. It was the fastest time of the pre-IAAF era, but it should be remembered that Shrubb had done much better, albeit unofficially, enroute to his 1-hour record.

Finland entered the picture a bit later but then lost little time in reaching the top. In 1910 one Hannes Kolehmainen ran the standard distances in 15:53.0 and 32:36.1, little more than a pale indication of what was to follow – more on him in the next chapter.

France already had good traditions, with the likes of Louis Bouchard and Emile Anthoine. The latter was credited with 15:29.0 (1909) and 32:57.0 (1903) as a "pro", but such times are viewed with some reservation by French statisticians. Anthoine was prominent also as a walker and later made his mark as a writer. In 1914 he edited an excellent book, "Athlétisme", which had a foreword by Henri Desgrange, first "patron" of Tour de France, the famous cycle race. In 1905 Gaston Ragueneau ran 10,000 metres in 32:36.0, a national record which was broken four years later by Jean Bouin – 32:13 3/5 enroute to a 1-hour run. As will be related soon, Bouin, a stout man from Marseille, was to make history in his alas too short career. South Africa had such good runners as Charles Hefferon and Kennedy McArthur, both of whom were to earn lasting glory as marathon runners. Best of the Americans was George Bonhag, who posted remarkable times on indoor circuits: 9:14 1/5 for 2 miles (1910), 14:29 2/5 for 3 miles (1910) and 30:42.0 for 6 miles (1909).

Rare longevity

The career of England's Joe Deakin was among those that make a durable imprint in athletics annals, even though he was in all probability a good but not exceptional talent. The history of sport, like that of humanity in general, is usually reserved to those who accounted for superlative deeds, yet Deakin's achievements cannot escape the attention of those who regard longevity as one of the most notable traits in the life of a sportsman.

Joseph Edmund Deakin was born at Shelton near Stoke-on-Trent on 6 February 1879. His biographer Kevin Kelly regarded him as a "living legend". Deakin's running career certainly ranks among the longest on record as it lasted no less than 90 years. (It may be rivalled by that of Abel Kiviat, an American miler, who in his youth had been a world record holder and an Olympic silver medallist. In 1984 Kiviat, well in his eighties, acted as torch bearer of the Olympic flame on the way to the Los Angeles Olympics. He died in 1991 at the age of 99 years and 2 months. Not long before he had revived his fame with an appearance in the popular Johnny Carson show on TV and was celebrated as the oldest of living American Olympians).

Joe Deakin ran his first (official) race at age 8, a 100- yard dash. But his true career began in 1900. His compass covered middle and long distances. At the AAA Championships he was 3rd in the 10 miles in 1905, 2nd in both 1 mile and 4 miles in 1907 , 2nd again in 1 mile and 10 miles in 1908. He had his most glorious days at the 1908 Olympics in London. After placing 6th in the 1500 metres, he contributed to Britain's victory in the 3-mile team race. In the latter he had the best time, 14:39 3/5, which according to Kelly could have been even faster if the time-keepers, carried away by their enthusiasm over Britain's incoming victory, had not forgotten to stop their watches at the right time, i.e. when Deakin crossed the finish line!

Deakin continued to run intensively even after the end of his competitive career. In the years between the two World Wars he ran the Polytechnic Harriers' Marathon, the most famous of British races at that distance. He settled for shorter races only in his fifties and sixties. Up to his 90th birthday in 1969, when he ran in the colours of his club, Surrey AC. He died, aged 93, on 30 June 1972.

THE FINNISH ERA: KOLEHMAINEN, THE IMMORTAL NURMI AND HIS HEIRS

The 1912 Olympics in Stockholm were the first truly modern version of the quadrennial event revived by Pierre de Coubertin in the last decade of the 19th century. Sweden could claim a pioneer role in promoting sport as an educational form, mainly thanks to Pehr Henrik Ling (1776-1839), who is commonly regarded as the father of modern gymnastics. This heritage and their devotion to sport made it possible for the Swedes to put on stage an edition of the Games that truly outshone in terms of technical efficiency all previous editions of the Games, invariably beset by sundry problems.

The Stockholm Games saluted the coming-of-age of a sporting country which at the time was not yet a nation in the political and formal sense of the word - Finland, then still a grand duchy of the Russian Empire, although enjoying a limited autonomy. The Finns had already made their presence felt at the Games of 1906 and 1908, e.g. with discus thrower Verner Järvinen, still revered in Finnish sport literature as "Isä (father) Järvinen" – head of one of the greatest athletic families the world has ever known. (three of his four sons became athletes of world class). For the Stockholm Games Finnish sports authorities were granted by Russia permission to field a team of their own, but this favour did not include the use of the Finnish flag. Even so, the small Nordic country (which was to become independent in 1917) really stole the limelight in the Stockholm Games. Their lead-off man was Johannes ("Hannes") Petter Kolehmainen (born at Kuopio on 9 December 1889; 1.69m. / 60 kg.) , who with his brothers Tatu, Viljami and Kalle and his sister Maiju formed the first of several famous "athletic families" from Suomi (Finland). A solid man of average height, he had discovered sport at an early age – first cross-country skiing, then marathon running. He tried the latter for the

first time in June 1907, when still 17, and finished third in 3 hrs 06:19 over a course of 40.2 km. (then standard distance for the marathon in Scandinavia). Before the end of the year he improved to 2 hrs 57:25.4. In 1909, over a period of three months he ran five marathons – a pantagruelian task for a boy of his age. In the fourth he was timed in 2 hrs 42:59 – this time in a 42,195 km. track race. Then he stayed away from marathons for .... 8 years, but in the intervening time he earned eternal glory in track events. I already made reference to his 1910 marks. The following year he did 8:48.5 for 3000 metres as well as 15:28:1 and 32:17.4 for the standard distances. By that time he received letters from his elder brother Viljami, who was in USA and used to give him an advice: "Do not neglect speed!" Hannes was eager to comply: the crazy marathoner of younger days had given way to a sage performer, who always liked to have something in reserve for a final sprint. Still in 1911 Hannes won his first international title: the AAA 4 miles. Time, 20:03 3/5. In the spring of 1912 he went to Berlin, where he met for the first time a man from sunny Marseille, Jean Bouin. The race was over a 7,500 metre course and the Finn won handily – 23:05 to 23:41. In a rehearsal for the Olympics in Helsinki the Finn ran the standard distances in 15:16.4 and 31:47.5 on consecutive days. By then virtually everybody in Finnish track circles was convinced that Kolehmainen was ready to put Suomi on the map of world athletics. Sports paper "Suomen Urheilulehti" was extolling the peculiar virtues of the Kolehmainen family with the following words: "There isn't a running quintette like them in the whole world", and gave their secrets in a nutshell: "Work, healthy life, good sleep, fresh air, suitable nourishment, regular sauna baths, gymnastic exercises, massage, lots of moving about in open air, and a running training based on theoretical and empirical research".

Just about the only man who looked capable of giving Hannes a good run for his money was Jean Bouin (born in Marseille on 20 December 1888; 1.68 m. / 66 kg.). He too had made his debut very early, winning a cross-country race in February 1904, when he was barely 15. He soon acquired a compass ranging from 800 metres to the longest track events, collecting his first national record in 1908: 15:48 4/5 for 5000 metres. He won his first national title in yet another cross country test in 1909. In the same year, on 30 May at Colombes, he set three national records in one gulp, when he covered 18,267 km. in 1 hour, with times of 15:38. 4/5 for 5000 m. and 32:13:3/5 for 10,000 metres enroute. In his preparation he indulged in a lot of gymnastics exercises and had muscle strength as his main "atout". After years of intense physical training he was so strong as to earn the label of "Hercule de Marseille".

By 1911 Bouin had become a household name even in international track circles. His pearls for the pre-Olympic season came late in the season. On 22 October in his hometown of Marseille he broke the French 1-hour record, covering 18,588 km. Enroute he was clocked in 31:21 1/5 at 10,000 metres for another national mark. In this race he was opposed to a famous "pro", Louis Bouchard, whom le left 580 metres behind. Of course, mixing with "pros" was against the rules even before the birth of the IAAF. However, the race was organized as a "bienfaisance" event for the benefit of the families of victims of a seafaring disaster. Be it as it may, Bouin's 1-hour record was ratified. Yet the best was yet to come: Bouin had a great day at Colombes on 16 November, when he chalked up history's first sub-31 minute mark for the 10,000 metres, a scintillating 30:58 4/5. Actually, his target in this race was the half-hour record, which he conquered by covering 9,721 km., with a frenzied sprint in the closing stage. Even so,

Kalevala

One of the reasons often brought up to explain why Finns love sport so much is their necessity to fight the harshness of the Nordic climate in which they live. A factor that leads them to cherish since boyhood all forms of physical exercise and open air motion. Another rather subtle reason may lie in the fact that few other countries have, like Finland, a sport tradition so closely intertwined with their culture. In this perspective one of their foremost authorities was philologist Elias Lönnrot (1802-1884), the author of "Kalevala" (literally: "Land of Heroes"), a national epic made of legends, popular ballads, folk songs and incantations, handed down by word of mouth from generation to generation by bards and ordinary people. Himself a strong advocate of open air activities, Lönnrot collected his material after travelling far and wide through Finland, the country of the countless lakes, on skis or by boat, treasuring the tales common people used to tell.

In 1936 Jack Schumacher of Switzerland, then holder of his country's national record in javelin throwing, wrote a book, "Die Finnen, das grosse Sportvolk" (The Finns, a great sporting nation), in which he wrote that in no other country one was likely to find such a close connection between sport and culture, reminding of ancient Greece.

In Finland, as in several other European countries, gymnastics acted as a sort of trail blazer for track and field athletics. Ironically enough, however, it fell to a man from Southern Europe, Italian Gioacchino Otta, a former officer of the Napoleonic army , pedagogue and master of fencing, to promote gymnastics in Finland, where in 1835 he became the first state-employed P.E. teacher in the annals of that country, then a grand duchy of the Russian Empire. In 1843 gymnastics was included in the standard programme of Finnish schools. Chiefly responsible for launching physical education on a large scale was a great Finn, Viktor Heikel. At the dawn of the 20th century skiing and athletics became Finland's national sports – a role they have preserved until today.

he managed to go on decently till the 10,000 metre tape. His kilometre fractions in what was virtually a "solo" effort were as follows:

1000 m.	2:49 1/5	
2000 m	5:49 3/5	(3:00 2/5)
3000 m	8:54 1/5	(3:04 3/5)
4000 m	11:59 4/5	(3:05 3/5)
5000 m	15:11 2/5*	(3:11 3/5)
6000 m	18:21.0	(3:09 3/5)
7000 m	21:28 2/5	(3:07 2/5)
8000 m	24:38 3/5	(3:10 1/5)
9000 m	27:49 1/5	(3:10 3/5)
10,000 m	30:58 4/5	(3:09 3/5)

* French record.
Enroute he did 29:51 3/5 for 6 miles, also a new world record.

In the early months of 1912 Bouin was not particularly brilliant, even apart from the above-mentioned defeat to Hannes Kolehmainen in Berlin. The Frenchman went to the Stockholm Olympics with seasonal bests of 15:14.0 and 32:56 4/5. For the Games he decided to concentrate on the 5000 metres, whereas his chief rival, Hannes Kolehmainen, took upon himself a very heavy task: doubling '5' and '10', plus 3000 metres (team) and cross-country races! Counting heats and finals he ran 6 races for a total of 45 kilometres in the space of nine days. Details:

7 July: 10,000 m. (heat) 1.Kolehmainen 33:49.0

8 July: 10,000 m. (final): 1.Hannes Kolehmainen (Fin) 31:20.8, 2.Louis

Hannes Kolehmainen winning the 10,000 metres at the 1912 Olympics in Stockholm. He inaugurated the Finnish era in long distance running.

25

Tewanima (USA) 32:06.6, 3. 3.Albin Stenroos (Fin) 32:21.8, 4.Joseph Keeper (Can) 32:36.2, 5.Alfonso Orlando (Ita) 33:31.2. Among those who dropped out was Tatu Kolehmainen, Hannes' brother. The winner ran the first half in 15:11.4, the second in 16:09.4 !

9 July: 5000 m (heats) Kolehmainen won ht .4 in 15:34.6 and Bouin ht.5 in 15:05.0, a new French record.

10 July: 5000 m. (final): 1.Hannes Kolehmainen 14.36.6 (new world record), 2.Jean Bouin 14:36.7, 3.George Hutson (GB) 15:07.6, 4.George Bonhag (USA) 15:09.8, 5.Tel Berna (USA) 15:10.0, 6.Mauritz Karlsson (Swe) 15:18.6, 7.Alexander Decoteau (Can), 8.Henry Louis Scott (USA). At 3 miles Bouin led in 14:07.2 (world best, but unofficial, hence not ratified) with Kolehmainen close in 14:07.4.

12 July: 3000 m. team race. Finland, second in its heat, did not qualify for the final. In that race, however, Kolehmainen was timed in 8:36.9, a new world record which was erroneously ratified by the IAAF as 8:36.8.

15 July: Croos-Country team race (8 km.): Sweden won from Finland and Hannes Kolehmainen had the fastest time, 45:11.6. Bouin dropped out.

The man who finished second in the '10', Louis Tewanima of USA, was a Hopi Indian, probably 24-years old at the time. A teammate of famous decathlete Jim Thorpe at Carlisle Indian School, he had placed 9th in the Olympic marathon of 1908 and 16th in the same event in Stockholm. In later years he was a high priest in his tribe, always very fit for his age. Recalling his younger days in an interview with an American magazine, he revealed that he used to train with rabbits, wild horses and antelopes. It is a known fact that American Indians have always worshipped physical fitness. Tewanima himself put it this way: "Body our temple".

The 5000 metre final was the "clou" of the Stockholm Games. In a way it can be said that it inaugurated a new era in distance running. At the start the ever smiling Finn looked surprisingly relaxed, while Bouin (who out of sheer superstition used to run with a toothpick in his mouth) appeared to be his usual earnest and absorbed self. The Finn

was the early leader, but Bouin soon took over and led till the final lap. It was only 20 metres from home that the Finn managed to inch his way ahead and finally won by a metre or so. Eye-witness Sven Lindhagen, a famous Swedish expert, supplied the following comment in one of his books many years later: "In those days no intermediate times were usually taken, or if they were, nobody cared to convey them to the public, who were by no means as knowledgeable as present-day crowds. Yet (on that day) we all felt that the two champions were travelling at a very fast pace". We do have some splits, supplied by French journalists watching from the stands: 2:45.5 (1000 m.), 4:17 (1500 m.), 5:47 (2000 m.), 7:17 (2500 m.), 8:46 (3000 m.), 11:40 (4000 m., estimated time). The final times "massacred" all previously known records. Prof. Lauri Pihkala, a well-known Finnish athlete (first sub-2 min. performer at 800 m. in his own country), journalist and humanist, sometimes referred to as "Finland's master mind in athletics", had this to say about the victory ceremony in "Suomen Urheilulehti": "A white, blue and red flag was hoisted on top of a pole, and underneah a little rag with the word – Finland. Our country is part of the Czarist Russian Empire and this shame had to be endured".

Following his glorious days in Stockholm (three gold medals , plus one silver for the team-race), Kolehmainen emigrated to USA, where he continued to break records, indoors and out, over an endless series of odd distances. His most significant times – all made in 1913:

3 miles, outdoors: 14:22 3/5 Celtic Park, NY, 17 August
indoors: 14:18 1/5 Brooklyn, NY, 12 February
6 miles, outdoors: 30:20 2/5* New York, 1 November
indoors: 30:24.0* Buffalo, NY, 1 February
10 miles, outdoors: 51:03 2/5 New York, 1 November
indoors: 51:06 3/5 Buffalo, NY, 1 February
* Intermediate time during a race over a longer distance.

Apart from a visit to Finland in 1914 , when he ran 10,000 metres in 31:27.4 at Tampere, one had to wait till 1920 to welcome him back to Europe.

Bouin had his greatest season in 1913, when between January and November he ran 28 races. He reached the peak of his career on 6 July in Stockholm with a new 1-hour world record of 19,021 km., leaving Albin Stenroos of Finland far behind (17,728 km.). He thus outshone Alfred Shrubb once more. While enroute, the Frenchman set two more world bests: 47:18.6 for 15,000 metres and 55:54.0 for 11 miles. However, his time at 10 miles (50:46.0) remained well below Shrubb's 50:40.6. The Stockholm race was on the 385-metre track of the Olympic Stadium. Bouin felt he could have done better but for the necessity of travelling around a host of lapped runners while enroute. Just like his great predecessor Alfred Shrubb, the man from Marseille was also a great cross-country runner. At the International Championhips he was second in 1909, then won for three years in a row, 1911-12-13 – the first non-Briton to annex that title.

After their epic duel at the 1912 Olympics, Kolehmainen and Bouin never met again. On 26 July 1914 Bouin won the 800 metres at the Belgium vs. France match in Brussels in 2:02.0. This was to be the last race of his life. World War I was by then making vicious inroads upon the lives of many young men all over Europe. Bouin was enrolled in a French infantry corps as "instructeur de sport des Armées". On 29 September, while engaged in courier duties during a furious battle at Saint-Mihiel , he fell victim to a tragic error of the French artillery, when a howitzer put a premature end to his life. He was not yet 26. "L'Auto" described him as "the most amazing pedestrian our country has ever had". Several stadia in France still bear his name.

George Hutson of Great Britain, the man who finished a distant third in the race of the famous Kolehmainen-Bouin classic, also died on a battle field in October 1914. He could point to four AAA championship titles: three at 4 miles and one over the mile (4:22.0 in 1914).

Birth of the IAAF

An important development for the world of athletics occurred during the 1912 Olympics in Stockholm: a group of outstanding lovers of the sport, spearheaded by officials of "Svenska Idrottsförbundet" (the Swedish Athletics Federation), conceived the idea of founding the "International Amateur Athletic Federation", which is still the governing body of the sport on a world-wide scale. (In 2001 the name was changed to "International Association of Athletics Federations", thereby preserving the original initials). The first congress of the IAAF in Stockholm was held three days after the conclusion of the Olympic track and field events in the Parliament building ("Riksdagshuset"), with delegations from 17 countries. The first president of the IAAF was J.Sigfrid Edström of Sweden, who in his younger days held the Swedish record for 150 metres (16.4 in 1891). The official constitution of the IAAF was put forward to the congress of 1913 in Berlin.

The declared aims of the newly-formed body were as follows: 1) To draw up and agree the rules and regulations for international athletics competition; 2) To register all World, Olympic and National Records and maintain a register of these at a central office; 3) To define "amateur" for international competition purposes. Beginnings were not easy and were made all the more difficult by World War I. Several years went by before point 1) could become effective. In USA , for example, the time honoured AAU remained loyal to its own rules, not always coherent with those of the IAAF. The problem of timing fractions was to remain confused for a long time to come. Finland and Sweden continued to stick to tenths of a second, rather than fifths as originally specified by IAAF rules.

The first official list of IAAF World Records was divulged in 1913. In principle it consisted of the best marks until then ratified by national federations. Some of these dated from the earliest years of the century, e.g. Alfred Shrubb's 2, 3 and 6 mile records. A few marks from the latter part of the 19th century were also included, e.g. a record for 20 miles walking made by Thomas Griffith of Great Britain in 1870.

Swedish sparkles in the gloomy years of WW1

World War I obviously reduced athletic activity to a minimum in most European countries. In England there were no AAA Championships from 1915 up to and including 1918. France had no national title meet for five years (1914-18). Germany somehow missed only one edition, 1914. Even in Finland, where the sport had received a great fillip through Kolehmainen's Olympic triumphs, there were no outstanding marks for several years. In such a situation, just about the only European country to enjoy a normal athletic activity during war years was neutral Sweden (the same will happen during World War II). Outstanding among Swedish stars of the time was John Zander (born in Stockholm on 31 January 1890; 1.80 m. / 66 kg.). He had signalled his presence on the international scene by winning the mile in 4:25 4/5 at the 1913 AAA Championships. In the following years this lanky Stockholm clerk collected Swedish records galore at distances ranging from 1000 to 5000 metres. No less than seven of these were also world records, no matter if only three were ratified as such by the IAAF. In the domain of distance running he did 8:35.7 (1917), 8:34.8 and 8:33.1 (both in 1918) for 3000 metres. The last one was at Stockholm on 7 August and was duly ratified as a world record, rounded up to 8:33.2. This was in a handicap race and Zander had halves of 4:13.7 and 4:19.4. He was perhaps at his best over 1500 metres: after placing 7th in the final of the Stockholm Olympics in 1912, five years later he succeeded Abel Kiviat of USA as a world record holder with 3:54.7. He more than held his own with the very best at 5000 metres, winning over this distance at the 1914 Baltic Games in Malmö in 15:26.6. By the way, this meet was probably the most important review of athletic talent during those gloomy years. In 1917 Zander became history's third sub-15 min. performer with 14:59.6. He improved to 14:57.5 in Stockholm on 17 August 1918. A typical front runner, Zander decided to call it quits at the end of the 1918 season, but two years later he was talked into giving it one more try in view of the Antwerp Olympics. Bothered by a leg injury, he made the 1500 metre final but was unable to finish.

Another outstanding Swede was Eric Backman (born at Acklinga on 18 May 1896). Endowed with plenty of talent, he was somewhat reluctant in taking adequate training loads. In 1918 he brought Sweden's 10,000 metre record to 31:13.7. 1919 was a bright year for Swedish long distance men. On 21 July in Stockholm three men ducked under 15 minutes over 5000 metres: 1.Rudolf Falk 14:54.3, 2.Backman 14:56.7, 3.Alf Halstvedt (Norway) 14:59.1. However, Backman had the last word: in the triangular match Sweden-Denmark-Norway at Stockholm on 31 August he did 14:51.0, leaving Falk and Halstvedt far behind.

In the meantime, "pros" had virtually disappeared from the scene. The best of them in those years was probably Jean Vermeulen of France, who ran 10,000 metres in 31:32 4/5 in 1913 and improved to 31:14.2 on an indoor circuit in Paris in 1914. In the latter race he beat one of Hannes Kolehmainen's brothers – Viljam . Curiously described as a "pseudo-pro" by Gaston Meyer, the dean of French journalists in athletics, Vermeulen was born in 1895 according to one French source – which, if correct, would make him the most fantastic junior of those days over the long distances.

The 1916 Olympics had been assigned to Berlin, but of course they had to be cancelled because of World War I. The sporting fraternity thus had to wait four more years for the next Olympic celebration. Antwerp was the venue of the 1920 Games and the Belgians, although beset by sundry problems, did their best to live up to the difficult task. Those Games brought to the fore new forces, even in the domain of distance running.

The incomparable Nurmi and his heirs

Hannes Kolehmainen's victories at the 1912 Olympics had a great impact on Finnish sport, and on the Finnish nation as a whole, yet one had to wait several years to see the fruits thereof. Finland was heavily affected by World War I and on top of that also had to endure the hardships of a civil war between "whites" and "reds". With the victory of the former the Nordic country finally won independence. In the midst of such vicissitudes and the state of poverty afflicting the country, there appeared a bright new running star who was to become Kolehmainen's rightful heir. This man was Paavo Johannes Nurmi (born at Turku on 13 June 1897, 1.74 m. / 65 kg.), the son of a carpenter who died of a pulmonary hemorrhage in 1910, just before turning 50, leaving his wife and four children in far from flourishing conditions. After completing his compulsory school term, young Paavo found a job as errand boy for a local wholesale dealer. Finnish stories tell of a boy pushing a handcart up a steep hill on the way to the Turku Railway station. Hard work kept him busy for the greater part of the day. In the evening, however, he would usually

stay away from the games and jokes other boys of his age liked to indulge in. He preferred to run all alone in nearby woods. Being by nature a man of rare words, he developed into a lone wolf after his father's death. A vegetarian by his own choice, he remained faithful to his philosophy for many years. In this connection it may be interesting to recall that Hannes Kolehmainen had tasted meat for the first time in 1916, aged 27, while a guest of Abraham L. Monteverde, a famous American specialist of "grand fond" racing.

Nurmi had his first "dialogue" with a stopwatch at the tender age of 10, when he ran 1500 metres in a time trial in 5:43. He is supposed to have improved to an almost unbelievable 5:02 when he was only 11. Then various circumstances, chiefly connected with the death of his father in 1910, held him back and his progress was rather slow, as can be gathered from the following table, showing his best marks up to and including 1920.

Year (Age)	3000 m	5000 m	10,000 m
1914 (17)	10:06.9	-	-
1915 (18)	9:30.6	15:57.5	-
1916 (19)	-	15:52.8	34:35.0
1917 (20)	9:47,8	15:47.4	-
1918 (21)	10:10.2	15:50.7	-
1919 (22)	8:58.1	15:31.5	32:56.0
1920 (23)	8:36.2 *	15:00.0	31:45.8

* Finnish record.

His training since he was 15 would usually consist of a race at distances ranging from 2 to 6 kms. no more than four times a week. For the rest he indulged in long walks, before or after his long working hours. The turning point came in 1919, when he moved to Pori to serve an 18-months period in the army. The new kind of life turned to his advantage as far as sport was concerned: he had more time to train to an extent finally compatible with his great – no matter if secret – ambition, that of emulating Hannes Kolehmainen.

The great Paavo Nurmi in his senior years, visiting Helms Hall in Los Angeles. He stands beside the huge Helms World Trophy, upon which his name has been engraved.

1911
1940

29

The first alarm bell was heard on 28 May 1920 in Turku, when he conquered his first Finnish record: 8:36.2 over 3000 metres, actually a few tenths under the time (8:36.8) credited to his boyhood hero at the 1912 Olympics, and only 3 seconds shy of John Zander's world record. In July of the same year at the Finnish trials for the Olympics he ran 5000 metres in 15:00.5, moving to 7th on the All Time World List. He went to Antwerp full of confidence, even though he lacked international experience. However, this condition was shared by most if not all his potential rivals on the eve of the first major post-war test. Nurmi's potential in terms of speed had not been discovered yet – he had a casual PB of 4:05.5 for 1500 metres (1920). Then he suffered from sea-sickness on his boat trip to Antwerp and after landing he had to work hard for several days to regain condition.

On the eve of the Antwerp Games Scandinavia seemed to have the best cards for the distance races with Paavo Nurmi and Eric Backman. The United States had Charles Hunter, who had been credited with a surprising 14:45.0 for 5000 metres on 26 June at Pasadena. This time was duly ratified by the AAU as a US record, yet some observers regarded it as doubtful. Be it as it may, at Antwerp he failed to survive the prelims. There was also an outsider from France, Joseph Guillemot (born at Dorat, Haute-Vienne, on 1 October 1899 / 1.62 m. / 55 kg.). Foreign authors have repeatedly stated that his heart was on the right side of his chest, an assumption French sources have never confirmed. Robert Parienté, the great French track historian, simply states that Guillemot had an extraordinary chest expansion and a heart beating at slow rhythms which allowed a very quick recovery. Others refer to his fascinating personality, in which generosity seemed to blend with a certain degree of mythomania. After serving in the French army in the latter stage of World War I he had grown up as a good runner, who was particularly at home in cross-country races. In 1919 he won the 5000 metres at the French Championships (15:51 1/5), a title he won again in 1920, this time with an eloquent 15:09 2/5.

French "revanche" – 8 years later

In spite of Guillemot's most recent progress, few international experts thought that he would be capable of taking revenge, in the name of France, for Jean Bouin's tantalizing defeat at the hands of a Finn in the 1912 Olympics. Yet such a miracle materialized on 17 August at Antwerp in the final of the 5000 metres. Confident Paavo Nurmi led for the greater part of the race. He covered the first half in 7:12, after which he had to slow down more than somewhat. The Frenchman was close on his heels for most of the time and waited till the last turn to launch his attack. He then forged ahead with surprising ease and finally won by a safe margin. Sweden's Backman never seemed to pose a real threat. He finished a distant third. It should be noted that this race came one day after the heats, in which both Guillemot and Nurmi had ostensibly bided their time. Details:

Antwerp, 17 August 1920 – 5000 metres: 1.Joseph Guillemot (Fra) 14:55 3/5, 2.Paavo Nurmi (Fin) 15:00.0, 3.Eric Backman (Swe) 15:13.0, 4.Teodor Koskenniemi (Fin) 15:17.0, 5.Charles Blewitt (GB) 15:19.0est., 6.William Seagrove (GB) 15:21.0; 7.Carlo Speroni (Ita), 8.Alfred Nichols (GB).

Paavo Nurmi lost little time in trying to even the count with his French rival. The 10,000 metres offered him an adequate chance to do so. On 19 August he "took a rest" in his own, pretty slow heat, while Guillemot qualified in another heat with a much faster time (32:08 4/5). Once again, the final was on schedule for the next day. In the early stages of the race Nurmi fell 20 metres behind James Wilson of Great Britain and Guillemot. This probably served to convey the impression that the 23-year-old Finn was in trouble. An impression that was soon corrected when the two leaders began to slow down and Nurmi, ever the master of pace judgment, rejoined them. Wilson lost contact right after the bell. What followed was a ding-dong battle all through the last lap between Nurmi and Guillemot. This time the Finn was not to be denied though. He went home the victor by a comfortable margin. A French report said that Guillemot found himself in trouble due to a bad digestion. Even so, he chalked up a new PB – as did his conqueror.

Details:

Antwerp, 20 August 1920 – 10,000 metres: 1.Paavo Nurmi (Fin) 31:45 4/5, 2.Joseph Guillemot (Fra) 31:47 1/5, 3.James Wilson (GB) 31:50 4/5, 4.Augusto Maccario (Ita) 32:04.0 est, 5.James Hatton (GB) 32:14.0 est, 6.Jean-Baptiste Manhès (Fra) 32:26.0 est, 7.Heikki Liimatainen (Fin), 8.Fred Faller (USA).

But Nurmi had more in mind. On 22 August he ran his fifth race in less than a week and won a cross-country competition (8 km.) in 27:15.0. His pursuers finished in the following order: Backman 27:17 3/5, Liimatainen 27:37 2/5, Wilson 27:45 1/5. Guillemot was in this race too but he did not finish. Finland won the team compettion and Nurmi, as the fastest finisher, secured two more gold medals under the rule then in force. Finland stayed away from the 3000 metre team competition, which was won by USA. In his first Olympic experience, Nurmi thus proved a worthy successor of Hannes Kolehmainen. The latter added one more pearl to his Olympic jewels of 1912 by emerging the winner in a fascinating and "long" marathon – over a course of 42,750 km. In his 11th marathon over a period of 13 years (1907-1920) he was timed in 2 hrs 32:35 4/5, at the end of a hot duel with Jüri Lossmann of Estonia (2 hrs 32:48 3/5). Such a feat, coming as it did eight years after his triumphs at Stockholm, certainly earned him eternal glory - in his own country and in the athletics world as a whole. Hannes was to compete in two more marathons, at the 1924 Paris Olympics and four years later in Finland, but in both cases he failed to finish.

Nurmi was to treasure his Antwerp experiences. He decided to work harder on "pace judgment": that was when he developed a habit of holding a watch in his hand in both training and competition. He also aimed at improving his basic speed and to that purpose he took more and more interest in middle distance races. He conquered his first world record at Stockholm on 22 June 1921 – 30:40.2 over 10,000 metres. In open contradiction with his own philosophy he covered the first kilometre in a fast 2:51.5, yet he could not shake off a bold companion, Eric Backman of Sweden. After which both had to settle for a more reasonable pace. The Swede held on for over half the distance, then Nurmi was on his own and easily succeeded Jean Bouin as world record holder.

Details:

Stockholm, 22 June 1921 – 10,000 metres: 1.Paavo Nurmi 30:40.2, 2.Eric Backman (Swse) 31:02.1, 3.Nils Bergström (Swe) 33:42.0.

Kilometre fractions:

1000 m	2:51.5	
2000 m	5:51.5	(3.00.0)
3000 m	8:54.4	(3.02.9)
4000 m	11:58.4	(3.04.0)
5000 m	15:06.1	(3.07.7)
6000 m	18:11.3	(3.05.2)
7000 m	21:16.9	(3.05.6)
8000 m	24:27.1	(3.10.2)
9000 m	27:35.6	(3.08.5)
10,000 m	30:40.2	(3.04.6)

Enroute Nurmi ran 6 miles in 29:41.2, also a new world record (not ratified by the IAAF).

This was the first link of a wondrous chain which was to be completed ten years later. The list of Paavo Nurmi's world records looks as follows:

Stockholm, 22 June 1921	6 miles	29:41.2* +
Stockholm, 22 June 1921	10,000 m	30:40.2
Kokkola, 10 August 1922	3 miles	14:14.4* +
Turku, 27 August 1922	3000 m	8:28.6
Tampere, 4 September 1922	2000 m	5:26.3°

Stockholm, 12 September 1922	3 miles	14:08.4* +
Stockholm, 12 September 1922	5000 m	14:35.3°
Stockholm, 23 August 1923	1500 m	3:53.0* +
Stockholm, 23 August 1923	1 mile	4:10.4
Stockholm, 24 Aug 1923	3 miles	14:11.2
Copenhagen, 17 September 1923	3000 m	8:27.8*
Helsinki, 19 June 1924	1500 m	3:52.6
Helsinki, 19 June 1924	3 miles	14:02.0* +
Helsinki, 19 June 1924	5000 m	14 :28.2
Kuopio, 31 August 1924	4 miles	19:18.7* +
Kuopio, 31 August 1924	5 miles	24:13.1* +
Kuopio, 31 August 1924	6 miles	29:07.1* +
Kuopio, 31 August 1924	10,000m	30:06.1°
Viipuri, 1 October 1924	4 miles	19:15.6 +
Viipuri, 1 October 1924	5 miles	24:06.1°
Berlin, 24 May 1926	3000 m	8:25.4
Stockholm, 13 July 1926	3000 m	8:20.4
Kuopio, 18 June 1927	2000 m	5:24.6
Berlin, 7 October 1928	15,000m	46:49.5° +
Berlin, 7 October 1928	10 miles	50:15.0 +
Berlin, 7 October 1928	19,210 km	1 hour
London, 9 June 1930	6 miles	29:36.4
Stockholm, 3 September 1930	20,000 m	1.04:38.4
Helsinki, 24 July 1931	2 miles	8:59.5°

+ Intermediate time during race at a longer distance.
° Time was ratified rounded up to nearest fifth-of-a-second , as per IAAF rule.
* Not ratified by the IAAF.

The above list has 29 world records but it should be noted that Nurmi broke two more as anchor leg man in 4x1500 m. relay races for his club, Turun Urheiluliitto: 16:26.2 (Stockholm, 12 July 1926) and 16:11.4 (Viipuri, 17 July 1926). In addition to this, he collected many world indoor records during his famous "tournée" of 1925 in USA, as will be related later in this chapter.

In 1923 Nurmi extended his sovereignity to the mile, a distance of great appeal to Anglo-Saxon fans. In the same year he also won the 800 metres at the Finnish Championships in 1:56.3 – good enough to earn him place no.20 in the 1923 World List for that distance.

1924 was Nurmi's greatest year, during which he reached heights he would never reach again. In the meantime the international scene had changed considerably. After his exploits of 1920, Joseph Guillemot began to fade, slowly but gradually, although it was only by 1927 that he disappeared from the picture completely. "Guigui", as the French called him, is remembered as a runner whose true potential was to remain untapped, chiefly if not entirely for his casual approach to training. Yet Nurmi was to find two serious rivals in his own geographical sphere: Edvin Wide and Ville Ritola.

Wide (born at Kemiö, Finland on 22 February 1896; 1.70 m. / 62 kg.) originally belonged to that Swedish language minority which is still present in Finland. As a youth he was divided between his sense of loyalty to his home country and his cultural and linguistic ties with Sweden. During the civil war rivalries in Finland ran high and Wide decided to move to Sweden. In the end, however, he always had "deux amours", and he showed that by refusing to compete in the Sweden vs. Finland classic, which is capable of evoking hot rivalries somehow reminiscent of those to be found in Italy in connection with the famed Palio horse race in Siena. Wide became a Swedish citizen in 1920 and ran for the yellow-blue colours at the Antwerp Olympics, where he contributed to Sweden's third place in the 3000 metre team race.

In 1923 Wide and Nurmi were engaged in a strong duel over 1 mile in Stockholm. They were the only competitors in the race which in a way brought back memories of the great match races of the 19th century among "pros". Nurmi won in world record time (4:10.4) and Wide was second in 4:13.1. They covered the last 109.35 metres separating the 1500 metres from the mile in 17.4 and 18.9 respectively. In those days even the greatest runners had a limited finishing power. Nurmi met tougher resistance from his compatriot Ville Ritola (born at Peräseinäjoki on 18 January 1896; 1.77 m./ 62 kg.), This runner's career unfolded for the most part in USA, where Ville – 14th in a poor peasant family of 20 children – emigrated at the age of 17. He led a precarious life for some time, mostly doing odd jobs and moving from one place to another. Although hampered by scarce education (just two years in elementary school) he managed to stay away from risky enterprises and finally developed into a good carpenter - and a fine runner as well.

The careers of Nurmi and Ritola were quite different from one another and their clashes were limited almost entirely to Olympic years, when Ritola would come to Europe to represent his mother country. Unlike his great countryman, Ville (known as Willie in the States) did not adhere to systematic training, yet he was able to surprise himself, and many others, when big competitions came

33

*A famous trio:
Ville Ritola
leading from
Paavo Nurmi
(both of Finland)
and Edvin Wide
(Sweden) in the
Olympic 5000
metres at
Amsterdam
in 1928.
They finished
in that order.*

around. He made his debut in a road race at New York in 1919. Soon afterwards he came into the orbit of the Finnish-American Athletic Club. Among his Finnish acquaintances there was a man who could give him sound advice – Hannes Kolehmainen. Following the philosophy of his "maestro", Ville alternated long walks with long races at a relatively slow pace. He had to stay away from the Antwerp Olympics due to his commitments in connection with work and marriage. By 1922 he was a well established quantity in the road racing department, notably with a second place in the Boston marathon of that year (2 hrs 21:44 4/5). In 1923 he picked up some notable US indoor records: 14:15 4/5 at 3 miles, 15:01 2/5 at 5000 metres and 19:27 4/5 at 4 miles. He came back to Finland shortly before the 1924 Olympics. On 25 May at Helsinki he introduced himself to his sport loving countrymen with a most brilliant performances – a new world record of 30:35.4 for 10,000 metres! In the process he succeeded none other than Nurmi himself. Details:

Helsinki, 25 May 1924 – 10,000 metres: 1.Ville Ritola 30:35.4, 2.Eero Berg 31:56.7, 3.Väinö Sipilä 32:05.3, 4.Heikki Liimatainen 32:28.4.

Kilometre fractions:

1000 m	2:56.0	
2000 m	6:00.8	(3:04.8)
3000 m	9:04.5	(3:03.7)
4000 m	12:08.5	(3:04.0)
5000 m	15:14.0	(3:05.5)
6000 m	18:22.0	(3:08.0)
7000 m	21:26.0	(3:04.0)
8000 m	24:32.0	(3:06.0)
9000 m	27:40.0	(3:08.0)
10,000 m	30:35.4	(2:55.4)

Enroute Ritola ran 6 miles in 29:38.5, also a new world record (not ratified by the IAAF).

Nurmi's reaction followed suit - at the very same venue, the Eläintarha (Zoological Garden) grounds in Helsinki on 19 June. The test was meant as a rehearsal for the forthcoming Paris Olympics (where he would have to face a similar time schedule): in the space of 55 minutes he tried the 1500 first, then the 5000, and set new world records in both with 3:52.6 and 14:28.2 respectively. Details on the longer race follow.

Helsinki, 19 June 1924 – 5000 metres: 1.Paavo Nurmi 14:28.2, 2.T.Berggren 15:57.8 , 3.Ilmari Jokinen 16:16.0.

Kilometre fractions:

1000 m	2:48.6	
2000 m	5:43.2	(2:54.6)
3000 m	8:40.3	(2:57.1)
4000 m	11:37.0	(2:56.7)
5000 m	14:28.2	(2:51.2)

Last 400 metres: 64.2
Enroute Nurmi ran 3 miles in 14:02.0, a new world record (not ratified by the IAAF).

The stage was set for captivating Olympic fireworks. On the Colombes track (then a 500-metre circuit) near Paris the finals of 1500 and 5000 metres were scheduled for the same afternoon, a trick Nurmi had purposely and successfully tried in his Helsinki rehearsal. Except that the weather in Colombes was considerably warmer. Nurmi stayed away from the 10,000 metres, scheduled for the first day, thus leaving the way free for Ritola, who in the meantime had endeared himself to many Finnish fans. Here is the detailed story of what happened in that momentous Olympic week.

6 July: 10,000 metres – 1.Ville Ritola (Fin) 30:23 1/5 (new world record), 2.Edvin Wide (Swe) 30:55 1/5, 3.Eero Berg (Fin) 31:43.0, 4.Väinö Sipilä (Fin) 31:50 1/5, 5.Ernest Harper (GB) 31:58 est, 6.Halland Britton (GB) 32:06est, 7.Guillaume Tell (Fra) 32:12est, 8.Earle Johnson (USA) 32:17est.

Kilometre fractions:

1000 m	2:47 4/5	
2000 m	5:45 1/5	(2:57 2/5)
3000 m	8:47 2/5	(3:02 1/5)
4000 m	11:52 3/5	(3:05 1/5)
5000 m	15:00 1/5	(32:07 3/5)
6000 m	18:05 3/5	(3:05 2/5)
7000 m	21:05 3/5	(3:00.0)
8000 m	24:14 1/5	(3:08 3/5)
9000 m	27:19 3/5	(3:05 2/5)
10,000 m	30:23 1/5	(3:03 3/5)

No 6-mile time for Ritola.

7 July: 3000 m Steeplechase (heats), Ritola won his in 9:59.0.
8 July: 5000 m (heats), Nurmi won his in 15:28 3/5, Ritola was 3rd in another heat.
9 July: 1500 m (heats), Nurmi won his in 4:07 3/5. 3000 m Steeplechase (final): 1.Ritola 9:33 3/5.
10 July: (at 19.05 hrs), 1500 metres (final): 1.Nurmi 3:53 3/5
(at 20.00 hrs), 5000 metres (final): 1.Paavo Nurmi (Fin) 14:31 1/5, 2.Ville Ritola (Fin) 14:31 3/5, 3.Edvin Wide (Swe) 15:01 4/5, 4.John Romig (USA) 15:12 2/5, 5.Eino Seppälä (Fin) 15:18 2/5, 6.Charles Clibbon (GB) 15:20 2/5est, 7.Lucien Dolquès (Fra) 15:22 3/5est, 8.Axel Eriksson (Swe) 15:38est.
11 July: 3000 m team race (heats). Finland qualified and Nurmi had the fastest time, 8:47 4/5.
12 July: Cross-Country race (10,650 km), 1.Nurmi 32:54 4/5, 2.Ritola 34:19 2/5.
13 July: 3000 m team race (final). Finland won and Nurmi had the fastest time, 8:32.0, with Ritola 2nd best (8:40 3/5).

Nurmi, at the peak of his form, really had a mammoth task. He won 5 gold medals (availing himself of the previously mentioned rule which allowed one to collect two medals in team races) and thereby outshone even the feats of Hannes Kolehmainen, his boyhood hero, in the 1912 Games. However, one should not underestimate – as some observers apparently did at the time – the part played by Ville Ritola, who collected 4 gold and 2 silver medals, truly a record, quantity-wise at least. And he was the only one who managed to give Paavo a good race for his money at least once, in the 5000 metre final. No matter if Nurmi, then running his second race in the space of an hour, was apparently content to win without straining himself unduly. Much easier was Nurmi's victory over Ritola in the cross-country race, which was run on a sultry day.
There was a lot of speculation in Finnish circles over Nurmi's absence in the 10,000 metres. Rumour had it that the "powers that be" of Finnish athletics wanted to reserve that event for Ritola, the "enfant prodigue" who had come all the way from America to earn glory for his mother country. There was also another rumour: somebody said that Nurmi, exactly at the time of Ritola's victory in the '10', ran the same distance inside 30 minutes in a secret time trial on his training ground .... Surely Nurmi had the potential of a sub-30 min. runner. After his return home he recaptured the world record, again in a virtual solo race, with 30:06.1. Splits are not available. We only know that Nurmi negotiated the first half in 14:52.5 and the second in 15:13.6. Details:
Kuopio, 31 August 1924 – 10,000 metres: 1.Paavo Nurmi 30:06.1 (officially ratified by the IAAF as 30:06 1/5), 2.Kalle Matilainen 33:36.1. While enroute, Nurmi also ran world bests for 4 miles (19:18.7), 5 miles (24:13.1) and 6 miles (29:07.1). none of which was ratified by the IAAF.
Nurmi and Ritola finally locked horns on Finnish tracks too, namely twice on consecutive days. In both Nurmi won a KO decision, as can be gathered from results:
Turku, 14 September, 5000 metres: 1.Nurmi 14:43.8, 2.Ritola 15 :03.8.
Tampere, 15 September, 10,000 metres: 1.Nurmi 30:20,9, 2.Ritola 30:44.5.
By then everybody knew who was the king of distance running.

Nurmi conquers America: 55 races in 5 months (and only 2 defeats)

The echo of Paavo Nurmi's deeds in Paris predictably reached the ears of American promoters and early in 1925 the "Silent Finn" – as he was then called in the rest of Europe – was invited to USA for a long "tournée". This turned out to be unique in terms of both quality and quantity. In the space of 5 months the man from Turku ran 45 races indoors and 10 outdoors! Of these he lost only two: on 17 March, during an indoor meet in New York he was pitted against Ville Ritola in the 5000 metres but had to drop out four laps from home due to a case of indigestion. Ritola won in 14:33.6. Nurmi did not lose again until his last appearance on American soil, in an outdoor meet at Bronx Baseball Stadium over a distance of 880 yards. The winner was America's premier specialist, Alan Helffrich, who finished in 1:56.8, leaving Nurmi 6 yards behind. On all other occasions the Finn was the undisputed master. He set American indoor records galore, which were actually world bests too for undercover competition, virtually ignored at that time in most other countries. It may suffice to list here his records at standard distances:

New York, 6 January		1500 m	3:56.0+
		1 mile	4:13.6
		5000 m	14:44.6*
New York, 15 January		3000 m	8:26.8
New York, 17 January		2000 m	5:33.0
New York, 28 January		2000 m	5:30.2
Boston, 31 January		2 miles	9:16.2
New York, 3 February		2 miles	9:09.2+
Brooklyn, N.Y., 7 February		2 miles	9:08.0
Buffalo, N.Y., 12 February		2000 m	5:22.4+
New York, 14 February		2 miles	8:58.2
Buffalo, N.Y., 7 March		1 mile	4:12.0
New York, 12 March		3000 m	8:26.4+
Buffalo, N.Y., 26 March		5000 m	14:38.0

+ Intermediate time in a race at longer distance.
* Won from Ritola (14:48.0)

Americans were particularly impressed by his sub-9 min. race over 2 miles, while Europeans were most appreciative of Ville Ritola's 14:23.2 for 5000 metres (New York, 24 February), which was faster than Nurmi's outdoor record. Both races were on an unbanked board track at Madison Square Garden (11 laps to the mile). Here again, Ritola's solid work deserves a detailed mention. He set new American indoor records at the following standard distances:

New York, 27 January	3 miles	14:04.0
New York, 4 February	5000 m	14:31.0
Buffalo, N.Y., 12 February	2 miles	9:03.8
New York, 14 February	3 miles	14:01.4
New York, 24 February	3 miles	13:56.2+
	5000 m	14:23.2

+ Intermediate time in a race at longer distance.

Especially in meets held at Madison Square Garden, which at the time had a capacity of 17,000 spectators, Nurmi's appearances invariably coincided with a "Sold Out" announcement. Wrote Wally Donovan, America's premier historian on indoor activities: "Several hours before his first meet there (January 6), fans waited in long lines outside the Garden for the doors to open. Late arrivals had to be quelled by special police when the fire department ordered the doors closed". Matti Hannus says: " In the chronicles of sports, Paavo Nurmi's American tour is still a special case , an unsurpassed cairn of human ability and probably craziness as well. Allegedly, largely thanks to his exploits the United States helped Finland through the big government loans in the 1920's". Especially in the latter part of his tour, which brought him to California, Nurmi became an attraction even for famous Hollywood movie stars.
Throughout his triumphal tour Nurmi had Hugo Qvist as manager and interpreter, a

man most capable of taking adequate care of his protégé. However, the great Finn had to pay a price for all this: such an overdose of races, many of which on board tracks, was to leave signs in his body and legs. In later years he no longer had the aura of an invincible man. Due to recurring bouts of rheumatism, he suffered some otherwise unexplainable defeats in the 1925 outdoor season. More of this was to follow in 1926, when in a major meet at Berlin he was badly beaten twice on consecutive days and lost two of his world records. On 11 September Otto Peltzer of Germany ran 1500 metres in 3:51.0, beating Edvin Wide of Sweden (3:51 4/5) and Nurmi (3:52 4/5). The following day, on the same track, Wide ran 2 miles in 9:01 2/5, with Nurmi second in 9:05.0.

Nurmi was in better shape when the 1928 Olympics in Amsterdam rolled around. Once again, Ritola and Wide were his main rivals. In the first round, over 10,000 metres, Ritola led the dance most of the way, passing the 5000 metre mark in a brisk 15:08. But with 100 metres to go Nurmi forged ahead and won safely. Wide wound up a distant third. Nurmi thus recaptured the title which had been his eight years before. Details:

Amsterdam, 29 July 1928 – 10,000 metres: 1.Paavo Nurmi (Fin) 30:18 4/5, 2.Ville Ritola (Fin) 30:19 2/5, 3.Edvin Wide (Swe) 31:00 4/5, 4.Jean-Gunnar Lindgren (Swe) 31:26.0, 5.Arthur Muggridge (GB) 31:31 4/5, 6.Ragnar Magnusson (Swe) 31:37 1/5, 7.Toivo Loukola (Fin) 31:39.0, 8.Kalle Matilainen (Fin) 31:45.0.

On 31 July, in the heats of the 5000 metres, Ritola, Wide and Nurmi all qualified without spreading themselves thin. The next day the two Finns won their respective heats of the 3000 metres steeplechase. Both were partly handicapped by the time they lined up at the start of the 5000 metre final on 3 August. They had supposedly suffered slight injuries in the prelims of the steeplechase: Ritola had a sore ankle and Nurmi a sore hip – probably as a result of their awkward technique in going over the barriers. After a "quiet" race for most of the way, Ritola finally had the upper hand and won comfortably, while Nurmi was content to shunt Wide to third. Details:

Amsterdam, 3 August 1928 – 5000 metres: 1.Ville Ritola (Fin) 14:38.0, 2.Paavo Nurmi (Fin) 14:40.0, 3.Edvin Wide (Swe) 14:41 1/5, 4.Leo Lermond (USA) 14:50.0, 5.Ragnar Magnusson (Swe) 14:59 3/5, 6.Armas Kinnunen (Fin) 15:02.0, 7.Stanislaws Petkevics (Lat), 8.Herbert Johnston (GB).

The two Finnish warriors had their last labours in the final of the 3000 metre steeplechase (4 August). Ritola, visibly in great pain, stayed with the leading group for a long time but finally had to drop out. Nurmi, notwithstanding his faulty technique over the hurdles, used his running talent to good advantage and finished second (9:31 1/5) well behind his countryman Toivo Loukola, probably the only "specialist" in the whole lot, who chalked up a world best of 9:21 4/5. (One had to wait till 1954 for a definitive codification of this event and the consequent introduction of official world records).

Willi Meisl, a well-known Austrian sports journalist (and a brother of Hugo, coach of the famous "Wunderteam" in football) wrote that one day, while watching a race from the press-box, he had the impression that Nurmi was not going all out. However, he had time to reconsider when at the end of it he saw "the greatest of them all" lying on the ground, exhausted and depressed as never before …

Nurmi's collection in three editions of the Olympic Games amounted to 9 gold and 3 silver medals – an incomparable record. Ritola, who was a front-line performer in two editions, had 5 gold and 3 silver medals, amply sufficient to be considered "history's greatest second" up to that time. It is curious to note that - contrary to the belief of posterity - neither of the two great Finns did ever mount an Olympic podium, simply because such a "gadget" was introduced only in 1932.

Nurmi allowed himself one more prowess before the end of the 1928 season: on 7 October in Berlin he succeeded Jean Bouin as holder of the world's 1-hour record by covering 19,210 km.

The three years that followed were rather calm for Nurmi, by then well in his thirties and rich in honours. The last of his world records occurred at Helsinki on 24 July 1931, when he beat three young Finnish lions in a 2-mile race in 8:59.5, still worse than his indoor mark of 1925 in America. In his wake, Lauri Lehtinen (9:00.5) , Lauri Virtanen (9:01.1) and the versatile Ilmari Iso-Hollo (9:06.6), who were looming as heirs apparent to his throne.

An unfulfilled dream

His many glory days notwithstanding, the man from Turku still had an unfulfilled dream: just like Hannes Kolehmainen, he wanted to crown his career with a victory in the marathon - at his fourth Olympics in Los Angeles, 1932. In the spring of that year, the ever methodical Paavo made a rehearsal at Viipuri over a distance of 40,200 km., which he covered in a most promising time - 2 hrs 22:03.8. As destiny would have it, however, he was denied the realization of his dream. Persistent rumours had been circulating for some time about alleged "purses" he had received for some of his appearances abroad. He was already on the spot, namely in Los Angeles, when it was announced that the IOC and the IAAF had decided to oust him from the amateur ranks. To him and to Finland this was sad news indeed. Urho Kekkonen, a former Finnish high jump champion who was then president of SUL, the Finnish athletics federation (and who was to become President of Finland) aired his views on the subject. He said it would henceforth be very difficult for any champion to train assiduously almost every day and still remain an amateur. He was instrumental in the decision of SUL to allow Nurmi to appear in meets on Finnish soil as a "national amateur". This allowed the old champion to have two more low-fire seasons. In 1933 he had his last glory day when he won the Finnish championship title at 1500 metres in 3:55.8, leaving behind the "nouvelle vague" of Finnish middle distance talent. In 1934 he closed his long career with times of 15:12.0 (5000 m.) and 31:39.2 (10,000 m.). He was 37 by then and the latter time ranked him 11th in the World List for that year.

Nurmi has committed to posterity some interesting revelations about his training methods. In his book "Olympiavoittajien Testamenttii" (Testament of an Olympic champion) he said that his physical fitness was largely a heritage of his many years of hard work as a teen-ager. He confessed that up to the age of 21 he had no idea of what "speed work" actually meant. "My training was perhaps too one-sided, mostly slow-pace running over long distances". In 1924 he adopted some new concepts though and from then on his training schedule was more or less as follows: an early morning walk of 10-12 km. with some sprints, then some gym work and a bath. After about an hour he started training on the track. Usually he ran 4-5 x 80-120 metre sprints, then a fast run over 400-1000 metres. Then 3000-4000 metre at even pace, with a fast last lap. His evening session consisted of cross-country running at distances ranging from 4000 to 7000 metres, always at faster speed in the closing range. He would usually close with 4-5 x 80-100 metre sprints. This daily training helped him to attain the condition he had at the 1924 Olympics in Paris.

Nurmi died at Helsinki on 2 October 1973, aged 76. He was given a state funeral, attended by over 2000 people, among them President Urho Kekkonen and other Finnish champions. On that occasion the main daily of his native town, "Turun Sanomat" (The Turku Herald) had two and a half pages on him. Equally if not more significant was the tribute paid by "The New York Times", which devoted three front-page columns to "The Silent Finn".

Paavo's heirs come along

1932 marked the end of the Nurmi era. The turning point became crystal clear on 19 June, when two of his world records were bettered at different venues. At Antwerp a small, slightly hunch-backed Pole, Janusz Kusocinski, ran 3000 metres in 8:18 4/5, with halves in 4:05 1/5 and 4:13 3/5. Almost at the same time, at the Eläintarha grounds in Helsinki, Lauri Lehtinen ran 5000 metres in 14:16.9, thus bettering Nurmi's record by over 11 sec-

A champion in discretion

For the major part of his life Paavo Nurmi exasperated newspaper men far and wide for his parsimonious speech. In his own country the so-called Fourth Estate seldom, if ever, secured confidential revelations from him. Foreigners had an even harder job: Finnish is to many people in the rest of Europe a virtually impenetrable language. As a result, little was said or written about his private life. As an adult he went back to school and eventually managed to earn himself a dignified place in life – even outside the world of sport. He was a businessman, a building contractor and in his later years he was generally regarded as a well-to-do person. As a young man he used to say that an athlete should preferably live as a poor man and feel like one – just to be able to endure sufferings.

To his credit it must be said that in the latter part of his life he helped his onetime rival Ville Ritola, who had come back from USA "with more wealth in his soul than in his bank account". Maybe Nurmi experienced his greatest disappointment when his son Matti finished only 9th in a 1500 metre race at Turku on 11 July 1957 when two Finns, Olavi Salsola and Olavi Salonen, finished one-two in that order, both with a new world record of 3:40.2. No matter if Matti set a new PB of 3:54.8 on that occasion.

onds. The latter race definitely marked the coming-of-age of a new generation. Lehtinen led for the greater part of the race , actually with a second half (7:07) faster than the first (7:10) and won from Volmari Iso-Hollo, who also bettered the previous record. Details:

Helsinki, 19 June 1932 – 5000 metres: 1.Lauri Lehtinen 14:16.9, 2.Volmari Iso-Hollo 14:18.3, 3.Lauri Virtanen 14:36.8, 4.Jalmari Kaila 14:55.0, 5.Hannes Piispanen 15:03.6.

Kilometre fractions:

1000 m	2:46.5	
2000 m	5:40.5	(2:54.0)
3000 m	8:36.0	(2:55.5)
4000 m	11:33.5	(2:57.5)
5000 m	14:16.9	(2:43.4)

Last 200 metres in 30.9.

Lehtinen's mark was rounded up to 14:17.0 as per IAAF rule. Enroute he was timed in 13:50.6 for 3 miles, also a world record.

The new record holders, Lehtinen and Kusocinski, lived up to their newly acquired status in the Los Angeles Olympics. First to do the job was the Pole (born in Warsaw on 15 January 1907; 1.67 m. /57 kg.), who upset his Finnish rivals in the 10,000 metres. He went into the lead early and ran the first 1500 metres in 4:17.0. At the half-way mark (14:56.6) he was closely followed by Iso-Hollo, Lauri Virtanen and John Savidan of New Zealand. The sturdy Pole knocked them out one by one. Iso-Hollo was last to give way. "Kuso" ran the last lap in 62.0. His final time, 30:11.4, was the second best ever up to that time. Details:

Los Angeles, 31 July 1932 – 10,000 metres: 1.Janusz Kusocinski (Pol) 30:11.4, 2.Volmari Iso-Hollo (Fin) 30:12.6, 3.Lauri Virtanen (Fin) 30:35.0, 4.John Savidan (NZ) 31:09.0, 5.Max Syring (Ger) 31:35.0, 6.Jean-Gunnar Lindgren (Swe) 31:37.0, 7.Juan Morales (Mex), 8.Calvin Bricker (Can).

Earlier in the season Kusocinski had won the 800 metres at the Polish Championships in 1:56.6. In addition to his world record for 3000 metres he could point to a good 3:54.0 in the 1500, a distance over which he had beaten Luigi Beccali of Italy late in 1931. (The latter went on to beat the cream of the world in the Olympic test at that distance).

At the Los Angeles Games Kusocinski did not run the 5000 metres. Here the Finns were ultra-confident in the capabilities of their new world record holder Lauri Lehtinen (born at Kerkkoo on 10 August 1908; 1.74 m. / 62 kg.). Much to their surprise, however, he found a very hard nut to crack in Ralph Hill of USA, a 4:12.4 miler (the world's fastest time in 1930), who at the US Olympic Tryouts had quali-

41

Little Kohei Murakoso (Japan) leading Finnish trio Askola-Salminen-Isohollo in the 10,000 metres at the 1936 Olympics in Berlin. The Japanese failed in his gallant attempt to break the Finnish hegemony and finished fourth behind his Nordic rivals. Salminen won in 30:15.4.

fied for the 5000 with an easy 14:55.7. He and Lehtinen were in the same heat on 2 August: they finished in that order (14:59.6 and 14:59.8 respectively) without straining themselves unduly. In the final (5 August) Lauri Virtanen and Lehtinen went into the lead early, while Hill was closing up the rear. But a hot, rather un-Finnish weather, forced the two Northerners to slow down: from 2:46 in the first kilometre, they had to settle for 2:59, 2:54 and 2:57 in the next three. With 1000 metres to go Hill was still in contention. And the first to lose contact was Virtanen. What then unfolded before the eyes of a large (80,000) crowd was a ding-dong battle between the record holder, Lehtinen, and his challenger, Hill. No matter how hard he tried, the Finn just could not get rid of the man "who was not supposed to be there". In the last lap the American twice tried to pass Lehtinen, first from the outside, then from the inside. Lehtinen held him off, but not without first swinging wide and then closing in. Hill was thus obliged to cut his stride, and when he tried to fight back it was too late. Lehtinen won by half a metre and the time for both was 14:30.0. Virtanen was third in 14:44.0. The judges finally decided not to charge Lehtinen with a foul, and the crowd, who in such cases are not apt to think twice, gave way to their feelings with loud boos. Announcer Bill Henry (a well-known sports writer who in 1948 was to author an excellent book, "A History of the Olympic Games") rose to the occasion and quieted down the masses with the words: "Remember, please, these people are our guests".

The winner negotiated the last kilometre in 2:54 and that tantalizing last lap in 69.2 – clear evidence that he and his great rival were by then on the verge of exhaustion. Details:

Los Angeles, 5 August 1932 - 5000 metres: 1.Lauri Lehtinen (Fin) 14:30.0, 2.Ralph Hill (USA) 14:30.0, 3.Lauri Virtanen (Fin) 14:44.0, 4.John Savidan (NZ) 14:49.6, 5.Jean-Gunnar Lindgren (Swe) 14:54.8, 6.Max Syring (Ger) 14:59.0, 7.J.Alex Burns (GB) 15:03est, 8.Daniel Dean (USA).

Fair play, vintage 1932

During the 1984 Olympics in Los Angeles I got a chance to meet, during a "Track & Field News" party in the proximity of the Memorial Coliseum, Ralph Hill, then 76 and ostensibly sad over the recent death of his wife (he himself was to pass away in 1994). During our conversation I invited him to give me a retrospective view of the most important venture of his athletic life, the Olympic 5000 metre final of 1932 right there in Los Angeles. Just as he had done at that time, he aired his viewpoint in consequent terms: "I don't think Lauri deliberately wanted to hinder me. As we were going down the homestretch he looked around to see where I was. I know from experience that a tired runner often happens to lose his sense of direction. Lehtinen was so exhausted that he was steering a blind course and balked in front of me, yet I think he had enough left to win anyhow. I did not file a protest because I was sure of that. I had found myself in similar situations."

Hill's decision not to file a protest surely led the jury to put out a verdict in favour of the "status quo".

Lehtinen and Hill met again over 5000 metres in a post-Olympic meet at Chicago on 18 August. The Finn, reportedly affected by what had been said and written about his conduct in the Los Angeles race, felt flat and did not finish. Yet the winner was not Hill but Poland's Janusz Kusocinski, who beat the American – 14:59.9 to 15:02.0. The Pole never rose again to his 1932 heights. In 1934 he was second in the 5000 metres at the European Championships, then recurring injuries made his career most precarious. He resurrected rather surprisingly in 1939, when he ran the 5000 metres in 14:24.2 in an international meet in Stockholm. He died during World War II as a fighter in the Polish "Résistance" movement. The most important event in the Polish track calendar is named Kusocinski Memorial Meet.

In the years after the Los Angeles Games Nurmi's Finnish heirs more than confirmed their superiority, no matter if they lost something along the way, as in the inaugural edition of the European Championships in Turin in 1934. Results of the two distance races there were as follows:

Turin, 7 September 1934 – 10,000 metres:
1.Ilmari Salminen (Fin) 31:02.6, 2.Arvo Askola (Fin) 31:03.2, 3.Henry Nielsen (Den) 31:27.4, 4. Georg Braathe (Nor) 32:20.0, 5.Jenö Szilágyi (Hun) 32:23.0.

Turin, 9 September 1934 – 5000 metres:
1.Roger Rochard (Fra) 14:36.8, 2.Janusz Kusocinski (Pol) 14:41.2, 3.Ilmari Salminen (Fin) 14:43.6, 4.Lauri Virtanen (Fin) 14:47.6, 5.Salvatore Mastroieni (Ita) 32:00.6.

The winner of the shorter race, Roger Rochard (born at Evreux on 20 April 1913) had his Day of Days on that occasion, equalling Jean Bouin's 22-year-old French record (which was 14:36.7 but, as previously related, it was rounded up to 14:36.8). A runner with a medium but very agile frame, he had emerged at the national level at the unripe age of 17. His victory in the Turin race, aged 21, came as a major surprise, but he was unable to live up to his reputation in the years that followed.

On the eve of the 1936 Olympics in Berlin the Finnish armour appeared to be stronger than ever. The above-mentioned Ilmari Salminen (born at Elimäki on 21 September 1902; 1.82 m. / 66 kg.) symbolized a metronome with the smooth and consistent succession of his long strides. He had a punishing kick too. In his younger years he had adopted the philosophy of patience and moderation, maybe as a result of several circumstances that delayed his development. Yet in 1928 he seemed ready for major tasks, but due to unexplained reasons he was not selected for the Amsterdam Olympics. In 1932, aged 30, he was barely seventh in the 5000 metres at the Finnish Olympic Trials. But his best days were yet to come ..... His breakthrough occurred at the 1934 Europeans, as related above. After which he went from strength to strength.

At the 1936 Olympics Finland reached the apex of its glory, winning 5 of the 6 medals at stake in the long distance events. In the 10,000 metres a trio made of Salminen, his nemesis Arvo Askola and the eccentric Volmari Iso-Hollo (the 1932 Olympic champion in the steeplechase, a title he was to retain in Berlin) turned out to have only one truly serious rival. This was not America's Don Lash as might be expected on the strength of his recent world record over 2 miles - 8:58.3 at Princeton on 13 June. But in the Olympic race he had to be content with an undistinguished rôle (eighth). The real threat came from a little Japanese, 31-year-old Kohei Murakoso, who had come to Berlin with the season's fastest clocking – 30:41.6. In the race that counted most he remained in the wake of the well-oiled Finnish trio and gave up only in the early stages of the last lap, when the tall Salminen launched his attack. Iso-Hollo was next to give up. Askola remained in contention till the end and lost by merely 0.2 sec. Details:

Berlin, 2 August 1936 – 10,000 metres:
1.Ilmari Salminen (Fin) 30:15.4, 2.Arvo Askola (Fin) 30:15.6, 3.Volmari Iso-Hollo (Fin) 30:20.2, 4.Kohei Murakoso (Jap) 30:25.0, 5.J.Alex Burns (GB) 30:58.2, 6.Juan Carlos Zabala (Arg) 31:22.0, 7.Max Gebhard (Ger) 31:29.0, 8.Don Lash (USA) 31:39.4.

The first half was covered in 15:01.0 and the second in 15:14.4.

The Finns were out for another grand slam in the 5000 metres. On 4 August Gunnar Höckert, Lehtinen and Salminen went through the heats hands down, but in the decisive race on 7 August things did not go smoothly all the way. The hitch was met with two laps to go, when Salminen collided with Lehtinen and fell. The winner of the '10' got up as quickly as he could but obviously had no time to make up for the lost ground and finished sixth. His two countrymen met some resistance from a Swedish "cousin", Henry Jonsson, but finally went home one-two, with Höckert outsprinting Lehtinen, the defending champion, with astounding ease. Don Lash had lost contact near the half-way mark. The impressive Höckert (born in Helsinki on 12 February 1910; 1.79 m./ 67 kg.) was in the opinion of Finnish experts, notably including Paavo

Nurmi, the greatest talent of them all, no matter if not always systematic in his training methods.

Berlin, 7 August 1936 – 5000 metres: 1.Gunnar Höckert (Fin) 14:22.2, 2.Lauri Lehtinen (Fin) 14:25.8, 3.Henry Jonsson (Swe) 14:29.0, 4.Kohei Murakoso (Jap) 14:30.0, 5.Józef Noji (Pol) 14:33.4, 6.Ilmari Salminen (Fin) 14:39.8, 7.Umberto Cerati (Ita) 14:44.4, 8.Louis Zamperini (USA) 14:46.8.

Kilometre fractions:

1000 m	2:49.0	
2000 m	5:45.6	(2:56.6)
3000 m	8:40.0	(2:54.4)
4000 m	11:37.5	(2:57.5)
5000 m	14:22.2	(2:44.7)

Höckert, a Finn of Swedish language, closed his 1936 account on very high notes, with two world records in the space of eight days, both in Stockholm: 8:14.8 for 3000 metres (16 September) and 8:57.4 for 2 miles (24 September). Recurrent bouts of rheumatism - a disease that affected him since boyhood - hampered him in the following years. He died on the Carelian front in 1940, the day before his 30th birthday.

In 1936 Finland was able to receive daily radio broadcasts from Berlin. Quite predictably, enthusiasm for the triumphs of Suomi champs ran high in every corner of the country. Salminen - who in the opinion of many, could have contributed to another sweep if he had not fallen in the closing stage of the 5000 metres - had begun to reveal his real talent rather late, yet his thirst was not quenched yet. His ambition was to succeed Nurmi as holder of the 10,000 metre world record. He succeeded in his quest in the summer of 1937 at Kouvola with a time of 30:05.5. Practically all the best distance men from Finland were in the race, which attracted 6000 spectators – more than the entire population of Kouvola! Details:

Kouvola, 18 July 1937 - 10,000 metres: 1.Ilmari Salminen 30:05.5, 2.Lauri Lehtinen 30:15.0, 3.Arvo Askola 30:34.2, 4.Veikko Tuominen 32:18.0.

Kilometre fractions:

1000 m	2:56.0	
2000 m	5:51.5	(2:55.5)
3000 m	8:56.0	(3:04.5)
4000 m	11:58.0	(3:02.0)
5000 m	15:01.0	(3:03.0)
6000 m	18:05.0	(3:04.0)
7000 m	21:10.0	(3:05.0)
8000 m	24:16.0	(3:06.0)
9000 m	27:11.0	(2:55.0)
10,000 m	30:05.5	(2:54.5)

Enroute he did 29:08.3 for 6 miles, also a new world record. Both this and the 10,000 time were rounded up to the nearest fifth in accordance with IAAF rules.

Mäki opens new frontiers

By that time another good runner was gathering momentum. His name was Taisto Mäki (born at Rekola on 2 December 1910; 1.73 m. / 64 kg.) and he was to be the last of Finland's pre-war aces. He too came up rather slowly, even though he ranked among Finland's best in 1934 and more so in 1936. For his real breakthrough one had to wait till 1938, when he won a continental crown in the 5000 metres and then broke Salminen's world record. The European Championships of that year were held at Stade de Colombes near Paris, theatre of the 1924 Olympics. The circumference of the track had been reduced to 400 metres, the new standard distance. In compliance with a well established Finnish tradition, Mäki and his compatriot Kauko Pekuri alternated in setting the pace, yet they met stubborn resistance from Henry Jonsson of Sweden. Mäki finally won but Pekuri had to give way to the Swede for second place. Details:

Colombes, 4 September 1938 – 5000 metres: 1.Taisto Mäki (Fin) 14:26.8, 2.Henry Jonsson (Swe) 14:27.4, 3.Kauko Pekuri (Fin) 14 :29.2, 4.Jack Emery (GB) 14:46.2, 5.Józef Noji (Pol) 14:47.8, 6.Morrison Carstairs (GB) 14:51.3, 7.András Csaplár (Hun) 14:52.4, 8.Roger Rochard (Fra) 14:55.6. The winner covered the last lap in 64.2.

In the 10,000 metres Ilmari Salminen had to

fight pretty hard to stay ahead of a very small Italian, 24-year-old Giuseppe Beviacqua, who was only 1.62 m. tall – hence 20 cm. shorter than the Finn. An odd scenario indeed. In the next-to-last kilometre Beviacqua was bold enough to forge ahead of the reigning Oympic champion and world record holder. But the Finn used his long legs to good advantage to reverse positions in the closing stage. It was a stirring duel, no matter if the time for the last lap, 67.8, may look unimpressive if seen through present-day lenses.

Colombes, 5 September 1938 - 10,000 metres: 1.Ilmari Salminen (Fin) 30:52.4, 2.Giuseppe Beviacqua (Ita) 30:53.2, 3.Max Syring (Ger) 30:57.8, 4.Jenö Szilágyi (Hun) 30:58.6, 5.Thore Tillman (Swe) 31:06.6, 6.János Kelen (Hun) 31:16.6, 7.Giuseppe Lippi (Ita) 31:51.6, 8. André Sicard (Fra) 32:09.6.

Before the end of the season Mäki launched an attack against Salminen's world record for the 10,000 metres. He reached the venue of the meet, Tampere, after a three-hour train trip from Helsinki, then he allowed himself an hour for rest before lining up at the start of the race. As usual, the best Finns were all there, including Salminen, the record holder. Yet the latter happened to have an off day and the others were not a match for the confident Taisto, who beat 3 minutes in four of his kilometre fractions, including the last one. He finally succeeded Salminen with 30:02.0. Fine running on a 333 1/3 m. track. Details:

Tampere, 29 September 1938 – 10,000 metres: 1. Taisto Mäki 30:02.0, 2.Kauko Pekuri 30:18.2, 3.Arvo Askola (Fin) 30:48.8, 4.Matti Laihoranta 30:50.6, 5.Ilmari Salminen 31:04.6, 6.Volmari Iso-Hollo 31:26.4. Virtanen and Lehtinen did not finish.

Kilometre fractions:

1000 m	2:58.0	
2000 m	5:55.0	(2:57.0)
3000 m	8:57.0	(3:02.0)
4000 m	11:57.0	(3:00.0)
5000 m	14:59.0	(3:02.0)
6000 m	18:01.0	(3:02.0)
7000 m	20:59.0	(2:58.0)
8000 m	24:01.0	(3:02.0)
9000 m	27:05.0	(3:04.0)
10,000 m	30:02.0	(2:57.0)

No time taken for 6 miles.

Kauko Pekuri, 26, was in the process of becoming Mäki's eternal second, the same rôle played by Askola vis-à-vis Salminen. As previously noted, Mäki and Pekuri were willing to share the "donkey work" in world record attempts. It was again so in 1939, when the former conquered the 5000-metre record as well. The race was at the new Olympic Stadium in Helsinki, which had been built for the 1940 Olympics – an event later cancelled by World War II. Mäki bettered Lehtinen's world record by no less than 8.2 secs., chiefly thanks to a last kilometre in 2:44.3. Old warrior Ilmari Salminen, third, astounded experts with a new PB of 14:22.0 – at age 37. Details:

Helsinki, 16 June 1939 – 5000 metres: 1.Taisto Mäki 14:08.8, 2.Kauko Pekuri 14:16.2, 3.Ilmari Salminen 14:22.0, 4.Veikko Tuominen 14:33.0, 5.Matti A. Järvinen 14:36.2, 6.Veikko Strömbäck 14:40.0, 7.Matti Laihoranta 14:41.0, 8.Viljo Heino 15:07.8. Lehtinen did not finish.

Taisto Mäki (Finland) nips Henry Jonsson (Sweden) in the 5000 metres of the dual meet between the two Nordic countries in Stockholm in 1939. Times: 14:17.8 and 14:18.8.

Kilometre fractions:

1000 m	2:46.0	
2000 m	5:39.0	(2:53.0)
3000 m	8:32.5	(2:53.5)
4000 m	11:24.5	(2:52.0)
5000 m	14:08.8	(2:44.3)

Enroute he did 13:42.4 for 3 miles, another world record.

Mäki, at the peak of his condition, went on to conquer another world mark – 8:53.2 for 2 miles at Helsinki on 7 July. On this occasion Veikko Tuominen gave him a good race for his money, finally succumbing by merely 0.3 sec. Pekuri was third in 8:54.8. All three bettered the previous record, (8:56.0) set by Miklós Szabó, a Hungarian middle distance ace, in 1937. A further proof of Mäki's splendid form was offered only three days later when he lowered his PB for 1500 metres to 3:53.5.

Henry Jonsson was considered by many the most serious threat to the new conqueror from Finland. The Swede had revealed his potential as a miler in 1937 by finishing close to Archie San Romani of USA in Stockholm – 4:08.8 to 4:08.4. In that summer he and Mäki met twice in the Swedish capital. The first round was in the eagerly awaited "Match" between the two Nordic countries and Mäki won – 14:17.8 to 14:18.8. Less than two months later a re-run saw them finish in the same order: 14:19.8 to 14:20.6. But Mäki was not through yet: just two days after his hard clash with Jonsson he returned to Helsinki's Olympic Stadium and put up what was to remain the greatest of his achievements. As the tale goes, in the morning of that day (17 September) he ran an ultra-easy 4:23.0 for the 1500 metres in a club race at nearby Käpylä. In the afternoon he lined up with some of Finland's best at the start of the 10,000 metres on the fast track of the Olympic Stadium. In cloudless, fairly warm weather he covered the first half in 14:58.2. His aim – break the half-hour barrier - began to look nearer as he negotiated the seventh kilometre in 2:54.0. Even though he was on his own in the closing stage, he was able to reproduce that pace in the last kilometre and the final result was a magnificent 29:52.6. Remarkably enough, his second half (14:54.4) was faster than the first. Details:

Helsinki, 17 September 1939 – 10,000 metres: 1.Taisto Mäki 29:52.6, 2.Tauno Kurki 30:16.0, 3.Ilmari Salminen 30:26.2, 4.Matti Laihoranta 31:15.2, 5.Evert Heinström 31:15.6.

Kilometre fractions:

1000 m	2:55.5	
2000 m	5:56.8	(3:01. 3)
3000 m	8:57.6	(3:00.8)
4000 m	12:00.6	(3:03.0)
5000 m	14:58.2	(2:57.6)
6000 m	18:00.0	(3:01.8)
7000 m	21:04.0	(3:04.0)
8000 m	23:58.0	(2:54.0)
9000 m	26:58.4	(3:00.4)
10,000 m	29:52.6	(2:54.2)

Enroute he did 28:55.6 for 6 miles, another world record.

At the end of that momentous season the 1939 World Lists had four Finns among the Top Ten in the 5,000 metres, namely in positions 1, 2, 4, 5; and six Finns among the Top Ten in the 10,000 metres, in positions 1, 2, 3, 4, 5, 10. In fact, runners from the "Rest of Europe" were overshadowed as never before. Unfortunately, World War II was to put an end to this flourishing era. In November 1939, Soviet armed forces attacked Finland by land, sea and air. This conflict between Goliath and David lasted a little more than one hundred days and at the end of it Finland had to cede to its neighbour the whole Karelian isthmus with the city of Viipuri. When Germany invaded USSR in June 1941, Finland decided to fight alongside Germany, mostly with the hope of recovering the lost land. Needless to say, throughout the war years track activity in Finland remained at a low ebb. Taisto Mäki, like other fine champions of his generation, never got a chance to vie for Olympic honours.

ZÁTOPEK – THE HALCYON DAYS OF THE HUMAN LOCOMOTIVE

The first half of the Forties, suffocated by World War II, saw a strongly reduced track activity in Europe. The vacuum was aptly filled by neutral Sweden, where excellent athletic talents came to the fore. They reached spectacular heights in the 1500 metres/1 mile departments but made notable inroads in the longer distances as well. The Swedish boom was favoured, to some extent, by the temporary absence from the athletic scene of other countries then engaged in fields of unfriendly strife. The above-mentioned Henry Jonsson (born at Kälarne on 12 May 1912, 1.81 m. / 70 kg.) changed his last name in 1940 and adopted that of his native village. In his youth he was rather frail, to the point of being rejected for military service. In later years, however, hard training eventually helped him to develop into a champion. His days of glory were mostly in 1940, when he was spurred by a coming great, Gunder Hägg, a hard front runner. On 14 August 1940 in Stockholm, Kälarne used the latter's pace work to finally emerge as a new world record holder for the 3000 metres in 8:09.0, with Hägg second in 8:11.8 - both well under Gunnar Höckert's 8:14.8. From that very moment, however, experts knew that the future belonged to Hägg. This runner (born at Sörbygden on 31 December 1918; 1.80 m. / 68 kg.) was in fact regarded as a wondrous talent. Although at his best in the 1500 metres / 1 mile department, in his banner year, 1942, he opened new frontiers in the 3000 and 5000 metres as well. On 28 August in Stockholm he ran the shorter distance in 8:01.2, annihilating Kälarne's record. Halves in 4:01.4 and 3:59.8 testified to his great potential.

A hint of Hägg's possibilities over longer distances was offered on 11 September of the same year in Stockholm. The race was over 5000 metres but he stopped at 3 miles – content with a new world record of 13:35.4,

seven seconds under Taisto Mäki's previous mark. But he reserved his "pearl" for a meet at Göteborg's Slottsskogsvallen track nine days later, when he broke the 14-minute barrier in the 5000 metres. He thus bettered by over 10 seconds the mark set in 1939 by his Finnish "cousin" Taisto Mäki. And he did so in what was practically a solo race! Details: Göteborg, 20 September 1942 - 5000 metres: 1.Gunder Hägg 13:58.2; 2.Bror Hellström 14:41.4, 3.Karl-Erik Larsson 14:42.6, 4.Gösta Östbrink 14:43.8.

Hägg's actual time, 13:58.1, was rounded up to 13:58.2 by Swedish officials, in accordance with the IAAF rule.

Kilometre fractions:

1000 m	2:40.0	
2000 m	5:27.0	(2:47.0)
3000 m	8:18.5	(2:51.5)
4000 m	11:09.0	(2:50.5)
5000 m	13:58.2	(2:49.2)

Enroute Hägg was timed in 13:32.4 for 3 miles, another world record.

In addition to being the world's fastest miler, Hägg had great endurance to speed, acquired through years of steady work under coach Gösta Olander, who operated in an idyllic tourist station - Vålådalen (Jämtland). This man, sometimes depicted as a humanist, preached a return to nature, i.e. to running without artificial limitations of time and/or distance. His idea of "Fartlek" (speed play) could only have originated in a natural atmosphere such as that of Vålådalen. In winter and summer, the running guests of that tourist resort (600 metres above sea level) would train down at the lakes and through the forests, mostly on undulating ground, never departing from the canons of "löparglädje" (joy of running). Thus they would sound out their possibilities. As time went on and their stamina increased, they would set themselves a goal and then go for it with ever-growing intensity. Hägg surely had the potential for even greater deeds at 5000 metres but was caught by a feeling of annoyance whenever he had to negotiate lap after lap at a pace which was not that of a born miler. For this reason, he made only a few more appearances in the 5000 metres.

In the meantime Finland had found a new talent, who was to be the last of her golden series for at least two decades to come. That was Viljo Akseli Heino (born at Iitti on 1 March 1914; 1.75 m. / 63 kg.). He emerged in 1939 with such times as 14:42.0 and 31:04.2, but was later hampered by various circumstances, notably including a wounded leg during the Winter War with USSR. He had to resort to intense gymnastic exercises to overcome his muscular stiffness, probably developed in years of hard work in a lumber yard. He was on the comeback trail by 1943 (14:34.6 and 30:15.2) and the following year he succeeded Mäki as holder of the world's 10,000 metre record with a time of 29:35.4 – a spectacular 17.2 secs. improvement vis-à-vis the previous mark.

Details:
Helsinki, 25 August 1944 – 10,000 metres: 1.Viljo Heino 29:35.4, 2.Gösta Pettersson (Swe) 30:22.6, 3.Kauko Pekuri 31:01.6, 4.Tauno Kurki (Fin) 31:39.6.

Kilometre fractions:

1000 m	2:56.0	
2000 m	5:52.4	(2:56.4)
3000 m	8:52.4	(3:00.0)
4000 m	11:51.4	(2:59.0)
5000 m	14:49.4	(2:58.0)
6000 m	17:49.4	(3:00.0)
7000 m	20:49.8	(3:00.4)
8000 m	23:45.8	(2:56.0)
9000 m	26:44.6	(2:58.8)
10,000 m	29:35.4	(2:50.8)

Enroute Heino did 28:38.6 for 6 miles, another world record.

Gunder Hägg was invited to the Finnish Championships at Helsinki on 24 September for a head-to-head confrontation with Heino. At the end of a relatively slow race the Swede beat his rival – 14:24.4 to 14:24.8.

The first major post-war event was the 1946 European Championships, held at Oslo's Bislett Stadium. Old and new faces appeared on the scene: young men from all corners of the continent were again able to express their "joie de vivre" on a field of friendly strife. There were some notable absentees though: ironically enough they represented neutral Sweden: Gunder Hägg, Arne Andersson (his main rival in the 1500 metres/mile department) and Henry Kälarne were ousted from the amateur ranks early in 1946. Through their sterling performances they had become so popular that Swedish promoters went out of their way to invite them to meets big and small. Inevitably, both sides committed financial abuses, which "Svenska Idrottsförbundet" could not tolerate.

At the Oslo rendez-vous Viljo Heino won the 10,000 metres hands down. After a hyperfast first half (14:35) he obviously had to slow down, yet none of his rivals was close enough to pose a threat. Even with a second half in 15:17 and a last lap in 75.0 he won by a wide margin in 29:52.0. Details:

Oslo, 22 August 1946 – 10,000 metres: 1.Viljo Heino (Fin) 29:52.0, 2.Helge Perälä (Fin) 30:31.4, 3.András Csaplár (Hun) 30:35.2, 4.Sven Rapp (Swe) 30:49.2, 5.Fyeodosiy Vanin (USSR) 30:56.2, 6.Charles Heirendt (Lux) 31:08.2, 7.Thorvald Wilhelmsen (Nor) 31:20.8, 8.Martin Stokken (Nor) 32:56.0.

Heino's visible sufferings in the closing part of the race were a prelude to what awaited him in the 5000 metre final, scheduled for the next day. Here he had to give way to fresh middle distance runners with plenty of basic speed.

Wooderson wins European 5000 m. title (eight years after his 1500 m. victory in Paris)

In the annals of the European Championships few feats are comparable to that of Sydney Wooderson at Oslo in 1946.

*Viljo Heino
(Finland) held
the world record
for 10,000
metres during
the Forties.*

51

This Briton (born in London on 30 August 1914; 1.67 m. / 56 kg.) won a great 5000 metres in 14:08.6 (then history's second best time) - eight years after his victory in the 1500 metres at the Europeans in Paris. The bespectacled Wooderson certainly did not have the semblance of a champion runner: pale, frail looking, with a chest expansion of only three inches (7.6 cms), But inside that deceptive body was an unprecedented combination of speed and endurance. A pupil of Albert Hill, a double Olympic champion (800/1500 m. in 1920), Wooderson emerged as a top miler before turning 20. In 1937 he conquered the world record for this classic distance with 4:06.4. The following year he captured the half-mile world record as well, with 1:49.2. Like many other champions he was probably deprived of his best years by World War II, yet he never really quit. In 1945 he resumed full training and the following year he began to focus his attention on the longer distances. He went to Oslo with a nice credential: a victory over Wim Slykhuis of Holland in the 3 miles of the AAA Championships – 13:53.2 to 13:54.2.

In the Oslo 5000 Heino was bold enough to go into the lead early. He passed 3000 metres in 8:32.5, but when the decisive battle flared up he could not respond to the challenge of men who were both faster and fresher. In the last lap it was simply a Wooderson vs. Slykhuis affair - two milers with a strong finishing kick. The Briton took the lead with 200 metres to go and won by a comfortable margin. He ran the last lap in 61.2. Surely he was literally exhausted at the end of it, but for a 32-year-old runner who had "lost" two editions of the Olympics on account of the war it would have been difficult to imagine a career ending on a higher note. Details:

Oslo, 23 August 1946 – 5000 metres: 1.Sydney Wooderson (GB) 14:08.6, 2.Wim Slykhuis (Hol) 14:14.0, 3.Evert Nyberg (Swe) 14:23.2, 4.Viljo Heino (Fin) 14:24.4, 5.Emil Zátopek (Cze) 14:25.8, 6.Gaston Reiff (Bel) 14:45.8, 7.Rikard Greenfort (Den) 14:46.0, 8.Raphaël Pujazon (Fra) 14:46.8.

Among the place-getters of the Oslo race there were two men bound to be heard from in the following years – Emil Zátopek of Czechoslovakia and Gaston Reiff. of Belgium. The former (born at Koprivnice, Northern Moravia, on 19 September 1922; 1.74 m. / 67 kg.) eventually developed into the first king of long distance running of the post-war period. In the earlier days of his career he had to fight against tremendous odds. His country happened to be in the midst of the horrors of war. Furthermore, Czechoslovakia was completely devoid of traditions in distance running. The national records of the pre-Zátopek era aptly tell the tale: 15:14.8 and 32:15.8. Emil's father, a factory worker, had no sporting background. As a youth Emil liked to play football, as was the case for most other boys of his generation. He made his debut in athletics at 19, when he worked as an apprentice in a shoe factory at Zlin. In his first race, on 27 April 1941, he finished second over an odd distance, 1400 metres. His best times in the early part of his career were not impressive and somehow remind one of Paavo Nurmi's best efforts at a similar age. The following chart gives his progression till 1947.

Year	Age	3000 m	5000 m
1942	20	9:12.2	16:25.0
1943	21	8:56.0	15:26.6
1944	22	8:34.8	14:54.9
1945	23	8:33.4	14:50.8
1946	24	8:21.0	14:25.8
1947	25	8:08.8	14:08.2

NB – In 1947 he also ran 1500 metres in 3:52.8 (Paris, 30 August), which was to remain his PB. In subsequent years he seldom tried this distance though.

It was only in 1945 that he got a chance to see a real champion. This was shortly after the end of World War II, when Arne Andersson of Sweden visited Czechoslovakia. From such a man, grown up in a highly competitive atmosphere, the Czech certainly had something to learn. Yet he adopted Swedish training methods only to some extent. At any rate he was inclined to intensify the quantity of his work. To this effect he shortened intervals between races and took a habit, especially in winter, to use heavy basket-ball shoes in training and even soldier's boots on rainy days. His daily running ration was increased gradually through the years. At the peak of his career he averaged over 1000 hours of running per year, 800 kilometres per month, i.e. well over half a marathon per day! His basic principle was to make his training so hard that competitive racing by comparison would come as a light matter to him. He was once quoted as saying: "It's important what you do in a crowded stadium, but it's far more important what you do in an empty one".

Zátopek was all but disappointed over his fifth place in the 5000 metres in the 1946 European Championships, especially when he heard somebody say that his time (14:25.8) was better than Paavo Nurmi's onetime world record. Amazingly enough, it was only in 1948 that Emil made his debut over 10,000 metres. This resulted in a most promising 30:28.4 (Budapest, 29 May). His next try (Prague, 17 June) yielded an astonishing 29:37.0, barely 1.6 sec. off Viljo Heino's world record! His third try coincided with a smashing Olympic victory in London's Wembley Stadium. On this occasion the 26-year-old Czech was pitted against Heino himself, then 34. After 7 kilometres the Finn collapsed under the combined effect of atmospheric heat and racing pace. Experts and laymen watching the race were strongly impressed by the Czech, as disgraceful in his running style as he was tenacious in his fighting spirit. They witnessed the advent of the "Human Locomotive", as he was to be known in track circles the world over. Details: London, 30 July 1948 – 10,000 metres: 1.Emil Zátopek (Cze) 29:59.6, 2.Alain Mimoun (Fra) 30:47.4, 3.Bertil Albertsson (Swe) 30:53.6, 4.Martin Stokken (Nor) 30:58.6, 5.Severt Dennolf (Swe) 31:05.0, 6.Ben Said Abdallah (Fra) 31:07.8, 7.Stanley Cox (GB) 31:07.0u, 8.Jim Peters (GB) 31:16.0u. First half in 14:54.0, second half in 15:05.6. Last lap: 66.6.

Zátopek allowed himself no extra time to rejoice. The preliminary round of the 5000 metres was scheduled for the next day. He went through his heat easily, as did the other top-ranking men. The final was on 2 August. And here even the great Czech found a hard nut to crack in the person of Gaston Reiff of Belgium (born at Braine-l'Alleud on 14 February 1921; 1.73 m. / 61 kg.), who could already point to a long career. He started in 1939, winning two cross-country races

Gaston Reiff (Belgium), the 1948 Olympic champion in the 5000 metres. Was also the first man to duck under 8 minutes in the 3000 metres.

53

in the space of 8 days. He shone in this particular field – so dear to the heart of Belgian runners – before turning his attention to track events. In 1946 he ran 5000 metres in 14:26.1, then finished sixth in the European Championship race at Oslo, right behind Zátopek. In the same year he also ran the 3000 metres in 8:08.8 to tie for first with Wim Slykhuis in the World Year List, and was timed in 3:51.6 for the 1500. In 1947 he improved to 3:48.4 at the latter distance, thus revealing his great potential in terms of speed. By then he was under the tutelage of Marcel Alavoine, a well-known coach.

"I have not forgotten"

In few other countries, if any, is cross-country running so popular as it is in Belgium. In the honour roll of the International Cross-country races one finds quite a few Belgian names. When this competiton was raised to the rank of a World Championship in 1973, the "première" was held at Waregem, Belgium. Most prominent among Belgian harriers was Gaston Roelants, a four-time winner of the event but also an excellent track runner – on flat courses and in the steeplechase. In some cases there have been Belgian runners who actually preferred the harrier version of the sport, e.g. Eric De Beck and Léon Schots, who won world C/C titles in 1974 and 1977 respectively but never attained major heights on the track. The great Gaston Reiff also had C/C as his "premier amour". As a youth he was coached in his native Braine-l'Alleud by Henri Gossiaux. In the book "100 ans d'athlétisme belge" he brings back memories of those years: "In training runs our group was preceded by Gossiaux's dog. Later on, when the poor animal lost his eye-sight, he used to follow us as if drawn along....... I have not forgotten".

In 1948 Reiff opened his Olympic season on a very high note: 14:14.2 for 5000 metres in Brussels – only to learn, a few days later, that down in Prague a Czech by the name of Zátopek had done 14:10.0. What is even worse, shortly afterwards he was involved in a traffic accident while waiting for a tramcar and thereby suffered injuries that forced him to stop for a while.

But on 2 August, the day of the Olympic 5000 metre final in London, the Belgian was ready. And so was Zátopek, of course. The race was marred by the rain, and conditions made the duel between these great champions truly dramatic. The tireless Czech set the pace with 2:48 (1000m), 5:38 (2000 m) and 8:33 (3000 m), with Reiff and Wim Slykhuis in his wake. When Reiff suddenly decided to attack, with 1800 metres to go, Zátopek surprisingly lost ground. That was when the Belgian increased his speed over one lap from 71.2 to 67.2. At the bell he led, with Slykhuis about 20 metres in arrear, and Zátopek another 20 metres further back. Whoever thought that Zátopek was "done" soon had to reconsider. With 300 metres to go the Czech surged like a fury, caught Slykhuis, then began to close the gap vis-à-vis Reiff. It looked as if he might finally prevail, but in the last stretch of land the Belgian rallied his last energies and finally won the day by a scant margin. Reiff ran the last lap in 69.6 Zátopek's time (not recorded officially) must have been considerably faster.

Details:

London, 2 August 1948- 5000 metres: 1.Gaston Reiff (Bel) 14:17.6, 2.Emil Zátopek (Cze) 14:17.8, 3.Wim Slykhuis (Hol) 14:26.8, 4.Erik Ahldén (Swe) 14:28.6, 5.Bertil Albertsson (Swe) 14:39.0, 6.Curtis Stone (USA) 14:39.4, 7.Väinö Koskela (Fin) 14:41.0, 8.Väinö Mäkelä (Fin) 14:43.0.

A few days later, in Prague, a rematch confirmed the Olympic verdict as Reiff again won – 14:19.0 to 14:21.2.

With one gold and one silver in his first Olympic experience, Zátopek had every reason to be satisfied with his 1948 season. Yet the first year of the Zátopek Era was 1949, when his premiership in the long distance department truly began to be unrivalled. He made his first inroad on the IAAF world record list in June of that year, opening a great series which was to end in 1955. Here is the complete list of his world records, in chronological order.

Ostrava,
11 June 1949   10,000m. 29:28.2

Ostrava,
22 October 1949   10,000m   29:21.2

Turku,
4 August 1950   10,000m   29:02.6

Prague,
15 September 1951   1 hour   19,558km+
                     20,000m   1.01:15.8

Stará Boleslav,
29 September 1951   10 miles   48:12.0+
                    20,000m   59:51.7+°
                    1 hour   20,052 km

Stará Boleslav,
26 October 1952   15 miles   1.16:26.4+
                   25,000m   1.19:11.8+
                   30,000m   1.35:23.7°

Stará Boleslav,
1 November 1953   6 miles   28:08.4+
                   10,000m   29:01.6

Colombes,
30 May 1954   5000m   13:57.2

Brussels,
1 June 1954   6 miles   27:59.2+
               10,000m   28:54.2

Celákovice,
29 October 1955   15 miles   1.14:01.0+
                   25,000m   1.16:36.4

+ Intermediate time during a race
at a longer distance.
° Officially rounded up to nearest fifth
as per IAAF rule.

In 1949 the world's 10,000 metre record was bettered on three occasions. Zátopek hit first, as follows:
Ostrava, 11 June 1949 – 10,000 metres: 1.Emil Zátopek 29:28.2, Frantisek Zanta 32:25.8.

Kilometre fractions:

1000 m	2:54.5	
2000 m	5:49.0	(2:54.5)
3000 m	8:43.0	(2:54.0)
4000 m	11:40.7	(2:57.7)
5000 m	14:39.5	(2:58.8)
6000 m	17:39.0	(2:59.5)

7000 m	20:37.0	(2:58.0)
8000 m	23:37.0	(3:00.0)
9000 m	26:36.0	(2:59.0)
10,000 m	29:28.2	(2:52.2)

No time taken at 6 miles.

Viljo Heino, then 35, allowed himself one "Last Hurrah" by bettering his rival's record by one second. The Finn gained that margin in the last kilometre, 2:49.8. This was to remain the real "Swan Song" of the Finnish era, at least for twenty-plus years to come.
Details
Kouvola, 1 September 1949 – 10,000 metres: 1.Viljo Heino 29:27.2, 2.Väinö Koskela 30:41.4, 3:Salomon Könönen 31:13.8.

Kilometre fractions:

1000 m	2:53.2	
2000 m	5:47.0	(2:53.8)
3000 m	8:47.8	(3:00.8)
4000 m	11:44.0	(2:56.2)
5000 m	14:44.0	(3:00.0)
6000 m	17:43.8	(2:59.8)
7000 m	20:40.2	(2:56.4)
8000 m	23:40.0	(2:59.8)
9000 m	26:37.4	(2:57.4)
10,000 m	29:27.2	(2:49.8)

Heino was timed in 28:30.8
for 6 miles, another world record.

But Zátopek had the last word. Still at Ostrava, in what was virtually a solo race, he offered a fine example of even pace running and clipped six seconds off Heino's mark. Details: Ostrava, 22 October 1949 – 10,000 metres: 1.Emil Zátopek 29:21.2, 2.Ladislav Klominek 32:24.2.

Kilometre fractions:

1000 m	2:55.0	
2000 m	5:50.9	(2:55.9)
3000 m	8:45.0	(2:54.1)
4000 m	11:42.0	(2:57.0)
5000 m	14:38.0	(2:56.0)
6000 m	17:36.0	(2:58.0)
7000 m	20:33.5	(2:57.5)
8000 m	23:33.0	(2:59.5)
9000 m	26:30.5	(2:57.5)
10,000 m	29:21.2	(2:50.7)

Once again, no time for 6 miles.

In 1949 Zátopek ran the '10' eleven times and the '5' twelve times - all this in the space of just over 5 months! And he mastered Heino easily in the Finland vs. Czechoslovakia match at Helsinki on 12 July – 29:58.4 to 30:12.2. The Czech went through the season undefeated at distances from 3000 to 10,000 metres. Taken for all in all, this was a superlative season.

Reiff mainly concentrated on shorter distances. He was first to break the 8-minute barrier in the 3000 metres with 7:58.7 at Gävle, Sweden, on 12 August (first half in 3:57.7, second in 4:01.0). In this race he won easily from Henry Eriksson of Sweden (8:30.6), the Olympic 1500 metre champion of 1948.

In 1950 Zátopek's superiority over his fellow travellers became, if possible, even more outrageous, to the point of giving the impression that they suffered from an inferiority complex. The Czech, by then regarded as a national hero, no longer had economic problems. Officially employed in the Army, he could devote to training all the time he deemed necessary and advisable. He happened to live in a favourable climate at home too as his wife Dana (née Ingrová) was herself a leading athlete, a javelin thrower of international caliber. As destiny would have it, they were "astrological twins" born on 19 September 1922, just a few hours (and miles) apart.

Just before the 1950 European Championships in Brussels, Zátopek sent a warning to his rivals by smashing his world record for 10,000 metres and he did so at Turku, the hometown of his great predecessor Paavo Nurmi. After covering the first half in 14:37, he shocked Finnish observers by negotiating the second half in 14:25.6. He thus shaved 18.6 secs. off his own record. Details:

Turku, 4 August 1950 – 10,000 metres:
1.Emil Zátopek 29:02.6, 2.Paavo Ukkonen 31:56.8.

Kilometre fractions:

1000 m	2:58.0	
2000 m	5:51.8	(2:53.8)
3000 m	8:46.0	(2:54.2)
4000 m	11:41.5	(2:55.5)
5000 m	14:37.0	(2:55.5)

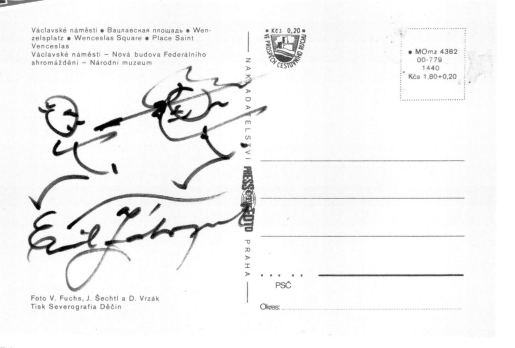

Emil Zátopek being chased by his wife Dana with her javelin. (Drawing given to the author by Zátopek himself in Prague, 1978).

Václavské náměstí ● Вацлавская площадь ● Wenzelsplatz ● Wenceslas Square ● Place Saint Venceslas
Václavské náměstí – Nová budova Federálního shromáždění – Národní muzeum

NAKLADATELSTVÍ PRESSFOTO PRAHA

Foto V. Fuchs, J. Šechtl a D. Vrzák
Tisk Severografia Děčín

PSČ
Okres:

Kčs 0,20
VE PROSPĚCH CESTOVNÍHO RUCHU

● MOmz 4382
00-779
1440
Kčs 1,80+0,20

6000 m	17:31.0	(2:54.0)
7000 m	20:24.0	(2:53.0)
8000 m	23:20.0	(2:56.0)
9000 m	26:15.0	(2:55.0)
10,000 m	29:02.6	(2:47.6)

No time for 6 miles.

In the European Championships at Brussels' Heysel Stadium the "Human Locomotive" proved head and shoulders above the rest of the field at both distances. On 23 August he won the 10,000 metres with astounding ease, leaving runner-up Alain Mimoun over 1 minute (exactly 1:09) behind! Details:
Brussels, 23 August 1950 – 10,000 metres: 1.Emil Zátopek (Cze) 29:12.0, 2.Alain Mimoun (Fra) 30:21.0, 3.Väinö Koskela (Fin) 30:30.8, 4.Frank Aaron (GB) 30:31.6, 5.Nikifor Popov (USSR) 30:34.4, 6.Martin Stokken (Nor) 30:44.8, 7.Marcel Vandewattyne (Bel) 30:48.6, 8.Osman Cosgül (Tur) 30:50.0.
First half 14:37.0, second half 14:35.0, last 400 metres 62.0.

As usual, the preliminary round of the 5000 metres followed the next day (24 August). Emil qualified easily, as did Gaston Reiff in another heat. The final was scheduled for 26 August. On the eve of the decisive race the Belgian was nursing a slight back injury, but on D Day he was feeling better and declared himself ready for action The race was witnessed by 60,000 spectators, most of whom cheered Reiff as he entered the stadium. The Big Two alternated in the lead throughout most of the journey. In the second half of the race the Belgian, spurred on by his many fans, repeatedly tried to "kill" Zátopek and at one time he had about 6 metres on him. But the Czech came back strongly and early in the last lap he "injected" into the struggle a tremendous burst of speed. To the dismay of the crowd the Belgian began to lose ground, gradually and irreparably. Zátopek went home a triumphant victor in his best-ever time, 14:03.0 - 4.8 secs. off Gunder Hägg's world record. Reiff was so tired that near the end he had to give way to Alain Mimoun in the battle for second place. Details:
Brussels, 26 August 1950 – 5000 metres: 1.Emil Zátopek (Cze) 14:03.0, 2.Alain Mimoun (Fra) 14:26.0, 3.Gaston Reiff (Bel) 14:26.2, 4. Väinö Mäkelä (Fin) 14:30.8, 5.Hannu Posti (Fin) 14:40.8, 6.Lucien Theys (Bel) 14:42.4, 7.Stevan Pavlovic (Yug) 14:50.2, 8.Alec Olney (GB) 14:51.8.
Kilometre splits. 2:48.0, 2:49.4, 2:49.8, 2:50.4, 2:45.4, last 400 metres 62.4.

Patriotism and sportsmanship

I have a warm personal recollection of the Zátopek vs. Reiff summit in Brussels in 1950. I reached Heysel Stadium on a tramcar crowded with Belgian fans who were mainly engaged in discussing the forthcoming event. From what I heard, it was obvious that just about everybody saw Gaston as a "sure-fire" bet. The magic power of patriotism! In the stadium, filled to capacity, Reiff was loudly cheered - from his first appearance on the track up to the tragic moment when he suddenly lost contact with his Czech rival. As the gap became wider and wider, it looked as if even the huge crowd had suddenly lost contact with the race. But a bunch of seconds later the sad silence was followed by a burst of cheers to salute Zátopek's fantastic performance. I was witnessing the European Championhips for the first time and such an experience made me appreciate the magic power of sportsmanship as well.

At that stage Alain Mimoun O'Kacha (born at El Telagh, Algeria on 1 January 1921; 1.69 m. / 57 kg.) could well be described as Zátopek's "eternal second", having played that rôle once at the London Olympics and twice at the Europeans in Brussels. This man of Algerian extraction was reportedly "proud of his loyalty to the French colours": in fact he had been a fighter for France during World War II and was seriously wounded in the battle of Cassino in Southern Italy. He recovered to raise himself to the rank of an Olympic medallist. But his greatest moment was yet to come: at the 1956 Olympics in Melbourne he won the marathon, beating among others one Emil Zátopek.
Emil's seasonal record for 1950 was superb:

20 races at 5000 metres and 7 at 10,000 metres – with no defeats. In the year that followed his "menu" was more frugal: 12 races at 5000, and 3 at 10,000 metres, still with no defeats. In search of new frontiers to conquer, on 29 September 1951 he set new world records for 10 miles, 20 kilometres and 1-hour running, (times as specified in a preceding chart). Besides breaking the half hour limit twice in close succession during his 20 km. journey , with 29:53.4 and 29:58.3 (a barrier that always eluded the great Paavo Nurmi in 10 km. races), he also conquered another milestone as he became the first runner to excel 20 kms. within 1 hour.

Notwithstanding the greatness of his achievements in 1950/51, Zátopek's most glorious days were yet to come! In fact, he reached the peak of his art at the 1952 Olympics in Helsinki, when he was close to his 30th anniversary. To tell the truth, the season had begun with uncertain omens for him. On 10 June at Kiev he was surprisingly beaten in a 5000 metre race by Vladimir Kazantsev of USSR, known chiefly as an excellent steeplechaser, and Nikifor Popov. The Czech had a crisis in the 3rd kilometre, then resurged near the end but could not catch the two Russians: Kazantsev won in 14:13.2 from Popov (14:16.0) and Zátopek (14:22.0). An imposing winning streak –49, between October 1948 and June 1952, thus came to an end. Two days later, on the same track, Zátopek met another tough opponent in the 10,000 metres – Aleksandr Anufriyev, a runner who was known for his over-abundant training rations. Here again, the Czech found himself well in arrear at one stage, but fought back in fine style and finally beat Anufriyev – 29:26.0 to 29:31.4. Czech sources claimed that Zátopek had lost part of his elasticity after embarking on a tough endurance programme in preparation for the Olympic marathon. It was no secret then that he intended to shoot for three gold medals at Helsinki, 5000, 10,000 metres and marathon, an exploit no one had ever accomplished. (Of course Hannes Kolehmainen could claim golds in all 3 events, but spread over two editions of the Games, eight years apart).

In Helsinki Zátopek really surpassed himself. In a memorable week he put a definitive seal to his fame as an All Time Great of distance running. Seven years had gone by since the end of World War II and competition in long distance running was fiercer than ever. Heino was no longer active and Reiff was in poor form, but new forces had come to the fore: Chris Chataway and Gordon Pirie of Great Britain, and Herbert Schade of Germany, plus of course the above-mentioned Russians. As for Mimoun, he looked stronger than ever. The best pre-Olympic mark over 5000 metres was credited to Schade – 14:06.6 in a great solo effort at Nienburg on 8 June. Incidentally, it should be noted that USSR was making its debut in the Olympic arena. Actually, that vast Euro-Asian country could have been on the entry list in 1948, being by then a member of the IOC, but the "powers that be" in Moscow decided to stay away.

Zátopek '52, a historic triple

In Helsinki, theatre of the 1952 Olympics, Zátopek, by then a major in the Czech army, was quick to dispel doubts still lingering in some quarters as to his condition. His grimaces and his running style may have looked as grotesque as usual, yet he was by then a wise veteran, with plenty of experience and more self-confident than ever before. In the 10,000 metres (20 July) he took the lead after six laps and was never threatened. His pace was swift enough to allow five of his distant pursuers to duck under 30 minutes. Mimoun and Anufriyev never looked like having a real chance and had to be content with second and third respectively. Details:

Helsinki, 20 July 1952 – 10,000 metres: 1.Emil Zátopek (Cze) 29:17.0, 2.Alain Mimoun 29:32.8, 3.Aleksandr Anufriyev (USSR) 29:48.2, 4.Hannu Posti (Fin) 29:51.4, 5.Frank Sando (GB) 29:51.8, 6.Valter Nyström (Swe) 29:54.8, 7.Gordon Pirie (GB) 30:04.2, 8.Fred Norris (GB) 30:09.8.

The heats of the 5000 metres (22 July) were won by Mimoun (14:19.0), Schade (14:15.4, a new Olympic record) and

*Emil Zátopek
(Czechoslovakia)
on his way to
victory in the
marathon of the
1952 Olympics
in Helsinki,
his third gold
medal in those
Games.*

59

Anufriyev (14:23.6). Zátopek was content to qualify as third in heat 3 (time, 14:26.0) As was his custom on such occasions, he would now and then talk to his rivals and cheer them up, if need be. Tips for the final (24 July) were generally in favour of Herbert Schade, the metronome type of runner: among his supporters were such people as Paavo Nurmi and Gunder Hägg. As it was, the German led for the longer part of the journey, with Zátopek relieving him now and then.With 500 metres to go Gaston Reiff, the defending champion, suddenly dropped out.At the bell Zátopek took the lead, followed by Chataway, Schade and Mimoun in that order. What followed still stands in my memory as one of the fiercest struggles of all-time in high-level competition. On the backstretch young Chataway challenged his more experienced rivals and took the lead, as Schade and Mimoun moved past Zátopek. No sooner had it appeared he might be beaten, the fantastic Czech began his fantastic kick. He swung wide around the last turn, running in the third lane. Halfway through the curve he regained the lead. From then on he was the dominant figure of the four-man field, no matter if Mimoun and Schade were in hard pursuit. It was at that stage that Chataway spilled to the infield and sprawled across the curb. Zátopek went home an imposing victor. Mimoun was once again loyal to his rôle as "eternal second", and Schade had to be content with third. The unlucky Chataway, looking very tired, was nipped by his countryman Gordon Pirie for fourth. (Wrote "Athletics World": "But for his fall Chataway would certainly have made a fourth but he himself is not prepared to say that he would have secured anything more than "perhaps" third place"). Zátopek ran the last lap in 58.1 and the last 200 in 28.3. Such times could well be viewed as an introduction to the new age of distance running. Details:

Helsinki, 24 July 1952 – 5000 metres: 1.Emil Zátopek (Cze) 14:06.6, 2. Alain Mimoun (Fra) 14:07.4, 3.Herbert Schade (Ger) 14:08.6, 4.Gordon Pirie (GB) 14:18.0, 5.Chris Chataway (GB) 14:18.0, 6.Leslie Perry (Aus) 14:23.6, 7.Ernö Béres (Hun) 14:24.8, 8.Åke Andersson (Swe) 14:26.0. After that incredible race, an elated but exhausted Zátopek quickly returned to the Olympic village (This was at Otaniemi for "Easterners", while "Westerners" were lodged at Käpylä). He was not bold enough to watch "de visu" the final of the women's javelin, in which his wife Dana was to face a highly touted Russian cohort. He followed the competition via radio, first with some apprehension and finally with great joy when Dana came out the winner. Only two "astrological twins" as they were could have expected to win an Olympic gold medal on the same day!

Having accomplished his mission on the track, Zátopek was now on the threshold of "No Man's Land". The marathon was just that for him, at least in terms of competition. One could of course wonder how many times he had run similar distances in training. Amazingly enough, on that 27 July 1952 he behaved as a veteran marathoner, or just about. After 15 kilometres a trio consisting of Jim Peters of Great Britain, Gustaf Jansson of Sweden and Zátopek, was in the lead, with the nearest pursuer over a minute behind. As the story goes, more or less at that stage the Czech addressed his companions in English with the following words: "I've never run a marathon before, but don't you think we ought to go a little faster ?" Much to their annoyance Jansson and Peters were unable to answer in the affirmative, and shortly afterwards Zátopek decided to do something about it and drew away from his rivals. He entered the stadium with more than 2 minutes to spare on his nearest pursuer, Argentina's Reinaldo Gorno. The knowledgeable Finnish crowd, who on the opening day had gone wild in cheering the last torch bearer, one Paavo Nurmi, now reserved a loud and long ovation to Zátopek. Home fans as well as guests from all over the world fully realized that they were witnessing what was most probably the greatest feat in the annals of the Games. The happy victor was very tired and had blisters in his feet, yet he could now indulge in relaxation: he embraced his wife Dana, ate an apple and offered an orange to runner-up Reinaldo Gorno of Argentina, who came home over 2 and a half minutes later. Zátopek's time, 2 hr 23:03.2, was the fastest ever recorded on an out-and-back course. Best on record for a point-to-point course was 2 hr 20:42.2 by Jim Peters, who in the Helsinki race retired after 30 kilometres. Before the race, the Englishman was quoted as saying: "I have no chance against Zátopek. He can run 2 hr 15".

In 1952 Zátopek ran the 5000 metres 15 times (with two losses, if we also consider a heat in Olympic competition) and the 10,000 metres 6 times. Figures apart, that will be remembered as his Golden Year. Even in 1953 his persistent winning habits continued to amaze experts. He went through 9 races at 5000 metres and 4 at 10,000 metres without a loss. He was scared only once, but that was a warning of things to come. On 5 August at Bucharest he made the acquaintance of one Vladimir Kuts, a young Ukrainian who was bold enough to challenge him from the earliest stages of a 5000 metre race. After the first kilometre Kuts had 15 metres on Zátopek and at the fourth kilometre the gap had widened to 40 metres. At that stage even József Kovács, a short (1.63 m.) Hungarian, was well ahead of Zátopek. But the Czech was able to stage a counterattack worthy of his tradition. At the bell he was still 25 metres behind the leader, yet he managed to swallow Kovács and even Kuts. The times: Zátopek 14:03.0, Kuts 14:04.0, Kovács 14:04.2. Aleksandr Anufriyev was 4th in 14:15.0. Emil thus had to equal his PB to stay ahead of his challengers. Four days later, still at Bucharest, the Czech easily held off Kuts in the 10,000 metres – 29:25.8 to 29:41.4. It should be noted, however, that earlier in the season Aleksandr Anufriyev had surprised a lot of people with a marvellous 13:58.8 for 5000 metres in Moscow, missing Gunder Hägg's world record by merely 0.6 sec. The Russian was actually ahead of Hägg's time-table at 4000 metres (11:06 to 11:09), but faded badly near the end.

Not to lose his good habits, Zátopek broke his own world record for 10,000 metres just before the end of the 1953 season. This was on his favourite track at Stará Boleslav, a 363.8 metre circuit. Details:

Stará Boleslav, 1 November 1953 – 10,000 metres: 1.Emil Zátopek 29:01.6, 2.Milos Tomis 31:12.2, 3.Jaroslav Liska 31:12.4.

Kilometre fractions:

1000 m	2:52.8	
2000 m	5:48.6	(2:55.8)
3000 m	8:43.8	(2:55.2)
4000 m	11:39.6	(2:55.8)
5000 m	14:34.8	(2:55.2)
6000 m	17:28.6	(2:53.8)
7000 m	20:24.0	(2:55.4)
8000 m	23:19.6	(2:55.6)
9000 m	26:16.8	(2:57.2)
10,000 m	29:01.6	(2:44.8)

At 6 miles he was officially timed in 28:08.4, another world record. Here Zátopek succeeded to Gordon Pirie of Great Britain, who earlier in the season had won the AAA title in 28:19.4 (London, 10 July).

The true worth of a champion

I am among the lucky track fans who saw Emil Zátopek in his Week of Weeks at the Helsinki Olympics in 1952, and about a quarter-of-a-century later I had a chat with him during the European Championships in Prague. I found him as kind and humorous as ever, even though he had gone through troubled times for siding with those who turned out to be the temporary losers during the Prague Spring of 1968.

I invited him to give me his retrospective views on his track career . What he said in reply was, in fact, a monument to his proverbial modesty. In sharp contrast to the type of champion from yesteryear who likes to take refuge in the "ivory tower" of his old days, he candidly told me: "I think I had a fair amount of luck. That was a time when track thrived at a low-fire temperature. Most countries still had to heal the wounds of World War II and the turnover in talent was relatively slow. Finland's great runners of the pre-war days had disappeared, apart from Viljo Heino, who was near the end of his career". Recalling the 1952 Olympic marathon he said: "In a way, that was probably my easiest victory. It was not the "new" distance that frightened me, but rather the possibility of a fast pace throughout – and nobody chose to impose that".

VLADIMIR KUTS, THE FIRST CZAR OF USSR

Vladimir Kuts, the virtual novice who had caused quite a stir in challenging the "Human Locomotive" at Bucharest in 1953, soon developed into a full-blooded champion himself. Some observers felt that the Zátopek Era was nearing its end, yet the old lion met the new challenge with his indomitable spirit. Ironically enough, 1954, the year that was to provide the turning point , saw him achieve the fastest times of his career at both 5000 and 10,000 metres. And he chalked up his two PB's in the space of 50 hours! On 30 May at Colombes he set a new world record for 5000 metres (incidentally the first of his career at this distance) with a time of 13:57.2, thus clipping a full second off Gunder Hägg's 12-year-old mark. Details: Colombes, 30 May 1954 – 5000 metres: 1.Emil Zátopek (Cze) 13:57.2, 2.Drago Stritof (Yug) 14:42.2, 3.Stevan Pavlovic (Yug) 14:45.6.

Kilometre fractions:

1000 m	2:47.2	
2000 m	5:34.4	(2:47.2)
3000 m	8:23.4	(2:49.0)
4000 m	11:13.4	(2:50.0)
5000 m	13:57.2	(2:43.8)

No time taken for 3 miles.

Barely 50 hours later, Zátopek was on the war-path again, this time at the Racing track in Brussels. It had been raining and the surface was water-logged. Emil lapped all his 11 opponents, covering the first half of his 10,000 metre journey in 14:27.6 and the second in 14:26.6. He thus broke the 29-minute barrier with 28:54.2. Details:
Brussels, 1 June 1954 – 10,000 metres: 1.Emil Zátopek 28:54.2, 2.Marcel Vandewattyne Bel) 30:50.0e.

Kilometre fractions:

1000 m	2:47.8	
2000 m	5:44.2	(2:56.4)
3000 m	8:38.2	(2:54.0)
4000 m	11:34.0	(2:55.8)
5000 m	14:27.6	(2:53.6)
6000 m	17:23.0	(2:55.4)
7000 m	20:16.4	(2:53.4)
8000 m	23:11.6	(2:55.2)
9000 m	26:07.4	(2:55.8)
10,000 m	28:54.2	(2:46.8)

Official 6 mile time, 27:59.2, another world record.

My friend André Greuze, Belgian journalist and statistician, told me that the following morning the indefatigable Emil had a session of interval training that included ten 200's and twenty 400's. Yet all this did not suffice to save him from the rolling stone of history..... The first alarm bell was heard on 3 July: in the 10,000 metres of the Hungary vs. Czechoslovakia match in Budapest, little József Kovács of the home team offered unsuspected resistance and emerged as a surprise winner – 29:09.0 to 29:09.8 – at the end of a furious struggle, mainly thanks to a 59.2 last lap. This put an end to Zátopek's "lucky streak" at that distance - 38 consecutive victories, a series that started with his debut in the '10' in 1948.

In the meantime British distance men seemed to be on the verge of a long-awaited revival. After James Wilson's bronze in the 10,000 metres of the Antwerp Olympics in 1920, the men from Albion had won no medals in the 5000/10,000 metre department in the quadrennial Games. In the 1954 AAA Championships at London's White City Stadium, Freddie Green and Chris Chataway staged a fierce battle in the 3 miles and finished in that order as both were timed in 13:32.2 for a new world record, the equivalent of 14:02/14:03 at 5000 metres. This was on 10 July and the two met again a month later in the Commonwealth Games at Vancouver, B.C. Here Chataway squarely evened the count, winning from Green, 13:35.2 to 13:37.2, as yet another Englishman, Frank Sando, wound up a close third in 13:37.4. Back in fourth was a novice from Kenya, Nyandika Maiyoro, in 13:43.8. This was in fact the first time a runner from the East African country entered the picture of international distance running. Much more was to come from there .....

Christopher John Chataway (born Chelsea, London on 31 January 1931; 1.75 m. / 69 kg.) had started as a middle distance runner, but in 1952, as previously related, he was one of the main characters in the play of the great 5000 metre final at the Helsinki Olympics, although still "green" if compared with his rivals. Early in 1954 he was second in two historic 1-mile races, in Roger Bannister's first sub-4 effort (3:59.4) at Oxford and to John Landy when the Aussie star lowered the record to 3:58.0 at Turku. Chataway's times were 4:07.2 and 4:04.4 respectively. On top of his basic speed he had built an adequate endurance, as shown by his tussles with Green over 3 miles. He was now regarded by some observers as Zátopek's most serious rival. It was rumoured that the Briton actually trained harder than he would generally admit in his casual utterances.

All this notwithstanding, the week of the European Championships at Berne's Neufeld Stadium began along a familiar pattern, i.e. with a sweeping victory for Zátopek. On a cold (12° C) and rainy summer day he outclassed the opposition in the 10,000 metres with history's second fastest time, 28:58.0. He did this with 14:28 in the first half and 14:30 in the second, plus a 63.0 last lap. His recent conqueror József Kovács was a well beaten second. Details:
Berne, 25 August 1954 – 10,000 metres: 1.Emil Zátopek (Cze) 28:58.0, 2.József Kovács (Hun) 29:25.8, 3.Frank Sando (GB) 29:27.6, 4.Herbert Schade (Ger) 29:32.8, 5.Franjo Mihalic (Yug) 29:59.6, 6.Peter Driver (GB) 30:03.6, 7.Öistein Saksvik (Nor) 30:04.4, 8. Aleksandr Anufriyev (USSR) 30:19.4.

But the 5000 metre final four days later was quite a different story. Vladimir Kuts, who had come to Berne with a seasonal best of 14:11.6, won his heat with a fast 14:18.8, while Zátopek in another heat ostensibly bided his time and was content to qualify in fifth place. Chataway too chose to qualify the easy way. In the decisive race on 29 August Kuts stayed in the wake of Britain's Freddie Green in the first 200 metres, then jumped into the lead and took command of the operations. At the end of the first lap he had 3 metres on a group led by Green. After 800 metres his lead had increased to 20 metres and many people were wondering if he knew what he was doing. Maybe Chataway and Zátopek belonged to the same school of thought ....Be it as it may, it was only in the fourth lap that Zátopek showed signs of life, by taking the lead of the pursuers' group, with Kovács and Chataway in his wake. But Kuts, after slowing down somewhat in the second kilometre, increased his pace again in the next and brought his lead to 120 metres. When the Czech finally decided to resort to a final spurt, it soon became apparent that he and Chataway would only fight it out for second. The indefatigable Ukrainian managed to stay ahead by nearly 90 metres and went home in world record time – 13:56.6. Chataway finally outsprinted Zátopek for the silver medal. The Englishman was easily the fastest of the three in the last lap (59.3). Kuts' superlative performance was all the more praiseworthy in view of the sultry weather (24° C.). And if anyone made a tactical mistake that day, it surely wasn't Kuts. Details:
Berne, 29 August 1954 – 5000 metres: 1.Vladimir Kuts (USSR) 13:56.6, 2.Chris Chataway (GB) 14:08.8, 3.Emil Zátopek (Cze) 14:10.2, 4.Vladimir Okorokov (USSR) 14:20.0, 5.Lucien Hanswyck (Bel) 14:25.6, 6.Frans Herman (Bel) 14:31.4, 7.Öistein Saksvik (Nor) 14:32.2, 8.Urho Julin (Fin) 14:32.4.

Kilometre fractions:

1000 m	2:44.0	
2000 m	5:36.7	(2:52.7)
3000 m	8:23.9	(2:47.2)
4000 m	11:12.3	(2:48.4)
5000 m	13:56.6	(2:44.3)

Kuts was timed in 13:27.4 for 3 miles, another world record. He ran the last lap in 64.8.

Fierce duel on a soggy track in London during the 1956 AAA Championships: Derek Ibbotson, left, wins 3 mile race from Chris Chataway. Time for both: 13:32.6.

The wounded but indomitable lion from Czechoslovakia tried to fight back immediately. On 3 September in Stockholm he attacked Kuts' fresh world record and almost made it! He stayed ahead of Kuts' pace at Berne up to the fourth kilometre (11:11), then faded a bit and finished in 13:57.0, barely 0.4 off his target!

The British were eager to see a rematch between Kuts and Chataway. The occasion was offered by a floodlight meet at London's White City Stadium on 13 October: the Inter City match London vs. Moscow. It was one of the most dramatic races ever seen on British soil. It was watched by 40,000 spectators on the spot and by an estimated 15 million televiewers all over Europe. As eyewitness Norris McWhirter put it, "Kuts' sustained bursts subjected Chataway to a profligate torture" Because the Ukrainian led the dance throughout the entire distance, with the Briton always in contention. Kuts hit the 3-mile mark in 13:27.0, a new world record, with Chataway (13:27.1) hot on his heels. It was only in the last 5 metres that Chataway, thanks to a superhuman effort, managed to inch his way ahead to earn the final verdict as well as the world record– 13:51.6 to 13:51.7. "Sitters" may not always be the favourites of pure track fans, yet it is unquestionable that every athlete has the right to pursue victory and happiness the best way he can. Details:

London, 13 October 1954 – 5000 metres: 1.Chris Chataway (GB) 13:51.6, 2.Vladimir Kuts (USSR) 13:51.7, 3.Peter Driver 14:29.2, 4.Vladimir Okorokov (USSR) 14:50.0.

Kilometre fractions:

1000 m	2:41.5	
2000 m	5:31.6	(2:50.1)
3000 m	8:16.5	(2:44.9)
4000 m	11:09.9	(2:53.4)
5000 m	13:51.6	(2:41.7)

Last lap. Chataway 60.1, Kuts 60.4.

The tenacious Kuts wanted to have the last word for that memorable season. Only ten days later he was in Prague for the Czechoslovakia vs. USSR match. Zátopek was there too, of course, but contrary to expectations this was clearly a "no contest". The emerging force simply outshone the older one. Zátopek, undefeated in his own country since 1948, just had no answer. Kuts resorted to his devastating tactics, soon piled up a sizable lead and won as he pleased. He also succeeded in recapturing the world record. Details:

Prague, 23 October 1954 – 5000 metres: 1.Vladimir Kuts (USSR) 13:51.2, 2.Emil Zátopek (Cze) 14:19.0, 3.Ivan Ullsperger (Cze) 14:25.2, 4.Vladimir Okorokov (USSR). 14:55.2.

Kilometre fractions:

1000 m	2:38.4	
2000 m	5:30.8	(2:52.4)
3000 m	8:22.6	(2:51.8)
4000 m	11:07.6	(2:45.0)
5000 m	13:51.2	(2:43.6)

Enroute Kuts was timed in 13:26.4 for 3 miles, another world record. Last lap: 68.0.

1954 thus went down in history as a memorable year. The world record for 5000 metres was broken four times by three different men. At the end of it Vladimir Kuts clearly emerged as the undisputed no.1. During the season he ran eight 5000 metre races and lost two (one to Vladimir Okorokov in early season, plus of course to Chataway in London), bettered the world record twice and won a smashing victory in the European Championships. Zátopek had a worthy successor.

To tell the truth, USSR could not point to a particularly great tradition in distance running. Only notable exceptions were the Znamenskiy brothers, Syerafim and Georgiy, who in 1939 chalked up remarkable 10,000 metre times, 30:44.8 and 30:45.8 respectively, good enough to be placed among the Top Ten in the 1939 World List. After which one had to wait till the advent of the abovementioned Aleksandr Anufriyev in 1953.

Vladimir Pyotrovich Kuts (born at Trostyanets, Ukraine, on 7 February 1927, 1.72 m. / 72 kg.) practised rowing, skiing and boxing as a youth. The last one probably marked his personality more than somewhat. Emil Zátopek, a fine humorist, was once quoted as saying that Kuts had discovered athletics just as Cristoforo Colombo discovered America – by mere chance. This happened when Kuts, then serving as a sailor, casually tried distance running. After a 15:34.8 for 5000 metres at the age of 23, he was heard from again two years later, in 1952,when he ran the standard distances in 14:32.2 and 31:02.4.This retarded but very effective burst was possibly favoured by his intense and multiform sport activity in his younger years He reached the higher echelons in 1953, with his first clashes with Zátopek. He used to explore the boundaries of endurance-to-fatigue – in training as well as in competition. But unlike Zátopek, who even in hot competitions occasionally found time for moments of light-hearted humour, Kuts always behaved like a true running machine, a sort of human metronome.

USSR experts understandably rejoiced over the fact that Kuts seemed to have all the qualities they had in vain sought in so many of their distance runners. His training methods were partly similar to Zátopek's in terms of massive doses of "Interval training", but while the Czech mostly confined himself to repetitions over 200 and 400 metres, Kuts would in the course of time move to longer distances: 800, 1200, 1600 and 2000 metres. Between 1951 and 1953 his general programme was as follows: for 3 months of the year he concentrated on gymnastics, weight lifting and jumping. For the following 6 months he would have one 10,000 metre run per day, generally at a fast pace. In the remaining 3 months he would concentrate on interval training. In later years he vastly increased his ration of muscle training. Of course there were experts who feared he might risk overwork.

1955 was another year of record-breaking feats, except that the lion's share in that department belonged to a Hungarian – Sándor Iharos. Along with István Rózsavölgyi and László Tábori he impersonated the "Three Musketeers" of the Magyar Army Club (Honvéd). The trio was coached by "Iron Sergeant" Mihály Iglói, who in his younger days had been a good 1500 metre man (3:52.2, the world's sixth best performer in 1937). The other two characters, Rózsavölgyi and Tábori, were usually at their best in the middle distances. Initially, Iharos had the same extraction. The following

record may be unique for three pupils of the same coach: all of them, at one time or another, held the world record for 1500 metres – Iharos and Tábori with 3:40.8 in 1955 and Rózsavölgyi with 3:40.5 in 1956. Iharos also managed to make successful inroads on the longer distances.

Sándor Iharos (born in Budapest on 10 March 1930; 1.80 m. / 65 kg.) was probably the least prominent of the three in terms of aggressiveness and competitive spirit, but he remedied to a great extent with his unrivalled dedication to the sport. In the course of his career he excelled at all distances from 1500 to 10,000 metres, with world records all along this range, as only Paavo Nurmi had been able to do. Iharos used to have two training sessions per day, practically with no break, i.e. for a total of about 700 training sessions per year! He spent 3 _ to 4 hours daily at training, always with a different programme for frequency and length of his repetitions. His position as an army officer certainly allowed him to concentrate on his "mission" with the best part of his physical and mental energies. Too bad his many records were not accompanied by equally brilliant performances in big competitions. However, one should allow for the fact that the Hungarian Revolution of 1956 greatly hampered his preparation for the Melbourne Olympics when he happened to be at the peak of his condition – to the point that he had to miss the Games altogether.

Iharos started his 1955 season in brilliant fashion, with a new world record for 3000 metres – 7:55.6 at Budapest on 14 May. Two weeks later in London he annexed the 2-mile record as well, with 8:33.4. Then he moved up to 5000 metres, at which distance his best at the end of 1954 was no better than 14:12.2. He showed great improvement in losing to Jerzy Chromik, a Polish steeplechaser, 13:56.6 to 13:55.2. A month later he rose to new heights with a record-breaking 13:50.8 in the Hungary vs. Czechoslovakia match at Budapest's Népstadion, thereby succeeding Kuts on the IAAF list. Details:

Budapest, 10 September 1955 – 5000 metres: 1.Sándor Iharos (Hun) 13:50.8, 2.Miklós Szabó II (Hun) 14:11.4, 3.Stanislaw Ozóg (Pol) 14:50.6.

Kilometre fractions:

1000 m	2:44.0	
2000 m	5:33.4	(2:49.4)
3000	8:23.2	(2:49.8)
4000 m	11:09.6	(2:46.4)
5000 m	13:50.8	(2:41.2)

Unofficial 3-mile time: 13:25.0

One did not have to wait long for Kuts' response. The Ukrainian fought back with the type of front race that was his unmistakable trademark. Details:
Belgrade, 18 September 1955 – 5000 metres: 1.Vladimir Kuts (USSR) 13:46.8, 2.Hubert Berta (Hun) 14:19.0, 3.Drago Stritof (Yug) 14:21.0.

Kilometre fractions:

1000 m	2:42.0	
2000 m	5:30.0	(2:48.0)
3000 m	8:16.0	(2:46.0)
4000 m	11:06.0	(2:50.0)
5000 m	13:46.8	(2:40.8)

No official time for 3 miles.

The last stroke of the season came from Iharos. In his attempt , during the Hungarian Championships in Budapest, he was ably seconded by his club mates, particularly by Tábori (who had run a 3:43.0 1500 metres the day before), who stayed with Iharos till 3900 metres. Then Sándor let himself go with a splendid 2:33.6 for the last kilometre and recaptured the world record with 13:40.6. Details:
Budapest, 23 October 1955 – 5000 metres: 1.Sándor Iharos 13:40.6, 2.László Tábori 13:53.2, 3.Miklós Szabó II 13:59.2, 4.József Kovács 14:07.2.

Kilometre fractions:

1000 m	2:42.0	
2000 m	5:28.0	(2:46.0)
3000 m	8:16.0	(2:48.0)
4000 m	11:07.0	(2:51.0)
5000 m	13:40.6	(2:33.6)

Official 3-mile time: 13:14.2,
another world record. Last lap: 59.6.

While this was going on, Zátopek, then 33, had an ordinary season, enlightened by two world records at 15 miles and 25,000 metres – the last ones of his career.

Prior to Iharos' last world mark at Budapest, Chris Chataway had been for a short time the holder of the 3-mile record: 13:23.2 in London on 30 July. Later in the season, the blond Briton lost to Tábori in a close duel over the same distance (13:44.6 to 13:44.5). It should be noted that both of them were members of the "Sub-4 Club" in the mile, a select group then numbering no more than 5 members.

At the dawn of the Olympic year another Englishman joined the record-breaking parade: Douglas Alastair Gordon Pirie (born at Leeds on 10 February 1931; 1.88 m./ 65 kg.), a filiform figure who had devoted himself to running at the unripe age of 10. Quite understandably, eight years went by before he could make an impact – that was when he ran 6 miles in 32:32.0. In 1951 his training programme became more and more intense, mostly along the tenets of Interval Training. In fact he was advised by Woldemar Gerschler, the onetime tutor of Rudolf Harbig and Roger Moens, both holders of the 800-metre world record. By the end of 1953, Pirie could point to PB's of 13:29.8 for 3 miles and 29:17.2 (10,000 metres) and also had a good 1:53.0 for the half mile. In that year he even tried a 2 hour-race, but he emerged from that experience with a vow: "Never again".

The first shock of 1956 was provided by a fierce duel between Kuts and Pirie at Bergen, Norway, in the evening of 19 June – distance, 5000 metres. It was a rainy day, with a temperature of barely 11° C. Almost a replica of the Kuts vs. Chataway affair in London two years earlier, in the sense that Pirie kept steadily in the wake of the Ukrainian for most of the distance, except for testing the reactive capacity of his rival on two occasions. The tall Englishman launched an all-out attack with 275 metres to go. To this Kuts had no answer and Pirie thus won the night, beating Iharos' world record as well. The Englishman owed his victory to his great finishing speed: last 800 metres in 1:55.0, last 400 in 55.0. Details:

Bergen, 19 June 1956 – 5000 metres: 1.Gordon Pirie (GB) 13:36.8, 2.Vladimir Kuts (USSR) 13:39.6, 3.Leif Egge (Nor) 14:32.0.

Kilometre fractions:

1000 m	2:36.0	
2000 m	5:22.0	(2:46.0)
3000 m	8:09.0	(2:47.0)
4000 m	10:57.0	(2:48.0)
5000 m	14:36.8	(2:39.8)

No official 3-mile time.

Taking full advantage of his euphoria, Pirie was on the trail again three days later at Trondheim, Norway, where he equalled Sándor Iharos' world record for 3000 metres, 7:55.6. The Englishman actually did 7:55.5, but his time was rounded up to 7:55.6 as per IAAF rule. He was obviously thriving in the atmosphere of Scandinavian summer evenings, often conducive to superlative efforts in distance running. On 4 September in Malmö he met Hungary's "Three Musketeers" in a 3000 metre race, and beat them all, lowering the world record to 7:52.7 (officially rounded up to 7:52.8). His Magyar rivals followed in this order: Rózsavölgyi 7:53.4, Iharos 8:05.8, Tábori 8:16.8.

Pre-Olympic fireworks had actually begun on 25 January right in Melbourne, venue of the Games, when Dave Stephens ran 6 miles in 27:54.0, the first world record conquered by a long distance man from Down Under. The 27-year-old Australian covered the first half in 13:59.0 and the second in 13:55.0. During the European summer Iharos and Kuts entered the picture and actually took turns in bettering the world's 10,000 metres record. The Hungarian caused quite a stir when he did 28:42.8 in the national championships at Budapest – a sound 11.4 secs. under Zátopek's record! But the world of track was really shocked two months later when Kuts pulverized Iharos' fresh record with a startling 28:30.4 in Moscow's Lenin Stadium before 100,000 spectators. Details:

Budapest, 15 July 1956 – 10,000 metres: 1.Sándor Iharos 28:42.8, 2. József Kovács 29:25.6, 3.Béla Juhász 30:59.6.

Kilometre fractions:

1000 m	2:47.6	
2000 m	5:37.0	(2:49.4)
3000 m	8:29.4	(2:52.4)
4000 n	11:20.0	(2:50.6)
5000 m	14:14.2	(2:54.2)
6000 m	17:04.0	(2:49.8)
7000 m	19:57.0	(2:53.0)
8000 m	22:50.0	(2:53.0)
9000 m	25:47.0	(2:57.0)
10,000 m	28:42.7*	(2:55.7)

* Officially rounded up to 28:42.8 as per IAAF rule. Enroute Iharos was timed in 27:43.8 for 6 miles, another world record.

Moscow, 11 September 1956 – 10,000 metres: 1.Vladimir Kuts 28:30.4, 2.Pyotr Bolotnikov 29:37.0, 3.Ivan Chernyavskiy 29:41.0.

Kilometre fractions:

1000 m	2:42.5	
2000 m	5:34.0	(2:51.5)
3000 m	8:25.0	(2:51.0)
4000 m	11:16.0	(2:51.0)
5000 m	14:08.0	(2:52.0)
6000 m	17:02.0	(2:54.0)
7000 m	19:54.5	(2:52.5)
8000 m	22:48.5	(2:54.0)
9000 m	25:42.5	(2:54.0)
10,000 m	28:30.4	(2:47.9)

No official 6-mile time.

Two K.O. victories for Kuts in Melbourne Olympics

The above-mentioned series of record performances led some observers to think that Europeans had spread themselves thin too early, underestimating the difficulties of the Olympic tests awaiting them in the Southern Hemisphere –at a time of the year which was clearly "out of season" for them. (But wasn't that a problem runners from Down Under had faced on many occasions in the annals of previous Games, all held in the Northern Hemisphere?). In fact, such a fear proved to

Alain Mimoun (France) was for years Zátopek's eternal second on the track but closed his career with a victory in the 1956 Olympic marathon.

be justified at least in the case of Gordon Pirie, who failed to reproduce the kind of form that made him well-nigh unbeatable during the European summer. As for Iharos, he did not go to Australia. His team-mates Tábori and Rózsavölgyi did make the trip, but only the former fared reasonably well – 6th in the 5000 metres, then 4th in the 1500. After the Games, Tábori chose to take political asylum in USA, along with his coach Mihály Iglói, whose teachings were to make a great impact there too.

Even so, the Melbourne races proved to be most attractive. Kuts reached the apex of his career, disposing of the opposition as he pleased over both distances. The onetime boxer literally K.O.'d all his rivals. In the 10,000 metres he ran away from Pirie, his last pursuer, with 5 laps to go, after subjecting

him to the torture of his repeated spurts. The Englishman was so exhausted that he finished no higher than 8th. After that he honestly commented: "He ran me off my feet".Local favourite Dave Stephens was a disappointing 20th, somehow fulfilling a prediction made by coach Percy Cerutty: "Stephens will either be in the first three or the last three".

On 26 November the fastest time in the heats of the 5000 metres was 14:14.2 by Albie Thomas, a tiny Australian. In the final two days later Kuts again used his patented tactics to get rid of his fiercest rivals, Englishmen Derek Ibbotson and Pirie, in the last kilometre. (In 1957 Ibbotson went on to break the world's 1-mile record with 3:57.2). The winner's post-race comment was terse: "My only strategy was to come first. I would have liked the British runners to fight me more at the finish". Kuts thus joined Kolehmainen and Zátopek in the tiny group of successful "doublers". Details:

Melbourne, 23 November 1956 - 10,000 metres: 1.Vladimir Kuts (USSR) 28:45.6, 2.József Kovács (Hun) 28:52.4, 3.Allan Lawrence (Aus) 28:53.6, 4.Zdzislaw Krzyszkowiak (Pol) 29:05.0, 5.Kenneth Norris (GB) 29:21.6, 6.Ivan Chernyavskiy (USSR) 29:31.5, 7.Dave Power (Aus) 29:49.2, 8.Gordon Pirie (GB) 29:49.5.
Kuts ran the last kilometre in 2:52.6, the last 400 metres in 66.7.

Melbourne, 28 November 1956 – 5000 metres: 1.Vladimir Kuts (USSR) 13:39.6, 2.Gordon Pirie (GB) 13:50.6, 3.Derek Ibbotson (GB) 13:54.4, 4.Miklós Szabó (Hun) 14:03.4, 5,Albert Thomas (Aus) 14:04.8, 6.László Tábori (Hun) 14:09.8, 7.Nyandika Maiyoro (Ken) 14:19.0, 8.Thyge Tögersen (Nor) 14:21.0.
Kuts ran the last kilometre in 2:42.2, the last 400 metres in 62.8. Unofficial 3-mile time, 13:13.0 (one timer only), inside the official world record.

In the final act of the Melbourne Olympics on 1 December veteran Alain Mimoun won the marathon in 2 hr 25:00, thereby closing his long career on a triumphal note. The olive-faced, Algerian-born Frenchman beat, among others, his perennial conqueror in so many past battles, Emil Zátopek, who finished sixth. Years later, in an informal talk

Devastating effects

Vladimir Kuts succeeded the legendary Emil Zátopek in the most theatrical fashion one could ever imagine – by beating him in a head-to-head confrontation over 5000 metres at the 1954 European Championships and at the same time depriving the Czech of his world record! However, this reasoning could well be reversed with a "bravo" for Zátopek, who managed to achieve his best times (at both 5000 and 10,000 metres) in that very year, aged 32, at a time when he was approaching the Sunset Boulevard of his glorious career.

In the years 1954-57 Kuts obviously became a subject of study for many observers, notably including his rivals. Australia's Dave Stephens, who in 1956 held the world's 6-mile record with 27:54.0, got a chance to closely follow Kuts' training in the days preceding the Melbourne Olympics (when Stephens was annihilated by the Ukrainian). Here is what he told Fred Wilt, author of "How They Train": "Concerning strategy, it is well known that Kuts runs the first half of his races at a speed which will exhaust his opponents (and himself). The motive for this is that his opponents become so completely demoralized in spirit that they run quite poorly for the remainder of the race – well below their own personal ability. They fail to realize that Kuts is also exhausted during the second half of his races." That is precisely what happened to Chataway and Zátopek at the 1954 European Championships, and to Pirie, Ibbotson, Kovács and others in the 1956 Olympics. Stephens added: "His strategy is to strike at the morale or spirit of his opponents – a very shrewd and devastating method. An athlete must be extremely fit and strong to use this strategy.......His will power and discipline are terrific. Yet he is human like anyone else. He gets quite nervous before a race – he sings to himself to try and forget the race and calm his nerves." Stephens was certainly right in his analysis of the devastating effects such a strategy could produce. However, this is partly contradicted by the fact that Kuts himself managed to finish some of his best races just as fast as he started them.

Vladimir Kuts (USSR) won 5000 and 10,000 m. at the 1956 Olympics in Melbourne.

with Ladislav Krnác, a leading Slovak expert, Emil recalled: " He (Mimoun) ran alongside me for a long time, but then I told him that I did not feel right and that he'd better go ahead by himself. He won, but then he stayed by the finish waiting for me until I came in 6th. That was the only time that he beat me, and when it was all over he told me I'd better congratulate him on the birth of his daughter, and that he'd named her Olympia". It should be said that Zátopek was operated on (hernia) earlier in the year: Also that Mimoun, then 35, had lowered his PB for 10,000 metres to 29:13.4 shortly before going to Australia.

1957 was by contrast a relatively quiet year. The Hungarians were virtually out of the picture after the diaspora caused by political events in their country. Kuts was once again the dominant figure and accounted for the only world record of the year. This was in a 5000 metre race at Rome's Stadio Olimpico on 13 October. Kuts had only one noteworthy opponent, his countryman Pyotr Bolotnikov, who had actually outsprinted him in the closing stage of the 10,000 metres at the USSR Championships earlier in the season (29:09.8 to 29:10.0). On that occasion Kuts was reportedly suffering from a stomach ailment. But he recovered well enough to return to his winning ways. In Rome he reverted to his devastating tactics of the year before and Bolotnikov lost contact after 2 kilometres. All on his own, Kuts continued to punish himself lap after lap, spurred on by a sympathetic crowd, who stirred him with a strange neologism: "Kuts-nik, Kuts-nik", an overt reference to satellite Sputnik very much in the news in those days. Kuts duly responded with a new world record. Details:

Rome, 13 October 1957 – 5000 metres: 1.Vladimir Kuts (USSR) 13:35.0, 2.Pyotr Bolotnikov (USSR) 14:06.6, 3.Urho Julin (Fin) 14:29.6.

Kilometre fractions:

1000 m	2:37.8	
2000 m	5:24.3	(2:46.5)
3000 m	8:08.7	(2:44.4)
4000 m	10:52.9	(2:44.2)
5000 m	13:35.0	(2:42.1)

No official 3-mile time.

Kuts closed his 1957 account with a low-key race in Genoa (29:10.4 for 10,000 metres). He was 30 by then, yet in 1958 most observers were surprised when his name suddenly sank into oblivion. News filtered of an "ordinary" 14:12.2 for 5000 metres in July, but that was all. His failing health, apparently caused by alcoholism, gave him much to think about. On 15 August 1975 the world of track was shocked by the news that he had passed away at 48, following a heart attack. Ten years later a monument was erected in his memory at Trostyanets, his native Ukrainian town.

The highlights of 1958 were provided by a couple of world records at non-standard distances by Albie Thomas of Australia (born in Sydney on 8 February 1935; 1.66 m. / 56 kg.). A protégé of Percy Cerutty – who also tutored John Landy, history's second sub-4 miler – Thomas ran 3 miles in 13:10.8 (Dublin, 9 July) and 2 miles in 8:32.0 (Dublin, 7 August). In the former race the Aussie star had mile fractions of 4:27.0, 4:25.0 and 4:18.8. That was a vintage season for distance runners from Down Under, mostly thanks to the stimulus provided by such coaches as Percy Cerutty and Franz Stampfl in Australia and Arthur Lydiard in New Zealand. Stampfl, a former Austrian, was essentially an advocate of Interval Training, by then a well established philosophy, whereas the other two experimented new ways and methods, particularly Lydiard. Himself a good marathoner (2 hr 41:29.8 in 1953, plus a 12th place at the 1950 Commonwealth Games), the New Zealander maintained that distance men could conquer new worlds if they succeeded to increase their stamina, that is their capacity to endure swift rhythms. He led his pupils to train over distances considerably longer than their "parade event". One of the runners who prospered most under his teachings was

Murray Halberg (born at Eketahuna on 7 July 1933; 1.80 m. / 62 kg.). At the age of 17 he suffered a serious injury while playing rugby football. At first it was feared that he would not live, and later, that he would remain an invalid for the rest of his life. But his dedication in trying to overcome his condition was such that not only was he restored to normal health, except for a withered arm, but also attained the highest honours one can hope for in athletics! His breakthrough as a class runner came in 1954, when he ran a mile in 4:04.4. In later years he began to explore longer distances and won his first international title at the 1958 Commonwealth Games at Cardiff, when he won the 3 miles in 13:15.0, beating the newly crowned world record holder Abie Thomas (13:24.4). Quite impressive on this occasion was Halberg's speed over the last three-quarter mile – 3:11.4.

The 1958 season in Europe offered exciting battles, especially at the continental championships in Stockholm. Zdzislaw Krzyszkowiak of Poland (born at Wielichowo on 3 August 1929; 1.72 m. / 59 kg.) was in all probability the most versatile distance runner since the days of Volmari Iso-Hollo. And just like the Finn he could play a leading rôle on the flat and in the steeplechase as well. The latter was in fact Krzyszkowiak's parade event, but in the Stockholm meet he chose to leave this to the expert care of his countryman Jerzy Chromik and opted for the flat events, aiming for a double. He succeeded in his quest, thus emulating the great Zátopek. As related in the adjoining aside, the 5000 metre final was run under adverse weather conditions. Details of both races follow.

Stockholm, 19 August 1958 – 10,000 metres: 1.Zdzislaw Krzyszkowiak (Pol) 28:56.0, 2.Yevgeniy Zhukov (USSR) 28:58.6, 3.Nikolay Pudov (USSR) 29:02.2, 4.Stanley Eldon (GB) 29:02.8, 5.Stanislaw Ozóg (Pol) 29:03.2, 6.John Merriman (GB) 29:03.8, 7.Alain Mimoun (Fra) 29:30.6, 8.Antonio Amorós (Spa) 29:31.4. Last 800 metres: 2:06.0, last 400 metres: 64.0.

Stockholm, 23 August 1958 – 5000 metres: 1.Zdzislaw Krzyszkowiak (Pol) 13:53.4, 2.Kazimierz Zimny (Pol) 13:55.2, 3.Gordon Pirie (GB) 14:01.6, 4.Peter Clark (GB) 14:03.8, 5.Aleksandr Artinyuk (USSR) 14:05.6, 6.Sándor Iharos (Hun) 14:07.2, 7.Miroslav Jurek (Cze) 14:12.2, 8.Friedrich Janke (GDR) 14:17.0. Last 400 metres: 56.4.

P.S. Zdzislaw Krzyszkowiak, known in non-Polish circles as the man with the unpronounceable name, returned to his "premier amour", the steeplechase, at the 1960 Olympics in Rome and won in superb style.

Mud baths, 1958 version

At the time of conventional (cinder) tracks a heavy and persistent rain could result in a water-logged surface, the equivalent of a mud bath for distance runners. Much in contrast to what happens nowadays with virtually rain-proof synthetic tracks. From personal experience I can recall two special cases. First, during the 5000 metre final of the 1958 European Championships in Stockholm. Prior to the race it had been raining cats and dogs and especially the inner lanes of the cinder track were particularly water-logged. To relieve the pains of competitors, the organizers resorted to an emergency solution: they decided to use the third lane as the inside one, with watering pipes marking the improvised border line. No more than 20 minutes were lost in the process of preparing and checking the whole thing, while seemingly frozen runners were patiently waiting. Even so, the runners splashed in water all along the race. The winner, Zdzislaw Krzyszkowiak of Poland, looked like an "ecce homo" as he crossed the finish line. And he did run the last 400 metres in a great 56.4.

Another personal recollection dates from 1989 and certainly provides a sharp contrast. It is relevant to the last day of the World Cup in Barcelona, when rains resembling a biblical deluge forced the organizers to delay all events for over an hour and a half. Yet, when the first event – 110 metre hurdles – got underway, the synthetic track had dried so well that Roger Kingdom of USA sped to 12.87, to this day history's fastest time, no matter if ruled out by a favouring wind of 2.6 m/s.

Page 74

Gordon Pirie (GB), world record holder for 3000 and 5000 metres in 1956.

The outstanding figure of 1959 was Pyotr Grigoryevich Bolotnikov (born at Zinovkino, Russia, on 8 March 1930; 1.73 m. / 64 kg.). He too emerged rather late, with 15:15.0 and 31:40.0 at age 24. He grew up in the shadow of the great Kuts, but later succeeded in replacing him in the hearts of USSR fans - at least to some extent. In 1959 he was a world leader in the 10,000 metres with 29:03.0. A teacher by profession, he was very strong but lacked the "animus pugnandi" (fighting spirit) of his predecessor. He had good basic speed – 3:46.0 for 1500 metres in 1961.

Halberg steals Rome race

At the 1960 Olympics in Rome Bolotnikov chose to concentrate on the 10,000 metres. Contrary to tradition, however, the 5000 metres came first. Here Murray Halberg was the favourite of experts. Early in the year, in New Zealand, he had done 13:11.4 in the 3 miles. The fastest time in the Olympic preliminary round was 14:01.2 by Hans Grodotzki (GDR). In this race Luigi Conti of Italy, spurred on by the home crowd, ran all out and finished close behind the German in 14:01.6, over 13 secs. below his own national record. A typically premature effort: two days later in the final he could do no better than 14:34.0 and 12th . The race was a splendid reflection of Halberg's well-known courage. The Kiwi ace was bold enough to run away from the rest with no less than 9 laps to go. He soon built up a lead which at one time was about 20 metres. He faded a bit near the end but still managed to stave off Grodotzki's strong closing burst. At the end the happy winner flopped to the ground exhausted. Details:
Rome, 2 September 1960 – 5000 metres: 1.Murray Halberg (NZ) 13:43.4, 2.Hans Grodotzki (GDR) 13:44.6, 3.Kazimierz Zimny (Pol) 13:44.8, 4.Friedrich Janke (GDR) 13:46.8, 5.Dave Power (Aus) 13:51.8; 6.Nyandika Maiyoro (Ken) 13:52.8, 7.Michel Bernard (Fra) 14:04.2, 8.Horst Flosbach (Ger) 14:06.6. Last kilometre, 2:41.7.

The 10,000 metres field initially had 44 entries and it was feared that a possible "traffic jam" would cause some problems. At the last moment, however, some of those who had run the 5000 or were planning to run the marathon, plus a few others, decided to scratch. The field was thus reduced to 32 runners, who were divided in two rows. The weather, relatively cool by Roman standards, promised to be conducive to fast times. So it was: most of the top finishers bettered their PB by several seconds. Among the exceptions was the 5000 metre champion, Murray Halberg, who barely missed his own in finishing fifth. Dave Power of Australia launched the fireworks with 7 laps to go. Only Bolotnikov, Grodotzki and Aleksey Desyatchikov of USSR stayed with him. With 700 metres to go Bolotnikov put on an impressive burst and ran away from the others to win by a convincing margin. After a 14:22.2 first half the winner ran the second in 14:10.0. Grodotzki was again second – in the best Mimoun style. The winner said: "I owe this victory to Kuts. He gave me advice and inspiration. Lacking his strength and fearing the heat of Rome, I chose to concentrate on one race." Details:
Rome, 8 September 1960 – 10,000 metres: 1.Pyotr Bolotnikov (USSR) 28:32.2, 2.Hans Grodotzki (GDR) 28:37.0, 3.Dave Power (Aus) 28:38.2, 4.Aleksey Desyatchikov (USSR) 28:39.6, 5.Murray Halberg (NZ) 28:48.8, 6.Max Truex (USA) 28:50.2, 7.Zdzislaw Krzyszkowiak (Pol) 28:52.4, 8. John Merriman (GB) 28:52.6. Last kilometre: 2:38.6, last 400 metres: 57.4.

Bolotnikov aptly closed his excellent season by succeeding Kuts also as a world record holder. To tell the truth he tried to do so at both distances but his first attempt, over 5000 metres, was not successful. At Kiev on 7 October he had to be content with 13:38.1, good enough to move him to 3rd in the All Time list. He had better luck the following week, still in the Ukrainian capital, when he ran 10,000 metres in 28:18.8, a good 11.6 secs. under Kuts' mark. Details:
Kiev, 15 October 1960 – 10,000 metres: 1.Pyotr Bolotnikov 28:18.8, 2.Aleksandr Artinyuk 29:08.6, 3.Yevgeniy Zhukov 29:08.6.

Kilometre fractions:

1000 m	2:43.0	
2000 m	5:31.0	(2:48.0)
3000 m	8:22.0	(2:51.0)
4000 m	11:13.0	(2:51.0)
5000 m	14:07.0	(2:54.0)
6000 m	16:57.0	(2:50.0)
7000 m	19:49.0	(2:52.0)
8000 m	22:42.0	(2:53.0)
9000 m	25:35.0	(2:53.0)
10,000 m	28:18.8	(2:43.8)

No official time for 6 miles.

1961 belonged to Halberg, an undisputed ruler in the 5000 metre department. Back to Europe, the Kiwi champion delighted Nordic crowds, ever ready to enthuse in the presence of long distance greats. Halberg got the ball rolling with a new world record for 2 miles – 8:30.0 at Jyväskylä on 7 July. He did this with two perfect halves, both in 4:15.0! Then he moved to Stockholm, where on 25 July he was engaged in a 5000 metre race. He passed the 3 mile mark in 13:10.0 for a new world record. In the eyes of metric-minded observers, though, his brilliant effort resulted in a failure, were it only by a tantalizing margin, for he was finally timed in 13:35.2 – two tenths shy of Kuts' world record! In this race the Olympic champion received useful help from his compatriot Barry Magee, a bronze medallist in the Rome Olympic marathon who had run the 10,000 metres in 28:50.8 at Helsinki in July. Maybe Magee had a chance vis-à-vis Halberg in the Stockholm race but, as historian P.N. Heidenstrom put it, "Magee is a Christian and, knowing the parable of the wedding rooms, decided to give up his own chances in order to pace Halberg's record attempt for as long as he was able". Magee stayed with Halberg for the major part of the race, but in the last 188 yards Halberg was on his own and barely failed to replace Kuts on the IAAF record list. No matter if he ran the last kilometre in 2:37.2. Magee was second in 13:39.2.

First to make the headlines in 1962 was an American, Jim Beatty, a pupil of Mihály Iglói. In a night meet at Los Angeles on 8 June, Beatty, a runner of medium build endowed with good basic speed, did 8:29.7 for 2 miles (halves of 4:15.4 and 4:14.3), a new world record. But in the hot part of the season Bolotnikov was again the leading figure. At the USSR Championships in Moscow he mastered a very large 10,000 metre field (25) and finally won in 28:18.2, six tenths under his own world record. The "depth" of USSR talent turned out to be quite impressive as no less than 12 men ducked under the half hour and the 17th finisher was timed in 30:04.0, i.e. under Paavo Nurmi's onetime world record. Details:

Moscow, 11 August 1962 – 10,000 metres: 1.Pyot Bolotnikov 28:18.2, 2.Yuriy Nikitin 29:07.0, 3.Leonid Ivanov 29:07.6, 4.Yuriy Zakharov 29:21.4, 5.Boris Yefimov 29:30.4.

Zdzislaw Krzyszkowiak (Poland) winning the European 5000 metre title under adverse weather conditions at Stockholm in 1958.

Kilometre fractions:

1000 m	2:41.5	
2000 m	5:30.0	(2:48.5)
3000 m	8:21.0	(2:51.0)
4000 m	11:12.0	(2:51.0)
5000 m	14:04.0	(2:52.0)
6000 m	16:57.0	(2:53.0)
7000 m	19:50.0	(2:53.0)
8000 m	22:41.5	(2:51.5)
9000 m	25:34.5	(2:53.0)
10,000 m	28:18.2	(2:43.7)

No official 6-mile time.

At the European Championships in Belgrade the man then hailed as "Kuts' heir apparent", Pyotr Bolotnikov, chose to compete in both 5000 and 10,000 metres. At the longer distance he won as he pleased in 28:54.0, with a last kilometre in 2:41.4. In the closing stage he did not go all out as he had in mind the heats of 5000 metres, scheduled for the following day. Here he qualified with an easy 13:53.4. Another two days later, in the final, the Russian for once decided to change his tactics and set a fairly fast pace from the beginning. However, when the final battle began to rage, under the leadership of Miroslav Jurek of Czechoslovakia, the Russian lost contact. Very soon it became apparent that Jurek had committed suicide (he finished 12th), but bare-footed Bruce Tulloh of Britain and Kazimierz Zimny of Poland had enough left to stay ahead and repulse Bolotnikov's counter-attack. Tulloh, who early in the season had run a mile in 3:59.3, covered the last 400 metres in a nifty 57.4. Once again it became apparent that Bolotnikov lacked Kuts' magic qualities. Details:

Belgrade, 12 September 1962 – 10,000 metres: 1.Pyotr Bolotnikov (USSR) 28:54.0, 2.Friedrich Janke (GDR) 29:01.6, 3.Roy Fowler (GB) 29:02.0, 4.Martin Hyman (GB) 29:02.0, 5.Robert Bogey (Fra) 29:02.6, 6.Leonid Ivanov (USSR) 29:04.8, 7.Frank Cervan (Yug) 29:07.6, 8.Michael Bullivant (GB) 29:13.4.

Belgrade, 15 September 1962 – 5000 metres: 1.Bruce Tulloh (GB) 14:00.6, 2.Kazimierz Zimny (Pol) 14:01.8, 3.Pyotr Bolotnikov (USSR) 14:02.6, 4.Lech Boguszewicz (Pol) 14:03.4, 5.Michel Bernard (Fra) 14:03.8, 6.John Anderson (GB) 14:04.2, 7.Siegfried Herrmann (GDR) 14:05.0, 8.Robert Bogey (Fra) 14:06.8.

The Commonwealth Games at Perth, Australia, closed the 1962 season on a brilliant note, mainly thanks to Murray Halberg, who won the 3 miles in 13:34.2, after covering the last quarter in a blazing 53.8. Next came two promising runners, Ron Clarke of Australia (13:36.0) and Bruce Kidd of Canada (13:36.4). Two days earlier Kidd, 19, had won the 6 miles in 28:26.2 from Dave Power of Australia (28:34.0). It was ironically noted that Kidd behaved like an "adult" in these Games. Unfortunately, he did not live up to his promises in the years that followed.

RON CLARKE, MAGNANIMOUS KING WITHOUT A CROWN

Very few long distance aces, if any, have had such a great impact on their generation as had Ron Clarke throughout most of the Sixties. First, for his many world records – only Paavo Nurmi and Emil Zátopek can vie with him in this respect. During his European tours he led and inspired distance men from different countries, extending them to new PB's and new national records, thanks to his bold front running tactics. Notwithstanding his great achievements against the clock, in the perspective of some observers Clarke is remembered as a prime example of the "good loser". Even though he won many fast races, he never went beyond a single bronze medal in the Olympic Games and four silver medals in the Commonwealth Games – a decidedly meager record for a champion of his stature. Of course one could argue that in the 1968 Olympics at Mexico City he was handicapped, like other runners from the "plains", by the rarefied atmosphere of the Mexican capital (2300 metres). Earlier in the same year, in European meets, Clarke looked better than ever and won highly competitive races from the likes of Kipchoge Keino and Naftali Temu, i.e. Kenyan "mountaineers" who were to conquer the world at Mexico City. Yet it is perhaps safer to look at it from another angle: for every Herb Elliott there is a Ron Clarke, i.e. two champion athletes from the same country yet entirely different in mentality and racing tactics. The former endowed with high doses of the so-called killer instinct, the latter apparently devoid of that quality and hence incapable of doing himself justice on "hot" occasions. Be it as it may, Clarke will stand – in the mind of those, like me, who got to know him – as the perfect embodiment of fair play and sportsmanship, the most important values in any athlete, let alone a champion.

Ronald William Clarke (born in Melbourne on 21 February 1937; 1.83 m. / 74 kg.) had a distant Irish extraction. His ancestors left the Emerald Isle in the 19th century and settled down in Australia. His great-grandfather was a man of great strength and stamina. He was working at the Australasian mine when it was flooded by an underground river but he managed to survive and eventually won credit for helping to rescue his mates. Ron's father, Tom, was a relatively small man who played Australian football and even tried the sprints in the famous "Stawell Gift", a professional race that dates back to the Gold Rush era. This heritage undoubtedly had useful effects on Ron and his elder brother Jack, who was the first to achieve fame in sports, namely in Australian football, which to many Aussies is almost a religion and – as Ron himself once put it – "nowhere was it more intensely worshipped than in the Clarke family". Of course Ron himself practised it for a while but lacking pronounced agility and flexibility he never went far in it. Jack was a very brilliant centreman and eventually became such a nationally prominent figure that for a long time to come even Ron the athlete was referred to in Australian sporting circles as "Jack's younger brother". Be it as it may, Ron soon found his right way – in athletics. In 1953, as a 16-year-old boy, he ran the half mile in 2:07.3 and the mile in 4:31.1. He once happened to run against John Landy, who was soon to become holder of the world 1-mile record. Predictably enough, the novice was soundly beaten and finished well behind Landy (4:18.0). Some time later, Ron was highly surprised when he received a wonderful gift from Landy: a letter in which the champion gave him a lot of useful advice on training. Even though he had occasionally met Percy Cerutty – coach of John Landy and Herb Elliott - Ron found the right inspiration early in 1955 when he got in touch with Franz Stampfl, the man who had been tutoring Roger Bannister, Landy's great rival. Coming under Stampfl's wing was tantamount to becoming an adept of Interval Training. Ron began to collect national junior

Closing stage of a great 5000 metres at the 1965 World Games in Helsinki: Ron Clarke is still leading from Michel Jazy, the eventual winner (13:27.6), and Kipchoge Keino, who will shunt Clarke to third.

records in 1955. Early in 1956 he conquered the world junior record for the mile with a brilliant 4:06.8. At that time he preferred distances ranging from 880 yards to 2 miles. The Melbourne Olympics came too early for him, yet his growing fame as a most promising youth caused him to be chosen as the last torch bearer on the opening day of the Games. Performing that task before 102,000 spectators certainly made his bond for athletics ever stronger. Even now, in recalling the episode, he says: "I get unfair recognition for carrying a torch and probably not enough recognition for my running all over the world, even though I broke many world records".

In the years that followed, Clarke's athletic life was spattered with roses as well as thorns. The 1958 Commonwealth Games and the 1960 Olympics went by and he was not selected for Australia's team. In 1957 he ran 3 miles in 14:01.6, but the subsequent seasons yielded disappointing results. In his autobiography "The Unforgiving Minute" he says: "Near the end of 1960, when I was nearly 24, I estimated I had another six years or so in which I could take part in top-class sport and many, many more years in which top sport would be impracticable. Should I waste those six years? It seemed that so many sportsmen later rued their early retirement. You have only one life and it's futile looking back upon it and regretting that you didn't do something when you were capable of doing it". Not by chance then, it was at that time that he changed his attitude and decided to pass from a purely recreational work to a methodical engagement implying intense and systematic training. He joined a group of running devotees known as the "Caulfield Mob" or, alternatively, as the "Ferny Creek Gang", so called after the Melbourne areas in which they used to train. Clarke began to have two regular training sessions per day, before and after his office hours as an accountant. He had at last decided to discover the depth of his potential. His real challenge was on. His progression over the long distances up to and including 1962 tells the subsequent story. (In 1958/59 he ran sparingly, mostly at shorter distances).

Late in 1962 he won his first medal in international competition: 2nd to Murray Halberg in the 3 miles of the Commonwealth Games in Perth – as related in the previous chapter. 1963 was the starting point of the Clarke Era in the IAAF record book. I deem it advisable to give here a résumé of his world records in chronological order.

Melbourne, 18 December 1963	6 miles	27:17.8+
	10,000 m	28:15.5°
Melbourne, 3 December 1964	3 miles	13:07.5°
Hobart, 16 January 1965	5000 m	13:34.7°
Auckland, 1 February 1965	5000 m	13:33.6
Mentone, Vic., 3 March 1965	10 miles	47:12.7°
Los Angeles, 4 June 1965	3 miles	13:00.4+
	5000 m	13:25.7°
Turku, 16 June 1965	10,000 m	28:14.0*
London, 10 July 1965	3 miles	12:52.4
Oslo, 14 July 1965	6 miles	26:47.0+
	10,000 m	27:39.4
Geelong, 27 October 1965	20,000 m	59:22.7°+
	20,232 m	1 hour
Stockholm, 5 July 1966	3 miles	12:50.4+
	5000 m	13:16.6
Västerås, 27 June 1967	2 miles	8:19.8
London, 24 August 1968	2 miles	8:19.6

+ Intermediate time during a race at longer distance.
° Time was rounded up to nearest fifth-of-a-second, as per IAAF rule.
* Not ratified by the IAAF.

Year	Age	3 miles	5000 m	6 miles	10,000 m
1957	20	14:01.6	-	-	-
1960	23	14:22.6	-	-	-
1961	24	-	14:23.0	-	30:36.0
1962	25	13:31.4	14:11.6	28:11.6	29:53.0

If one adds the following indoor bests he set in USA, the total of Ron Clarke's world records comes up to 21.

New York,
22 February 1964 3 miles   13:18.4

San Francisco,
25 February 1966 2 miles   8:28.8

Oakland,
24 January 1969 3 miles   13:12.6

The first world record of 1963 was set up by a Frenchman, Michel Jazy (born at Oignies, Pas-de-Calais on 13 June 1936; 1.75 m. / 65 kg.), the offspring of a Polish couple who had migrated to France. As a youth he was lucky enough to come under the tutelage of Gaston Meyer, chief editor of "L'Equipe", the famous sports daily, who offered Jazy a part-time job as a printer, thus leaving him plenty of time to train, mostly in the Marly forest. His coach was René Frassinelli, a Frenchman of Tuscan extraction. Jazy soon developed into an excellent middle distance runner, reaching worldwide recognition in 1960, when he finished second to Herb Elliott of Australia in the 1500 metres of the Rome Olympics with a time of 3:38.4, a new European record. In later years Jazy began to explore the longer distances. In 1962 he broke two world records with 5:01.5 for 2000 metres and 7:49.2 for 3000 metres. All this while remaining faithful to the 1500, his first love: still in 1962 he was crowned European champion at this distance. The following year he ran the 5000 metres in 13:50.2 and conquered the world's 2 mile record with 8:29.6.
The outstanding effort of 1963 was at any rate Ron Clarke's first world record, made at Melbourne's Olympic Park. A fantastic "solo" race over 10,000 metres ...witnessed by a handful of spectators! Details:
Melbourne, 18 December 1963 – 10,000 metres: 1.Ron Clarke 28:15.5, 2.Robert Ward 31:28.0, 3.Tom Kelly 31:56.0.

Kilometre fractions:

1000 m	2:44.0	
2000 m	5:31.0	(2:47.0)
3000 m	8:25.0	(2:54.0)
4000 m	11:15.0	(2:50.0)
5000 m	14:06.5	(2:51.5)
6000 m	17:01.0	(2:54.5)
7000 m	19:54.5	(2:53.5)
8000 m	22:50.0	(2:55.5)
9000 m	25:40.0	(2:50.0)
10,000 m	28:15.5*	(2:35.5)

* Officially rounded up to 28:15.6 as per IAAF rule.
Official 6-mile time, 27:17.8, another world record.

Remarkably enough, only three days earlier Clarke was outsprinted by little Albie Thomas in the closing stage of a 5000 metre race – 13:51.6 (still a PB for Ron) to 13:51.4. Enroute Clarke led at the 3-mile mark in 13:27.5, another PB.
That year also saw a new world 1-hour record: 20,190 kms. by Bill Baillie of New Zealand (Auckland, 24 August), stimulated by a Japanese marathoner, Kokichi Tsuburaya (20,083 kms.).

Tokyo '64: two American stars

In 1964 the scene was centered on the Tokyo Olympics, the first ever held in Asia, and new emerging forces entered the picture. The new cast notably included runners from USA, a country of great athletic traditions but not in this department. Prior to 1964 Americans had won only two Olympic medals – both silver, with Louis Tewanima in the 10,000 (Stockholm 1912) and Ralph Hill in the 5000 (Los Angeles 1932).
The Games were scheduled for October and quite a few things happened in the long pre-Olympic period. However, the only new world record was a 2-mile mark of 8:26.3 by Bob Schul of USA on 29 August in Los Angeles. Billy Mills was a distant second in 8:45.6. Both men were to play prominent rôles in Tokyo.
Robert Keyser Schul (born at West Milton, Ohio, on 28 September 1937; 1.84 m./ 66 kg.) had grown in stature under the tutelage of Mihály Iglói, onetime coach of the three Hungarian "Musketeers". He first made the headlines as a steeplechaser (8:47.8 in 1961). Endowed with a great finishing "kick", Schul made his debut over 5000 metres early

in 1964 with an excellent 13:38.0 at Compton, California. This was to remain the world's fastest time for 1964. At the US Olympic Trials Schul and Bill Dellinger deliberately tied for first in 13:55.6 "after having a good chat on the last lap" (62 secs).

William Mervin Mills (born at Pine Ridge, South Dakota, on 30 June 1938; 1.80 m. / 68 kg.) had 7/16 Sioux blood as a descendant of an Indian chief. An orphan at the age of 12, he began to be acquainted with adequate training when he joined the Marine Corps. He first tried his favourite distance, 10,000 metres, in 1963 and chalked up a good 30:08.0. He offered a greater glimpse of his potential on 12 August 1964 in Los Angeles when he ran 6 miles in 27:56.4. But the status of US distance men was then on the upgrade and he finished only second to Ron Larrieu, 27:54.0. The latter, 15 cms. shorter than Mills in height, really had his day of days on that occasion. At the US Olympic Trials both these men were baffled by 18-year-old Gerry Lindgren (1.67 m.) who won in 29:02.0, with Mills (29:10.4) and Larrieu (30:20.4) in his wake. On the eve of the Games American experts favoured Schul for gold in the 5000 metres but seemed to underestimate Mills at the double distance, where Ron Clarke was understandably the pick of many. In addition to his world 10,000 metre record late in 1963, the Australian could point to a recent 13:39.0 in the 5000 meters in losing to Pyotr Bolotnikov (13:38.6) at Zurich. Other possible favourites were Michel Jazy, who finally opted for the 5000; Mohamed Gammoudi of Tunisia, redoubtable for his finishing kick; veteran Bolotnikov, then 34; and the ever dangerous Murray Halberg. Hence, an intriguing multi-national scenario.

The 10,000 metres came first on the Olympic timetable. The final was a race of upsets. Clarke particularly feared well-established quantities like Halberg and Bolotnikov, yet the real danger came from others. The Australian tried to inject his usually hot pace. In fact, the time at 8000 metres (22:47.0) was three seconds faster than his clocking at the same stage in his record-breaking race in Melbourne. But it was not enough to discourage Mills and Gammoudi. Going round the last turn the 26-

A blanket finish in the 5000 metres of the 1964 Olympics in Tokyo, with 2.2 secs. covering the first six. From left to right: Norpoth (Ger), 2nd; Bob Schul (USA), 1st; Jazy (Fra) 4th; covering Keino (Ken), 5th; Dellinger (USA), 3rd, partly covering Baillie (NZ), 6th. Winner's time: 13:48.8.

year-old Tunisian grabbed the lead. Mills was at first taken by surprise yet he was quick to recover, so well in fact that he shot ahead of Gammoudi with 50 metres to go. Clarke, surely the least agile of the three, had to be content with a disappointing (for him) third. Gammoudi in second and Mamo Wolde of Ethiopia in fourth served evidence that the African giant was waking up. An elated Mills said: "I'm flabbergasted. I can hardly believe it." As for Clarke, the following figures should aptly tell the tale: in the last two kilometres he "lost" more than 13 secs. vis-à-vis his record breaking race at Melbourne in 1963. Details:

Tokyo,14 October 1964 – 10,000 metres: 1.Billy Mills (USA) 28:24.4, 2.Mohamed Gammoudi (Tun) 28:24.8, 3.Ron Clarke (Aus) 28:25.8, 4.Mamo Wolde (Eth) 28:31.8, 5.Leonid Ivanov (USSR) 28:53.2, 6. Kokichi Tsuburaya (Jap) 28:59.4, 7.Murray Halberg (NZ) 29:10.8, 8.Tony Cook (Aus) 29:15.8. Mills ran the last kilometre in 2:41.4.

Two days later, the fastest time in the heats of the 5000 metres was 13:48.4 by (guess who?) Ron Clarke in finishing ahead of Kipchoge Keino of Kenya (13:49.6). Another two days later, a cold, rainy weather made things difficult for the finalists. Incidentally, the Tokyo Olympics were the last to be contested on a conventional cinder track Gammoudi had to scratch due to an injury. Clarke again set the pace and reached 3000 metres in 8:22.2, with Jazy and Harald Norpoth, a tall thin German, in his wake, while Schul was in sixth place. Clarke, apparently confused after his disappointing experience in the 10,000 metres, slowed to a 70secs. lap at one stage, allowing his rivals to breathe. In the last lap Jazy, the best miler of them all, really let himself go. And Clarke was his first "victim". The Frenchman grabbed the lead and had nearly 10 metres on Schul at one time. But the American began to close the gap. Jazy, by then exhausted, looked back as Schul was closing fast on him. With 50 metres to go the American took the lead and won comfortably. Jazy was passed also by Norpoth and, right on the finish line, by Bill Dellinger too. (At the end of his career Dellinger was to become a famous coach).

"Nous tombions de trop haut"

Throughout most of his career Michel Jazy had an expert and passionate counselor in Gaston Meyer, a famous sport journalist, affectionately known as "le Pape" in his profession. For many years Meyer was the "cantor" of athletics in the columns of the Paris sports daily "L'Equipe". He was also a lively "animateur" – a promoter of young talents. His favourite theory, fascinating but perhaps controversial, was that the greats of the middle distances could contribute to the popularity of athletics better than champions from any other segment of the sport. He had a loyal and intelligent pupil in Marcel Hansenne, a bronze medallist in the 800 metres at the 1948 Olympics and later his colleague at "L'Equipe". Another Meyer protégé was Michel Jazy, who in his second Olympic venture (Rome 1960) was unlucky enough to be opposed to one of the all- time greats of the 1500 m./ mile, Herb Elliott. On the eve of the 1964 Olympics in Tokyo Jazy and his clan were facing a hard choice: should he choose the 1500 or the 5000 metres? True, he had made notable progress in the latter: shortly before leaving for Tokyo he did 13:46.8 easily in a special rehearsal (Fontainebleau, 26 September). The theory of those who still regarded him primarily as a miler stumbled on the bare fact that if he chose the 1500 metres he would face one Peter Snell of New Zealand, regarded by many as well-nigh untouchable, as was Herb Elliott in 1960. That was probably the reason why Jazy finally opted for the 5000 metres, an event without a steadfast favourite. At any rate, his clan had an unlimited faith in Michel. They thought that in a not-too-fast race to be decided in the last lap, Jazy's great basic speed (1:47.1 for 800 metres in 1962) would finally win the day. Alas, it wasn't so. Jazy launched his final attack too soon and in the final section of the homestretch he ran out of gas. In the space of a few seconds he sank from first to fourth. Disappointment in the French section of the press box ran high. It was admirably summed up by Marcel Hansenne: "Nous tombions de trop haut" (free translation: the greater the expectations, the bigger the disappointment).

Schul ran the last 400 metres in 54.8, the last 300 in 38.7 – a tremendous finish under those conditions. For Clarke, whose last lap took 64 secs., the closing stage of the race was a real Odyssey. "I have to learn how to finish fast", he said. Details:

Tokyo, 18 October 1964 – 5000 metres: 1.Bob Schul (USA) 13:48.8, 2.Harald Norpoth (GFR) 13:49.6, 3.Bill Dellinger (USA) 13:49.8, 4.Michel Jazy (Fra) 13:49.8; 5.Kipchoge Keino (Ken) 13:50.4, 6.Bill Baillie (NZ) 13:51.0, 7.Nikolay Dutov (USSR) 13:53.8, 8.Thor Helland (Nor) 13:57.0, 9.Ron Clarke (Aus) 13:58.0. Schul ran the last kilometre in 2:32.6.

By then it became obvious to most observers that Clarke could not adapt to the sudden changes of rhythm that are characteristic of highly competitive races. He took a partial revenge just before the end of the year in Melbourne on 3 December when he broke the world's 3-mile record with 13:07.5, after his countryman John Coyle had set the pace in the first half of the journey. Clarke's mile splits were: 4:21.0, 4:27.0, 4:19.5. Theoretically, that was more or less what he should have done in Tokyo .....A declining Murray Halberg was second just ahead of Tony Cook (Australia), both in 13:31.0.

1965 was a memorable, unique year. In the range 3000-to10,000 metres no less than four-teen world records were broken! (not counting one that remained unofficial). As if that was not enough, even the 1-hour record was bettered. Clarke opened the parade in his usual style, bet-tering the 5000 metre record three times (in the space of five months) with just as many run-away victories. Details:

Hobart, 16 January 1965 – 5000 metres: 1.Ron Clarke 13:34.7, 2.Tony Cook, 350 m. back.

Kilometre fractions:

1000 m	2:43.8	
2000 m	5:27.4	(2:43.6)
3000 m	8:11.8	(2:44.4)
4000 m	10:54.9	(2:43.1)
5000 m	13:34.7*	(2:39.8)

* Officially rounded up to 13:34.8 as per IAAF rule.
Official 3-mile time, 13:10.5. Auckland, 1 February 1965 – 5000 metres: 1.Ron Clarke 13:33.6, 2.Neville Scott (NZ) 13:45.0.

Kilometre fractions:

1000 m	2:39.6	
2000 m	5:21.5	(2:41.9)
3000 m	8:09.5	(2:48.0)
4000 m	10:55.6	(2:46.1)
5000 m	13:33.6	(2:38.0)

Official 3-mile time, 13:08.0
Last 440 yards, 64.0.

Los Angeles, 4 June 1965 – 5000 metres: 1.Ron Clarke 13:25.7, 2.Neville Scott (NZ) 13:59.4, 3.Dave Ellis (Can) 14:03.6.

Kilometre fractions:

1000 m	2:39.1	
2000 m	5:20.4	(2:41.3)
3000 m	8:04.1	(2:43.7)
4000 m	10:48.7	(2:44.6)
5000 m	13:25.7*	(2:37.0)

* Officially rounded up to 13 :25.8 as per IAAF rule.
Official 3-mile time, 13:00.4, another world record. Last 220 yards, 25.3.

Fully conscious of his "état de grâce", the Aussie champion re-visited his beloved Scandinavian shores. In Turku he turned his attention to the 10,000 metres and improved on his world record of 1963 with 28:14.0. However, the mark never made the IAAF record book due to a formal failure: his permission to participate was not registered early enough to be in accordance with requirements. Details:

Turku, 16 June 1965 – 10,000 metres: 1.Ron Clarke 28:14.0, 2.Matti Utriainen (Fin) 30:26.4, 3.Simo Saloranta (Fin) 30:51.8.

Kilometre fractions :

1000 m	2:43.4	
2000 m	5:29.6	(2:46.2)
3000 m	8:19.0	(2:49.4)
4000 m	11:10.6	(2:51.6)
5000 m	14:02.0	(2:51.4)
6000 m	16:51.8	(2:49.8)
7000 m	19:45.6	(2:53.8)
8000 m	22:39.4	(2:53.8)
9000 m	25:32.6	(2:53.2)
10,000 m	28:14.0	(2:41.4)

Official 6-mile time, 27:22.6

Jazy: a meaningful revenge

Michel Jazy was thirsty for revenge after his tragic Olympic failure. In 1965 he got the ball rolling on 23 June at Melun, breaking two world records in the same race: 7:49.0 for 3000 metres and 8:22.6 for 2 miles. His rivals in this race were Ron Clarke and Mohamed Gammoudi. The former was outpaced in the closing stage and finished second in 8:24.8, also under the previous record. Gammoudi was a distant third in 8:37.8. More was to follow from the Frenchman, but in strict chronological order it must be said that in the AAU Championships at San Diego on 27 June two Americans broke Clarke's 6-mile world record as Olympic champion Billy Mills beat Gerry Lindgren in a hair-raising finish, 27:11.5 to 27:11.6. Of course, Mills' time was officially rounded up to 27:11.6, so that both got credit for the record. The Bulova Photo Timer actually "saw" only 6 hundredths of a second between them as they crossed the finish line. Bill Morgan was third in 28:33.8. The second half (13:31.7) was considerably faster than the first (13:39.8). The last mile took only 4:21.6. Little Lindgren was trailing Mills as the bell rang and ran the last lap in 57.9 - not enough to overhaul his rival. The day before, Bob Schul had won the 3 miles in 13:10.4, a new US record, after a fierce fight with Neville Scott of New Zealand (13:10.8) and Ron Larrieu (13:11.4).

The highlight of that unforgettable summer unfolded in Finland, namely in a 5000 metre race at Helsinki's World Games on 30 June. The cast included Jazy, Clarke, Kipchoge Keino of Kenya, as well as the two Americans who had won gold medals in the Tokyo Olympics, Schul and Mills. The last two performed well below expectations though: maybe they had not fully recovered from their efforts at the AAU meet in San Diego on a hard asphalt track and their subsequent trip from California to Finland. The eagerly awaited Helsinki "summit" was very exciting and served as a reminder that highly competitive races can have a unique flavour even without the benefit of a record breaking time. True to his habits, Ron Clarke set the pace for most of the race but was again sub-merged in a hectic finish. Jazy went into the lead with 500 metres to go, i.e. even earlier than in Tokyo, but this time he held on up to the end. A vastly improved Keino shunted Clarke to third. This was nice revenge for the Frenchman, whose winning time – 13:27.6 – was the second best ever. Details:

Helsinki, 30 June 1965 – 5000 metres: 1.Michel Jazy (Fra) 13:27.6, 2.Kipchoge Keino (Ken) 13:28.2, 3.Ron Clarke (Aus) 13:29.4, 4.Mike Wiggs (GB) 13:33.0, 5.Thor Helland (Nor) 13:37.4 .... 8.Billy Mills (USA) 13:42.2, ... 10.Bob Schul (USA) 13:49.8. Enroute, 3-mile times were as follows: Jazy 13:04.8, Keino 13:04.8, Clarke 13:05.0, Wiggs 13:08.6. Jazy ran the last kilometre in 2:37.4.

The indomitable Clarke, vanquished but not discouraged, responded in his usual way – with two world records in close succession! At the AAA Championships in London he brought a vast crowd to its feet as he broke the 13-minute barrier for the 3 miles. Four days later in Oslo he was even more impressive as he broke another barrier, 28 minutes for 10,000 metres, bettering his previous mark by 34.6 seconds! Details:

London, 10 July 1965 – 3 miles: 1.Ron Clarke (Aus) 12:52.4, 2.Gerry Lindgren (USA) 13:04.2, 3.Lajos Mécser (Hun) 13:07.6, 4.Derek Graham (GB) 13:15.8. Clarke's 1-mile splits: 4:15.4, 4:20.8, 4:16.2.

Oslo, 14 July 1965 – 10,000 metres: 1.Ron Clarke (Aus) 27:39.4, 2.Jim Hogan 29:19.6, 3.Claus Börsen (Den) 31:03.2.

Kilometre fractions:

1000 m	2:41.5	
2000 m	5:25.0	(2:43.5)
3000 m	8:11.0	(2:46.0)
4000 m	10:58.0	(2:47.0)
5000 m	13:45.0	(2:47.0)
6000 m	16:33.0	(2:48.0)
7000 m	19:23.0	(2:50.0)
8000 m	22:13.0	(2:50.0)
9000 m	24:59.0	(2:46.0)
10,000 m	27:39.4	(2:40.4)

Official 6-mile time, 26:47.0, another world record.

An electronic device used as a "reserve" gave Clarke's final time as 27:39.89.

Prior to the Oslo race no one had ever run the first or second half of a 10,000 metres race in less than 14 minutes. The Aussie ace turned the trick twice in the same race, with 13:45.0 and 13:54.4 ! The crowd at Bislett stadium cheered him no end as he was hugged by rivals and .. judges.

Keino, first of the great Kenyans

One who shared a minor part of the great vintage of 1965 was Siegfried Herrmann (GDR), who shaved 3.1 secs. off Michel Jazy's recent 3000 metre world record with 7:45.9. a time which was rounded up to 7:46.0 as per IAAF rule. The race was on a 500 metre-track at Erfurt on 5 August and was characterized by an impressive crescendo with a second half (3:49.3) much faster than the first (3:56.6). This was yet another short-lived record though. The chief tenor in the latter part of the year was a Kenyan, Hezekiah Kipchoge Keino (born at Kipsamo in the Nandi Hills region on 17 January 1940; 1.78 m. / 66 kg.). His life as a boy was quite different from that of most of his rivals from Europe, North America and Oceania. He was only 4 when his mother died. At 10 he was experienced enough to tend a flock of goats all by himself. As legend has it, he ran the fastest run of his young life the day he came face to face with a leopard which was eating a goat. He entered his first official race at 16, spurred on by his father, and finished fifth in a 3-mile race. However, he came to know serious training not at school but after joining the Police Corps, which has remained to this day the main storehouse of Kenyan athletics. His marks at age 19 were all but impressive: 4:38 for 1 mile and 16:17 for 3 miles. Only three years later he was rated good enough to earn selection in Kenya's national team for the Commonwealth Games in Perth, where he finished 11th in the 3 miles in 13:50.0. In 1964, by then a family man but also the owner of a house he had built for himself, he was 5th in the 5000 metres at the Tokyo Olympics, as previously related. He also tried the 1500 metres but was eliminated in a semi-final (3:41.9). I have already hinted to

his excellent 5000 metre race at Helsinki in 1965, where he lost to Jazy but finished ahead of Clarke. He closed the season with two world records, a truly impressive crescendo. At Hälsingborg, Sweden, on 27 August he ran 3000 metres in 7:39.5 (halves of 3:49.5 and 3:50.0). Then, during a brief visit to New Zealand, he succeeded Clarke as holder of the world's 5000 metre record with 13:24.2. Details:

Auckland, 30 November 1965 – 5000 metres: 1.Kpchoge Keino (Ken) 13:24.2, 2.Bill Baillie (NZ) 14:01.2, 3.Franc Cervan (Yug) 14:02.0.

No intermediate times for the metric distances. 1-mile splits: 4:16.0, 8:33.8 (4:17.8), 12:58.6 (4:24.8). Keino covered the last 171.96 metres in 25.6.

Africa thus entered the picture of élite distance running - a wave that was to mount relentlessly in the years to come. As far as Kenya is concerned, however, Keino had a predecessor of minor yet notable class in Nyandika Maiyoro, who earned honorable placings in the 5000 metres in two editions of the Olympic Games (7th in 1956 and 6th in 1960).

Prior to losing his 5000 metre record, Clarke had conquered yet another world mark: 20,232 km. for 1 hour at Geelong, Victoria, on 27 October. A summary of his strenuous work in 1965 may be in order: he competed in 51 races, winning 37 and losing 14. His defeats occurred, for the most part, in middle distance races, save for a half-hearted effort in the Fukuoka marathon (he did not finish). But he also lost four 5000 metre races, ending up on the losing side with both Jazy (0-1) and Keino (1-3). His record over 10,000 metres was peerless: two races - with just as many world records!

1966 was by comparison a quiet year, during which attention was mainly focussed on two big events: the Commonwealth Games at Kingston, Jamaica, and the European Championships in Budapest. Only two men made successful inroads on the world record department: the indefatigable Clarke and Gaston Roelants of Belgium. The former delivered his big blows during the Scandinavian summer. Just as he had done the previous year, he first went to USA, where he suffered a defeat against a fine steeplechaser, George Young, in a 5000

metre race – 13:40.6 to 13:40.2, as both left behind Billy Mills and Roelants. In Europe the Aussie champion had a busy schedule, as per his well-known generosity. Once again, he lost some races, e.g. in Berlin on 26 June, when he bowed to Keino in the 5000 metres – 13:28.4 to 13:26.6, as both beat Harald Norpoth and Naftali Temu. After a Gargantuan menu of 4 races in just as many countries in the space of 4 days, Clarke allowed himself a rich 5-days rest, then exploded into another world record at Stockholm: 13:16.6 for 5000 metres. Details:
Stockholm, 5 July 1966 – 5000 metres: 1.Ron Clarke (Aus) 13:16.6, 2.Lech Boguszewicz (Pol) 13:51.8, 3.Tony Cook (Aus) 13:52.6, 4.Bill Baillie (NZ) 13:56.2, 5.Keisuke Sawaki (Jap) 13:58.2.

Kilometre fractions:

1000 m	2:40.2	
2000 m	5:16.4	(2:36.2)
3000 m	7:57.4	(2:41.0)
4000 m	10:39.0	(2:41.6)
5000 m	13:16.6	(2:37.6)

Official 3-mile time, 12:50.4, another world record.

It should be said that Bodo Tümmler of Germany, a topclass 1500 m./1 mile performer, played an important rôle in the Stockholm race, setting the pace for half the distance before stepping out.
Such was Ron Clarke's passionate commitment to running that he gave at times the impression of failing to distinguish between important and not-so-important races. For instance, he went to Kingston, Jamaica, for the Commonwealth Games after strenuous tours to USA, Europe and back to USA – 17 meets in the space of six weeks! After which he allowed himself less than two weeks of much-needed rest before meeting the Kenyans at Kingston. A hot temperature close to 30 °C. plus a high humidity made conditions very difficult. The well-known ability of his rivals did the rest. Even so, Clarke's first defeat was rather unexpected: on 6 August he was badly beaten by Naftali Temu in the 6 miles, 27:39.4 to 27:14.6. Ironically enough, Clarke's time was equal to his .... 10,000 metre world record of the year before! Once

again, the Australian set the pace and reached the half-way mark in a fast 13:24.4, with the 21-year-old Kenyan still in his wake. Then Clarke began to alternate spells of fast and slow running. When Temu chose to inject a 62.6 lap in the last mile, Clarke dropped behind and finally lost by a huge margin - 150 yards. Jim Alder of Scotland was third (28:15.4) and Pascal Mfyomi of Tanzania fourth (28:38.0). The winner (born at Kisii on 20 April 1945; 1.71 m. / 60 kg.) was a major sensation, even though he had shown great promise as a junior in 1964 with a 28:30.4 six-mile time. In the same year he competed in the Tokyo Olympics: he dropped out of the 10,000 metres with just two laps left and finished 49th in the marathon in 2 hrs 40:47. In 1965 he improved to 28:18.6 over 6 miles and also ran 13:57.6 for 5000 metres.
Two days later, in the 3 miles, Clarke evened the count with his young conqueror yet lost once more – quite predictably to Kipchoge Keino. A deadly 56.3 last quarter by the Kenyan was too quick for the Australian. Times: 12:57.4 and 12:59.2. Place-getters also put up significant marks: 3.Allan Rushmer (England) 13:08.6, 4. Temu 13:10.4, 5.Ian McCafferty (Scotland) 13:12.2 , 6.Dick Taylor (England) 13:12.4. Keino's superiority in basic speed was undisputable. Five days later he also annexed the 1-mile title in 3:55.3. Clarke closed his disappointing week with a low-key appearance in the marathon, in which he dropped out after 19 miles.
The distance races at the European Championships in Budapest later in August were exciting too. Michel Jazy for once decided to vie for a double: 1500/5000 metres. Chronologically, the 10,000 metres came first though. The winner was Jürgen Haase of the GDR (born at Friedersdorf on 19 January 1945; 1.76 m. / 62 kg.), who had started as a 1500 metre man, moving to the longer distances at 19/20 years of age. In 1965 he could point to such times as 13:49.8 (5000) and 29:04.4 (10,000) and 3:41.8 in the "metric" mile. He was essentially a "sitter" who relied on his tremendous finishing kick to win highly competitive races. He behaved exactly that way in Budapest, where he ran the last kilometre in 2:36. Details:
Budapest, 30 August 1966 – 10,000

metres: 1.Jürgen Haase (GDR) 28:26.0, 2.Lajos Mécser (Hun) 28:27.0, 3.Leonid Mikityenko (USSR) 28:32.2, 4.Manfred Letzerich (Ger) 28:36.8, 5.Allan Rushmer (GB) 28:37.8, 6.Bruce Tulloh (GB) 28:50.4, 7.János Szerényi (Hun) 28:52.2, 8.Gaston Roelants (Bel) 28:59.6.

Michel Jazy failed in his first attempt to hit gold. In the 1500 metre final he had to be content with second behind Bodo Tümmler of Germany, a powerful man with a strong finishing kick. Three days later the Frenchman tried again in the 5000 metres and here he won from another German, Harald Norpoth, with a long sustained drive (last 400 metres in 55.5). It was clear by then that he was finally at home in the 5000 as he had ever been in the 1500. Norpoth too had tried the double 1500/5000, winning medals in both (bronze at the shorter distance). Details:
Budapest, 4 September 1966 – 5000 metres: 1.Michel Jazy (Fra) 13:42.8, 2.Harald Norpoth (FRG) 13:44.0, 3.Bernd Diessner (GDR) 13:47.8, 4.Derek Graham (GB) 13:48.0, 5.Lajos Mécser (Hun) 13:48.0, 6.Bengt Nåjde (Swe) 13:48.2, 7.István Kiss (Hun) 13:48.2, 8.Jean-Luc Salomon (Fra) 13:52.0 .... 11.Jürgen Haase (GDR) 13:55.6.

Both Keino and Jazy went through the entire season without a loss as far as the 5000 metres was concerned. As usual their "pensum" was lighter than that of Ron Clarke, who ran 19 races at 3 miles/5000 metres and 7 at 6 miles/10,000 metres. Ever since 1948 the US magazine "Track & Field News" had been publishing a World Ranking of the Top Ten in every event, based on the following criteria: 1) Honours won, 2) Winloss record, 3) Sequence of marks. A "cage" through which only a reasonable minimum of "subjective thinking" was likely to pass. In 1966 these Rankings saw Clarke second in both 5000 and 10,000 metres, behind Keino and Temu respectively. Quite obviously, the outcome of the Commonwealth Games races played a decisive rôle.
Before closing with 1966 mention should be made of Gaston Roelants' 1- hour world record: 20,664 at Louvain on 28 October, a remarkable improvement vis-à-vis Clarke's

previous mark. Roelants (born at Opvelp on 5 February 1937; 1.74 m. / 58 kg.) was a versatile runner who could hold his own against the best in the world over a wide range of distances – with or without hurdles, on the track and on the road. He was at his best in the steeplechase (1964 Olympic champion) and as a harrier (fourtime winner of the International Cross-Country title between 1962 and 1972), but had a good competitive record in the marathon as well.
The two years that followed – 1967 and 1968 – saw a further decrease in the number of record shattering achievements. "Hurricane Clarke" closed his phenomenal series with two world records, both at 2 miles: 8:19.8 at Västerås on 27 June 1967 and 8:19.6 in London on 24 August 1968. These were achieved with partly different patterns: 4:11.5 + 4:08.3 in the former race and 4:08.9 + 4:10.7 in the latter. In 1967 Clarke had 14 races at 3miles/5000 metres, suffering only one defeat – to Kip Keino at Los Angeles, 13:40.0 to 13:36.8. He earned the no.1 spot in the World Ranking of "Track & Field News". The Kenyan chiefly concentrated on the1500 metres/ 1 mile, where he fought for world supremacy with Jim Ryun of USA. Over longer distances Keino lost three times to lesser quantities in home meets. Still in 1967, Clarke ran the 6 miles just once (27:21.6) and never tried the 10,000 metres.
The most important event of 1967 was the inaugural America vs. Europe match at Montreal in August. Lajos Mécser of Hungary won the 5000 metres in 14:01.8 from Roelants (14:02.0), while Haase took the 10,000 in 29:05.4. Schul and Mills had by then disappeared from the scene.
1968 was to go down in history as a most controversial year. The Olympic Games were at Mexico City, which is 2300 metres above sea level. As proven on some occasions in the past (e.g. in the Pan American Games of 1955, also held in the Mexican capital), the rarefied atmosphere turned out to be most favourable to events falling in the anaerobic sphere (sprints and horizontal jumps) and decidedly unfavourable to those of the aerobic (with oxygen) sphere, i.e. the long distances. Most of the runners from the "plains" obviously ran into trouble. An Australian medical authority calculated that the decrease in performances

at 5000 metres would be about 8% for acclimatised runners and 12% for unacclimatised ones. The relative figures for 10,000 metres were 11% and 18% respectively.

Among those who suffered most in the Olympic races were Jürgen Haase, Gaston Roelants and ... Clarke. One bright exception was Mohamed Gammoudi of Tunisia, whose only notable experience with running at high altitude was during a sojourn at Font-Romeu (1850 m.) in the Pyrenees region of Southern France. Clarke had only one previous experience under similar circumstances, right in Mexico City back in 1966, when he ran second to Gammoudi in a 5000 metre race – 14:41.2 to 14:40.6. Still there, he had done no better than 4:38.0 in a 1-mile time trial.

Yet Clarke looked better than ever during the pre-Olympic season in Europe , especially in competitive terms, as can be gathered from the following results:

Stockholm, 3 July 1968 – 5000 metres: 1.Mécser (Hun) 13:29.2, 2.Clarke 13:29.8, 3.Gammoudi 13:30.8 .... 7.Norpoth (Ger) 13:35.2, 8.Temu (Ken) 13:37.6.

Oslo, 10 July 1968 – 5000 metres: 1.Clarke 13:33.6, 2.Keisuke Sawaki (Jap) 13:41.8, 3.Keino (Ken) 13:43.4.

Oslo, 11 July 1968 – 10,000 metres: 1.Clarke 28:18.6, 2.Temu 28:27.4, 3.Keino 28:51.6.

Stockholm, 18 July – 5000 metres: 1.Clarke 13:30.4, 2.Keino 13:35.8, 3.Mécser 13:40.6, 4.Gammoudi 13:41.6.

Mexico '68: High altitude "speaks" African

In the Mexico Olympics, however, Ron Clarke went through gloomy days. In his first test, the 10,000 metres, he lost contact with the leading group with two laps to go, when Naftali Temu launched his attack. Mamo Wolde of Ethiopia was the only one who managed to remain in contention. The two Africans finished in that order, after covering the last 400 metres in about 57 seconds. Mohamed Gammoudi of Tunisia completed Africa's medal sweep by taking third. Completely exhausted, Clarke dropped to sixth. European champion Jürgen Haase had lost contact even earlier. He finished a dismal 15th. The second half (14:32.4) was faster than the first (14:55.0). Details:

Mexico City, 13 October 1968 – 10,000 metres: 1.Naftali Temu (Ken) 29:27.4, 2.Mamo Wolde (Eth) 29:28.0, 3.Mohamed Gammoudi (Tun) 29:34.2, 4.Juan Martinez (Mex) 29:35.0, 5.Nikolay Sviridov (USSR) 29:43.2, 6.Ron Clarke (Aus) 29:44.8, 7.Ron Hill (GB) 29:53.2, 8.Wohib Masresha (Eth) 29:57.0.

Kipchoge Keino was in the race too but a stomach cramp forced him to veer off the track and tumble onto the grass with just

Mohamed Gammoudi (Tunisia) on his way to victory in the 5000 metres at the 1968 Olympics in Mexico City, followed by Kenyans Kipchoge Keino and Naftali Temu, who will take second and third in that order. Winner's time: 14:05.0.

under three laps to go. Stretcher-bearers rushed out to help him but much to their surprise he waved them away and resumed running. But he had been disqualified, of course, and did not finish the race anyway. In the following days he fought back splendidly though – to the point of winning two medals! Counting preliminary rounds and finals, he ran six races in the space of a week (13/20 October) passing from a DNF in the 10,000 metres to silver in the 5000 and winding up with gold in the 1500. If there had ever been a crescendo, that was it!

The heats of the 5000 metres (15 October) were won by Keino (14:28.4) from Gammoudi and Wolde; Temu (14:20.4) from Clarke; and Jean Wadoux of France (14:19.8). Two days later, in the final, Clarke was his usual self in going into the lead early, but when the final battle flared up he was literally submerged by the African Wave and also by an "enfant du pays", Juan Martinez of Mexico, who wound up fourth, just as he had done in the 10,000 metres. In a furious battle for top honours, Gammoudi narrowly edged Keino, with Wolde third, for another great African sweep. The winner ran the last lap in 54.8, (Clarke, fifth, needed about 61 seconds to cover the same distance). Details:

Mexico City, 17 October 1968 – 5000 metres: 1.Mohamed Gammoudi (Tun) 14:05.0, 2.Kipchoge Keino (Ken) 14:05.2, 3.Naftali Temu (Ken) 14:06.4, 4.Juan Martinez (Mex) 14:10.8, 5.Ron Clarke (Aus) 14:12.4, 6.Wohib Masresha (Eti) 14:17.6, 7.Nikolay Sviridov (USSR) 14:18.4, 8.Fikru Deguefu (Eti) 14:19.0. Mamo Wolde (Eti) did not start, Harald Norpoth (GFR) did not finish. The winner's proper name was Mohamed Tlili Ben Abdallah, known as "Gammoudi" (born at Sidi Aich Gafsa on 2 November 1938; 1.72 m./ 61 kg.). Contrary to his Kenyan and Ethiopian rivals, he was not born and raised at altitude. He emerged in 1962 with such times as 14:18.8 and 29:50.8 and in 1964 he won a silver medal in the 10,000 metres at the Tokyo Olympics, as previously related. In 1967 he competed in a pre-Olympic meet at Mexico City, outsprinting Jürgen Haase in the 10,000 metres, 30:16.0 to 30:16.2. Yet his comment after the Olympic race was: "I was definitely most fearful of the altitude-trained Kenyans". Notwithstanding different levels of adaptation to the rarefied atmosphere, it is obvious that conditions at Mexico City penalized distance runners considerably. 1500-metre runners also suffered, but here again Africa supplied a very bright exception – Keino, who scored a K.O. victory over world record holder Jim Ryun of USA, 3:34.9 (Olympic record) to 3:37.8. A résumé of Keino's labours during those Games may be in order.

13 October – 10,000 m. Did not finish.
15 October – 5000 m. Heat: 1st in 14:28.4.
17 October – 5000 m. Final: 2nd 14:05.2.
18 October – 1500 m. Heat: 1st 3:46.9.
19 October – 1500 m. Semi-final: 2nd 3:51.4 (behind J.Ryun, 3:51.2).
20 October – 1500 m Final: 1st in 3:34.9.

Even though he had suffered crushing defeats in the Olympic races, Clarke was ranked no.1 for the year by "Track and Field News" in both 5000 and 10,000 metres. In the eyes of their World Ranking compilers, his victories over Gammoudi, Keino and Temu in Europe and his clear superiority in sequence of marks more than counter-balanced his Mexico débacles. In 1968 the Australian ran 18 races at 3 miles/5000 metres and six at 6 miles/10,000 metres.

Clarke was to remain no.1 in 1969 too. During that year he ran 16 races at 3 miles/5000 metres and seven at 6 miles/10,000 metres. At the shorter distance he lost three- to Jürgen May of the GDR in Stockholm (13:33.8 to 13:33.0) and twice in Australia, both times to his compatriot Kerry O'Brien, a steeplechaser. At the longer distance he lost one – to Dick Taylor of Britain in London (28:21.0 to 28:06.6).

The second (and last!) Europe vs. America match was held in Stuttgart. It offered little Gerry Lindgren of USA a chance to shine at the international level as he won the 5000 metres in 13:38.4 from Jürgen May (13:40.8), an excellent miler who could hold his own against the very best even at this distance. In the 10,000 metres Jürgen Haase and Gaston Roelants finished in that order – both in 28:51.4.

The 1969 European Championships (first to be held in an odd year) were at Athens. Sultry weather conditions were not conducive to fast times in the long distance department. Both finals were characterised by hectic finishes. Haase injected life into an otherwise dull 10,000 metre race with a 55.8 last lap and won comfortably. At the shorter distance the real battle began earlier and Ian Stewart of Britain won the day with a 1:58.8 in the last 800 metres and 56.6 in the last 400. Details:

Athens, 16 September 1969 – 10,000 metres: 1.Jürgen Haase (GDR) 28:41.6, 2.Mike Tagg (GB) 28:43.2, 3.Nikolay Sviridov (USSR) 28:45.8, 4.Drago Zuntar (Yug) 28:46.0, 5.Gaston Roelants (Bel) 28:49.8, 6.Mike Freary (GB) 28:49.8, 7.René Jourdan (Fra) 28:57.0.

Athens, 19 September 1969 – 5000 metres: 1.Ian Stewart (GB) 13:44.8, 2.Rashid Sharafyetdinov (USSR) 13:45.8, 3.Alan Blinston (GB) 13:47.6, 4.Bernd Diessner (GDR) 13:50.4, 5.Dane Korica (Yug) 13:51.4, 6.Giuseppe Ardizzone (Ita) 13:51.8, 7.Emiel Puttemans (Bel) 13:53.2.

1970 marked the closing stage of Ron Clarke's phenomenal career. As it happens in the world of sport, his decline coincided with the appearance of bright new talents, mostly from Great Britain. European 5000 metre champion Ian Stewart (born at Handsworth, Birmingham, on 15 January 1949; 1.77 m. / 64 kg.) lived in Scotland and well personified the type of distance runner so prevalent in the British Isles: a strong competitor as well as a fast finisher. In 1969, the year of his breakthrough in the 5000 metres of the European Championships, he also ran the 1500 in 3:39.1. He was to have his best season in 1970, when only 21 years of age. He and two Scotchmen really stole the show at the Commonwealth Games in Edinburgh – for the happiness of the large audiences gathered at the beautiful Meadowbank Stadium. Weather conditions, with intermittent rain and wind, seemed not conducive to classy performances, yet the standard was invariably high. In the 10,000 metres (29 entries!) Lachie Stewart, described as "Scots through and through", ran the race of his life and emerged the winner in 28:11.8, beating the great Ron Clarke (28:13.4). True, the Australian tried to run away from his rivals with 3000 metres to go, but as in many similar instances in the past he did not succeed. He thus lost his last chance of finally winning a gold medal in major international competition. Because few observers, if any, expected him to do himself justice in the 5000 metres seven days later - in the presence of fast milers like Kipchoge Keino and Ian Stewart. The latter, he too inspired by an enthusiastic crowd of 30,000, finally emerged a superb victor in 13:22.8. Another Scotchman, Ian McCafferty, shunted the great Keino to third, while Clarke had to be content with fifth. The last kilometre was run in a brisk 2:30.8, the last 400 in 55.4 and the last 200 in 26.4. Details:

Edinburgh, 18 July 1970 – 10,000 metres: 1.Lachie Stewart (Sco) 28:11.8, 2.Ron Clarke (Aus) 28:13.4, 3.Dick Taylor (Eng) 28:15.4, 4.Roger Matthews (Eng) 28:21.4, 5.John Caine (Eng) 28:27.6, 6.John Ngeno (Ken) 28:31.4.

Dave Bedford (GB), always great in "solo" efforts, here winning a 5000 metre race in Rome, 1971.

The dilemma of a giant

Ron Clarke has been one of those (relatively rare) champions who can talk candidly with members of the fourth estate. My friend Jon Hendershott, Associate Editor of "Track & Field News", took full advantage of this when he interviewed him at length for his delightful book "Ron Clarke Talks Track". It may be of interest to quote here Clarke's answer to a particularly intriguing question.

H – (summing up Clarke's experience) "Was it worth it? What did you get out of it? Would you do it again?"

C - "It's just fantastic what I got out of it. First, I had the chance to travel overseas. Second, the most important thing in life besides your family is the chance to make friends. To my mind, friends are what you measure your life-span by, not the amount of possessions you gain but the number of friends you make, the people you meet and the experiences you have. Track did all this to me. Track turned my whole world upside down. I kept at it because I loved it so much. I knew this was a chance I would never get again once it stopped ………. I fear, though, that my reputation will grow as an athlete who did not succeed. I noticed that when Dave Bedford ran sixth in the European 10,000 in 1971, his performance was likened to one of mine . I never missed a place in any of the big races I ran in. Again take away altitude, I always ran pretty close to my records. To be likened to a giant and yet have the reputation of someone who just did not make the big time will grow rather than recede. This is where I get a little sour and frustrated I did not get the opportunity to compete at Munich instead of Mexico City (for the 1968 Olympics)".

Edinburgh, 25 July 1970 – 5000 metres: 1.Ian Stewart (Sco) 13:22.8, 2.Ian McCafferty (Sco) 13:23.4, 3.Kipchoge Keino (Ken) 13:27.6, 4.Allan Rushmer (Eng) 13:29.8, 5.Ron Clarke (Aus) 13:32.4, 6.Dick Taylor (Eng) 13:33.8, 7.Dick Quax (NZ) 13:43.4.

I had a chance to talk to Clarke during those Games - one of the most enjoyable track festivals I can remember, at least in terms of sportsmanlike atmosphere. Always kind to interviewers, he seemed to be concerned with the performances of his younger teammates Kerry O'Brien and Tony Manning much as he was with his own – if not more. Even though he did not say that in explicit terms, I was under the impression that he considered himself "over the hill". That was in fact his last major season. I deem it advisable to give here a summary of his placings in "Track & Field News" World Ranking (Top Ten).

Year	5000 m.	10,000 m.
1963	-	1.
1964	2.	3.
1965	3.	1.
1966	2.	2.
1967	1.	*
1968	1.	1.
1969	1.	1.
1970	8.	4.

* As a matter of fact Clarke had the world's fastest 6-mile time (27:21.6 on 19 December in Melbourne) for 1967.

At that time, however, the Ranking was published in November and so Clarke's time could not be taken into consideration. However, it counted for the Ranking of the following year as one of the Australian marks for the 1967-68 season Down Under.

The revelation of 1970 was an Englishman, David Bedford (born in London on 30 December 1949; 1.83 m. / 63 kg.), a slim, long-haired fellow who was to inject new life into the time-honoured passion of his countrymen for long distance running. In fixing his training loads he used to lay a stress on quantity. At the peak of his career he covered an average of 200 miles (321 km.) per week in the early part of the year, when his training was at its most intense. His work was a mixture of Endurance Training and Interval Training, as set out by his coach Bob Parker. Just before turning 20 he ran the 10,000 metres in 28:24.4 and in 1970 he improved to 28:06.2 – a world best for that year! But just like Clarke, and even more so, he was to prove quite vulnerable in top-class competition.

LASSE VIREN,
A LONE WOLF FROM FINLAND

The great Finnish tradition had dried up after the days of Viljo Heino, who was a worthy successor of his ancestors clock-wise but not as great in big-time competition. (It must be said, however, that the cancellation of the 1944 Olympics possibly deprived him of his best chance). For no less than six editions of the Olympic Games – 1948/1968 – there had been no medals for Finland in the 5000/10,000 metres department. A fourth place by Hannu Posti in the 10,000 metres of the 1952 Games in Helsinki was the best Finland could be proud of. At the European Championships, from 1950 up to and including 1969, the Nordic country had won only one bronze medal (Väinö Koskela in the 10,000 metres in 1950). A very slim record for the fatherland of Paavo Nurmi. Several reasons were brought up to explain this vacuum. In early post-war years Finland was in harsh economic conditions and young men, once they had taken care of their daily needs, turned their attention to lighter pastimes rather than work hard on distance running. The time-honoured ideal of the distance runner who must be prepared to toil and suffer, so dear to Nurmi in his younger days, seemed to have little impact on post-war generations. Another reason, possibly the most important, lay in the fact that the map of athletics had begun to widen considerably throughout the Fifties and Sixties and it seemed just logical that a small country such as Finland could no longer maintain in the distance department her quasi-monopoly of pre-war days. Even so, there had been from time to time some echoes of past glory, for instance in the 1500 metres and the marathon. Arthur Lydiard, the prophet of Endurance Training, lived and worked in Finland between 1967 and 1969. His teachings to young Finns were lively discussed and sometimes criticized, maybe as a token of national pride on the part of his hosts. As time went by, however, his merits were duly acknowledged. Typical in this respect is the following salute by Finnish historian Matti Hannus: "Thank you, Arthur – you did your job even better than we could appreciate at the time."

At any rate the early Seventies witnessed a revival in Finnish long distance running. The man who got the ball rolling was quite different from the Finnish greats of pre-war years, in both outlook and mentality - Juha Väätäinen (born at Oulu on 12 July 1941, 1.72 m. / 60 kg.) had the features of a "wild rascal" in his boyhood years. By 1958, however, he showed signs of a radical change – and the merit for this was attributed to his budding love for athletics. He started as a sprinter, then gradually moved up to the longer distances. In 1960 he won the 400 metres hurdles in 56.2 at the Finnish Junior Championships. His tutor in those days was Paavo Meskus, who gradually turned him into a fully engaged and responsible athlete. At the 1965 Finnish Championships he won the 800 metres and two years later he ran the same distance in 1:48.4. At that time he covered an average 150 kilometres per week in training. Loyal to his "savage" origins he liked to sport a vest with the words "Julma-Juha" (Cruel Juha). He first tried the 10,000 in 1966, aged 25, and did 30:54.0. As destiny would have it, his coach died three years before Juha's greatest triumphs. A onetime sprinter of national class (11.1 and 22.1), Väätäinen eventually became a world class distance runner. In 1970 he ran the classic distances in 13:43.2 and 28:19.6. The man with fierce looks and a long beard had his glory days at the 1971 European Championships in Helsinki. He came to the big rendez-vous with a rather unimpressive seasonal record. Experts generally favoured Jürgen Haase, Emiel Puttemans of Belgium and Dave Bedford, who had won the 10,000 metres at the AAA Championships (Portsmouth, 10 July) with a new European record of 27:47.0. This was built through a fast first half (13:45.4). While enroute he also broke the European 6 mile record with 26:51.6. Much credit was given to Jean Wadoux of France, who could claim a recent victory over Kipchoge Keino in the 5000 metres and was known as a middle-distance runner of world caliber thanks to his European 1500 metre record – 3:34.0 in 1970.

The glory days of "Cruel Juha"

The "explosion" of the 30-year-old Väätäinen at the European Championships in Helsinki caused quite a stir in continental track circles. And obviously repaid Finnish fans for years of abstinence from success in the department they loved most. The 10,000 metres came first and Bedford, as generally expected, took upon himself the task of leading the pack. The first half was covered in 13:54.4. The Englishman was still the leader at the bell but like the great Ron Clarke he knew he could finish relatively fresh but he also knew that he could not measure up to the feared turn of speed of most of the five men still in his wake. That is what happened: one by one the five passed him! Most foreign onlookers thought that defending champion Jürgen Haase, a big kicker, would again prevail. But they did not reckon with the man who had prepared, lived, eaten and slept this race for over a year – Juha Väätäinen. The onetime sprinter from Oulu . He went past Haase in the last turn and a capacity crowd of 40,000 literally went wild. The overwhelming Finnish majority cheered him chorally with the words: "Julma-Juha!" And cruel he was for he covered the last lap in 54.0 – a truly staggering finish in a 10,000 metres race. The 28-minute barrier was broken by five men and all of them set new national records! Ironically enough, European record holder Bedford, sixth, was over that limit. But he was great in his comment: "I think the loss did me more good than anything else could have. Now I realize

that I'm human and can be beaten also".
Details:
Helsinki, 10 August 1971 – 10,000 metres: 1.Juha Väätäinen (Fin) 27:52.8, 2.Jürgen Haase (GDR) 27:53.4, 3.Rashid Sharafyetdinov (USSR) 27:56.4, 4.Dane Korica (Yug) 27:58.4, 5.Mariano Haro (Spa) 27:59.4, 6.Dave Bedford (GB) 28:04.4, 7.Mike Tagg (GB) 28:14.8, 8.Seppo Tuominen (Fin) 28:18.0... ....17.Lasse Viren (Fin) 28:33.2.

The 5000 metre heats two days later were won by Wadoux (13:44.2), Väätäinen (13:47.6) and Puttemans (13:50.4). The final (14 August) was characterized by a relatively slow pace for the greater part of the distance and a mad finish. The last kilometre was run in 2:28.6, the last 800 in 1:56.6 and the last 400 in 53.4! Even in the presence of two milers like Wadoux and Harald Norpoth, local matador Väätäinen won as he pleased. Here too he set a new Finnish record. Emiel Puttemans, one of the hottest pre-race favourites, was only sixth: he disappointed Belgian fans just like Bedford's demise in the 10,000 metres had been frustrating to the British. Details:
Helsinki, 14 August 1971 – 5000 metres: 1.Juha Väätäinen (Fin) 13:32.6, 2.Jean Wadoux (Fra) 13:33.6, 3.Harald Norpoth (FGR) 13:33.8, 4.Daniel Korica (Yug) 13:35.0, 5.Javier Alvarez (Spa) 13:35.8, 6.Emiel Puttemans (Bel) 13:36.6, 7.Lasse Viren (Fin) 13:38.6, 8.Bronislaw Malinowski (Pol) 13:39.4.

Emiel Puttemans partly made amends for his Helsinki failure when he lowered the world's 2-mile record to 8:17.8 in the Highland Games at Edinburgh on 21 August. Enroute he clocked 7:44.3 for 3000 metres.

Väätäinen's belated explosion had no sequence. Somebody ventured the opinion that he had made acquaintance with the sufferings of a distance runner too late and at 30 probably had no ambition to go further. But then his memorable days in Helsinki could well suffice to crown his long, strange career in a most impressive way. The image of long-haired "Julma-Juha" with a red rose in his mouth basking in the applause of a devoted crowd was resembling that of Santa Claus, the patron saint of children from Northern countries.

Be it as it may, the double European champion did act as a spark which was to be followed, just a year later, by a blazing fire – still made in Suomi. The man for the job was Lasse Viren (born at Myrskylä on 22 July 1949; 1.80 m. / 61 kg.), an entirely different type of man: cool, reserved, with a vaguely ascetic look, he somehow reflected the landscape of the forest region in which he was born and brought up, a region where the climate is harsh for the greater part of the year. He became involved in distance running much earlier than Väätäinen. In 1965, aged 16, he ran 3000 metres in 9:33.8. Two years later he ducked under 15 minutes in the 5000 metres. His progression before 1972 was as follows:

Year	Age	5000 m.	10,000 m.
1967	18	14:59.4	-
1968	19	15:07.8	32:18.8
1969	20	13:55.0	-
1970	21	13:43.0	29:15.8
1971	22	13:29.8	28:17.4

At the 1971 European Championships in Helsinki he was outshone by Väätäinen and many others: 17th in the 10,000 metres, then 7th in the 5000. By then, however, his training loads were becoming progressively heavier. Rolf Haikkola, his coach, and Pentti Vuorio, a well-known sports journalist, wrote a book on him, "Lasse Viren, kullatut sekunnit" (Golden Seconds). Among other things they give the total of his training loads in the twelve-month period October-to-September (of the following year) in what we may call his build-up years:

1967-68	1940 km.
1968-69	2967 km.
1969-70	3728 km.
1970-71	5332 km.
1971-72	7348 km.

Even more interesting perhaps is his detailed load for the period Oct. 71/Sep. 72.

October '71	392 km.
November '71	532 km.
December '71	739 km.
January ,72	636 km.
February '72	844 km.
March '72	824 km.
April '72	630 km.
May '72	589 km.
June '72	489 km.
July ,72	558 km.
August '72	676 km.
September '72	439 km.

Basically, he was an adept of the endurance training. As for competition, in his best year, 1972, Viren ran 46 races, at distances ranging from 800 to 10,000 metres. He went to the Munich Olympics (early September) with seasonal bests of 7:43.2 (3000 m.), 13:19.0 (5000 m.) and 27:52.4 (10,000 m.) – all of which were new Finnish records. He suffered some defeats in June and early July, but then he rounded into high gear and set his first world record in Stockholm on 14 August: 8:14.0 for 2 miles, with halves of 4:09.4 and 4:04.6. In so doing he beat a crack field, notably including Emiel Puttemans (2nd in 8:17.2, under his own world record), Swedish steeplechaser Anders Gärderud, Ian Stewart, Dick Quax of New Zealand and Dave Bedford. No doubt a great fillip in view of the forthcoming battles in the Olympic arena. On the eve of the Games in Munich the 23-year-old Finn was obviously counted among the top favourites, along with Puttemans, Bedford, Haase, Gammoudi and an American, Steve Prefontaine, who had reached high levels of popularity in his home state, Oregon. "Pre", as he was known to track fans from the West Coast, had qualified with a good 13:22.8 in the 5000 metres at the US Olympic Trials, held in his home town of Eugene, which was branded as the Mecca of US track & field. On the eve of the Munich Games, however, the best seasonal marks belonged to Bedford, who had scored an impressive double at the AAA Championships with 13:17.2 and 27:52.4 (on consecutive days). The latter equalled Viren's seasonal best.

Viren falls yet wins in WR time

For he first time since 1920 the Olympic schedule called for a preliminary round in the

1972 Olympics in Munich. Lasse Viren (Finland) no.228, leading a great 5.000 metre field in the closing stage. He won in 13.26.42. Others from left are: M. Gammoudi (Tunisia) 2nd; I. Stewart (GB), partly covered, 3rd; E. Puttemans (Belgium), 5th; and S. Prefontaine (USA), 4th.

10,000 metres. Such heats yielded surprisingly fast times: all 15 qualifiers broke Billy Mills' Olympic record (28:24.4) ! Puttemans won heat 1 in 27:53.4, with Bedford 2nd (27:53.6); Gammoudi won heat 2 in 27:54.8, with Viren fourth (28:04.4); and Miruts Yifter of Ethiopia won heat 3 in 28:12.2. Three days later, in the final, Viren outshone all his rivals and won in 27:38.4, a new world record. The circumstances surrounding his feat make it an indelible souvenir. After 4500 metres there was a collision. With several runners running too close to one another, Viren fell down, blocking veteran Gammoudi, who was thrown onto the infield. The veteran Tunisian, apparently dazed, struggled to his feet and ran for another 600 metres before giving up. Viren lay sprawled on the track for a few seconds before bounding to his feet and setting out after the pack, some 10 metres ahead. Without panicking, he managed to rejoin the leaders about half a minute later. Meanwhile, Bedford was leading, just as he had done at Helsinki the previous year. At 5000 metres he was timed in 13:43.9, but during the 8th kilometre he lost contact. Five men – Viren, Haro, Yifter, Puttemans and Shorter – were left to fight it out for top honours. With two laps to go they were still closely bunched, but with 600 metres left Viren began a murderous drive. One by one he knocked out all his rivals and won in superb style. Puttemans and Yifter finished in that order for the remaining medals. Viren's new world record was officially announced as 27:38.4, but the actual electronic time in hundredths of a second was 27:38.35. His tremendous crescendo was reflected in the following figures: last kilometre, 2:29.2; last 800 metres, 1:56.4; last 400 metres, 56.4. (Puttemans 57.2, Yifter 58.2, Haro 63.6). Details:

Munich, 3 September 1972 – 10,000 metres: 1.Lasse Viren (Fin) 27:38.4, 2.Emiel Puttemans (Bel) 27:39.6, 3.Miruts Yifter (Eti) 27:41.0, 4.Mariano Haro (Spa) 27:48.2, 5.Frank Shorter (USA) 27:51.4, 6.Dave Bedford (GB) 28:05.4, 7.Dane Korica (Yug) 28:15.2, 8.Abdelkader Zaddem (Tun) 28:18.2..... DNF: Mohamed Gammoudi (Tun).

Kilometre fractions:

1000 m.	2:36.9	
2000 m	5:18.8	(2:41.9)
3000 m	8:06.4	(2:47.6)
4000 m	10:55.6	(2:49.2)
5000 m	13:43.9	(2:48.3)
6000 m	16:35.8	(2:51.9)
7000 m	19:27.8	(2:52.0)
8000 m	22:17.8	(2:50.0)
9000 m	25:09.2	(2:51.4)
10,000 m	27:38.4	(2:29.2)

The 5000-metre field included Juha Väätäinen, but any hope that he may revive memories of Helsinki '71 was short lived. He did win his heat in 13:32.8, but in the decisive race he never entered the picture and finished 13th and last. Other heat winners (7 September) were Gammoudi (13:49.8), Puttemans (13:31.8, a new Olympic record), Ian McCafferty (13:38.2) and Viren (13:38.4). The controversial circumstances surrounding Yifter's failure to show up at the start of his heat will be related in a forthcoming aside dealing with curious aspects of his career.

The final (10 September) was dominated by Viren. The initial pace was not unduly fast, save for a thrust by Steve Prefontaine in the fourth kilometre, when things really began to happen. Going into the last lap, the American led from Viren and Gammoudi. The Finn grabbed the lead as they were going down the backstretch and from then on he was never threatened. Gammoudi made amends for his unlucky experience in the 10,000 metres and took second, just ahead of Ian Stewart. The winner's time, 13:26.4, was a new Olympic record Details: Munich, 10 September 1972 – 5000 metres: 1.Lasse Viren (Fin) 13:26.4 (electronic time, 13:26.42), 2.Mohamed Gammoudi (Tun) 13:27.4, 3.Ian Stewart (GB) 13:27.6, 4.Steve Prefontaine (USA) 13:28.4, 5.Emiel Puttemans (Bel) 13:30.8, 6.Harald Norpoth (Ger) 13:32.6, 7.Per Halle (Nor) 13:34.4, 8.Nikolay Sviridov (USSR) 13:39.4...... 12.Dave Bedford (GB) 13:43.2.

An additional note may be in order re: Kipchoge Keino. Even though he did not compete in the classic distance events, he added considerably to his fame as well as to his medal collection. After winning the steeplechase in 8:23.6, the 32-year-old Kenyan was second in the 1500 metres. He was definitely the first in a long line of Kenyan Greats.

Viren/Puttemans: quick repartee

Post-Olympic weeks in Northern Europe offered plenty of remarkable action and the world record for 5000 metres was broken twice. Viren hit first: just four days after his last triumph in Munich, on a freezing cold evening in Helsinki he brought a large crowd to its feet with a time of 13:16.3. The fans had assembled to thank him for his Olympic exploits, so this was an extra bonus – so much more gratifying as the last Finn to hold the global mark for the '5' had been Taisto Mäki thirty-three years ago. Dave Bedford was the leader for a sizable part of the race but in the fourth kilometre he had to give way to a superlative Viren. Details:
Helsinki, 14 September 1972 – 5000 metres: 1.Lasse Viren (Fin) 13:16.3, 2.Dave Bedford (GB) 13:30.0, 3.Juha Väätäinen (Fin) 13:35.4, 4.Seppo Tuominen (Fin) 14:10.6.

Kilometre fractions:

1000 m	2:36.6	
2000 m	5:18.5	(2:41.9)
3000 m	8:00.3	(2:41.8)
4000 m	10:42.6	(2:42.3)
5000 m	13:16.3*	(2:33.7)

No official time for 3 miles.
* Officially rounded up to 13:16.4 as per IAAF rule.

On the same day at Aarhus, Denmark, Emiel Puttemans broke the world's 3000 metre record with 7:37.6 (halves: 3:48.0 and 3:49.6). The Belgian, at the top of his condition, conceived the plan of giving Viren a quick repartee for his 5000 metre mark at Helsinki. The record attempt took place in Brussels on 20 September. Dave Bedford was in this race too, but for once he left to others the rôle of acting as trail blazers.

Michel Bernard of France, René Goris and André De Hertoghe of Belgium led in the early goings at a very fast pace. Puttemans took the lead just before the halfway mark and finally shaved 3.4 seconds off Viren's fresh record. Details:
Brussels, 20 September 1972 – 5000 metres: 1.Emiel Puttemans (Bel) 13:13.0, 2.Paul Thys (Bel) 13:33.4, 3.Dave Bedford (GB) 13:39.0, 4.Jon Anderson (USA) 13:55.8.

Kilometre fractions:

1000 m	2:33.7	
2000 m	5:12.0	(2:38.3)
3000 m	7:51.2	(2:39.2)
4000 m	10:35.6	(2:44.4)
5000 m	13:13.0	(2:37.4)

Official 3-mile time: 12:47.8, the last world record at this distance. (In 1976 the IAAF decided that performances made over yard distances should no longer qualify for record purposes. The only exception was made for the classic 1-mile distance).

"Some like to sow, others prefer to pick"

With his late season exploit over 5000 metres, Puttemans brought to four the collection of his world records. This runner (born at Leuven on 8 October 1947; 1.71 m. / 58 kg.) had made his debut on the front stage of international athletics at the 1968 Olympics in Mexico, aged 21, finishing 12th in the 5000 metres. In subsequent years, as related above, he had his share of international honours, chiefly if not exclusively in the record-breaking department – in addition to those mentioned above he was to collect between 1973 and 1976 no less than 12 world indoor records. (Further on I will give details on the most important ones). Even so, the bare fact that this hyper-active record-breaker never earned a gold medal in big-time competition led some observers to classify him in the "good losers" category. Talking about different types of runners, he once said, with a similitude from the world of flowers: "Some like to sow, others prefer to pick".

The Belgians are fond of records though and on that 20 September in Brussels they were offered a royal treatment. About an hour after Puttemans' 5000 metre record, Gaston Roelants broke the world's 1-hour record on the same track, covering 20,784 km.

Before closing with 1972, mention should be made of another fast 5000 metre race that took place at Rome's Stadio Olimpico on 13 September. Steve Prefontaine and Juha Väätäinen fared better, clock-wise at least, than in the Olympic final, yet they had to bow to a 29-year-old Italian, Gianni Del Buono, who won in 13:22.4, a time that ranked him 6th in the All Time World List. The American (13:26.4) and the Finn (13:28.4) followed in that order. For Väätäinen it was, at any rate, a new personal best. Del Buono, who covered the last kilometre in 2:33.0, had chosen the 1500 metres in the Olympics (eliminated in the semi-finals). Now he had reasons to believe that he had made the wrong choice.

Puttemans had an excellent season in 1973. The light-footed, galloping Belgian was at his best on small indoor tracks. He thus had a great undercover campaign. At Leiden on 11 February he ran 3000 metres in 7:45.2. Exactly a week later in Berlin, on a 180-metre track, he ran 2 miles in 8:13.2, after doing 5:00.0 for 2000 metres and 7:39.2 for 3000 while enroute. All of these marks were new world indoor records. It should be noted that his 2-mile time was better than Lasse Viren's outdoor record (8:14.0 in 1972). However, it is risky not to say impossible to make comparisons between outdoor and indoor records, given the notable difference in running surfaces. In the outdoor season Puttemans ran the 5000 metres seven times, with no defeats. His best was at Stockholm on 7 August when he did 13:14.6 and won from an excellent New Zealand miler, Dick Quax (13:18.4).

Another prominent runner was Brendan Foster of Great Britain (born at Hebburn on 12 January 1948; 1.78 m. / 68 kg.), an entirely different type of runner if compared with Dave Bedford and much faster than the latter as a middle distance man. He was one of those relatively rare runners who can combine the capacity of setting a hot pace with a fast finishing kick. Thanks to the latter he won the 5000 metres in the final of the 1973 European Cup at Edinburgh, a "tactical" race in which he beat Harald Norpoth among others. This team competition, with one man per country in every event, was introduced in 1965. The stress was laid on the necessity of scoring as many points as possible for one's country. Middle and long distance races often resulted in slow tactical affairs characterized by hectic finishes. Foster's time in the Edinburgh race was an ordinary 13:54.8, after a 57.6 last lap, much in contrast with a funeral 75.2 for the first lap. Back in fifth place with 14:18.2 was double Olympic champion Lasse Viren. For the great Finn this was the onset of a lethargy that was to last till 1976, save for an excellent performance at the 1974 European Championships. Throughout this long period of time Viren was beset by physical problems, notably including leg surgery in January 1975. While healing his wounds he did a fair amount of travelling and put up a family. Some also said that he showed declining interest in athletics. But in 1976 the world was to hear from him again.....

The only world record of 1973 over the classic distances went to the credit of Dave Bedford, always at his best in races where he could freely express the enormous potential gathered through hours and hours of intensive training without having to worry about dreadful kickers. In what was to remain his greatest race, the Englishman succeeded Lasse Viren as holder of the 10,000 metre record. Details:

London, 13 July 1973 – 10,000 metres: 1.Dave Bedford (GB) 27:30.8 (actually 27:30.80 electronic time), 2.Tony Simmons (GB) 28:19.2, 3.Bernard Plain (GB) 28:30.2, 4.Seppo Tuominen (Fin) 28:32.8, 5.Lachie Stewart (GB) 28:40.8.

Kilometre fractions:

1000 m	2:39.8	
2000 m	5:23.2	(2:43.4)
3000 m	8:08.4	(2:45.2)
4000 m	10:54.6	(2:46.2)
5000 m	13:39.4	(2:44.8)
6000 m	16:26.0	(2:46.6)
7000 m	19:14.2	(2:48.2)
8000 m	22:02.0	(2:47.8)
9000 m	24:50.4	(2:48.4)
10,000 m	27:30.8	(2:40.4)

*Heat of the
10,000 m.
at the 1980
Olympics in
Moscow.
Werner
Schildhauer
(East Germany)
leading from
Lasse Viren
(Finland).*

Unofficial 6-mile time, 26:38.6 (actually better than Ron Clarke's world record, but the British no longer had records for yard distances other than the mile).

1974 featured two major events: the Commonwealth Games at Christchurch, New Zealand and the European Championships in Rome – over 7 months apart. Brendan Foster, at the peak of his form, came very close to winning a double 5000 metre crown. In the first "leg" he narrowly lost to a new star from Kenya, Benjamin Wabura Jipcho (born at Vasin Gishee in the region of Mount Elgon on 1 March 1943; 1.78 m. / 72 kg.). This gifted runner had made his first major appearance at the 1968 Olympics in Mexico City, acting as Kipchoge Keino's "hare" in the 1500 metres. Four years later at the Munich Olympics he was second to Keino in the 3000 metre steeplechase. In 1973 he was good enough to be elected "Athlete of the Year" by "Track & Field News" as world's no.1 performer in both 1500 metres and 3000 steeplechase. In the latter event he twice bettered the world record (8:19.8 and 8:14.0). In addition he ran 5000 metres in 13:30.0. At the 1974 Commonwealth Games the Kenyan had a busy schedule. He began by winning the steeplechase handily in 8:20.8 on 26 January. The following day he went through the prelims of the 5000 just as easily with 13:57.2, while Foster won another heat in 13:45.6. Foster's flowing style led observer Arthur Lydiard to say that it looked as though he had 20 seconds tucked up his sleeve. Quite true, because in the final (29 January) Foster ran faster than he had ever done before, but he did not win. The race began with a short-lived thrust by Dave Bedford. In the last two laps Jipcho followed Foster and it was only in the last stretch of land that the Kenyan edged ahead to win – 13:14.4 to 13:14.6, second and third fastest ever. Jipcho ran the last 400 in 55.0. After his second gold medal, Jipcho was asked what his best event was. He smiled and said: "At the moment I'm in favour of almost everything". Details:
Christchurch, 29 January 1974 – 5000 metres: 1.Benjamin Jipcho (Ken) 13:14.4, 2. Brendan Foster (Eng) 13:14.6, 3.David Black (Eng) 13:23.6, 4.Suleiman Nyambui

(Tan) 13:35.0, 5.Ian Stewart (Sco) 13:40.4 .... 11.Dave Bedford (Eng) 14:18.8.
Jipcho and Foster went through two other races: prelims (31 January) and final (2 February) of the 1500 metres. In the latter they were third and seventh respectively, both with new national records (3:33.2 and 3:37.6). Prior to all this, namely on 25 January, Richard Tayler of New Zealand had won the 10,000 metres in 27:46.4 from Black (27:48.6) and Richard Juma of Kenya (27:57.0). Bedford had to be content with fourth (28:14.8).

Royal Consent

The British Commonwealth was from its very origin a heterogeneous political entity. The Games - held for the first name at Hamilton, Ontario, Canada in 1930 – reflect in their ever (slightly but significantly) changing name the fluidity that seems to distinguish any political aggregation capable of having a free development. Through the years the official name of the Games changed thus:

1930-1950
British Empire Games

1954-1966
British Empire
and Commonwealth Games

1970-1974
British Commonwealth Games

From 1978 onwards
Commonwealth Games

A proposal to drop the word British was first advanced in 1970 but was rejected. Four years later it was put forward again and this time it received 18 "yes" and 7 "nos". Prince Philip of Edinburgh, president of the Games Federation, reportedly sided with the "abolitionists".

The European Championships were held at Rome's Stadio Olimpico in the first week of September. The meet offered exciting competition, even though weather conditions –

hot and humid - were not ideal, especially for distance runners. The closing stage of the 10,000 metres offered two distinct battles: one for first place between Manfred Kuschmann of the GDR and small Tony Simmons of Great Britain, and the other for third between Giuseppe ("Pippo") Cindolo of Italy and steeplechaser Bronislaw Malinowski of Poland. The climate was not conducive to fast times. Simmons led at the halfway point in 14:16.6. As usual under such circumstances, the real battle flared up in the last lap. When Kuschmann made his move and surged past some lapped runners, Simmons lost several metres. Yet the diminutive Briton closed the gap and finally lost by less than half a metre. Both were timed in 28:25.8 and the winner ran the last lap in 55.3. Cindolo came from behind to pass Malinowski in the homestretch. The Italian was timed in 54.1 for the last 400. (Five days later Malinowski won the 3000 metres steeplechase). Lasse Viren, nursing a bad leg, courageously tried to stir things up between 7000 and 8000 metres but finally had to be content with seventh. Details:

Rome, 2 September 1974 – 10,000 metres – 1.Manfred Kuschmann (GDR) 28:25.8, 2.Tony Simmons (GB) 28:25.8, 3.Giuseppe Cindolo (Ita) 28:27.2, 4.Bronislaw Malinowski (Pol) 28:28.0, 5.Nikolay Puklakov (USSR) 28:29.2, 6.Knut Börö (Nor) 28:29.2, 7.Lasse Viren (Fin) 28:29.2, 8.Mariano Haro (Spa) 28:36.0.

The 5000 metre final was a different type of race. Brendan Foster showed that it was still possible to win a highly competitive race with an offensive strategy – something Ron Clarke and Dave Bedford never managed to do. The Briton had come to Rome after a great "rehearsal", a new world record of 7:35.1 (officially rounded up to 7:35.2) on his favourite track at Gateshead on 3 August, with halves of 3:49.0 and 3:46.1. In the Rome race he led from the start. In what to Italian fans looked like a replica of Vladimir Kuts' record race on the same track in 1957, the Briton went on relentlessly. He delivered the KO blow in the eighth lap, covered in 60.4. Viren tried to hang on but had to surrender. Foster went home an easy victor in 13:17.2 (last lap in 62.2). Kuschmann closed fast to take second, while Viren was third in

13:24.6 - 1.8 secs. faster than his winning time in the 1972 Olympics. Details:
Rome, 8 September 1974 – 5000 metres: 1.Brendan Foster (GB) 13:17.2, 2.Manfred Kuschmann (GDR) 13:24.0, 3.Lasse Viren (Fin) 13:24.6, 4.Jos Hermens (Hol) 13:25.6, 5.Ilie Floroiu (Rum) 13:27.2, 6.Arne Kvalheim (Nor) 13:27.2, 7.Stanislav Hoffman (Cze) 13:29.0, 8.Klaus-Peter Hildenbrand (FRG) 13:32.0.

1975 was practically devoid of superlative performances, clock-wise at least. The sole exception was offered by Jos Hermens: on 28 September at Papendal the 25-year-old Dutchman covered 20,907 km. within 1 hour. In the last decades of the century he was to become one of the best known managers in the world of athletics. (With the advent of professionalism most if not all prominent athletes tend to have a representative who looks after their business).

A surplus lap "by inertia"

Indoor meets, usually held on small tracks, generally have the 3000 metres as the longest standard distance. Not the last reason for this may be found in a desire not to bore runners and/or spectators unduly with an immoderate number of laps .... 5000 and 10,000 metre races are an absolute rarity. The brightest exception was provided by Emiel Puttemans, the galloping Belgian, who between 1973 and 1976 amassed a great array of world indoor bests. On 22 February 1975 he showed up for a 10,000 metre race at Porte de Pantin in Paris. To cover the distance on that small board track – 166.66 metres in circumference - he had to negotiate no less than sixty laps. Puttemans went to work very earnestly. Lap after lap, he was finally driven by inertia to cover 61 of them...... As it was, lap counters apparently lost control of the situation and forgot to ring the bell in due time. Fortunately enough, timers were up to the task and clocked Puttemans at the end of the 60th lap in 28:12.4 (halves of 14:03.8 and 14:08.6). Not bad, especially if you consider that at the time the world outdoor record was 27:30.80.

From the standpoint of competition, the best of 1975 was offered by the final of the European Cup at the new, magnificent Parc de l'Ouest in Nice on 16/17 August. On the first day Karl-Heinz Leiteritz of the GDR won the 10,000 metres in 28:37.2 from Dave Black (28:42.2). Hero of the next day was Brendan Foster with another devastating 5000 metre race. He worked hard as usual: after injecting a couple of 61/62 sec. laps he found he had no other company than Lasse Viren. But the Finn did not have enough money to pay for the pace when Foster, after passing 3000 metres in 8:17.8, put in a 58.2 lap and went home a splendid winner in 13:36.2. Viren, obviously not at his best, faded so badly that he wound up 5th in 13:49.8.

Henry Rono (Kenya) set 4 world records in 4 different distance events in 1978, his banner year.

Foster made his debut over 10,000 metres on 29 August in London with a sterling performance: 27:45.4, good enough to place him 7th in the All Time World List. He had to run that fast though, because he was up against Frank Shorter (USA), the Olympic marathon champion of 1972. The American finished a close second in 27:46.0.

At any rate, in 1975 no distance runner had a seasonal record even remotely approaching the standard (quality + quantity) once achieved by Ron Clarke. However, it may be worth mentioning that Rod Dixon of New Zealand, one of the world's fastest milers, moved up to the 5000 metres and won three good races in Europe, his best being 13:21.6. In the Olympic year 1976 the world of track saw Lasse Viren at his best again. After three years of generally obscure performances, mostly due to physical problems, the lone wolf from Myrskylä was back where he belonged. True, he did not beat his PB's from 1972, but then records had never been his prime objective. What is more important, he achieved unprecedented heights as a big-time competitor.

The year began with another solitary exploit by Emiel Puttemans: a world indoor record of 13:20.8 for 5000 metres, on the Porte de Pantin track in Paris on 10 January. Springtime competition outdoors yielded what was to remain the only world record of the year: 20,944 km. within 1 hour by Jos Hermens at Papendal on 1 May. While enroute he reached 20,000 metres in 57:24.2, with halves in 28:35.2 and 28.49.0.

Montreal 1976: boycott enters the picture

The 1976 Olympics in Montreal unfortunately marked the opening of a series of politically inspired boycotts, a phenomenon which was to affect several other editions. To be sure, a warning of things to come had been served four years earlier in Munich with an attack on the Israeli quarters by Palestinian terrorists. In Montreal profound political differences besetting the world reverberated on sport in a more extensive manner. Twenty-two African countries plus Guyana decided at the last minute to boycott the Games on the grounds that New Zealand – whose rugby team had recently toured South Africa, a country still practising Apartheid policies – should have been expelled from the Games. The CIO insisted that the actions of rugby teams were outside its jurisdiction. No last-minute agreement was reached, hence the walkout, which resulted in the absence of leading distance runners like Miruts Yifter of Ethiopia, Henry Rono and John Ngeno of Kenya. The last one had been credited with 13:20.6 for 5000 metres in a pre-Olympic meet at Montreal ...

Over and above such unfortunate facts, it must be said that Lasse Viren really stood head and shoulders above the rest of the field – more so than four years earlier in Munich. He had shown a good return to form in previous weeks with 13:24.8 and 27:43.0. The heats of the 10,000 metres (23 July) were won by Carlos Lopes of Portugal (28:04.53); Marc Smet of Belgium (28:22.07) from Brendan Foster (28:22.19); and Tony Simmons (28:01.82). In the last one Viren (28:14.95) and Puttemans (28:15.52) qualified without spreading themselves thin. In the final (26 July) Viren had things well under control from start to finish. When he launched his attack in the next-to-the-last kilometre, only a small Portuguese, 29-year-old Carlos Lopes, managed to remain in his wake. But he had to surrender shortly before the bell. Viren wound up an undisturbed first. His superiority was reflected in his phenomenal second half , 13:31.44 (after 14.08.94 in the first). He covered the last kilometre in 2:38 and the last 400 in 61.3, for a final time of 27:40.38. (Incidentally, electronic timing in hundredths of a second was by then the rule, at least in major competitions). Lopes and Foster, both clearly outclassed, took second and third in that order. "Viren is the best runner there has ever been", said Foster. Details:

Montreal, 26 July 1976 – 10,000 metres: 1.Lasse Viren (Fin) 27:40.38, 2.Carlos Lopes (Por) 27:45.17, 3.Brendan Foster (GB) 27:54.92, 4.Tony Simmons (GB) 27:56.26, 5.Ilie Floroiu (Rom) 27:59.93,

6.Mariano Haro (Spa) 28:00.28; 7.Marc Smet (Bel) 28:02.80, 8.Bernie Ford (GB) 28:17.78....... DNF: Emiel Puttemans (Bel). Viren's task in the 5000 metres was more difficult though. Here he was pitted against such top-class milers as Dick Quax and Rod Dixon of New Zealand. The heats (28 July) were won by Quax (13:30.85); Willy Polleunis of Belgium (13:45.24); and Foster (13:20.34, a new Olympic record) from Dixon (13:20.48). Here too Viren qualified easily, as 4th in heat 1 (13:33.39). In the final (30 July) the Finn once again relied on his progressive acceleration in the latter stage of the race. It was in the last two kilometres that he set the world on fire with 2:39.3 and a punishing 2:29.5. He was timed in 1:57.5 for the last 800 metres and

Brendan Foster leading Nick Rose in the 5000 metres of the 1976 AAA Championships. Foster won in 13:33.0.

in 55.4 for the last lap. Quax, Germany's Klaus-Peter Hildenbrand and Dixon somehow managed to keep close to him, but that was all they could do. Said Dixon, a 3:53.62 miler (1975): "I was really amazed that Viren had that kind of speed over the last 400 metres". Details:

Montreal, 30 July 1976 – 5000 metres: 1.Lasse Viren (Fin) 13:24.76, 2.Dick Quax (NZ) 13:25.16, 3.Klaus-Peter Hildenbrand (FRG) 13:25.38, 4.Rod Dixon (NZ) 13:25.50, 5.Brendan Foster (GB) 13:26.19, 6.Willy Polleunis (Bel) 13:26.99, 7.Ian Stewart (GB) 13:27.65, 8.Aniceto Silva Simoes (Por) 13:29.38.

Two 5000/10,000 metre doubles in successive editions of the Games was an unprecedented feat and experts were obviously lavish in praising Viren, even though there were some who paradoxically branded him as "the man who could only win in the Olympics" or simply as "the opposite of Ron Clarke". But there were also people who wondered how he could always be at his best at the right time and ventured the opinion that "blood doping" may have something to do with it. This was known in medical circles as auto-hemotransfusion, a process whereby a certain quantity of blood – roughly 1/5 of the body's total - was extracted two-to-four weeks before D-day (big competition). Deprived of this oxygen-carrying hemoglobin, the body works to make up the deficit and does so at a steady rate. Then the extra blood, unfrozen from storage, is reinjected, increasing the body's total capacity to utilize oxygen. This procedure, totally legal at the time, was said to accomplish more or less what distance runners tried to achieve with long sessions of altitude training - but without any of the toil. When a journalist asked Viren about this, the Finn calmly replied: "I run 8000 kilometres a year. That is enough for me". Later, in a more ironical vein, he said that his secret weapon was reindeer milk. "We drink it daily. The only trouble is that you go bold". (Be it as it may, it was only in the late Eighties that the IAAF added the following sentence to art.144 of its rule book: "The practice of blood doping is forbidden"). Less than 24 hours after his victory in the 5000 metres, Viren tried the seemingly impossible as he lined up at the start of the

marathon – a distance he had never tried before in competition. Maybe in his heart of hearts he nurtured the hope of emulating Zátopek's famous triple at the 1952 Olympics. The Finn ran bravely but had to be content with fifth place in 2 hr 13:11. A superhuman effort, no doubt: after the race, in the dressing room, he tried to fill his dehydrated body with water and ice-cream, only to throw up, again and again .... (In fairness to him it must be said that back in 1952 Zátopek had a more comfortable interval – 3 days – between 5000 metres and marathon).

YIFTER,
AN AGELESS BLITZ

The early stages of 1977 were marked by two exploits which led to a further advancement, albeit infinitesimal, of the world records for the two classic distances. As often in the past, both occurred in Scandinavia. The first blow was delivered by a little known Kenyan, Samson Kimobwa (born in a village of the Marakwet region, altitude 600 metres, on 15 September 1955; 1.67 m. / 55 kg.), then a sophomore in agronomy at Washington State University in the North-West of the United States. That was the "nest" of a group of excellent distance runners from Kenya. Yves Pinaud, French statistician and historian and a great connoisseur of African athletics, had termed USA the "pouponnière" (kindergarten) of Kenyan athletics. Spurred on by scholarships, earned as often as not through their athletic performances, many young athletes from the mountain regions of Kenya were joining US colleges, where they could further their athletic ability but also acquire a good level of education. Kimobwa had been recommended by John Chaplin, track coach at Washington State University, who already had in his team men like John Ngeno, Joshua Kimeto and Henry Rono. In 1976 Kimobwa ran the 5000 metres in 13:56.4 and the following year he won the 10,000 at the NCAA Championships in 28:10.3. These credentials were not good enough to prepare the track world for what was to follow. On 30 June Kimobwa entered the 10,000 metres at the World Games in Helsinki and bettered Dave Bedford's world record, were it only by three tenths of a second, with a surprising 27:30.47. Pace-setters in the early goings were Franco Fava of Italy and Tony Simmons of Britain and the halfway point was reached in 13:48.7. Kimobwa took the lead after 6200 metres and was on his own for the rest of the race. His teammate Mike Musyoki shot ahead of Fava and Simmons to finish

second. Details:
Helsinki, 30 June 1977 – 10,000 metres:
1.Samson Kimobwa (Ken) 27:30.47, 2.Mike Musyoki (Ken) 27:41.92, 3.Franco Fava (Ita) 27:42.65, 4.Tony Simmons (GB) 27:43.59, 5.Toshiaki Kamata (Jap) 27:48.63, 6.Hideki Kita (Jap) 28:05.62, 7.Lasse Orimus (Fin) 28:05.72, 8.Kunimitsu Ito (Jap) 28:05.93.

Kilometre fractions:

1000 m	2:45.2	
2000 m	5:28.2	(2:43.0)
3000 m	8:14.3	(2:46.1)
4000 m	11:01.4	(2:47.1)
5000 m	13:48.7	(2:47.3)
6000 m	16:35.7	(2:47.0)
7000 m	19:17.4	(2:41.7)
8000 m	22:00.5	(2:43.1)
9000 m	24:45.9	(2:45.4)
10,000 m	27:30.47	(2:44.6)

After becoming famous almost overnight, Samson Kimobwa lived up to his newly acquired status only for a short time. His incredible "day-after" experience is told in the adjoining aside.

A precise man

Puttemans' mantle as holder of the world record for 5000 metres was taken over by Theodorus Jacobus Leonardus ("Dick") Quax of New Zealand. This former miler was born at Den Helder, Holland on 1 January 1948 and had an impressive build (1.83 m. / 65 kg.). His progress was at first delayed by recurrent injuries. At the 1972 Olympics he was eliminated in the prelims of the 5000 metres. Four years later, shortly before the Montreal Olympics, he came dangerously close to Puttemans' world record for 5000 metres with 13:13.10 (Stockholm, 5 July) –

Mad carrousel

As was to be expected, Samson Kimobwa's 10,000 metre record at Helsinki caused quite a stir in European track circles. He was swarmed with invitations to appear here and there and everywhere. The inexperienced Kenyan was involved in a mad carrousel. See what he did in the days that followed (the first of these races came 48 hours after his Helsinki triumph):

Milan (Italy),
2 July – 5000 metres: 13:21.9 (PB), 1st.

Raahe (Finland),
3 July – 5000 metres: 13:53.1, 2nd .
Won by Josh Kimeto (Ken), 13:42.2.

Stockholm (Sweden),
4 July – 10,000 metres: 27:37.28, 1st.

Turku (Finland),
5 July – 5000 metres:
13:32.48, 3rd. Won by Franco Fava
(Ita), 13:21.98 from John Ngeno (Ken),
13:28.72

Nyköping (Sweden),
6 July – 5000 metres: 13:43.9, 1st.

One can easily imagine what this implied in terms of air trips, etc. Then he took a few days' rest, of course. But he was back in harness soon and resumed competition all over Europe. Quite predictably, he lost form and in his last race, a '10' in London on 9 September, he finished 11th in 28:15.97 (Brendan Foster won in 27: 36.62 from Henry Rono, 27:37.08).
In 1977, his banner year, Kimobwa ran 14 races at 5000 metres, losing 8; and 9 races at 10,000, losing the last two. In the following years he was seldom heard from. After his meteoric career, however, he made an excellent impact as coach and official of the Kenya Amateur Athletic Association.

formally just outside the Belgian's hand-timed 13:13.0 of 1972. In Montreal, as previously related, he was a brilliant second to Viren over the same distance.
Exactly a year after his tantalizing failure at Stockholm, Quax went back to the old Olympic Stadium of the Swedish capital, just to try again. This time he did not fail and had the electronic apparatus stop at 13:12.86. Wondrous precision: he "beat" Puttemans by one tenth of a second! He received valuable help from his countryman Rod Dixon up to 3000 metres and was on his own for the rest of the way, apart from a brief spell when Karl Fleschen of Germany forged ahead of him with one kilometre to go. But Quax quickly recovered and won comfortably. Details:
Stockholm, 5 July 1977 – 5000 metres: 1.Dick Quax (NZ) 13:12.86, 2.Karl Fleschen (Ger) 13:13.88, 3.Peter Weigt (Ger) 13:14.54, 4.Manfred Kuschmann (GDR) 13:19.51, 5.Toshiaki Kamata (Jap) 13:25.41, 6.Hideki Kita (Jap) 13:27.44. DNF: Rod Dixon (NZ).

Kilometre fractions:

1000 m	2:39.21	
2000 m	5:18.42	(2:39.21)
3000 m	7:55.93	(2:37.51)
4000 m	10:38.92	(2:42.99)
5000 m	13:12.86	(2:33.94)

In 1977 the IAAF calendar had a new competition – the World Cup. Conceived along the same lines as the European Cup, with one man per team in every event, it was open to the countries that finished first and second in the European Cup (held earlier in the year), USA, Asia, Africa, Oceania, plus a team for the Rest of Europe and one for the Rest of America. The "première" was held at Düsseldorf and saw the first major international successes of Ethiopia's Miruts Yifter, by then in his thirties. He scored a fine double, exhibiting his main weapon, a fulminating "Blitz" over the last 300/400 metres. In the 10,000 he ran the last lap in 54.3 and the last 200 in 25.1. In the 5000 metres he was opposed to America's premier miler, Marty Liquori, who had beaten him in Zurich a few days earlier (13:16.00 to 13:18.12, with Quax second in between the two in

Miruts Yifter (Ethiopia) no. 191, flanked by Aleksandr Fyedotkin (USSR) in the 5000 metre final of the 1980 Olympics in Moscow. The Ethiopian, then 36, won a 5000/10,000 double in those Games.

13:17.32, and Kimobwa fifth). The Ethiopian turned the tables on Liquori with a devastating finish: 53.9 in the last 400 (Liquori 54.9) and 26.5 in the last 200. Details:

Düsseldorf, 2 September 1977 – 10,000 metres: 1.Miruts Yifter (Eti/Afr) 28:32.3, 2.Jörg Peter (GDR) 28:34.0, 3.Jos Hermens (Hol/Eur) 28:35.0.

Düsseldorf, 4 September 1977 – 5000 metres: 1.Miruts Yifter (Eti/Afr) 13:13.82, 2.Marty Liquori (USA) 13:15.06, 3.David Fitzsimons (Oce/Aus) 13:17.42.

Miruts Yifter (born at Adrigat, a village in the Tigre region, on 15 May 1944; 1.62 m. / 53 kg.) could point to a career of incredible mishaps, as related in the adjoining aside. Even his date of birth was a matter of controversy. The version given above is the one commonly accepted by the Association of Track & Field Statisticians (ATFS). Prior to 1977, his best credential was a bronze medal in the 10,000 metres at the 1972 Olympics. In 1977 no less than 18 men ran the 10,000 metres inside 28 minutes, a frontier first conquered by Ron Clarke in 1965.

1978 belonged to a talented Kenyan, Henry Rono (born at Kaprirsang in the Nandi Hills on 12 February 1952; 1.70 m. / 63 kg.). Just like Kimobwa, he belonged to the Kenyan group attending Washington State University and was coached by John Chaplin. He began to seriously explore the track world at the age of 20, yet his progress was relatively slow. He had some success as a steeplechaser and in 1976 he won this event at the Kenya Trials for the Montreal Olympics in 8:29.0. But, like many other Africans, at the last moment he had to stay away from the Games. However, it was dur-

A comedy of errors

Miruts Yifter, a small, solid and seemingly ageless Ethiopian, had to wait for many years before entering the spotlight of international athletics. This belated recognition was partly due to a series of unhappy events, almost a comedy of errors. Here they are, in chronological order:

July 1971 – Durham, North Carolina, USA vs. Africa dual meet. In his first appearance before a large international audience Yifter was opposed in a 5000 metre race to Steve Prefontaine, to this day probably the most popular distance runner America has ever had. On a sultry day, Yifter launched his attack with little more than 650 metres to go – in what he thought was the last lap. He ran away from "Pre" with a brisk burst and opened a 20 metre lead, then crossed what he thought was the finish line, threw up his hands in triumph and stopped running. When the starter fired the gun for the real last lap, Yifter, apparently not aware of the situation, could not be convinced to run another lap. Prefontaine plodded through a 70-seconds final lap to win unopposed in 13:57.6. Yifter made amends for his error the next day, when he was added to the 10,000 metre field as a non-scorer and won in 28:53.2, outsprinting Frank Shorter of USA (28:54.0).

September 1972 – Munich, Olympic Games. In his first experience at the quadrennial Games Yifter won a bronze medal in the 10,000 metres, finishing behind Lasse Viren and Emiel Puttemans. His time, 27:41.0, was to remain the best of his long career. Four days later he was to run a heat of the 5000 metres but failed to reach the starting line in due time. Officially the Ethiopian management stated that he was late to arrive as he was delayed in the washroom. There were (obviously unofficial) rumours that he had been deliberately withheld as he was accused of wearing track shoes not made by the company that officially sponsored the Ethiopian team.

July 1976 – Montreal, Olympic Games. A few days before the opening ceremony it was announced that many African countries, including Ethiopia, had decided to boycott the Games (for reasons explained earlier in this book). The news must have deeply saddened Miruts Yifter, who just a few days earlier had run the 5000 metres in 13:24.4 during a pre-Olympic meet in Montreal.

Even so, Yifter managed to survive all mishaps and finally did himself justice – especially, as we will see, in the 1980 Olympics in Moscow.

ing his sojourn in Canada in pre-Olympic weeks that he first met John Chaplin, who was instrumental for Henry's enrollment at WSU. In 1977 he did 8:31.1 in the steeplechase, then showed fine progress during a European tour with times of 13:22.1 and 27:37.08 in the classic distances, the latter in losing to Brendan Foster (27:36.62).

Rono: four world records in 80 days

1978 was a memorable year in the career of Henry Rono, and in the annals of distance running as a whole. Between January and November he ran 52 races on track and road, indoors and out. He reached the apex of his condition between April and June and broke world records in four different events. Details follow: Berkeley, 8 April 1978 – 5000 metres: 1.Henry Rono (Ken) 13:08.4, 2.Joshua Kimeto (Ken) 13:58.0, 3.Samson Kimobwa (Ken) 14:03.0.

Kilometre fractions:

1000 m	2:42.0	
2000 m	5:18.0	(2:36.0)
3000 m	7:57.5	(2:39.5)
4000 m	10:34.5	(2:37.0)
5000 m	13:08.4	(2:33.9)

Estimated 3 mile time, 12:42.9; last 400 metres, 59.4.
A well-known speaker, Bob Steiner, was doing his job at Berkeley that day. He was so impressed by Rono's form that he began to "call" a world record after only three laps!
At Seattle on 13 May Rono annexed another world record, bettering Anders Gärderud's mark for the 3000 metre steeplechase by nearly 3 seconds with 8:05.4. Then he moved to the European theatre of operation. His next "coup" was in a 10,000 metre race at Vienna. Jos Hermens of Holland set the pace for 8 1/2 laps, after which Rono was on his own. After a 13:49.0 first half he increased his speed so well that the second half took only 13:33.4, which would have been a world record for 5000 metres till June 1965! Details:

Vienna, 11 June 1978 – 10,000 metres: 1.Henry Rono (Ken) 27:22.4, 2.Domingo Tibaduiza (Col) 27:53.0, 3. Joel Cheruiyot (Ken) 27:58.9. DNF: Jos Hermens (Hol).

Kilometre fractions:

1000 m	2:47.5	
2000 m	5:30.2	(2:42.7)
3000 m	8:13.6	(2:43.4)
4000 m	11:04.6	(2:51.0)
5000 m	13:49.0	(2:44.4)
6000 m	16:35.7	(2:46.7)
7000 m	19:20.0	(2:44.3)
8000 m	22:02.1	(2:42.1)
9000 m	24:45.5	(2:43.4)
10,000 m	27:22.4	(2:36.9)

The photo finish apparatus failed, and hand timing was used for ratification purposes. A photo-cell timer caught Rono in 27:22.47.
At Oslo on 27 June Rono concluded his memorable record-breaking spree with 7:32.1 for 3000 metres, 3.1 seconds under Brendan Foster's world record. Here again his second half (3:42.5) was considerably faster than the first (3:49.6).
Even apart from his record performances, Rono maintained his form throughout the greater part of the season. He ran the 5000 metres on 12 occasions and the 10,000 on five – with no defeats. In the steeplechase, his boyhood favourite, he had no less than 12 competitions, losing two. His superlative campaign included two victories in the Commonwealth Games at Edmonton, Canada : with 8:26.54 in the steeplechase (7 August) and 13:23.04 in the 5000 metres (10 August). In the latter he easily disposed of his countryman Mike Musyoki (13:29.92) and England's Brendan Foster (13:31.35). He did not run the 10,000 (6 August), which went to Foster (28:13.65), with Musyoki second (28:19.14). Two well-known New Zealanders were among the "also ran": Rod Dixon 8th in the 5000 metres and Dick Quax 9th in the 10,000.
Italy entered the picture in 1978 with the first of five men who were to play important rôles for several years to come. The country on the Mediterranean Sea had previously had only one performer of good international caliber, "Nini" Beviacqua, second in the

10,000 metres at the 1938 European Championships. In 1978 the ice was broken by Venanzio Ortis (born at Paluzza, Udine, on 29 January 1955; 1.79 m./ 63 kg.), a quiet forestry student from Padua. At 23 he could already point to a decade of athletic activity. As befits an Italian from the North East, he had some success in cross-country skiing before turning to track. At 19 he had such times as 3:48.1, 8:09.0 and 14:11.0. Guided by coach Franco Colle, he finally settled for the long distances, with slow but steady progress. He did not go beyond the 5000 metre prelims at the 1976 Olympics. By the end of 1977 he had PB's of 13:33.9 and 28:34.0. In 1978, unquestionably his best year, he started with 13:27.1 as fifth in a 5000 metre race Down Under. This was his first experience in a tight finish at such levels and the race was won by Rod Dixon (13:25.2), with Dick Quax second and one Lasse Viren ninth. In Europe he beat Viren again in the Finland vs. Italy dual meet at Kouvola, with 13:27.9, then he lost to his countryman Luigi Zarcone in the 10,000 metres at the Italian Championships (28:05.2 to 28:04.5). His last pre-Europeans test was a high-level 5000 in the famous Zurich meet (16 August), where he finished third in 13:20.82, a new Italian record, behind Henry Rono (13:16.12) and amazing Markus Ryffel of Switzerland (13:19.97).

With Viren by then a shadow of his former self, Finland's hopes for the forthcoming Europeans rested on Martti Vainio (born at Vehkalahti on 30 December 1950; 1.92 m. / 71 kg.), one of the tallest men ever seen in élite distance running. In 1976 he had such times as 13:35.3 and 28:07.4, but he too could not go beyond the 10,000 metre prelims in the Montreal Olympics. Shortly before the continental championships in Prague a highly touted candidate was of course Brendan Foster, who brought the British 10,000 metre record to 27:30.3 (London, 23 June).

First on the European Championships schedule was, as usual, the 10,000 metres. After a steady rhythm throughout, with Ilie Floroiu of Romania as the most active pace-setter (13:44.8 at 5000 metres), the battle flared up in the last lap. Going round the last turn, Vainio jumped into the lead. Ortis and Aleksandr Antipov (USSR) offered stubborn resistance but could not close the gap. Yet this trio surprisingly relegated Foster to fourth. It was possibly the greatest mass finish in the history of distance running, with the first four in a 1.66 secs. blanket. Details: Prague, 29 August 1978 – 1.Martti Vainio (Fin) 27:30.99, 2.Venanzio Ortis (Ita) 27:31.48, 3.Aleksandr Antipov (USSR) 27:31.50, 4.Brendan Foster (GB) 27:32.65, 5.David Black (GB) 27:36.27, 6.Gerard Tebroke (Hol) 27:36.64, 7.Ilie Floroiu (Rom) 27:40.06. 8.Enn Sellik (USSR) 27:40.61.

In the preliminary round of the 5000 metres (31 August) there was a very fast heat, won by Aleksandr Fyedotkin in 13:24.10 from Ryffel (13:24.71) and Ortis (13:26.7). The final two days later was less impressive clock-wise but offered great competition. The early pace was slow and with one lap to go seven men were still in contention, closely bunched. Vainio was first to attack, but Ryffel and Ortis passed him. The Italian finally won by the narrowest of margins. Aleksandr Fyedotkin also closed fast and earned a tie for second with the Swiss, while Vainio faded to sixth. As a blanket finish this was even greater than the one over 10,000 metres: less than 3 tenths of a second covered the first four and poor Vainio was sixth barely 1.1 secs. behind the winner ! Ortis ran the last 400 in 57.0. Details: Prague, 2 September 1978 - 5000 metres: 1. Venanzio Ortis (Ita) 13:28.57, 2(tie) Markus Ryffel (Swi) and Aleksandr Fyedotkin (USSR) 13:28.66, 4.John Treacy (Ire) 13:28.8, 5.Ilie Flroiu (Rom) 13:29.3, 6.Martti Vainio (Fin) 13:29.7, 7.Nick Rose (GB) 13:32.8, 8.Enn Sellik (USSR) 13:35.8. In later years Ortis was hampered by recurring injuries and seldom, if ever, managed to reproduce his 1978 form.

The last world record of 1978 was an 8:13.51 for 2 miles by Steve Ovett of England. It was bound to remain unofficial as the IAAF had resolved (in 1976) that times made over English distances, except the mile, should no longer qualify for record purposes. The meet was held in London on 15 September. Ovett, one of the world's fastest milers, won from Rono (8:14.66) and Bronislaw Malinowski of Poland (8:18.43). The second half (4:04.4) was faster than the first (4:09.1).

In 1979 Henry Rono performed at notably lower levels, save perhaps for a good 13:19.65 for 5000 metres at Rieti on 21

July. In the major test of the year, the second edition of the World Cup at Montreal, Miruts Yifter re-emerged in a most impressive fashion. On 24 August he won the 10,000

Run for tea

In 1978 track observers found it difficult to explain what kept Henry Rono so furiously at work all over Europe for several months, even after conquering 4 world records in just as many events and winning major titles at the American NCAA Championships, the African Championships and the Commonwealth Games. People who knew him ventured the opinion that the reason behind such a frantic activity was to be found in his ambition to enlarge a tea plantation he owned back home at Kapsabet, which in his absence was run by his family. European meets were by then pretty lucrative, no matter if money still had to be handed "under the table". By mid-August Rono allowed himself a 20-days break from of his European labours to visit his family and study ways and means to make his dream come true. As a good patriot he also visited the grave of Jomo Kenyatta, President of Kenya. All this obviously kept him away from training for a while. Back to Europe he was no longer at his best, yet he took part in 8 meets in various parts of the continent - all in the space of 15 days! Inevitably, he suffered several defeats, even though he managed to beat Ortis and Vainio, the newly crowned European champions. His seemingly endless season closed on a tragicomical note. He competed in the NCAA Cross-Country Championships at Madison, Wisconsin on a cold day in November. At one time he stepped in a hole and injured an ankle. He got a little frostbite on his hands and feet. He wound up 237th of 241 finishers.

In the years that followed Rono probably felt the effects of his mad campaign (52 races) of 1978. Apart from a brief (but splendid) spell in 1981, he was never his old self again. And once his career was over his addiction to alcoholic drinks was to put him in trouble in more than one way.

metres in 27:53.07 from Craig Virgin of USA (27:59.55) and two days later he easily disposed of Valeriy Abramov (USSR) in the 5000 – 13:35.9 to 13:37.6. Markus Ryffel of Switzerland was third (13:38.6). Once again, Yifter's finishing speed made the difference: 54.3 (last 400) and 25.5 (last 200) in the longer race; 53.3 and 25.8 in the 5000 metres. Throughout the season, Yifter lost only once - to Thomas Wessinghage of Germany in the 5000 metres at the Zurich meet, 13:38.3 to 13:37.5. Details of the World Cup races:

Montreal, 24 August 1979 – 10,000 metres: 1.Miruts Yifter (Eti/Afr) 27:53.07, 2.Craig Virgin (USA) 27:59.55, 3.Aleksandr Antipov (USSR) 28:25.17.

Montreal, 26 August 1979 – 5000 metres: 1.Yifter (Eti/Afr) 13:35.9, 2.Valeriy Abramov (USSR) 13:37.6, 3.Markus Ryffel (Eur/Swi) 13:38.6.

As one can see from the statistical section, the fastest times of 1979 at the standard distances were posted by Suleiman Nyambui of Tanzania (13:12.29) and Karl Fleschen of Germany (27:36.8).

In 1980 Yifter, 36, obviously aimed at the highest honour – Olympic gold, which for previously related reasons had escaped him in 1972 and '76. He knew this was his last chance. He had a good rehearsal at Bratislava on 7 June when he ran 5000 metres in 13:16.38, which was to remain the fastest time of the year. Even the Moscow Olympics happened to be damaged as a result of the perverse boycott game. This time it was the turn of USA and some of their allies from the Western bloc to stay away from the Games as a protest against the invasion of Afghanistan by Soviet troops. The measure was advocated by Jimmy Carter, President of USA, and subsequently backed by the US Olympic Committee. Among countries that joined in the boycott were Germany, Japan, Kenya, Canada and New Zealand. The Olympic Committees of Great Britain and Italy refused to bow to political pressure from their governments and sent teams to Moscow. In the long distance department the most notable absentees were Craig Virgin of USA, who had the year's fastest 10,000 metre time, 27:29.16 (Paris, 17 July), Thomas Wessinghage of

Eamonn Coghlan (Ireland) winning the 5000 metres at the 1983 World Championships in Helsinki.

Germany and several Africans, e,g. Henry Rono, who started on a high note with 27:31.68 over 10,000 metres (Melbourne, 6 February) but faded to sixth in a 5000 metre race at Oslo on 15 July, won by Nat Muir of Great Britain (13:17.9) from Filbert Bayi (13:18.2) and Nyambui (13:18.6) both of Tanzania.

It is highly doubtful, however, if any of the absentees could have threatened Yifter in Moscow. The "ageless" Ethiopian was at his very best in those days and looked virtually unbeatable in hectic finishes. Among his rivals in the 10,000 metres was Lasse Viren, the champion of 1972 and '76. When the Finn, then 31, took the lead in the next-to-the-last lap, quite a few of his admirers probably thought that a new miracle was in the making. In fact, winning a distance title for the third straight time would amount to just that. But it was, alas, a short-lived hope. The Viren bubble burst early in the last lap, when Yifter launched his attack and soon built up a lead, as three others – Kaarlo Maaninka of Finland, Mohammed Kedir and Tolossa Kotu of Ethiopia also ran away from Viren. Yifter ran the last 400 metres in 54.4 for a final time of 27:42.69, his second best ever. A first half in 14:03.0 was followed by a brisk second in 13:39.7. The runner-up, relatively little known Maaninka, was a major surprise. Details:

Moscow, 27 July 1980 – 10,000 metres: 1.Miruts Yifter (Eti) 27:42.69, 2.Kaarlo Maaninka Fin) 27:44.28, 3.Mohammed Kedir (Et) 27:44.64, 4.Tolossa Kotu (Eti) 27:46.47, 5.Lasse Viren (Fin) 27:50.46, 6.Jörg Peter (GDR) 28:05.53, 7.Werner Schildhhauer (GDR) 28:10.91, 8.Enn Sellik (USSR) 28:13.72 .... 11.Brendan Foster (GB) 28:22.54,.... 13.Martti Vainio (Fin) 28:46.22.

Five days later, Yifter completed his double with a victory in the 5000 metres. He ran along the same pattern, with a decisive burst 260 metres from home. He met strong resistance from another African, Suleiman Nyambui of Tanzania, but finally won by a safe margin. His time for the last 400 was 54.9 (Nyambui 55.5). Maaninka amazed once more by finishing third. Details:

Moscow, 1 August 1980 – 5000 metres: 1.Miruts Yifter (Eti) 13:20.91, 2.Suleiman Nyambui (Tan) 13:21.60, 3.Kaarlo Maaninka (Fin) 13:22.00, 4.Eamonn Coghlan (Ire) 13:22.74, 5.Markus Ryffel (Swi) 13:23.03, 6.Dietmar Millonig (Aut) 13:23.25, 7.John Treacy (Ire) 13:23.62,

8.Aleksandr Fyedotkin (USSR) 13:24.10.
At 36 Yifter thus joined the four men who had previously scored a 5000/10,000 double in the Olympics - Kolehmainen, Zátopek, Kuts and Viren (twice). He paid tribute to his teammates Kedir, Kotu and Yohannes Mohammed, with whom he took turns leading "to make the races harder for our adversaries". In the space of a week, Yifter ran five races, counting preliminary rounds and finals, as follows:
24 July: 10,000 m (heat) 28:41.68 (1st)
27 July 10,000 m (final) 27:42.69 (1st)
28 July 5000 m (heat) 13:44.4 (1st)
30 July 5000 m (semi-final) 13:40.0 (2nd)
1 August 5000 m (final) 13:20.91 (1st)
When it was all over, Yifter said: "I would have made it at Montreal in 1976, if allowed to compete".

Posthumous confession

Ethiopia had happy days in Moscow, yet the real upset of the Games came from a little known, 27-year-old Finn, Kaarlo Maaninka, who won silver in the 10,000 metres and bronze in the 5000, both times with new PB's – 27:44.28 and 13:22.00 respectively. He was in the pink of condition at the right time, in the best Viren style. His performances before and after the Games were on a lower scale ("Track & Field News" World Ranking had him 4th in the 5000 metres and 5th in the 10,000). In subsequent years he quickly sank into oblivion.
Maybe some track observers were still raving about his Moscow heroics several years later when Maaninka made the headlines again – this time with a confession. He said that in 1980 he resorted to blood doping to enhance his performance before the Moscow Olympics. His admission came as part of a spiritual reconsideration of his rôle in life, and sports as well. (The IAAF included blood doping among "prohibited techniques" only in the late Eighties).
The most important event of 1981 was the third World Cup, held in Rome in the first week of September. Up to then the most talked of man of the year had been Fernando Mamede, a 30-year-old distance runner from Portugal, endowed with a great potential but seldom, if ever, at ease in "hot" competition. On 30 May at Lisbon he was credited with a nifty 27:27.7 for 10,000 metres, but in a race over the same distance in Florence on 10 June he was badly beaten by Mohammed Kedir, the Olympic bronze medallist – 27:55.6 to 27:47.0. However, the Portuguese did not compete in the World Cup, which projected new forces into the limelight. One of these was Werner Schildhauer (born at Dessau on 5 June 1956; 1.81 m. / 68 kg.), an electronics worker from the GDR. In 1980, aged 24, he was seventh in the 10,000 metres at the Moscow Olympics. In Rome he ran the same distance in 27:38.43, after sprinting the last 100 metres in 13.2, good enough to get rid of Olympic bronze medallist Kedir, and Alberto Salazar of USA. The latter was a native of Cuba whose family landed in USA when he was two. He grew up as an athlete at Eugene (Oregon), known as the Mecca of US track and field, mostly thanks to local hero Steve Prefontaine, a very popular runner who was to lose his life in a traffic accident on 30 May 1975. Details of the Rome race follow:
Rome, 4 September 1981 – 10,000 metres:
1.Werner Schildhauer (GDR) 27:38.43, 2.Mohammed Kedir (Eti/Afr) 27:39.44, 3.Alberto Salazar (USA) 27:40.69, 4.Venanzio Ortis (Ita) 27:42.70, 5.Martti Vainio (Fin/Eur) 27:48.62, 6.Toomas Turb (USSR) 27:54.18.
Two days later an entirely different cast offered a poor tactical race in the 5000 metres. The battle for points flared up only in the closing stage. Not surprisingly, the winner was a strong Irish miler, Eamonn Coghlan (born in Dublin on 21 November 1952; 1.77 m. / 63 kg.). He covered the last 400 in 53.2 and the last 200 in 25.9, which barely sufficed to beat Hansjörg Kunze of the GDR in a spirited sprint. Details:
Rome, 6 September 1981 – 5000 metres:
1.Eamonn Coghlan (Ire/Eur) 14:08.39, 2.Hansjörg Kunze (GDR) 14:08.54, 3.Vittorio Fontanella (Ita) 14:09.06, 4.Valeriy Abramov (USSR) 14:09.85, 5.Tolossa Kotu (Eti/Afr) 14:11.14, 6.Matt Centrowitz (USA) 14:11.14.

By the way, the Rome edition fielded 9 entries (teams) per event, instead of 8 as usual. Dr. Primo Nebiolo of Italy, who in those days was to succeed Adriaan Paulen as President of the IAAF, had conceived the idea of adding a ninth lane to accommodate the team of the host country (Italy had not qualified, finishing no better than fifth in the European Cup). This allowed Venanzio Ortis, the European 5000 metre champion of 1978, to briefly reappear in élite ranks with the second fastest 10,000 metre time of his career.

Rono:
Five hectic days

The most notable absentees at Rome's World Cup were Miruts Yifter and Henry Rono. The former, well satisfied with his 1980 crop, continued for a couple of years with such 10,000 metre performances as 28:03.23 in 1981 and 28:31.4 in '82, then close to his forties he decided to call it quits. Rono had a disappointing record in 1979-80. Early in 1981 he ran three 5000 metre races, all in the 14-plus class, which prompted an American observer to call this "Rono's Last Hurrah". He was through with his studies at WSU and was about to return to Kenya when some European promoters happened to remember him .... Once in Europe, he regained form gradually: fifth in the 5000 metres at the AAA Championships in 13:26.45; fourth over the same distance in Zurich, time 13:27.71 (winner in both races was Eamonn Coghlan with 13:20.36 and 13:19.13). He began to show glimpses of his 1978 form at Koblenz on 26 August, when he won in 13:12.15. Not selected for the World Cup, he took revenge in his own way with three superb 5000 metre performances in just as many countries over a 5-days' period. Details:
Rieti, 9 September 1981 – 5000 metres: 1.Hansjörg Kunze (GDR) 13:10.40 (new European record), 2.Valeriy Abramov (USSR) 13:11.99, 3.Henry Rono (Ken) 13:12.47, 4.Thomas Wessinghage (FRG) 13:13.47, 5.Venanzio Ortis (Ita) 13:19.19. The Kenyan set the pace for the greater part of the race but was finally outsprinted by a couple of dreadful kickers.
London, 11 September 1981 – 5000 metres: 1.Henry Rono (Ken) 13:12.34, 2.Julian Goater (GB) 13:15.59.
On his third attempt, in Norway, he bettered his own world record:
Knarvik, 13 September 1981 – 1.Henry Rono (Ken) 13:06.20, 2.Kipsubai Koskei (Ken) 13:36.00.

Kilometre fractions:

1000 m	2:38.5	
2000 m	5:17.0	(2:38.5)
3000 m	7:55.0	(2:38.0)
4000 m	10:33.0	(2:38.0)
5000 m	13:06.20	(2:33.2)
Last 400 m:	56.0	

In this race three Britons – James Espir, Ian Stewart and Steve Cram - alternated in helping Rono in the first four laps, and at least one of them did so again after he had been lapped. After viewing a film of the race, however, the IAAF decided that everything was OK and Rono's time was ratified.

In 1982 Rono had a good but not exceptional season. That was the end of a strange career. Just like Kimobwa and even more so, Rono was a "spendthrift", who used to run too often when he was at his peak. No matter how great his achievements in 1978 and partly in 1981, one was left with the impression that Rono somehow dilapidated his resources. The highlights of 1982 were the European Championships at Athens in September and the Commonwealth Games at Brisbane in October. Such big events were preceded by intense fireworks in European invitationals. The first blow came as a surprise to many: a new world's 5000 metre record by David Moorcroft of Great Britain (born at Coventry on 10 April 1953; 1.80 m. / 68 kg.) at Oslo's famous Bislett stadium on 7 July. He had been practising middle and long distance running from the earliest days of his career. Until then he appeared at his best in the 1500 metres: 7th at the 1976 Olympics in Montreal, 1st at the 1978 Commonwealth Games and 3rd at the European Championships of the same year. In that department, however, he was unlucky enough to be up against two phenoms like Seb Coe and Steve Ovett, milers de

luxe both. That led Moorcroft to devote more attention to longer distances. He reached the semi-finals of the 5000 metres at the 1980 Olympics in Moscow and was 1st over the same distance in the European Cup of 1981. No matter how good these credentials, what he did at Oslo in 1982 really went beyond expectations. He shaved twenty seconds off his previous 5000 metre best (13:20.51 in 1981) and almost six seconds off Rono's world record! Even more appalling perhaps was the fact that he took the lead after 800 metres and never relinquished it. He did all this in the presence of Henry Rono himself, who finished a distant fourth. At the end Moorcroft was so far ahead that the second man, Ralph King of USA, mistook him for a lapped runner! Said the winner: "I knew it would be a world record with one lap to go".
Details:
Oslo, 7 July 1982 – 5000 metres: 1.David Moorcroft (GB) 13:00.41, 2.Ralph King (USA) 13:20.85, 3.Nick Rose (GB) 13:21.29, 4.Henry Rono (Ken) 13:25.14, 5.David Clarke (GB) 13:26.22.
Kilometre fractions:

1000 m	2:38.0	
2000 m	5.:12.6	(2:34.6)
3000 m	7:50.2	(2:37.6)
4000 m	10:28.7	(2:38.5)
5000 m	13:00.41	(2:31.7)

Last 400 metres, 58.5; last 200, 29.1.

Moorcroft certainly had a grand season, albeit not perfect. He chalked up new PB's of 1:46.64 (800 m.), 3:33.79 (1500 m.), 3:49.34 (1 mile) and 7:32.79 (3000 m.). The last one (London, 17 July) was a new European record.

Another continental best was credited to Fernando Mamede of Portugal: 27:22.95 for 10,000 metres in Paris on 9 July (halves of 13:42.7 and 13:40.3) – just a few tenths off Rono's world record. An untimely injury kept him away from the European Championships, which took place in Athens at the new Olympic Stadium, a massive construction with a capacity of 80,000. Top favourites for the longer race were Carlos Lopes of Portugal and Werner Schildhauer of the GDR, who had seasonal bests of 27:24.39 (Oslo, 26 June) and 27:33.66 (Jena, 29 May) respectively.

Italy could not count on Venanzio Ortis, injured, but at the right moment another Italian jumped into the limelight – Alberto Cova (born at Inverigo, Como, on 1 December 1958; 1.76 m. / 58 kg.). An accountant by profession, he was the type of runner who can use legs and brain in a perfect synthesis. He was coached by Giorgio Rondelli, who had carefully studied Gerschler's Interval Training as well as Lydiard's Endurance Training, trying to mould them into a single "school of thought". Cova started at 15 but did not try the long distances until he was 18. In 1977 he was fifth in the 5000 metres at the European Junior

Alberto Cova (Italy) winning the 10,000 metres at the 1984 Olympics in Los Angeles.

Championships in Donyetsk with 14:04.4, a PB. What seemed then a coincidence was to become his trademark as he always proved capable of rising to the occasion in big competition. In 1981 he had seasonal bests of 13:27.20 and 28:29.12.

Enter Cova, the King of Finish

1982 was the first of Cova's four golden years. His new dimension first became apparent in a meet in Florence on 25 May when he ran the 10,000 metres in 27:56.37, finishing second to David Clarke of Great Britain (27:55.77) but leaving behind, among others, Henry Rono, Martti Vainio and Venanzio Ortis. Shortly before flying to Athens, Cova lowered his 5000 metre best to 13:26.85.

The final of the 10,000 metres in Athens was contested while the temperature was 27° C. Quite understandably, the early pace was relatively slow (first half in 14:04.7), with Lopes and Schildhauer alternating in the lead and Cova biding his time. A crisp change of rhythm was registered after 6400 metres, under Lopes' thrust. The last lap was dramatic: it began with Lopes still in the lead, followed by Schildhauer, Vainio and Cova. First to lose contact, with 200 metres to go, was Lopes. Entering the homestretch, Vainio had to give up in the struggle for gold, which thus became a Schildhauer vs. Cova affair. The tall German seemed on his way to victory as per pre-race predictions, but in the last stretch of vital land Cova offered the first sample of his "atout maître", a deadly finishing kick. He collared his rival with 50 metres to go and surged ahead to win by a narrow margin, 0.18 secs. When it was all over, Schildhauer's apparent incredulity was in sharp contrast with Cova's ecstasy. The Italian ran the last 400 metres in 56.7 and the last 200 in 26.8. Perhaps even more important, the second half was run in 13:36.3. Details:

Athens, 6 September 1982 – 10,000 metres: 1.Alberto Cova 27:41.03, 2.Werner Schildhauer (GDR) 27:41.21, 3.Martti Vainio (Fin) 27:42.51, 4.Carlos Lopes (Por) 27:47.95, 5.Julian Goater (GB) 28:10.98, 6.Salvatore Antibo (Ita) 28:21.07, 7.Steve Jones (GB) 28:22.94, 8.Charles Spedding (GB) 28:25.91.

The heats of the 5000 metres (8 September) featured many of the leading figures of the '10' – plus world record holder David Moorcroft and Thomas Wessinghage of Germany, i.e. two excellent milers. Moorcroft won heat 1 in 13:30.28 from Schildhauer. Heat 2 was livelier, with Wessinghage first in 13:26.48 and eight others inside 13:30. The final three days later was a harsh affair with plenty of jostling as elbows seemed to work harder than legs. Cova was involved in a rough "bagarre" with Hansjörg Kunze of the GDR and was subsequently disqualified (after finishing 10th). In an inevitably hot finish Moorcroft was outshone by two Germans, Wessinghage and Schildhauer, and the latter was again second. Winner Wessinghage, a doctor from Mainz, covered the last lap in 54.6. Details:

Athens, 11 September 1982 – 5000 metres: 1.Thomas Wessinghage (FRG) 13:28.90, 2.Werner Schildhauer (GDR) 13:30.03, 3.David Moorcroft (GB) 13:30.42, 4.Yevgeni Ignatov (Bul) 13:30.95, 5.Dietmar Millonig (Aut) 13:31.03, 6.Valeriy Abramov (USSR) 13:31.26, 7.Tim Hutchings (GB) 13:31.83; 8.Martti Vainio (Fin) 13:33.69, 9. Hansjörg Kunze (GDR) 13:35.71....Disqualified: Alberto Cova (Ita) 13:35.9.

The following month the British were at Brisbane for the Commonwealth Games. Unfavourable weather conditions, coupled with the strains of a long European campaign, prevented better performances. Moorcroft closed his masterful year with an easy victory in the 5000 metres (13:33.00), beating his teammate Nick Rose (13:35.97) and Peter Koech of Kenya (13:36.95). Tanzania scored a valuable one-two in the 10,000 metres with Gidamis Shahanga (28:10.15) and Zakaria Barie (28:10.55). Julian Goater of England was third (28:16.11).

RISE OF THE AFRICAN WAVE: SAID AOUITA ET ALTERA

1983 saw the birth of a new global competition: the World Championships in athletics. Formally, this was a novelty in the sense that the IAAF, contrary to international federations of several other sports, had never had its own championship meet. In actual fact, however, Rule 10, paragraph 2 of its rule book stated: "The Olympic Games shall be regarded as World Championships in track and field athletics". However, the growth of the sport at all levels inevitably led to the birth of a proper IAAF World Championship meet, as did the necessity of having a "world summit" more frequently , rather than every fourth year as in Olympic celebrations. At first the new World Championship meet was scheduled for pre-Olympic years. The first three editions thus took place in 1983, 1987 and 1991, after which a biennial frequency in odd years was introduced. At the present time only one year out of four is without a global meet (Worlds or Olympics).

The inaugural edition of what is now, in track jargon, the "Worlds" was held at Helsinki in August 1983. The choice of the venue was a tribute to the great traditions of Finland - in the sport as a whole and in long distance running in particular. From the very beginning it became apparent that an autonomous event of the kind would better preserve the sport from the hideous games of international politics, which had ruined the most recent editions of the Olympic Games. In this respect the Helsinki event was truly representative of world athletics as it featured 1572 athletes from 153 countries.

However, the most resounding achievements of 1983, clock-wise at least, occurred before the Helsinki rendezvous, at the hands of two Portuguese veterans, Fernando Mamede and Carlos Lopes. The former (born at Beja on 1 November 1951, 1.75 m. / 59 kg.) could by then look back to a long career, rich in terms of classy times but devoid of honours in big-time competition. He started as a middle distance runner with a time of 1:47.5 in a heat of the 800 metres at the 1974 European Championships in Rome and 3:37.98 in a heat of the 1500 at the 1976 Olympics in Montreal – but failing to qualify for the respective finals. At the 1978 European Championships in Prague he moved up to the 5000 metres and wound up 15th in the final. In the early stages of 1983 he showed excellent form. On 30 June at Lausanne he ran the 10,000 metres in 27:36.80, beating European champion Alberto Cova, 27:37.59 (Incidentally, the latter was to remain Cova's best ever). On 9 July at Oslo, Mamede lost to his countryman Carlos Lopes – 27:25.13 to 27:23.44. Both went to Helsinki highly confident. And both qualified for the final with ease: Mamede as first in Heat 1 (27:45.54), ahead of Cova (27:46.61). Hansjörg Kunze (GDR) was first in Heat 2 with 28:04.69, ahead of Lopes (28:05.62).

Cova noses out Schildhauer

Gidamis Shahanga of Tanzania was the early leader in the final (9 August). As it happens more often than not, the second half turned out to be much faster than the first. World record holder Mamede was first to lose contact and the same happened to his teammate Lopes when the final battle began, with little more than one lap to go. Schildhauer took the lead, followed by Kunze, Vainio, Shahanga and Cova. The Italian was still fifth as they entered the homestretch, but he put on a devastating finish which allowed him to pass his rivals one by one, up to and including Schildhauer, again the toughest nut to crack. Finishing in lane 4, Cova won by 0.14

sec., even less than the tiny 0.18 secs. which had earned him victory vis-à-vis the same rival at the 1982 European Championships in Athens. Cova ran the first half in 14:08.1 and the second in 13:53.0. He covered the last 400 metres in 53.9 and the last 300 in 38.7 – a finish worthy of the best milers. Another great mass finish, with only 0.89 covering the first five! Details:

Helsinki, 9 August 1983 – 10,000 metres: 1.Alberto Cova (Ita) 28:01.04, 2.Werner Schildhauer (GDR) 28:01.18, 3.Hansjörg Kunze (GDR) 28:01.26, 4.Martti Vainio (Fin) 28:01.37, 5.Gidamis Shahanga (Tan) 28:01.93, 6.Carlos Lopes (Por) 28:06.78, 7.Nick Rose (GB) 28:07.53, 8.Christoph Herle (Ger) 28:09.05, 9.Mohammed Kedir (Eti) 28:09.92. ...... 14.Fernando Mamede (Por) 28:18.39.

Cova and Mamede did not run the 5000 metres, which unfolded in three rounds – heats on the 10th of August, semi-finals on the 12th and final on the 14th. Fastest qualifier in the heats was Valeriy Abramov with 14:12.61; in the semis the fastest time was 13:31.40 by Dmitriy Dmitriyev. Such a heavy schedule did not seem conducive to a fast final. Wodajo Bulti led at 4000 metres in 11:03.3. Dmitriyev attacked with 500 metres to go. The quickest in following him was Eamonn Coghlan, who shot ahead with 150 metres to go. Earlier in the year the Irishman had become the first sub-3:50 miler indoors (3:49.78). Schildhauer closed even faster but had to be content with (yet another!) second. Coghlan ran the last 400 metres in 57.3 and the last 200 in 28.7 (Schildhauer 57.0 and 27.7 respectively). The winner covered the last kilometre in an amazing 2:24.77 – which would have been a world record for that distance up to 1930. To the immense delight of the crowd, veteran Vainio nipped Dmitriyev for the bronze medal right on the finish line. The first World Championship titles in long distance running thus went to two renowned kickers, Cova and Coghlan. The Irishman said he was astonished at the slow pace: "They played right into my hands. I don't care about the time". Details:

Helsinki, 14 August 1983 – 5000 metres: 1.Eamonn Coghlan (Ire) 13:28.53, 2.Werner Schildhauer (GDR) 13:30.20, 3.Martti Vainio (Fin) 13.30.34, 4.Dmitriy Dmitriyev (USSR) 13:30.38, 5.Doug Padilla (USA) 13:32.08, 6.Thomas Wessinghage (Ger) 13:32.46, 7.Wodajo Bulti (Eti) 13:34.03, 8.Dietmar Millonig (Aut) 13:36.08.

Schildhauer finally found partial relief for his many tantalizing seconds as he nosed out his arch-rival Cova in the 10,000 metres of the European Cup at London's Crystal Palace, were it only by a flimsy 0.02 sec. – 28:02.11 to 28:02.13.

In "Track & Field News" World Ranking for 1983 Fernando Mamede was no.1 in the 5000 metres. His late season marks (13:09.92 at Rieti and 13:08.54 at Tokyo) aptly completed his immaculate seasonal records: 4 races, including one at Zurich's "Weltklasse" meet, and no losses. One could maliciously add - with the complicity of his absence from the World Championship race at Helsinki ..... (He did run the longer event at Helsinki and finished no higher than 14th). Ranking leader here was Schildhauer, 1-1 vs. Cova but with a better seasonal record than his Italian rival.

1984 provided a new guiding light – Said Aouita of Morocco (born at Kenitra on 2 November 1959; 1.75 m. / 58 kg.), an exceptional talent who in his career was to prove capable of competing with the very best in the world at distances ranging from 800 to 10,000 metres. He first emerged in the late Seventies, then he moved to France, where he competed for a Marignane club near Marseille. In 1983 he transferred to Italy and took residence in Siena. His progression up to that time was as follows:

Year	Age	1500 m.	5000 m.
1978	19	-	14:10.0
1979	20	3:42.3	13:48.5
1980	21	3:37.08	-
1981	22	3:37.69	14:14.2
1982	23	3:37.37	14:05.7
1983	24	3:32.54	-

He was at home in the middle distances, and in 1983 he also ran the 800 metres in 1:44.38. Essentially a self-made man, he improved by dint of hard work and thanks to his perceptiveness. His breakthrough at international levels coincided with the 1983 World Championships in Helsinki, where he finished third in the 1500 metres. Yet at the dawn of 1984 he was uncertain whether to choose the 1500 or the 5000 for the Los Angeles Olympics. On 13 June in Florence he made the grade at the longer distance with an impressive 13:04.78, beating among others Wodajo Bulti of Ethiopia (13:10.08). But on 6 July at Hengelo he proved equally strong in the 1500, winning in 3:31.54, with the runner-up almost 6 seconds behind. On the eve of the Games he was the world's no.1 performer in both events. Hence, no easy choice. He finally opted for the 5000 metres, where competition appeared to be just a bit softer.

Also outstanding in pre-Olympic weeks was Fernando Mamede. After posting an excellent 13:12.83 for the 5000 at Oslo (28 June), four days later he set a new world record for 10,000 metres at Stockholm, shaving over 8 secs. off Henry Rono's mark. In this race the 33-year-old Portuguese was aptly seconded by a group of compatriots, notably including Carlos Lopes. The operation "assault on Rono's world record" was directed by Mario Moniz Pereira, a Portuguese coach. Steeplechaser Guilherme Alves was the early leader, then came along Ed Eyestone of USA and did his share of the "donkey work". Lopes took the lead at the halfway mark (13:45.40 – 3.6 secs. under Rono's time at the same distance in 1978). Mamede forged ahead with two laps to go, ran the last 800 metres in 2:00 and the last 400 in 57.5. The second half was covered in a sizzling 13:28.41. Even Lopes, second, bettered Rono's previous mark (He was to reach the apex of his long career at the Los Angeles Olympics, when he won the marathon at 37 years of age). Details:

Stockholm, 2 July 1984 - 10,000 metres: 1.Fernando Mamede (Por) 27:13.81, 2.Carlos Lopes (Por) 27:17.48, 3.Mark Nenow (USA) 27:40.56, 4.Gianni De Madonna (Ita) 28:04.60, 5.Salvatore Nicosia (Ita) 28:05.35, 6.Seppo Liuttu (Fin) 28:06.58, 7. Mohamed Ali Chouri (Tun) 28:07.24.

Kilometre fractions:

1000 m	2:49.40	
2000 m	5:34.45	(2:45.05)
3000 m	8:16.41	(2:41.96)
4000 m	11:00.47	(2:44.06)
5000 m	13:45.40	(2:44.93)
6000 m	16:30.08	(2:44.68)
7000 m	19:16.62	(2:46.54)
8000 m	21:58.25	(2:41.63)
9000 m	24:41.09	(2:42.84)
10,000 m	27:13.81	(2:32.72)

Cova opened his 1984 account with an indifferent 29:17.43 for 10,000 metres, finishing third behind two other Italians. He showed marked improvement at Oslo on 21 July, winning a 5000 metre race easily in 13:18.24. However, the most brilliant Italian in those days was Salvatore Antibo, who on 13 June in Florence ran 10,000 metres in 27:48.02, finishing second to Martti Vainio (27:41.75).

A politically inspired boycott was to make ravages once more. This time it was the turn of countries from the Communist bloc to stay away from the Olympics, officially for "safety reasons" but evidently as a revenge against USA and other NATO countries who had boycotted the 1980 Games in Moscow. Athletes from USSR and its allies did not go to Los Angeles. The only "transgressors" were the Romanians, who were obviously greeted with cheers by the predominantly American crowd at the Los Angeles Coliseum.

In the prelims of the 10,000 metres (3 August) Mamede won heat 1 in 28:21.87 and Cova was first in heat 2 in 28:26.10. The fastest qualifier was Sosthenes Bitok of Kenya, who won heat 3 in 28:12.17. The final, three days later, offered two distinctly different phases: one pretty slow , with John Treacy as the leader at 5000 metres in 14:19.9, and the other extremely hot. Vainio took upon himself the task of changing the rhythm of the race. One by one he shook off all his rivals except one – Cova. The little Italian launched his attack going round the last turn and ran away from an exhausted Vainio with supreme ease. He ran the last 200 metres in 27.7, as opposed to Vainio's 31.4. After negotiating the first half of the

Said Aouita, the first Moroccan male athlete to win an Olympic title -5000 metres in Los Angeles, 1984. (Hurdler Nawal El Moutawakel had turned the trick on the women's side a few days earlier).

race in a leisurely 14:20.6, the Italian covered the second in a sizzling 13:27.0 – a time which would have been good enough to win the Olympic 5000 metre title up to and including 1968! Vainio said he had leg problems in the last kilometre. A few days later he was disqualified after laboratory analysis showed he had taken anabolic steroids. He was thus deprived of the silver medal. Mike McLeod of Great Britain and Mike Musyoki of Kenya thus advanced to second and third respectively . Salvatore Antibo of Italy missed bronze by four hundredths of a second. What happened to world record holder Fernando Mamede is told in the adjoining aside. Details:

Los Angeles, 6 August 1984 – 10,000 metres: 1.Alberto Cova (Ita) 27:47.54, 2.Mike McLeod (GB) 28:06.22, 3.Mike Musyoki (Ken) 28:06.46, 4.Salvatore Antibo (Ita) 28:06.50, 5.Christoph Herle (Ger) 28:08.21, 6.Sosthenes Bitok (Ken) 28:09.01, 7.Yutaka Kanai (Jap) 28:27.06, 8.Steve Jones (GB) 28:28.08...... DNF: Fernando Mamede (Por). Martti Vainio finished second in 27:51.10 but was disqualified.

Said Aouita lined up at the start of the 5000 metre final as the no.1 favourite of experts. His recent 13:04.78 was second only to David Moorcroft's world record (13:00.41) in the All-Time List. And Moorcroft was not in his best form, having resumed full training too late due to an injury. However, there were also observers who had doubts about Aouita, considering his lack of experience in the 5000 metre department. On 8 August he qualified with astounding ease (4th in 13:45.66) in a heat won by Mats Erixon of Sweden in 13:44.45. Fastest qualifier was Ezequiel Canario of Portugal in 13:43.28. In the semi-finals (9 August) Aouita was much faster and went through in 13:28.39, just ahead of Moorcroft (13:28.44) and John Walker of New Zealand (13:28.48), a great miler who in the closing stage of his career had decided to try the 5000. In the final (11 August) everything went smoothly for Said

Even champions can have different gears

The history of athletics offers several examples of world record breakers who were unable to do themselves justice in major competitions. Long distance races, no matter if governed (generally but not always) by the philosophy of even pace, make no exception to the rule. I have dealt with the cases of Ron Clarke, who did win medals but no gold, and Dave Bedford, who never went beyond honourable placings. The case of Fernando Mamede stands apart though as it is obvious that he had two different gears: a high one in "cold" races in which he was able to reach exceptional standards clock-wise and even beat famous runners. Let's not forget, for example, that Alberto Cova – World, Olympic and European champion – ran the fastest 10,000 metre time of his career in losing to Mamede at Lausanne in 1983. But Mamede always showed a low gear in big-time competitions where major laurels were at stake – episodes I have dealt with earlier in this book.

The high-gear version was in full view when Mamede broke the world's 10,000 metre record with 27:13.81 at Stockholm in 1984, after covering the last kilometre in 2:32.72. On the eve of the Los Angeles Olympics this feat led some observers to forget about his past failures in big meets and give him as the no.1 favourite. After going through the preliminary round unscathed, the 33-year-old Lusitanian met tragedy in the final. He looked surprisingly "tame" from the beginning, as he placed himself at the rear of the pack. The pace was all but swift. The leader hit the halfway mark in 14:19.9, with Mamede well behind in 14:22.7. (In his record race at Stockholm he had done 13:45.40). Shortly afterwards he swung out across the track and ran into the exit tunnel. As a witty observer put it, "his speed in the tunnel indicated an urgent need to go".

All this probably boils down to the fact that in major international competitions a correct psychological approach is of fundamental importance if one wants to express his full potential. Mamede, who even consulted medical experts about his problem, will forever remain a most peculiar case in this respect.

Aouita. Ezequiel Canario of Portugal set a fairly swift pace in the first 2000 metres (5:17.8), then his countryman Antonio Leitao took over (4000 in 10:38.8). After following these men with no apparent effort, Aouita made his move halfway down the backstretch of the final lap, swallowed Leitao and went on to win as he pleased. Markus Ryffel closed quite decently to take second. The Moroccan ran the last 800 metres in 1:55.2, the last lap in 55.0 and the last 200, easing up, in 27.7. Somebody asked him why he did not try harder, with the world record only 5 seconds away. His answer surprised his listeners: " Why should I break my head already? I am very young". At 25 he obviously felt he had a bright future to look forward to. He did not forget to add that had he run the 1500 metres he would have won it ! Supreme confidence was his trademark. Ryffel ran the race of his life, six years after winning the silver medal at the European Championships. Details:
Los Angeles, 11 August 1984 – 5000 metres: 1.Said Aouita (Mor) 13:05.59, 2.Markus Ryffel (Swi) 13:07.54, 3.Antonio Leitao (Por) 13:09.20, 4.Tim Hutchings (GB) 13:11.50, 5.Paul Kipkoech (Ken) 13:14.40, 6.Charles Cheruiyot (Ken) 13:18.41, 7.Doug Padilla (USA) 13:23.56, 8.John Walker (NZ) 13:24.46....... 14.David Moorcroft (GB) 14:16,61. DNS: Martti Vainio (Fin).

Star of the post-Olympic meets in Europe was ...... Fernando Mamede, who did 13:18.18 for 5000 metres in Rieti on 2 September and 27:47.19 for 10,000 in Paris two days later! In "Track & Field News" World Ranking he had to be content with second in both events, behind Aouita and Cova respectively.

There were no global titles at stake in 1985, yet the atmosphere was kept warm thanks to a series of fast races, the best of which was at magic Bislett stadium in Oslo on 27 July. Said Aouita lived up to his avowed optimism and succeeded David Moorcroft as holder of the world's 5000 metre record, were it only by the proverbial whisker – one hundredth of a second! Bob Verbeeck of Belgium set the stage for things to come by assuring a fast pace in the first two kilometres. Aouita forged ahead with his flowing style shortly

before 3000 metres and had things well under control for the rest of the journey. He ran the last kilometre in 2:28.24, the last 400 metres in 54.44 and the last 200 in 26.7. Sydney Maree, an American of South African extraction, he too a great miler, finished a strong second. Alberto Cova , a well beaten third, ran his fastest race ever. Details:
Oslo, 27 July 1985 – 5000 metres: 1.Said Aouita (Mor) 13:00.40, 2.Sydney Maree (USA) 13:01.15, 3.Alberto Cova (Ita) 13:10.06, 4.Nat Muir (GB) 13:18.47, 5.John Treacy (Ire) 13:19.11, 6.Christoph Herle (Ger) 13:19.25, 7.Steve Plasencia (USA) 13:19.37.

Kilometre fractions:

1000 m	2:35.14	
2000 m	5:13.82	(2:38.68)
3000 m	7:51.00	(2:37.18)
4000 m	10:32.16	(2:41.16)
5000 m	13:00.40	(2:28.24)

It should perhaps be added that 11 days before the Oslo race the Moroccan was involved in a torrid 1500 metre battle with Steve Cram at Nice. The Briton launched his attack with a lap to go and built up a sizable lead. Aouita fought back bravely and closed the gap steadily – but not entirely. They were rewarded with history's first sub-3:30 times (Cram 3:29.67, Aouita 3:29.71). The Moroccan was the faster of the two in the closing stage – 39.6 vs. 40.0 in the last 300 metres, 13.0 vs. 13.5 in the last 100.

1985 was the fourth and last year of Alberto Cova's glorious period. After scoring a fantastic 10,000 metre triple (1982 Europeans, 1983 Worlds and 1984 Olympics), this time he concentrated on the European Cup, a team competition so dear to countries of the "Old" continent. In the final round, scheduled for mid-August in Moscow, Italy was in danger of being demoted to the "B" group for the following year - a destiny reserved to the last two of the eight teams in competition. Cova thus took upon himself the task of piling up as many points as possible. Italy escaped such a calamity and remained in the "A" group thanks to his double – on the first day (17 August) he won the 10,000 metres in 28:51.46 from – guess who? – Werner Schildhauer (28:56.57) and the next day he took the 5000 after a wild battle with miler Thomas Wessinghage of Germany, 14:05.45 to 14:05.72. Contrary to his habits, Cova for once helped in setting the pace in both races, ostensibly to calm down his rivals and reach the closing stage with his reserves fully untapped …. It may be interesting to note that Cova, although a winner of the 10,000 metres in the three major title meets, never held the Italian record for the distance. He did break the national record for the 5000 though (13:10.06 in Aouita's world record race at Oslo in 1985).

1985 also saw the inaugural edition of the IAAF/Mobil Grand Prix, a series of international meets which offered prize money to athletes with the highest point score at the end of such series. This was of course a major innovation and practically marked the end of the amateur era – the official end, of course, because that time-honoured philosophy had been buried long ago with the practice of payments made "under the table". As far as distance races were concerned, the new policy led to a wider use of "hares" likely to set a fast pace and thereby help the best runners towards the achievement of record breaking performances. The highest point scorer of 1985 in the 5000 metre department was Doug Padilla of USA, whose best effort clock-wise was a good but not exceptional 13:15.44 at the World Games in Helsinki. This ranking earned him $10,000. Since he was first also in the Overall Ranking (embracing all events) he got an additional $25,000.

1985 closed with the fourth edition of the World Cup, held at Canberra, capital of the Commonwealth of Australia. Wodajo Bulti of Ethiopia won the 10,000 metres in 29:22.96 from Pat Porter of USA and Werner Schildhauer. Padilla won the 5000 in 14:04.11 from Stefano Mei of Italy and Bulti. As usual, these were "waiting" races characterized by short finishing bursts. Inevitable when ranking points are the prime concern.

The most notable happening of 1986 was the debut of Said Aouita over 10,000 metres. This was at Oslo on 5 July and the Moroccan won as he pleased in 27:26.11 from Mark Nenow of USA (27:28.80), Salvatore Antibo and Stefano Mei, both of Italy, and 36-year-old Martti Vainio, reinstated to compete after the disqualification he suffered in 1984. When the race was over Aouita, hampered by a sore ankle, said: "If I had to assign values to races I'd say that the 1500 is the greatest, the most beautiful of distances, the 5000 is the toughest and the 10,000 is the easiest. No, I must persist: the 10,000 is nothing at all". Well, that probably explains why he did not try the 10,000 again.

On 6 August at La Coruña the Moroccan ace came dangerously close to his own 5000 metre record with an excellent 13:00.86. His nearest rival, Antonio Leitao of Portugal, finished in 13:16.02.

1986 marked the beginning of Cova's decline, yet his first defeat in a big championship race over 10,000 metres curiously coincided with the brightest day in the annals of Italian distance running. This was at the European Championships at Stuttgart in August, but a warning of things to come had been served near the end June at the Italian Championships in Cesenatico, when Stefano Mei won the 5000 metres in 13:36.73, with Antibo and Cova next in that order. However, things seemed to change in the Zurich meet (13 August) when the big kicker was again on tops, winning the 5000 in 13:15.86, just ahead of Pierre Délèze of Switzerland (13:16.00) and Mei (13:16.28).

At the Europeans the 10,000 metre title was awarded on 26 August. During the race Cova was aptly flanked by his team-mates Stefano Mei and Salvatore Antibo. This trio took command with 600 metres to go. Down the backstretch of the final lap tall Mei forged ahead of Cova and for once the latter was beaten at his own game as his 56.8 for the last 400 metres definitely paled vis-à-vis Mei's 55.2. Antibo was good enough to stave off the attack of Sweden's Mats Erixon and took third. The first 5000 was covered in 14:13.74, the second in 13:43.05. This was the first 1-2-3 by one and the same country in the annals of track events at the European Championships. Curiously enough, such a record was equalled two days later when Sebastian Coe, Tom McKean and Steve Cram did the same for Great Britain in the 800 metres.

Stefano Mei (born at La Spezia on 3 February 1963; 1.82 m. / 66 kg.), a precocious talent if ever there was one, finished 8th in the 3000 metres at the European Junior Championships in 1979, when barely 16. He improved to 4th in the 1981 edition of the same meet. After dwelling for the most part in the 1500 metres (1982 Europeans, 1983 Worlds and 1984 Olympics, never going beyond the semifinals) with times constantly in the 3:36/3:37 range, he began to pay more attention to the 5000, with 13:29.61 in 1984 and 13:21.05 in '85. In the latter year he tried the 10,000 for the first time: 30:14.72. In the summer of 1986 he improved to 27:43.97 in placing fourth in the Oslo race won by Aouita.

Details of the Stuttgart race:

Stuttgart, 26 August 1986 – 10,000 metres: 1.Stefano Mei (Ita) 27:56.79, 2.Alberto Cova (Ita) 27:57.93, 3.Salvatore Antibo 28:00.25, 4.Mats Erixon (Swe) 28:01.50, 5.Domingos Castro (Por) 28:01.62, 6.John Treacy (Ire) 28:04.10, 7.Martti Vainio (Fin) 28:08.72, 8.Jean-Louis Prianon (Fra) 28:12.29...... DNF: Hansjörg Kunze (GDR) (He was spiked).

The 5000 metres was in two rounds: heats on the 28th of August, final on the 31st. The favourites went through the prelims without hitches, but in the decisive race only one of the three Italians, Stefano Mei, managed to reach the podium again. And he too had to bow to a better "sprinter" in the closing stage. Jack Buckner of Great Britain, 24, ran the last 400 metres in 56.2, as opposed to Mei's 57.4. The last kilometre took only 2:28. Details:

Stuttgart, 31 August 1986 – 5000 metres: 1.Jack Buckner (GB) 13:10.15, 2.Stefano Mei (Ita) 13:11.57, 3.Tim Hutchings (GB) 13:12.88, 4.Yevgeni Ignatov (Bul) 13:13.15, 5.Antonio Leitao (Por) 13:17.67, 6.Martti Vainio (Fin) 13:22.67, 7.Pierre Délèze (Swi) 13:28.80, 8.Alberto Cova Ita) 13:35.86 .... DNF: Steve Ovett (GB), Markus Ryffel (Swi).

Prior to the Europeans, another classic had been heavily damaged by one more politically inspired boycott. In the Commonwealth Games, held at Edinburgh in July, no less than 32 countries stayed away as a protest against the Apartheid policies of South Africa. Although deprived of many talents, especially from Africa, the distance events offered good competition. On 26 July Jon Solly of England won the 10,000 metres in 27:57.42 from Steve Binns, also of England (27:58.01) and Steve Jones of Wales (28:02.48). On 31 July miler Steve Ovett used his speed to good advantage to win in 13:24.11 from Jack Buckner (13:25.87) and Tim Hutchings (13:26.84), while veteran John Walker was fifth. It should be noted that 23-year-old Solly had done even better clock-wise in winning the AAA title in 27:51.76. He did not run in the Europeans.

Said Aouita was once again the dominant figure of the Grand Prix circus. He twice threatened Henry Rono's world record for the 3000 metres with 7:32.54 at Zurich on 13 August and 7:32.23 at Cologne four days later. In the last meet of the series in Rome on 10 September he won the 5000 metres in 13:13.13, outsprinting Mei (13:14.29) and Sydney Maree of USA (13:14.62). "Track & Field News" World Ranking for 1986 had Aouita first in both classic distances. He ran five races at 5000 metres and one at 10.000 and won them all. Second at the longer distance was Mark Nenow of USA, who had to his credit the year's fastest time, 27:20.56 (Brussels, 5 September).

In 1987 the Italian phalanx was reduced as a result of tendon problems necessitating surgery for both Cova and Mei. Antibo had a relatively indifferent season. To make up for these failures at least in part there came another "azzurro", Francesco Panetta (born at Siderno Marina, Reggio Calabria, on 10 June 1963; 1.72 m. / 63 kg.), who was coached, just like Cova, by Giorgio Rondelli. He alternated flat events with the steeplechase: in the latter he could point to a second place at the 1986 European Championships in Stuttgart. His best 10,000 metre time up to then was 27:44.67 (1985). On the eve of the 1987 World Championships he boldly decided to enter both events. He went to Rome with a bright credential: a new Italian record of 27:26.95, set on 30 June at Stockholm, which was to remain the fastest time of the year: This was an impressive performance, with Mark Nenow a distant second (27:48.94) and Cova a poor 9th.

The no.1 runner at 5000 metres was once again the incomparable Aouita. He first stole the headlines with a best-on-record time for the 2 miles: 8:13.45 at Turin on 28 May. Statisticians remembered a faster time though: 8:13.2 by Emiel Puttemans in an indoor meet at Berlin in 1973.

Aouita collected another world mark on 16 July in Paris: 4:50.81 for 2000 metres. Then he came to Rome for the Golden Gala on 22 July, with a precise aim in mind: break the 13-min. barrier in the 5000 metres. Weather conditions that evening (28° C., humidity 80%) did not seem conducive to fast times. Aouita had two friends from the Maghreb area as his "aids-de-camp": first his countryman Brahim Boutayeb, then Fethi Baccouche of Tunisia. The latter reached 3000 metres in 7:46.37. Said did the rest, covering the last two kilometres in 5:12 and the last 400 in 57.4. This allowed him to finish in 12:58.39. Forty-five years after Hägg's first sub-14 min. mark, another barrier was thus broken. A good runner like Sydney Maree, second, was left more than 26 seconds behind. Said Maree after the race: "Aouita just defies all logic. He's determined, he's prepared and he's willing to suffer. His range is what really does it for him. In my view, he is the best of all time". Details: Rome, 22 July 1987: 5000 metres: 1.Said Aouita (Mor) 12:58.39, 2.Sydney Maree (USA) 13:24.97, 3.Ezequiel Canario (Por) 13:39.60..... DNF: Brahim Boutayeb (Mor) and Fethi Baccouche (Tun).

Kilometre fractions:

1000 m	2:35.35	
2000 m	5:13.03	(2:37.68)
3000 m	7:46.37	(2:33.34)
4000 m	10:26.05	(2:39.68)
5000 m	12:58.39	(2:32.34)

All this happened while Aouita still held the world's 1500 metre record (3:29.46 in 1985). Obviously, he looked like an odds-on favourite for the 5000 metre crown at the forthcoming World Championships, still at Rome's Stadio Olimpico. But first came the 10,000 metres, which was wide open. At the last moment the organizers managed to do away with the preliminary round, which played into Panetta's hands as he planned to run both this and the steeplechase. But in his first try the Italian ran into a Kenyan then at the peak of his condition, Paul Kipkoech (born at Kapsabet on 6 January 1963; 1.73 m. / 58 kg.). This man could point to notable achievements: from 9th at the 1983 Worlds to 5th in the 1984 Olympics, always in the 5000 metres, then twice second in the World Cross-Country Championships (1985 and '87). He had PB's of 13:14.40 (1984) and 27:43.31 (1986). He came to Rome with seemingly modest seasonal credentials: 28:20.5 at the Kenya Trials and 28:34.77 at the African Games. However, both meets were at high altitude, hence in rarefied atmosphere, a negative factor in the domain of aerobic running. It was by then a known fact that runners who were born and brought up under such conditions could later find it easier to perform at or near sea level. Quite a few Europeans and Americans had developed a habit of training at high altitude in preparation for big meets to be held in the plains.

At the Worlds the 10,000 metre race was featured by a relatively slow pace in the first half (14:13.07), with Arturo Barrios of Mexico in the lead. Then Kipkoech surged ahead and things began to liven up. One by one his rivals lost contact. Panetta was the last to do so, with about 3 kilometres to go. The Kenyan went on to win easily in 27:38.63. The trailers were partly misled by an overeager lap-counter and Hansjörg Kunze put on a dazzling sprint down the stretch to the bell, only to realize soon afterwards that he still had a lap to go. In the meantime Panetta had moved to second, a position he held to the end. The winner proved the very model of humility at the press conference. To interviewers who wondered if he might possibly become more talkative, he simply replied: "I'm just not used to situations like this". In 1988 he was again second in the World Cross-Country Championship. In later years recurrent bouts of malaria precluded what might have been a longer winning spell. Tuberculosis put a premature end to his life: he passed away on 13 March 1995, aged 32.

Page 133

John Ngugi (Kenya) leads from team-mate Paul Kipkoech in the 1988 World Cross-Country Championships at Auckland. They finished 1st and 2nd in that order. Both also won "global" titles on the track. Kipkoech died in 1995, aged 32.

His fantastic second half in Rome (13:25.56) will be remembered. (Panetta was able to win another medal, this one gold, in the 3000 metre steeplechase six days later). Details:

Rome, 30 August 1987 – 10,000 metres: 1.Paul Kipkoech (Ken) 27:38.63, 2.Francesco Panetta (Ita) 27:48.98, 3.Hansjörg Kunze (GDR) 27:50.37, 4.Arturo Barrios (Mex) 27:59.66, 5.Steve Binns (GB) 28:03.08, 6.Martin Vrábel (Cze) 28:05.59, 7.Spyros Andropoulos (Gre) 28:07.17, 8.Steve Plasencia (USA) 28:11.38.... DNF: Martti Vainio (Fin).

The 5000 metre final was not a particularly exciting race. Aouita, hampered by an injury in August, waited for others to set the pace. His rivals, overwhelmed by his reputation as world record holder, expected just the same from him. With Aouita constantly looking around to watch his opponents, it looked as if he was saying: "Please keep quiet because I want to win". The result of this "waiting game" was a slow race, with a 2:50 first lap. The tempo picked up later, but only a little. Near the end of it, Aouita used his superior speed to full advantage, covering the last 400 metres in 53.2 and the last 200 in 26.0. He won easily from Domingos Castro and Jack Buckner. His final time was actually slower than Kipkoech's second half in the 10,000 metres! Among the "also ran" were such prominent athletes as milers Steve Ovett and Sydney Maree, and cross-country "king" John Ngugi of Kenya, who finished tenth, eleventh and twelfth respectively. Details:

Rome, 6 September 1987 – 5000 metres: 1. Said Aouita (Mor) 13:26.44, 2.Domingos Castro (Por) 13:27.59, 3.Jack Buckner (GB) 13:27.74, 4.Pierre Délèze (Swi) 13:28.06, 5.Vincent Rousseau (Bel) 13:28.56, 6.Yevgeni Ignatov (Bul) 13:29.08, 7.Tim Hutchings (GB) 13:30.01, 8.Dionisio Castro (Por) 13:30.94.

After yet another superlative season, Aouita could look back to a fantastic sequence: 44 consecutive victories over the past 26 months at distances ranging from 800 to 10,000 metres ! As if he was looking for a possible defeat, he went to Latakia, Syria, for the Mediterranean Games and elected to run the 3000 metre steeplechase. He improved on his personal best but lost to Alessandro Lambruschini of Italy, one of the world's best harriers – 8:21.92 to 8:19.72. Aouita had last tried that event as a junior in 1979 (8:40.2). In 1987 Aouita ran five 5000 metre races and won them all, thus confirming his mastery of the event.

Head and legs

About ten years after his halcyon days as a distance runner, I got a chance to talk to Alberto Cova again. (In 1994 he became a member of the Italian Parliament in the ranks of "Forza Italia"). Ever ready to exchange views on his favourite sport and as discreet in behaviour as he once was in his running tactics, he readily answered some questions.

Q – How do you view your athletic career in retrospect? With your excellent triple in the 10,000 metres (1982 Europeans, 1983 Worlds and 1984 Olympics) you won practically everything at this distance. Did you really have a preference for the '10' vis-à-vis the '5' ?

A - No. Frankly speaking, I wish I had been successful in the 5000 metres as I was at the longer distance. (Note – He actually was, but only clock-wise: his PB of 13:10.06 is worth just a little more than his 27:37.59, according to the latest IAAF Scoring Table). In those days, however, there were some very good milers in the 5000 metre department and competition was extremely tough. My coach Giorgio Rondelli and I came to such a conclusion after the final of the 1981 European Cup at Lille, where I placed fifth in the 5000. Further analyses confirmed that the '10' were better suited to my characteristics as a runner.

Q – In the opinion of many it is more important, and more gratifying, to win major titles rather than break world records. In this respect, how do you view cases like those of Ron Clarke, Dave Bedford and Fernando Mamede, all very clever in collecting records but inexplicably unable to do themselves justice in big-time competition?

A - I think such cases can only be connected with psychological factors. Apparently no one of them was able to face big-time competition with a cool-headed approach. As for my case, I readily admit that I mostly relied on a sudden change of gear in the conclusive stage of the race. I don't think I had the potential to break world records. Maybe I did not have them in my head either. Be it as it may, I am well satisfied with what I was able to reap in athletics.

Q – Looking at the years that lie ahead, do you think Europe may be able to field distance men likely to challenge the all-conquering Africans? Or do you think that the case of Dieter Baumann of Germany (1992 Olympic champion in the 5000 metres) is likely to remain an exception for a long time to come?

A - I hope not. Here in Europe there are no doubt prospects who can live up to the task, although not as many as in Africa. In Italy, for example, we have some promising talents, but in our present-day society it is not easy to find young men willing to put in years and years, perhaps a decade, of work, sweat and tears in order to reach the top. Even though prizes at stake are a lot higher than they were ten years ago. Then I think our young men should not stay away from international competition. Of course it is important to have definite goals and go after them earnestly.

The African Wave rose spectacularly during the Olympic year 1988, no matter if Said Aouita changed direction and chose the 800 metres as his "horse" for the Seoul rendezvous. Despite a far from perfect physical condition, the Moroccan ran that distance in 1:43.86 and later managed to win a bronze medal at the Games.

The pre-Olympic season seemed to augur well for European distance men. Eamonn Martin of Great Britain, a tall man who was working as a testing engineer at Ford Motors, had been signalled as a possible comer as early as 1983 when he ran 5000 metres in 13:20.94. Persistent tendon trouble had delayed his further progress though. He finally had his day at Oslo on 2 July 1988, when he won a classy 10,000 metre race with a new British record of 27:23.06, after covering the last 400 in 56.4. Salvatore Antibo of Italy was a fairly close second in 27:24.79, which time allowed him to succeed Panetta as Italian record holder. Arturo Barrios of Mexico was third in 27:25.07, followed by veteran Hansjörg Kunze (27:26.00) and Brahim Boutayeb (27:39.12), a young Moroccan.

The fastest 5000 metre time of pre-Olympic weeks was 13:15.62 by José Regalo of Portugal (Brussels, 19 August). One of the

Ngugi, a great harrier, did himself justice on the track at least once, winning the 5000 metres at the 1988 Olympics in Seoul.

135

most talked-of candidates was John Ngugi of Kenya (born at Nyahururu on 10 May 1962; 1.78 m. / 62 kg.), a member of the Kikuyu tribe who had great credentials as a harrier for his three consecutive victories at the World Cross-Country Championships (1986-87-88). With his long, galloping strides he surely seemed more at ease on up-and-down slopes than on perfectly flat surfaces. As a matter of fact this impression was never denied. In later years he brought to five his collection of World Cross-Country titles, thanks to his victories in 1989 and '92. But he allowed himself one bright exception, and that was at the Seoul Olympics. His best 5000 metre time going into that meet was 13:17.95.

African domination in the Games was first assured by a Moroccan, Moulay Brahim Boutayeb (born at Khemisset on 15 August 1967; 1.78 m. / 61 kg.), then affiliated to a flourishing Spanish club, Larios. He had made the headlines in 1987 with such times as 13:17.47 and 28:40.34. His 10,000 metre best in 1988 prior to the Seoul Games was 27:39.12 in finishing fifth at Oslo, as previously related. The fastest man in the Olympic heats (23 September) was Kipkemboi Kimeli of Kenya with 28:00.39. Boutayeb won his own heat in 28:17.61. The best European at this distance seemed to be Salvatore Antibo, who followed up his Italian 10,000 metre record at Oslo (27:24.79) with a good 13:16.1 in the 5000 metres. He went through the Seoul prelims easily, while Alberto Cova, ostensibly over the hill, was eliminated.

In the final (26 September) Antibo boldly put his opponents to test in the very first lap (62.2). He injected another fast one (62.4) a few laps later and this discouraged all except three of his rivals: Moses Tanui and Kipkemboi Kimeli of Kenya, plus a runner "who looked like Aouita", Boutayeb. Eamonn Martin dropped out just after the halfway mark. At that stage Kimeli was in the lead (13:35.32), with Boutayeb in his wake, while Tanui and Antibo followed not far behind. When the Moroccan took command of the operation early in the second half, nobody was able to answer. He slowed down a bit in the last lap (65.2) but won by a comfortable margin. Antibo closed fast to take

second ahead of Kimeli. The winner, a lanky figure with the green Moroccan shirt, actually looked to casual observers like a replica of the great Said. He was in any case the youngest and fastest Olympic 10,000 metre champ ever. Details:
Seoul, 26 September 1988 – 10,000 metres: 1.Brahim Boutayeb (Mor) 27:21.46, 2.Salvatore Antibo (Ita) 27:23.55, 3.Kipkemboi Kimeli (Ken) 27:25.16, 4.Jean-Louis Prianon (Fra) 27:36.43, 5.Arturo Barrios (Mex) 27:39.32, 6.Hansjörg Kunze (GDR) 27:39.35, 7.Paul Arpin (Fra) 27:39.36, 8.Moses Tanui (Ken) 27:47.23 ...... DNF: Eamonn Martin.

Some of these runners were bold enough to compete also in the 5000 metres, but a schedule implying three rounds between 27 September and 1 October was very tough indeed. Antibo did not survive the semi-finals. Martin, Eamonn Coghlan and Vincent Rousseau of Belgium also failed to make the final. In the decisive race (1 October) Ngugi electrified spectators and terrified most of his rivals just before the end of the first kilometre when he moved up from the rear and injected a terrific 57.8 lap. His second kilometre was a fast 2:32.2 and by then he was well in the lead - almost a replica of the Murray Halberg operation at the 1960 Olympics, except that Ngugi's "fatal injection" came even earlier. The Kenyan went on and on with his galloping stride. He closed with a 60.3 last lap and a final time of 13:11.70, easily his best ever. Way behind him, three Europeans engaged a furious battle for second: Dieter Baumann of Germany, 23, outsprinted Kunze and Castro. Details:
Seoul, 1 October 1988 – 5000 metres: 1.John Ngugi (Ken) 13:11.70, 2.Dieter Baumann (FRG) 13:15.52, 3. Hansjörg Kunze (GDR) 13:15.73, 4.Domingos Castro (Por) 13:16.09, 5.Sydney Maree (USA) 13:23.69, 6.Jack Buckner (GB) 13:23.85, 7.Stefano Mei (Ita) 13:26.17, 8.Yevgeni Ignatov (Bul) 13:26.41.

Both Ngugi and Boutayeb won Olympic gold with the fastest time of the year in their respective events. But Said Aouita was once again first in the more lucrative overall ranking of the Grand Prix series, thanks to his feats in the middle distances. The Moroccan returned to the 5000 metres in 1989 and punctually regained his leadership of the period 1984-87. He did suffer a defeat though, his first at this distance since 1979, at the hands of a little Kenyan, Yobes Ondieki. It happened at Seville on 20 June and Ondieki won by a wide margin - 13:12.12 to 13:23.96. In fairness to Aouita it should be said that earlier in the year he picked up a virus in Brazil and spent four weeks in bed. He resumed training less than a week before the Seville race. Ondieki, at any rate, went on to record a creditable 13:04.24 at Oslo on 1 July, winning easily from Jack Buckner (13:17.82).

Two Italians, Salvatore Antibo and Francesco Panetta, played prominent rôles in 1989. The latter was an excellent steeplechaser, 1987 world champion in this event, of which he sometimes said jokingly: "I'd be fond of the event if it weren't for the barriers". Now he wanted to concentrate on the flat route. The two "azzurri" had a big day at the World Games in Helsinki on 29 June. Antibo was admittedly aiming at the world record (27:13.81 by Fernando Mamede). Things did not go exactly as he expected though: apart for some help given him in the early goings by Barnabas Korir of Kenya, the Italian was on his own for over half the race. He reached the halfway mark in 13:34.4, a swift pace he could not maintain till the end. A second half in 13:42.1 allowed him no better than 27:16.50, still history's second best ever and, of course, a new Italian record. Addis Abebe of Ethiopia was second (27:17.82) and Panetta third (27:24.16, a new PB). Hammou Boutayeb of Morocco took fourth (27:50.04). Back in ninth place, Mamede (28:17.22), lucky for keeping his record. Boutayeb, said to be 33, provided a nice example of an athlete suddenly emerging at such a ripe age. He had been talked into taking up athletics by Said Aouita.

The central part of the season offered two world records. On 20 August at Cologne it was Aouita's turn again. He succeeded Henry Rono as holder of the 3000 metre mark with a scintillating 7:29.45, leaving Dieter Baumann (7:40.37) and Sydney Mareee (7:40.67) far behind. The Moroccan ace was helped by hares in the first two kilometres (2:31.53 and 2:30.37) then took command and covered the last kilometre in 2:27.55.

The other global mark was credited to Arturo Barrios (born in Mexico City on 12 December 1963; 1.74 m. / 60 kg.), then living in USA, where he took a degree in mechanical engineering. He had a solid reputation as a road runner and his record in that department included a 27:41 for 10,000 metres at Phoenix, Arizona, in 1986 – best on record for a loop course. But he also had excellent credentials on the track: fourth at the 1987 World Championships and fifth at the 1988 Olympics, always over 10,000 metres. His day of glory was at Berlin on 18 August 1989 when he attacked Mamede's world record for the distance. He and his Polish coach Tadeusz Kepka had mapped out a plan, and two Americans, Doug Padilla and Steve Plasencia, were to cooperate with them. The latter led Barrios at the halfway point in 13:32.39: that was a huge advantage vis-à-vis Mamede's pace. Once on his own, Barrios managed to save at least part of that to finish in 27:08.23. Details:

Berlin, 18 August 1989 – 10,000 metres:
1.Arturo Barrios (Mex) 27:08.23, 2.Kipkemboi Kimeli (Ken) 27:52.28, 3.Francesco Panetta (Ita) 28:06.71, 4.Andy Bristow (GB) 28:28.04.

Kilometre fractions:

1000 m	2:42.41	
2000 m	5:25.42	(2:43.01)
3000 m	8:08.10	(2:42.68)
4000 m	10:49.91	(2:41.81)
5000 m	13:32.39	(2:42.48)
6000 m	16:15.52	(2:43.13)
7000 m	19:01.14	(2:45.62)
8000 m	21:47.01	(2:45.87)
9000 m	24:32.56	(2:45.55)
10,000 m	27:08.23	(2:35.67)

Barrios ran the last 400 metres in 59.5.

The previous month in London, Barrios had lowered his 5000 metre best to 13:07.79. Yet he was no match for Said Aouita when they met over that distance in the final of the Grand Prix at Monaco (1 September). The Moroccan won as he pleased, 13:06.36 to 13:21.37.
Salvatore Antibo closed his 1989 account on brilliant notes. At Brussels on 25 August he ran the 10,000 metres in 27:27.66. Only

two days later at Rieti he suffered his only defeat of the year over 5000 metres as Brahim Boutayeb nosed him out, 13:16.52 to 13:17.03. Barrios was in the race too but had to be content with fourth (13:19.37). The Mexican did not compete in the most significant test of the year – the World Cup at Barcelona early in September. Too bad because his duel with Antibo in the "10" would have been a major attraction. As it was, the Italian outsprinted Addis Abebe of Ethiopia, 28:05.26 to 28:06.43, at the end of a typically slow "Cup race". Antonio Prieto of Spain was third (28:07.42). This was on 8 September. Two days later Said Aouita won a similar race over 5000 metres in 13:23.14. All he needed to vanquish his rivals was a 55.8 last lap. Next came John Doherty (Ire/Eur) 13:25.39, José Luis Carreira (Spa) 13:25.94 and Jack Buckner (GB) 13:26.89.

This earned Said Aouita his third victory in

A versatile talent

Said Aouita can easily be rated as one of the most versatile runners of all time. In modern times no one has been able to compete with the best in the world at distances ranging from 800 to 10,000 metres – as he did in the second half of the Eighties. Virtually perfect as a running machine, he appeared to some observers more difficult to define as to character and personality. I got a chance to talk to him at some length in the spring of 1986, when he lived in Siena, in the heart of Tuscany. Besides Arab, his mother tongue, Aouita was then fluent in French and also spoke some English, Spanish and Italian. Here are excerpts of said interview.

Q – How is the Aouita who races on the track similar to the Aouita off the track? How is he different?

A - No one should confuse Aouita the runner with the Aouita off the track. They are fundamentally different; I guess that's just part of the sport as I see it. However, while gathering more and more experience as an athlete, my mentality has been influenced accordingly. Very positively, I'd say. As a person, I feel like a pure Moroccan and a pure Arab. My character leads me to solve my problems independently, with no excessive attachment to other people's advice.

Q – Is it true that basically you coach yourself?

A - Yes, I've never had a coach. But I also never let myself be influenced or guided by the methods of other athletes. "Jamais" (never).

Q - What can you tell us about your most dangerous rivals? (At the time he preferably concentrated on the 1500 metres/1 mile).

A - Steve Cram "c'est un bon athlete". So are Seb Coe, Sydney Maree and Alberto Cova – good athletes whom I respect to the fullest. But there also are athletes "qui ne sont pas bien" – they are not normal. They use "other things" to enhance their performance. I don't like to talk about them at all.

Q – What have the reactions to your successes been like from the people of Morocco, especially after your Olympic win in 1984 and your world records?

A – The people have been very kind to me, particularly His Majesty King Hassan II. He has helped me and Nawal El Moutawakel (women's 400 metre hurdles champion at the 1984 Olympics) a great deal, assuring us a comfortable life and providing the best conditions possible for our training. He protects and loves us as if we were his own children.

Q – You have spoken in the past of how much you do for your country. Why, then, don't you live and train in Morocco?

A – I live and train in Morocco during the winter. But I come to Siena to tune up for competition. Here I am in close contact with the rest of Europe- and that is where most of the best action takes place.

PS. In the early Nineties Aouita has been doing useful work for "Fédération Royale Marocaine d'Athlétisme".

Page 141

1993 World Championships in Stuttgart:, 10,000 metres: Moses Tanui (Kenya) in second place with shoe missing. He lost to Haile Gebrselassie (Ethiopia).

the Overall Grand Prix. In "Track & Field News" World Ranking the Moroccan was an easy first in the 5000 metres. Barrios edged Antibo in the 10,000: both undefeated, the former's world record was the decisive factor.

After seven years (1983 through '89) at the highest international levels, the great Aouita inevitably began to show signs of impending decline. As it often happens, this trend became apparent after recurrent tendon injuries. In the meantime, however, other talents were emerging in Morocco. Brahim Boutayeb was of course one. Another consistent and highly competitive performer was Khalid Skah . Veteran Hammou Boutayeb had a good season in 1990 and a young athlete, Mohamed Issangar, showed good promise. All of this made up at least in part for the decline of the incomparable Aouita.

1990 opened with the Commonwealth Games, which were held at Auckland, New Zealand. The 10,000 metre title (27 January) went to veteran Eamonn Martin of England, who used a fine burst of speed over the last half-lap (25.8) to win in 28:08.57 from Moses Tanui of Kenya (28:11.56) and Paul Williams of Canada (28:12.71). Out of the ever impressive Kenyan reservoir there came a 17-year-old boy, Joseph Kibor, who was fifth in 28:27.56. In the 5000 metres (1 February) a more famous Kenyan, Olympic champion John Ngugi, had to surrender to an outsider, Andre Lloyd of Australia, by a tantalizing margin – 13:24.94 to 13:24.86. Third went to Ian Hamer of Wales (13:25.63). Well-known runners like Moses Tanui (5th), Yobes Ondieki (9th) and Jack Buckner (12th) were involved in separate falls early in the race.

The African wave continued to rise at a relentless pace, yet the best distance man of 1990 was Salvatore Antibo of Italy (born at Altofonte, Palermo, on 7 February 1962; 1.70 m. / 59 kg.), a precocious talent who first emerged at 19, finishing second in the 5000 metres at the 1981 European Junior Championships. A year later he was sixth over 10,000 metres at the European Championships. His performances in subsequent years have been recounted already. He was at his best in 1990, when he had an

immaculate record: nine races at 5000 metres and three at 10,000, with no defeats. He opened his international account at Oslo on 14 July with an attempt to break Arturo Barrios' 10,000 metre record. He expected to receive some help from veteran Hammou Boutayeb, but his hopes soon vanished as the Moroccan himself elected to take refuge in a waiting race. The Italian tried to speed things up, notably with a fifth kilometre in 2:35.8, Boutayeb stayed in his wake till the end though and Antibo had to be content with a narrow victory – 27:25.16 to 27:25.48. Thierry Pantel of France was third (27:31.16). Four days later Antibo competed in the classic Golden Gala, which for once was not held at its normal venue, Rome's Stadio Olimpico (then being refurbished for the forthcoming World Soccer Cup) but in Bologna. He ran a great 5000 metres: after trailing Jonas Koech of Kenya in the first 2400, he forged ahead and a last kilometre in 2:34.03 plus a last lap in 57.8 carried him home in 13:05.59, a new Italian record. He won by a street from Cyrille Laventure of France (13:23.92) and Stefano Mei (13:25.59). Antibo thus rose to no.5 on the All Time World List. His mark was to remain the fastest of 1990, no matter if Yobes Ondieki came dangerously close to it when he did 13:05.60 at Brussels on 10 August.

Arturo Barrios returned to Berlin on 17 August, hoping to find the same inspiration that led him to a world record for 10,000 metres in 1989. But this time he could do no better than 27:18.22, which at any rate remained the fastest time of the year.

The European Championships were held at Split, Yugoslavia, a country then threatened by incoming political and military bouleverse-ments. Salvatore Antibo was at the peak of his condition and scored an impressive 5000/10,000 double, a trick last turned by Finland's Juha Väätäinen in 1971. At the longer distance (27 August) he played "à la Kuts", i.e. running away from the rest at an early stage. He ran the first 800 metres in 2:06.3 – that was enough to discourage the opposition. He reached the half-way mark in 13:39.74, then continued to plod on in splendid isolation. He faded a bit near the end but still managed to win by a wide mar-gin in 27:41.27. Then came the 5000

metres: heats on 30 August and final on 1 September. The latter provided drama from the very beginning. There was a collision between Antibo and Marcus O'Sullivan of Ireland and both fell. The former hit the curb yet he did not panic (maybe sometime some-where he had seen a film of Lasse Viren's similar adventure at the 1972 Olympics….). The Irishman was first to recover, but dropped out later in the race. Antibo bided his time but eventually rejoined the leading pack a lap later. In the closing stage he was involved in a furious battle with Gary Staines of Great Britain and Dionisio Castro of Portugal (a twin of Domingos, mentioned earlier in the text). In the backstretch of the final lap the Italian dangerously found his way by bolting between the two. In doing so he sent Castro to the infield. Then he shot ahead of Staines and maintained a narrow lead till the end, after covering the last 200 metres in 26.76. He was somehow repaid for his mishap in the early stage as the judges did not deem it advisable to penalize him for pushing Castro in the last lap. The Portuguese recovered quickly and had a strong finish, but he missed third and the bronze medal by a narrow margin. Details:

Split, 27 August 1990 – 10,000 metres: 1.Salvatore Antibo (Ita) 27:41.27, 2.Are Nakkim (Nor) 28:04.04, 3.Stefano Mei (Ita) 28:04.46, 4.Antonio Prieto (Spa) 28:05.35, 5.Richard Nerurkar (GB) 28:07.81, 6. José Manuel Albentosa (Spa) 28:11.00, 7.Ezequiel Canario (Por) 28:11.95, 8.Martin ten Kate (Hol) 28:12.53.

Split, 1 September 1990 – 5000 metres: 1.Salvatore Antibo (Ita) 13:22.00, 2.Gary Staines (GB) 13:22.45, 3.Slawomir Majusiak (Pol) 13:22.92, 4.Dionisio Castro (Por) 13:23.99, 5.Jonny Danielson (Swe) 13:24.16, 6.Risto Ulmala (Fin) 13:25.08, 7.Stefano Mei (Ita) 13:27.13, 8.Harri Hänninen (Fin) 13:28.22, …. 13.Eamonn Martin (GB) 13:34.62.

In "Track & Field News" World Ranking Antibo earned first place in both events.

The opening stage of 1991 was marked by a new world record for 1-hour running. A French meet promoter put together a classy field on 30 March at La Flèche near Le Mans. Arturo Barrios, who undoubtedly was

Yobes Ondieki (Kenya) breaks the 27-minute barrier in the 10,000 metres at the Bislett Games in Oslo, 1993.
Time: 26:58.38.

143

at his best in racing against the clock, received some assistance from Vincent Rousseau of Belgium in the first 10 kilometres, then went on in his solitary journey till the fateful hour, during which he covered 21,101 kilometres. He thus eclipsed Jos Hermens' 15-year-old world record (20,944 km:). While enroute the Mexican was timed in 56:55.6 for 20,000 metres, another world record (with 10,000 metre halves of 28:19.8 and 28:35.8). It should be noted that Barrios became the first man to run a half-marathon (21,097 km.) in less than 1 hour. In recent years the 1-hour record has seldom, if ever, been on the mind of leading distance runners. This obviously explains why Barrios' 1991 mark is still unsurpassed at the time of writing.

1991 is to be remembered as an important year in the history of long distance running as it provided the turning point in the balance of powers between Europe and Africa. That was when the so-called African Wave was definitely submerging the "Old Continent" in terms of both quality and quantity of leading marks. Kenya and Ethiopia, the driving forces, were joined by Morocco, Algeria, Tanzania and other countries. The 1991 World Championships in Tokyo were to put the seal on this reversal. Such a trend had been anticipated by the results of the World Cross-Country Championships, in which the last victory by a European dated from 1985 (Carlos Lopes of Portugal). From then on, Africa always supplied the winner, leaving to Europe only 2 of the18 medals at stake between 1986 and 1991 included!

The early fireworks of 1991 on the track were provided by a young Kenyan, Richard Chelimo (born at Kapyego near Kapcherop in the Marakwet district on 24 April 1972; 1.65 m. / 55 kg.). He first made the headlines at the 1990 World Junior Championships in Plovdiv, Bulgaria: first in the 10,000 metres in 28:18.57. He won from .... his younger brother Ismael Kirui (28:40.77), supposed to be only 15 at the time. Based in London for some time, he was very successful in cross-country running. He opened his 1991 account with an impressive double in the high altitude of Nairobi: 13:35.1 and 28:16.7 on consecu-

tive days. Then he came to Europe and on 25 June at Hengelo he ran 10,000 metres in 27:11.18 (first half in 13:32) – a new world junior record. He won easily from Hammou Boutayeb of Morocco (27:45.35). The young lion then bowed to a more mature performer, Moses Tanui, at the National Championships, were it only by a narrow margin – 28:08.7 to 28:07.5.

Moses Tanui (born in the Nandi district on 20 August 1965; 1.65 m. / 65 kg.) was, in fact, a better known quantity at the international level. Over 10,000 metres he progressed from 28:53.1 in 1987 to 27:40.59 in 1988, when he also finished eighth at the Seoul Olympics. He lived and trained in Italy as a member of a club coached by Prof. Gabriele Rosa, a physician from Brescia who ran a well-equipped sports medicine centre.

The powerful Kenya team had another excellent performer in Yobes Ondieki (born in the Kisii district on 21 February 1961; 1.70 m. / 55 kg.). While attending Iowa State University in USA in the mid-Eighties he earned a reputation as a cross-country runner and as a tough trainer. He later transferred to Albuquerque, New Mexico, where he could practice altitude training, of which he was a strong advocate. Early in 1990 he married Lisa Martin of Australia, one of the world's best marathoners. Ondieki was at his best in the 5000 metres, at which distance he progressed from 13:49.5 in 1982 to 13:04.24 in 1989, when as previously related he scored an upset victory over Said Aouita at Seville. In 1990 he ran the 1500 metres in 3:34.36, an excellent speed credential for a long distance runner. He showed further progress in 1991: on 5 August in Zurich he lowered his 5000 metre best to 13:01.82, annihilating a trio from Morocco: Skah (second in 13:19.18), Brahim and Hammou Boutayeb.

Salvatore Antibo went to Tokyo for the World Championships with good but non-winning credentials: 27:24.55 for 10,000 metres in Oslo (6 July), behind strong finisher Khalid Skah (27:23.29), and 13:10.10 for 5000 metres in Rome (17 July), losing to a klittle known Kenyan, Ibrahim Kinuthia (13:09.76). It is true, however, that in the Oslo race he beat among others Arturo Barrios and Addis Abebe, and in Rome he left behind Brahim Boutayeb and Richard Chelimo. On the eve of the Worlds "Track & Field News" picked Antibo for the 5,000 metres and Skah for the 10,000. Barrios had to stay away due to a foot injury.

In Tokyo 10,000 metre candidates had to go through heats (24 August) and final (26 August). All the favourites qualified without undue trouble, the fastest times being 28:23.28 by Skah in heat 1 and 28:23.77 by Abebe in heat 2. In the final young Chelimo fired things up by running laps 3 through 6 in 4:15, a seemingly foolish pace that earned him a sizable lead. At the half-way mark (13:30.3) he was about 2 seconds ahead of Barrios' pace in his world record race and had 20 metres on Tanui. The latter rejoined his young countryman near the seventh kilometre. Their nearest rival, Skah, was 50 metres back. The Moroccan, then living in Norway, was reputed to be almost unbeatable as a "finisseur" but had difficulties when the pace was hot throughout. His companion at that stage, Thomas Osano of Kenya, was not willing to help him close the gap that separated them from the leading (Kenyan) duo. Tanui eventually outsprinted Chelimo in the last lap (61.3 to 62.0) and won comfortably in 27:38.74. Skah gained ground considerably in the closing stage, yet he could do no better than third. Antibo, one of the pre-race favourites, was a dismal 20th in 28:52.41. In pre-Tokyo weeks he had been bothered by such diverse evils as muscular ailments, herpes and tracheitis. After 13 laps the European champion was third, some 40 metres behind the Kenyan fugitives, Tanui and Chelimo. Then he suffered a mental blackout that forced him to slow down to a dog trot for a while. He later admitted he had no clear remembrance of what happened to him in those fateful seconds. He finished like an automaton, i.e. moving without active intelligence. From a medical check-up it emerged that following an auto accident that befell him as a child he had suffered brain injuries which occasionally caused a state of mind known as "momentary absence". He well recovered from his Tokyo mishap but never regained his brilliant form of 1990. Details:

Tokyo, 26 August 1991 – 10,000 metres:
1.Moses Tanui (Ken) 27:38.74, 2.Richard Chelimo (Ken) 27:39.41, 3.Khalid Skah (Mor) 27:41.74, 4.Thomas Osano (Ken) 27:53.66, 5.Richard Nerurkar (GB) 27:57.14, 6.Aloÿs Nizigama (Bur) 28:03.03, 7.Mathias Ntawulikura (Rua) 28:10.38, 8.Hammou Boutayeb (Mor) 28:12.77.

In the 5000 metres (heats on 30 August, final on 1 September) something rather unusual happened. Yobes Ondieki killed the race very early, simply by injecting a second lap in 60 secs. Only Fita Bayissa of Ethiopia and Skah managed to stay in contention but not for long. At 3000 (7:46.1) Ondieki led by 60 metres and was actually ahead of Said Aouita's pace in his world record venture of 1987. Skah had a crisis, even greater than the one that had befallen him in the 10,000

Dieter Baumann (Germany) emerging the winner in a furious battle over 5000 metres at the 1992 Olympics in Barcelona.

metres. The courageous Ondieki faded considerably in the closing stage (last kilometre in 2:45.4). Young Bayissa could only get nearer but had to settle for second. Brahim Boutayeb, third, was followed by an up and coming German, Dieter Baumann. Antibo had wisely decided to stay away. The times were excellent in view of the warm (30° C.) humid weather. Said the winner about his bold tactics: "I was thinking many times that maybe this was a mistake, and I can't keep on till the end ...... I didn't know where the others were, because I didn't look back". Details:

Tokyo, 1 September 1991 – 5000 metres: 1.Yobes Ondieki (Ken) 13:14.45, 2.Fita Bayissa (Eti) 13:16.64, 3.Brahim Boutayeb (Mor) 13:22.70, 4.Dieter Baumann (Ger) 13:28.67, 5.Domingos Castro (Por) 13:28.88, 6.Khalid Skah (Mor) 13:32.90, 7.Risto Ulmala (Fin) 13:33.46, 8.Dionisio Castro (Por) 13:35.39.

The most notable happening of post-Tokyo meets was Dieter Baumann's victory over world champion Ondieki in a 3000 metres race at Cologne 7:33.91 to 7:34.74.

1991 was a triumphal year for Africa's distance runners. The following figures can aptly tell the tale. In the World Year Lists that continent had 11 of the top 20 in the 5000 metres and 13 of the top 20 in the 10,000. What is more, Africa won all six medals at stake in the World Championships.

Following the dismantling of USSR, in 1992 athletes from its republics combined for the last time to form a so-called Unified Team and competed under such a provisional banner at the Barcelona Olympics. Africa continued to rule the roost, yet a European managed to steal the show in at least one important race, the Olympic 5000 metre final at Barcelona. The man who turned the trick was Dieter Baumann of Germany (born at Klingenstein on 9 February 1965; 1.75 m. / 60 kg.), a photographer who was coached by his wife, Isabell Hozang. He first emerged in 1985 with 13:48.0 in the 5000 metres and I have already referred to his second place in the 5000 metres at the 1988 Seoul Olympics, well behind John Ngugi. He was good in the middle distances too, with PB's of 1:48.40 in the 800 metres and 3:33.54 in the 1500. He opened his account for the

Olympic season of 1992 on a high note, with 13:09.03 in the 5000 metres at Seville (6 June), all the more significant in view of the men he beat in a hectic finish: Skah (13:09.10), Ondieki (13:09.72) and Arturo Barrios (13:11.86). Three days later, at the Golden Gala in Rome, there was another mass finish. A relatively little known Welshman, Ian Hamer, 27, won the 5000 metres in 13:09.80 from a seemingly resurging Antibo (13:10.08), Rob Denmark (13:10.24) and Jack Buckner (13:10.47) both of Great Britain, Barrios (13:10.52) and Jonah Koech of Kenya (13:10.88). Six men wrapped up in just over a second!

This was only the start of a frantic season. The Oslo meet (4 July) offered further food for Olympic thought as Paul Bitok of Kenya won the 5000 metres from a redoubtable finisher like Khalid Skah – 13:08.89 to 13:09.74. In the same meet Fita Bayissa upset Richard Chelimo in the 10,000 – 27:14.26 to 27:15.53. The last pre-Olympic spark came from the untiring Ondieki, who lowered the world's seasonal best for 5000 metres to 13:03.58 (Lausanne, 8 July).

On the eve of the Games at Barcelona the field of possible winners was larger than it had ever been in he past. Chief victim of the 10,000 metre prelims (31 July) was Eamonn Martin, not new to similar mishaps though. The final three days later turned out to be a controversial affair, one of those races rabid track fans are apt to remember and discuss again and again. In the early stages the pace was all but scorching. Chelimo led at the halfway mark in 13:53.66. By then Barrios and Antibo had already lost contact. The same happened shortly afterwards to Tanui, Bayissa and Abebe. With three kilometres to go Chelimo and Skah were left alone to battle it out. The Moroccan took the lead after 19 laps, only to inject a sleep-denying pace with a 69.1 lap. A while later he moved to lane 2 and invited Chelimo to pass on the inside. An expert and witty observer said it looked as if Skah might have said to his Kenyan companion: "I'd like you to meet a friend of mine". Because right in front of them, waiting to be lapped, was bolding Hammou Boutayeb of Morocco. What followed was a sour intermezzo, with Boutayeb

Closing stage of a controversial 10,000 metre race at the 1992 Olympics in Barcelona. From left: Hammou Boutayeb (Morocco), a lapped runner, Richard Chelimo (Kenya) and Khalid Skah (Morocco), the eventual winner.

swinging out when Chelimo tried to pass and forcing the Kenyan to break his rhythm. Chelimo later had this to say: "He knocked me off balance, bumped me three times, and gave me a shot with his elbow". Boutayeb received a verbal caution, but in the meantime his countryman Skah went on to win with a 59.3 last lap, as opposed to Chelimo's 60.4. Many of us who saw the race interpreted that interlude as the interference of a third party, by then "hors jeu", in the Skah vs. Chelimo duel. Most probably, Boutayeb felt bound to act the way he did, and Chelimo, obviously frightened, was no longer in the mood to try hard till the end. Immediately after the race, while the crowd was still in a turmoil, Skah was disqualified. But he was reinstated as winner and Olympic champion when the Moroccan delegation appealed against the verdict. High officials simply pointed out to the fact that there were no rules against conspiracies. Maybe they thought that if there had been someone openly acting as an offender that was Boutayeb and not Skah. No doubt Chelimo was ostensibly harassed and damaged at a crucial stage, yet even under normal circumstances it is doubtful whether he could have beaten Skah, known as a strong finisher. Maybe the Kenyan had to blame himself for not imposing a faster pace throughout.

Antibo had to be content with fourth behind Addis Abebe. Following Skah's disqualification, the Italian was for a short time the recipient of a bronze medal. When he heard that the Moroccan had been reinstated, he simply commented: "I wouldn't be interested in a medal won on the judges' table. When I meet Skah, I'll simply offer him my congratulations".

Details:

Barcelona, 3 August 1992 – 10,000 metres: 1.Khalid Skah (Mor) 27:46.70, 2.Richard Chelimo (Ken) 27:47.72, 3.Addis Abebe (Eti) 28:00.07, 4.Salvatore Antibo (Ita) 28:11.39, 5.Arturo Barrios (Mex) 28:17.79, 6.German Silva (Mex) 28:20.19, 7.William Koech (Ken) 28:25.18, 8.Moses Tanui (Ken) 28:27.11. .... DNF: Hammou Boutayeb (Mor).

Khalid Skah (born at Midelt on 29 January 1967; 1.72 m. / 60 kg.) could look back to

an honourable career. In the 5000 metres he had progressed from 14:28.4 in 1986 all the way to 13:09.55 in 1990, when he ranked no.1 in the event at the Grand Prix. In the same year he tackled the 10,000 for the first time and a year later he surprisingly won a bronze medal at the World Championships in Tokyo. He earned fame thanks to his smashing victories in the World Cross-Country Championships (1990 and '91), baffling on both occasions powerful Kenyan cohorts. As previously hinted, he lived in Norway for the greater part of the year. Feared for his burning turn of speed in the closing stage, he could point to a 1500 metre best of 3:42.06 (1990).

At Barcelona the 5000 metre field also included some runners who had not competed at the longer distance: Kenyans Ondieki and Paul Bitok, a 22-year-old airman from the Nandi tribe, Brahim Boutayeb and Dieter Baumann, the only European who was given a chance against Africa's marvels. Antibo and Bayissa were among those who tried to "double", while Skah and Chelimo decided to stay away. Two Britons were the most notable victims of the heats (6 August): the declining Jack Buckner and Ian Hamer, shooting star of the Golden Gala. Baumann had the fastest time (13:20.82) in this preliminary round.

"I have always thought a European could run as well as an African"

The final two days later was shaping up as an Africa vs. Baumann affair. Knowing and fearing the German's finishing kick, Africans should have set a fast pace throughout. That is what Dominic Kirui of Kenya tried to do from the beginning. After 3000 metres (7:55.0) Ondieki took over. At that stage the leading pack consisted of Ondieki, Bitok of Kenya, Bayissa and Worku Bikila of Ethiopia, Boutayeb of Morocco and Baumann, i.e. five Africans and one European. First to lose contact was Bikila. When the final battle flared up along the last backstretch, the German was boxed in and

his rivals allowed him no space to break through, within the rules that's true. On the last turn he seemed doomed. Viewing this from the stands, Isabell, his wife and trainer, was shuddering ... but a while later Baumann escaped through the rear of the box, swung out wide, passed Ondieki, then Boutayeb and Bayissa. Only Bitok was still ahead, but the German collared him in the last 10 metres and won by 1 1/2 metres, maybe less. He covered the last 400 metres in 56.1 and the last 200 in a sizzling 24.9. (Bitok 25.4, Bayissa 25.6). Only 0.75 secs. covered the first four. When it was all over the German said: "I have always thought a European could run as well as an African".

Details:

Barcelona, 8 August 1992 – 5000 metres: 1.Dieter Baumann (Ger) 13:12.52, 2.Paul Bitok (Ken) 13:12.71, 3.Fita Bayissa (Eti) 13:13.03, 4.Brahim Boutayeb (Mor) 13:13.27, 5.Yobes Ondieki (Ken) 13:17.50, 6.Worku Bikila (Eti) 13:23.52, 7.Rob Denmark (GB) 13:27.76, 8.Abel Antón (Spa) 13:27.80.

A notable absentee was the nth up and coming Kenyan, Moses Kiptanui (born at Elgeyo, Marakwet district, on 1 October 1970; 1.79 m. / 69 kg.), a corporal from the famous Nandi tribe. True, he was known mostly as a steeplechaser (8:06.46 in 1991), but he was unlucky enough to place only fourth in this event at the Kenyan Trials and did not go to Barcelona. After the Games he came to Europe "thirsty for revenge" and beat all the Olympic medal winners in the steeplechase, bringing the world record to 8:02.08. Three days later, namely on 22 August at Cologne, he conquered another world mark with a nifty 7:28.96 for 3000 metres flat, outclassing the likes of Bitok, Ondieki and Baumann. He thus succeeded Aouita, covering the first half in 3:47.6 and the second in a swift 3:41.4. He decided to take advantage of his splendid condition with an attack on another world record, Aouita's 5000 metre mark. This was in Brussels on 28 August and he had to be content with 13:00.93, good enough to place him third in the All Time World List. In this race he "murdered" Yobes Ondieki (13:09.72). Along with his countryman Henry Rono,

Kiptanui is to this day the only runner to have ever held the world record for 3000 metres with and without hurdles.

By comparison, other post-Olympic meets yielded indifferent performances. Brahim Boutayeb won a relatively slow 5000 (13:45.42) in the final of the Grand Prix in Turin, beating Bitok (13:45.90). Long distance races at the World Cup, held at Habana late in September, were penalized by a hot weather. Winners were Ethiopians Bayissa in the 5000 metres (13:41.23) and Addis Abebe in the 10,000 (28:44.38).

Leaders in "Track & Field News" World Ranking were Baumann in the 5000 metres and Skah in the 10,000, both with an immaculate record.

For the third consecutive year there was a global championship event in 1993 (the Worlds at Stuttgart), which had never happened before in the history of athletics. Yes, because the IAAF had decided that the World Championships should henceforth be a biennial event. Considering that this came on top of an intense Grand Prix circus, one can easily understand why long distance men of the Nineties really had their hands full. No matter if Grand Prix races – same as those of the indoor circus – were mostly contested at distances no longer than 3000 metres. Under such circumstances of growing physical and psychological engagement it was not surprising that several athletes alternated busy seasons with others in which they had "to take ten" because of injuries, the prevalent kind being the so-called stress fractures. Olympic champion Dieter Baumann, for example, had to bypass the 1993 season due to an injury. Early in the same year John Ngugi was involved in an unpleasant intermezzo when an IAAF officer, John Whetton (a former European 1500 metre champion) paid him a visit to conduct a random test. Ngugi refused to provide the sample and the IAAF inflicted him a four-year suspension. This decision caused quite a stir in Kenyan athletics circles. In May 1995, after reviewing the case, an IAAF spokesman said that lack of information from the Kenya AAA concerning the nature of the IAAF out-of-competition testing programme as well as language difficul-

ties had made it hard for Ngugi to understand what was going on. As a result of this, the IAAF concluded that Ngugi had suffered enough for his mistake and reinstated him under its "exceptional circumstances" rule. By then, however, Ngugi was past his athletic peak, mentally if not physically, and decided to quit.

In 1993 Scandinavia was once again the hotbed of major activity and the world's 10,000 metre record was bettered on two occasions. The first strike came from Chelimo at Stockholm on 5 July. After trailing John Doherty of Ireland and Charles Cheruiyot of Kenya in the initial stages of the race, the 21-year-old Chelimo forged ahead after 4600 metres and reached the half-way mark in 13:33.8. And he managed to go on at virtually the same pace till the end! That's how he eclipsed Arturo Barrios' record, were it only by 0.32 secs. In this race, however, Chelimo beat the holder himself by nearly half a minute. The hard-working Kenyan thus joined the select group of distance runners capable of "constructing" a global record mainly if not entirely by themselves. In a retrospective view he probably repented of not daring to act likewise in the Olympic final at Barcelona, where he did no better than 13:54 in the second half, as opposed to 13:34.1 here. Details:

Stockholm, 5 July 1993 – 10,000 metres: 1.Richard Chelimo (Ken) 27:07.91, 2.Arturo Barrios (Mex) 27:34.27, 3.Domingos Castro (Por) 27:34.53, 4.Paul Evans (GB) 27:47.79, 5.German Silva (Mex) 28:03.64..... DNF: John Doherty (Ire) and Charles Cheruiyot (Ken).

Kilometre fractions:

1000 m	2:44.9	
2000 m	5:26.0	(2:41.1)
3000 m	8:08.0	(2:42.0)
4000 m	10:50.8	(2:42.8)
5000 m	13:33.8	(2:43.0)
6000 m	16:15.9	(2:42.1)
7000 m	18:59.3	(2:43.4)
8000 m	21:43.4	(2:44.1)
9000 m	24:28.5	(2:45.1)
10,000 m	27:07.91	(2:39.4)

Chelimo ran the last 400 metres in 60.9.

149

"They had never seen a man run faster"

In his excellent book "Train hard, win easy – the Kenyan way" (published by Tafnews Press in 1997) Toby Tanser tells the following story about Richard Chelimo: "The people of the town where he lives, Iten, remember him more for an off-track incident than for his world record heroics. Late one night Chelimo parked the business' pickup truck outside the house. Just as he was locking the car door some machete-wielding robbers pounced upon him. Chelimo was forced to surrender both the automobile and the cash he was carrying. As the thieves made their getaway, Chelimo, dressed in his business suit, gave pursuit on foot. Townsfolk recollect the flash of light as Chelimo shot by, most swearing they had never seen a man run faster. A few moments after the vehicle had passed the regional police station – a couple of kilometres from Chelimo's home – Richard was in the same office registering an urgent complaint. The stolen car, cash and the criminals were soon captured and retrieved".

At 21 Chelimo became the youngest ever world record setter over 10,000 metres. His record had a very short life though. Five days later the magic Bislett track in Oslo acted as the ideal vehicle for another record breaking performance at the same distance – by another Kenyan! The man in question was 32-year-old Yobes Ondieki, who was barely at his third attempt over the distance. Moroccan Khalid Skah, a resident of Norway, changed his mind at the last moment and stayed away from the race. He ran the 5000 metres instead but here too he chanced upon a Kenyan, Paul Bitok, who ran the last 200 in 26.4 and beat Skah – 13:08.68 to 13:09.35. In the 10,000 metre race Ondieki got a helping hand from a compatriot, William Sigei, who earlier in the season had won over the same distance with an excellent 27:25.23 at the African Championships, held at Durban, the chief seaport of South Africa. Isaac Garcia of

Mexico and John Doherty of Ireland led in the early stages but Sigei soon forged ahead, with Ondieki in his wake. The would-be record breaker took the lead at the half-way mark (13:28.05). Apart from a brief thrust by Sigei in the sixth kilometre, Ondieki retained the lead for the rest of the journey. He showed his extraordinary endurance by covering the second half in 13:30.33. That's how he became the first man to break the 27-minute barrier, his final time being 26:58.38. Since the heydays of Paavo Nurmi, 69 years ago, the world record had advanced by nearly three minutes and ten seconds … Details:
Oslo, 10 July 1993 – 10,000 metres: 1.Yobes Ondieki (Ken) 26:58.38, 2.William Sigei (Ken) 27:16.81, 3.Alejandro Gómez (Spa) 27:39.38, 4.Richard Nerurkar (GB) 27:40.03, 5.Todd Williams (USA) 27:40.37, 6.Mathias Ntawulikura (Rua) 27:47.59, 7.Armando Quintanilla (Mex) 27:51.41, 8.Katsuhiko Hanada (Jap) 28:11.60.

Kilometre fractions:

1000 m	2:41.2	
2000 m	5:22.0	(2:40.8)
3000 m	8:02.8	(2:40.8)
4000 m	10:47.0	(2:44.2)
5000 m	13:28.05	(2:41.1)
6000 m	16:10.9	(2:42.8)
7000 m	18:53.6	(2:42.7)
8000 m	21:35.2	(2:41.6)
9000 m	24:20.2	(2:45.0)
10,000 m	26:58.38	(2:38.2)

Ondieki ran the last 400 metres in 60.6 and the last 200 in 29.6.

Skah was back in the news when he ran 2 miles in 8:12.17 at Hechtel on 31 July, a best-on-record performance at that distance, no longer on the IAAF list. Four days later he won an important 5000 metre race in Zurich with a new PB of 13:04.67. He won from Ondieki (13:05.09), Chelimo (13:05.14), one Haile Gebrselassie of Ethiopia (13:05.39), Ismael Kirui of Kenya (13:06.50) and Francesco Panetta (13:06.76). The Italian was back on the track after several unsuccessful attempts to join the world's élite in the marathon, and he chalked up his best-ever time.

THE ALL-CONQUERING GEBRSELASSIE

Yobes Ondieki failed to show up at the 1993 World Championships in Stuttgart. Rumour had it that he did so for lack of adequate incentives provided by the IAAF. A "bras-de-fer" had been going on between the international organ and some of the leading managers. The bone of contention concerned prizes to be awarded to athletes. Finally the parties agreed on a compromise, obviously suggested by the very venue of the championships: every winner would receive a Mercedes car.

Khalid Skah stayed away from the 10,000 metres as he chose the 5000. For once the shorter distance was first on the time schedule. The fastest qualifying time, 13:25.27, was turned in by a relatively little known Ethiopian, Haile Gebrselassie. At the time the spelling of his last name was rather controversial. I have adopted the version provided by German journalist Robert Hartmann, an eminent Africa hand. In the final two days later it soon became apparent that Kenyans had a well defined strategy: set a fast pace throughout in order to take the sting out of their feared Moroccan rival Khalid Skah, just to avoid a replica of Barcelona 1992. First to take up the task was Mike Chesire, who covered the first kilometre in 2:31.8. After 1500 metres Ismael Kirui took over and after injecting a 60.2 lap he reached 2000 metres in 5:11.3. This earned him a 20 metre lead vis-à-vis a group consisting of Skah and three Ethiopians – Gebrselassie, Bayissa and Worku Bikila. The man several observers rated as Kenya's first string, Paul Bitok, had lost contact. Kirui passed 3000 metres in 7:45.6 and 4000 in 10:26.9. At that stage the young Kenyan visibly began to suffer, yet his pursuers delayed their counterattack till 600 metres from home. It was there that Bayissa and Gebrselassie ran away from Bikila and Skah and started to earnestly chase Kirui. The Kenyan lost the greater part of his lead but rallied his remaining energies,

running the last 400 metres in 60.0 and the last 200 in 29.1. This allowed him to win by 0.42 sec. from Gebrselassie, whose corresponding splits were 56.5 and 27.4 – through which the young Ethiopian presented his "personal card" for the first time. Details:

Stuttgart, 16 August 1993 – 5000 metres: 1.Ismael Kirui (Ken) 13:02.75, 2.Haile Gebrselassie (Eti) 13:03.17, 3.Fita Bayissa (Eti) 13:05.40, 4.Worku Bikila (Eti) 13:06.64, 5.Khalid Skah (Mor) 13:07.18, 6.Brahim Jabbour (Mor) 13:18.87, 7.Aloÿs Nizigama (Bur) 13:20.59, 8.Paul Bitok (Ken) 13:23.41.

Kirui, 18 years 5 months, was the youngest winner in the history of the Worlds. Among place winners there were several Africans still in their early twenties. The rivalry between Kirui and Gebrselassie had flared up for the first time at the 1991 World Cross-Country Championships, junior class, when the Kenyan was seventh and the Ethiopian eighth. The following year, in the same class of the harriers' title meet, they finished in the same order: Kirui first and Gebrselassie second. The Ethiopian began to turn the tables on his rival in a very close finish at the 1992 World Junior Championships in Seoul – 13:36.06 to 13:36.11. Gebrselassie had previously won the 10,000 metres in 28:03.99, with Kirui not in the race. They met again at the 1993 World Cross-Country Championships, senior race, with Kirui third and Gebrselassie seventh. Two bright new stars were born, except that Kirui was to remain on top for a couple of years, whereas Gebrselassie was to dominate the scene of distance running for nearly a decade.

Ismael Kirui (born in the Marakwet district on 20 February 1975; 1.60 m. / 54 kg.) was a younger brother of Chelimo, as well as a cousin of Moses Kiptanui. To tell the truth, some people doubted the correctness of his "official" date of birth, as they did for Chelimo's. Here is Kirui's progression up to and including 1993:

Year	Age	5000 m	10,000 m
1990	15	13:59.6	28:40.77
1991	16	-	-
1992	17	13:15.67	29:35.0
1993	18	13:02.75	28:07.1

Haile Gebrselassie (born at Arssi, Asela on 18 April 1973; 1.64 m. / 53 kg.), a young policeman, was by then looming as Miruts Yifter's heir apparent. His progression:

Year	Age	5000 m	10,000 m
1992	19	13:36.06	28:03.99
1993	20	13:03.17	27:30.17

Ismael Kirui (Kenya) winning the 5000 metres at the 1995 World Championships in Göteborg.

Kirui elected not to try the 10,000 metres in Stuttgart, even though he had run the distance in 28:07.1 at Nairobi, a most valuable performance at high altitude. That was probably a wise choice though. The fastest qualifier was Antonio Silio of Argentina with 28:16.62. The final two days later was run on a warm day, maybe not the last reason why it was initially "quieter" than expected. Bayissa led the field at the half-way mark (13:59.4) but inexplicably dropped out a while later. Chelimo led the parade in the next two kilometres but after 7600 metres he too lost contact. Two men, Moses Tanui and Gebrselassie, were left alone to fight it out for gold. The Ethiopian trailed his rival till the bell, when things really began to happen. Tanui burst into a sprint to pull away but hitched his stride when Gebrselassie stepped on his left foot. The Kenyan's shoe flew off as he kicked it high into the air. While the crowd was roaring Tanui built up a 10-metre lead going round the last turn. When it seemed all over, the Ethiopian began to eat up the track with long, highly effective strides. He was even greater than in the closing stage of the 5000 metres and collared Tanui to finally forge ahead for a narrow but highly significant win. It was really a hectic finish: Gebrselassie ran the last 400 metres in 55.0 and the last 200 in 26.6 – as opposed to 55.4 and 28.0 for Tanui, running with only one shoe. In retrospect, the two warriors viewed the race from different angles. The winner said: "It was my tactic to follow the leader all the time. I always do that. I'm sorry Tanui lost his shoe, but he was slowing just in front of me and I was running faster". Tanui, obviously angry, said: "He kept stepping on my feet. I asked him to go ahead and take the lead, but he always refused. He finally stepped on my shoe and that was the only way he could beat me". Details:
Stuttgart, 22 August 1993 – 10,000 metres: 1.Haile Gebrselassie (Eti) 27:46.02, 2.Moses Tanui (Ken) 27:46.54, 3.Richard Chelimo (Ken) 28:06.02, 4.Stéphane Franke (Ger) 28:10.69, 5.Aloÿs Nizigama (Bur) 28:13.43, 6.Francesco Panetta (Ita) 28:27.05, 7.Todd Williams (USA) 28:30.49, 8.Antonio Silio (Arg) 28:36.88 ..... DNF: Fita Bayissa (Eti).
In the final of the Grand Prix in London (10

September) Kirui won the 5000 metres from Chelimo – 13:23.26 to 13:24.30. The title won in Stuttgart earned the "green" Kenyan place no. 1 in "Track & Field News" World Ranking. At the longer distance Ondieki was rated no.1 on the strength of his sub-27 min. race in Oslo, ahead of world champion Gebrselassie. In an overall view of both distances, however, the Ethiopian was clearly the dominant figure. That was for him the beginning of a glorious, long era. Only thing, it is interesting to note that Stuttgart 1993 was to remain the first and last time he ever tried for a double in a global meet.

1994 did not offer a global test (it is difficult to give such a status to the somewhat devalued World Cup) but plenty of excellent performances and stirring competition. The Grand Prix circus again provided new world records at both the classic distances. Times under 13 minutes in the 5000 metres and under 27 in the 10,000 became accessible to a growing number of runners, as it always happens once a barrier is broken. The vintage season opened on 4 June at Hengelo during the Adriaan Paulen Memorial, commemorative of the late Dutch President of the IAAF. Haile Gebrselassie conquered his first world record, succeeding the great Said Aouita as holder of the 5000 metre mark. After receiving useful help from his countryman Worku Bikila in the initial stages, the 1993 world champion was on his own for more than half the distance, thus showing that like all truly great runners he could be masterful in more than one rôle. Actually, he won his battle vis-à-vis Aouita in the second part of the race. Details:

Hengelo, 4 June 1994 – 5000 metres: 1.Haile Gebrselassie (Eti) 12:56.96, 2.Worku Bikila (Eti) 13:10.33, 3.Vener Kashayev (Rus) 13:33.42.

Kilometre fractions:

1000 m	2:36.6	
2000 m	5:13.7	(2:37.1)
3000 m	7:50.9	(2:37.2)
4000 m	10:28.3	(2:37.4)
5000 m	12:56.96	(2 28.7)

Gebrselassie ran the last 200 metres in 29.2.

A month later Khalid Skah made a record attempt over the same distance but failed, yet lowered his PB to 13:00.54 (Villeneuve d'Ascq, 8 July). He won from Bob Kennedy of USA (13:05.93).

Next on the line of prospective record-breakers was William Sigei of Kenya (born at Kericho on 11 October 1969; 1.78 m. / 57 kg.), a civil servant in the Army Corps, who enjoyed a good reputation, mostly earned with two victories in the World Cross-Country Championships (1993 and '94). His progression:

Year	Age	5000 m	10,000 m
1989	20	13:44.6	-
1990	21	-	-
1991	22	13:56.3	-
1992	23	13:15.01	28:35,0
1993	24	13:07.35	27:16.81

Richard Chelimo (Kenya) held the 10,000 m. world record for five days in 1993.

In 1994 he offered a glimpse of things to come with a new PB of 13:06.72. This was in London on 15 July and he beat, among others, Gebrselassie (4th in 13:11.87). On 22 July Sigei was in Oslo, where he lined up at the start of a 10,000 metre race with 17 others. Included in the group were two "hares", Paul Donovan of Ireland and William Mutwol of Kenya. They were pretty serious in doing their job and the latter led the dance till 6000 metres. At that stage, however, Sigei was more than 3 secs. down vis-à-vis Ondieki, the listed record holder. Once on his own, Sigei did the rest in superb style. He was visibly suffering in the closing stage, but the enthusiastic support of the crowd (18,270) carried him home in 26:52.23, more than 6 seconds under Ondieki's world record. He had covered the second 5000 in a phenomenal 13:19.52, which would have been a world record for that distance up to the end of 1965! Details: Oslo, 22 July 1994 – 10,000 metres: 1.William Sigei (Ken) 26:52.23, 2.William Kiptum (Ken) 27:17.20, 3.Armando Quintanilla (Mex) 27:18.59, 4.Aloÿs Nizigama (Bur) 27:20.51, 5.Paul Tergat (Ken) 27:29.45, 6.Mathias Ntawulikura (Rwa) 27:41.09, 7.Ondoro Osoro (Ken) 27:42.47, 8.Carlos de la Torre (Spa) 28:09.63.... DNF: Paul Donovan (Ire) and William Mutwol (Ken).

Kilometre fractions:

1000 m	2:42.3	
2000 m	5:24.3	(2:42.0)
3000 m	8:05.9	(2:41.6)
4000 m	10:50.8	(2:44.9)
5000 m	13:32.7	(2:41.9)
6000 m	16:14.1	(2:41.4)
7000 m	18:53.7	(2:39.6)
8000 m	21:36.0	(2:42.3)
9000 m	24:18.4	(2:42.4)
10,000 m	26:52.23	(2:33.9)

Sigei ran the last 400 metres in 56.8.

The new record holder was very humble in commenting his feat: "It wasn't so easy to run so many laps all by myself and I never expected to beat the record by such a big margin". To achieve his goal he had to rely on his innate pacing sense. " I never heard my split time. It was so noisy".

Before the big mid-summer events there was room for two more best-on-record performances. On 30 July at Hechtel Moses Kiptanui, who already held the global marks for 3000 metres with and without barriers, ran 2 miles in 8:09.01, the fastest time on record. The European carrousel held another upset in store: on 2 August at Monaco a great Algerian talent, Noureddine Morceli, lowered the world's 3000 metre mark to 7:25.11. For years the undisputed king of 1500 metres/1 mile runners, Morceli was helped by Joseph Chesire of Kenya and Mohamed Choumassi of Morocco in the first two kilometres (2:29.0 and 2:32.1), then completed the job with a last kilometre in 2:24.0.

Morceli 's "kick of kicks": last 400 metres in 52.2

Noureddine Morceli (born at Ténès on 28 February 1970; 1.72 m. / 62 kg.) had won the 1500 metres twice at the World Championships (1991 and '93). He held the world record at 3:28.86 (1992) and that of the mile as well, with 3:44.39 (1993), both at Rieti, a town in Central Italy (altitude 402 metres) which could then be regarded as an "Oslo of the South" - its track had acted as a useful vehicle for Seb Coe, Steve Ovett and others on their way to new PB's over the "metric mile". Morceli had tried the 5000 metres in 1990 (13:25.20) and was very confident about his possibilities at this distance. He wasn't wrong and proof was served at Zurich on 17 August 1994 when he won an important race in 13:03.85 from the likes of Fita Bayissa (13:07.70) and Khalid Skah (13:07.84).On that occasion the Algerian ran the last 800 metres in 1:53.8 and the last 400 in a sizzling 52.2, while Bayissa and Skah could do no better than 55.7 and 55.9 respectively. All this on a cold, rainy day. Morceli quickly admitted: "I need more experience. This is a different world". He tried once more later in the season at Rieti and did 13:07.88. But that was all. He never ran that distance again: apparently he was not so eager to explore the new world. He thus left his admirers guessing as to what he might have done if.....

The European Championships in Helsinki, eagerly expected as the meet of the year, were rather disappointing, at least in the domain of the distance races. It became apparent that European shares were at an-all time low, especially if compared with Africa's ever rising standards. The 10,000 metres was a tactical race with a slow first half (14:12.84), partly enlightened by a hectic finish which turned in favour of a 32-year-old Spaniard, Abel Antón, who was to attain even greater heights in the marathon, at which distance he won world titles in 1997 and '99. Second went to another veteran, Vincent Rousseau of Belgium, who had a reputation as marathon runner. Details:

Helsinki, 7 August 1994 – 10,000 metres: 1.Abel Antón (Spa) 28:06.03, 2.Vincent Rousseau (Bel) 28:06.63, 3.Stéphane Franke (Ger) 28:07.95, 4.Robert Stefko (Svk) 28:08.02, 5.Paulo Guerra (Por) 28:10.18, 6.João Junqueira (Por) 28:10.55, 7.Jan Pesava (Cze) 28:10.73, 8.Carlos de la Torre (Spa) 28:10.77. DNF: Francesco Panetta (Ita). Antón ran the last 400 metres in 56 secs.

The 5000 metre final a week later followed the same pattern. The race marked the comeback of the 1992 Olympic champion, Dieter Baumann, who had lost the 1993 season through injury. True to his trademark, he settled the issue with a hard finishing kick. Yet his time was no better than 13:36.93. Curiously enough, José Ramos of Portugal had run faster in the prelims three days earlier (13:30.33) – but he finished only 14th in the race that mattered most. Second went to Rob Denmark of Britain, who at the Worlds of the previous year was no better than 9th - but first of the Europeans! Antón, third, won another medal. Details:

Helsinki, 14 August 1994 – 5000 metres: 1.Dieter Baumann (Ger) 13:36.93, 2.Rob Denmark (GB) 13:37.50, 3.Abel Antón (Spa) 13:38.04, 4.Abdellah Béhar (Fra) 13:38.36, 5.John Nuttall (GB) 13:38.65, 6.José Carlos Adán (Spa) 13:39.16, 7.Risto Ulmala (Fin) 13:40.84, 8.Anacleto Jiménez (Spa) 13:41.60.

The Commonwealth Games followed later in the same month at Victoria, British Columbia. In the 5000 metres the Helsinki silver medallist Rob Denmark was in the front row again and with a faster time. He won in 13:23.00 from Philémon Hanneck of Zimbabwe (13:23.20) and John Nuttall of England (13:23.54). It is to be noted, however, that Kenya was generally represented at these Games by second-rate performers. Yet the East-African country provided the winner of the 10,000 metres with Lameck Aguta (28:38.22) who beat Tendai Chimusasa (28:47.72) of Zimbabwe and Fackson Nkandu (28:51.72) of Zambia.

Africa's dominance was confirmed by the results of the Grand Prix final in Paris (3 September). Khalid Skah emerged the winner by the narrowest of margins in a hectic 5000 metre battle as he nosed out his countryman Khalid Boulami – 13:14.63 to 13:14.64. Only four days earlier in Berlin there had been another very close finish, with local matador Dieter Baumann edging Skah – 13:12.47 to 13:12.74. Moses Kiptanui was third (13:14.93). By comparison the last important test of the season, the World Cup race in London (11 September), was a low-fire affair, won by Brahim Lahlafi of Morocco in 13:27.96 from John Nuttall (13:32.47)

Morceli, with only two races at the distance, was ranked no.1 in the 5000 metres by "Track & Field News", ahead of Khalid Skah. In the 10,000 metres Sigei, on the strength of his world record, was preferred to Gebrselassie.

The 1994 World Lists showed 9 Africans among the Top Ten in both 5000 and 10,000 metres!

Gebre's Golden Year

1995 was a momentous year for top distance runners. And a man proved to be head and shoulders above the rest: the light-footed Haile Gebreselassie from Ethiopia. By then 22 and stationed in Holland as the chef-de-file of manager Jos Hermens' team, he warmed up with a worthy opener at Kerkrade on 28 May: 8:07.46 for 2 miles, best ever at that distance which was no longer recognized by the IAAF. Enroute he passed 3000 metres in 7:36.37. This was meant merely as a test for a major record attempt over 10,000 metres scheduled for 5 June at Hengelo, still in Holland. Paul Donovan of Ireland and Worku Bikila of Ethiopia acted as "hares". The latter led his countryman till 6000 metres. Gebrselassie completed the task in a masterful way, his last kilometre (2:34.7) being the fastest of all. The final result was a new world record of 26:43.53, nearly 9 seconds under William Sigei's mark. Details:

Hengelo, 5 June 1995 – 10,000 metres: 1.Haile Gebreselassie (Eti) 26:43.53, 2.Assefa Mezegebu (Eti) 27:59.63, 3.Antonio Pinto (Por) 28:06.18.

Kilometre fractions:

1000 m	2:42.3	
2000 m	5:22.3	(2:40.0)
3000 m	8:01.2	(2:38.9)
4000 m	10:39.4	(2:38.2)
5000 m	13:21.4	(2:42.0)
6000 m	16:03.3	(2:41.9)
7000 m	18:43.2	(2:39.9)
8000 m	21:26.2	(2:43.0)
9000 m	24:08.8	(2:42.6)
10,000 m	26:43.53	(2:34.7)

Gebrselassie ran the last 400 metres in 60.2. NB: Splits given above are for Gebrselassie himself and were supplied by A.Lennart Julin (ATFS/Sweden).

At that stage the Ethiopian held the world records for both classic distances, but he retained this privilege for only three days. At the Golden Gala in Rome (8 June) Moses Kiptanui ran 5000 metres in 12:55.30. For this race the Kenyan had enlisted the help of his younger countryman Daniel Komen. "If I don't get the record, then you will", he told Daniel before the race. In fact the latter turned out to be so good that he led until midway in the last turn! 45,000 spectators went wild as the two engaged a furious battle down the homestretch. Kiptanui finally won the day by a fairly comfortable margin as both bettered Gebrselassie's 1-year-old mark. A similar trick was last turned in 1956 by Gordon Pirie and Vladimir Kuts at Bergen. Details:

Rome, 8 June 1995 – 5000 metres:

1.Moses Kiptanui (Ken) 12:55.30, 2.Daniel Komen (Ken) 12:56.15, 3.Worku Bikila (Eti) 12:57.23, 4.Salah Hissou (Mor) 13:02.25, 5.John Nuttall (GB) 13:16.70, 6.Stéphane Franke (Ger) 13:17.25, 7.Gennaro Di Napoli (Ita) 13:17.46.

Kilometre fractions:

1000 m	2:35.2	
2000 m	5:11.8	(2:36.6)
3000 m	7:47.0	(2:35.2)
4000 m	10:23.2	(2:36.2)
5000 m	12:55.30	(2:32.1)

Kiptanui ran the last 400 metres in 58.2.

Daniel Kipngetich Komen (born at Mwen on 17 May 1976; 1.70 m. / 55 kg.) had created a sensation at the 1994 World Junior Championships in Lisbon by scoring a great double: 28:29.74 on 20 July and 13:45.37 on 24 July, when only 18 years of age. In the spring of 1995 at Nairobi he ran 5000 metres in 13:29.33, good running in high altitude, and just three days before the Rome meet he did 3:34.63 for 1500 metres in Moscow for a world junior best, which was not ratified by the IAAF as no doping test was conducted after the race.

Moses Kiptanui, who continued to ride two horses – flat and steeplechase - moved to second on the All Time World List for 3000 metres flat with 7:27.18 (Monaco, 25 July). On the eve of the World Championships in Göteborg he opted for the steeplechase though. Gebrselassie gave up the idea of trying for a double and elected to run the 10,000 only – a tactic he was to follow even in later years. He won the world title with yet another exhibit of great finishing speed – last 400 metres in 56.0, last 200 in 25.1. Even Khalid Skah, himself a big kicker , had no answer to that.

Ismael Kirui, the Kenyan who had beaten Gebrselassie on more than one occasion in the past, won the 5000 metres, he too with a blistering finish: 56.6 for the last 400 metres, 26.6 for the last 200. Dieter Baumann was a shadow of his former self: he finished ninth, yet first of the Europeans! Details:

Göteborg, 8 August 1995 - 10,000 metres: 1.Haile Gebrselassie (Eti) 27:12.95,

2.Khalid Skah (Mor) 27:14:53, 3.Paul Tergat (Ken) 27:14.70, 4.Salah Hissou (Mor) 27:19.30, 5.Josephat Machuka (Ken) 27:23.72, 6.Joseph Kimani (Ken) 27:30.02, 7.Stéphane Franke (Ger) 27:48,88, 8.Paulo Guerra (Por) 27:52.55. Last kilometre: Gebrselassie 2:33.71.
Göteborg, 13 August 1995 – 5000 metres: 1.Ismael Kirui (Ken) 13:16.77, 2.Khalid Boulami (Mor) 13:17.15, 3.Shem Kororia (Ken) 13:17.59, 4.Ismail Sghyr (Mor) 13:17.86, 5.Brahim Lahlafi (Mor) 13:18.89, 6.Worku Bikila (Eti) 13:20.12, 7.Bob Kennedy (USA) 13:32.10, 8.Fita Bayissa (Eti) 13:34.52, 9.Dieter Baumann (Ger) 13:39.98.

Zurich: not a gloomy night after all

Gebrselassie badly wanted to recapture the world's 5000 metre record. An ideal chance was offered him at the classic "Weltklasse" meet in Zurich, where he met Kirui among others. Three days after his victory at the Worlds, the Kenyan was not ready for such a battle. His Ethiopian rival had once again enlisted the help of his compatriot Worku Bikila, who was well-nigh perfect in rendering his service – he led till 3400 metres. Each of the first two kilometres was run in 2:34-plus, well under Kiptanui's schedule in his record race in Rome. Then Gebrselassie took over and ran the last two kilometres in 5:01.4 – which would have been a world record for such a distance till the end of 1954. He finished in 12:44.39, thus shaving nearly 11 seconds off Kiptanui's mark. In the process he massacred a classy field, notably including new star Daniel Komen, who finished 11th. A resurging Baumann outsprinted Kirui for second as both finished the whale of a distance behind the winner, no matter if the German set a new national record. Said the ever smiling Gebrselassie: "I was afraid to slow down. There were 10 Kenyans in the race". Details:
Zurich, 16 August 1995 – 5000 metres: 1.Haile Gebrselassie (Eti) 12:44.39, 2.Dieter Baumann (Ger) 13:01.72, 3.Ismael Kirui (Ken) 13:02.75, 4.Bob Kennedy (USA) 13:03.37, 5.Stéphane Franke (Ger) 13:03.76, 6.Ismail Sghyr (Mor) 13:05.10, 7.Josephat Machuka (Ken) 13:06.69, 8.Paul Tergat (Ken) 13:07.49 .... 11.Daniel Komen (Ken) 13:14.94.

Kilometre splits:

1000 m	2:34.3	
2000 m	5:09.0	(2:34.7)
3000 m	7:43.0	(2:34.0)
4000 m	10:14.2	(2:31.2)
5000 m	12:44.39	(2:30.2)

The above splits are for Gebrselassie himself. He ran the last 200 metres in 29.7.

This phenomenal record had the power of blowing up the Hungarian scoring table, which rated it the equivalent of such times as 3:24.29 (1500 metres), 1:40.49 (800) and 19.39 (200). A fully revised table was adopted by the IAAF soon afterwards ....

Haile Gebrselassie (Ethiopia), the greatest distance runner of our time, seen here in his 10,000 m. victory at the 1999 World Championships, the fourth of a unique series.

157

In that memorable night in Zurich something out of the ordinary happened to Moses Kiptanui: he lost his 5000 metre record but bettered his own world record for the steeplechase, breaking the 8-minute barrier for the first time (7:59.18). Just for good measure, both he and Gebrselassie picked up bonuses which included $50,000 in cash and a 1-kilo ingot of gold. Not a gloomy night after all.

Another fast 10,000 metre time was registered at the Van Damme Memorial in Brussles on 25 August. Worku Bikila, for once enjoying a duty-free session in the absence of his master Gebrselassie, won a narrow but significant victory over Ismael Kirui – 27:06.44 to 27:06.59. But Gebrselassie had the last word anyhow: at Berlin on 1 September he finally met Moses Kiptanui in the 5000 metres and scored a decisive victory – 12:53.19 to 13:00.90. A 28 secs. 200 up to the bell gave the Ethiopian a 20-metre lead going into the last lap, which he covered in 56.6 just for good measure.

1996 was not comparable with its predecessor in terms of records, yet it offered exciting races galore. Early in the year Haile Gebrselassie allowed himself two digressions indoors and set new world records for that kind of competition – 13:10.98 for 5000 metres (Sindelfingen, 27 January) and 7:30.72 for 3000 metres (Stuttgart, 4 February). These were his first experiences ever on banked board tracks. In the shorter race he outclassed Fermin Cacho of Spain (7:36.61), the 1992 Olympic 1500 metre champion.

Daniel Komen had his best ever season clock-wise but he lacked consistency up to the big summer meets. He started in mediocre fashion, suffering bad losses in his first three races over 5000 metres. The last of these was at the Kenya Trials for the Atlanta Olympics and he was only fourth in 13:32.50 behind Tom Nyariki (13:28.30), Paul Bitok (13:29.25) and Shem Kororia (13:30.23). Consequently, he failed to qualify for the Games.

The best 5000 metre mark of the pre-Olympic season was posted by Salah Hissou of Morocco at the Golden Gala meet in Rome on 5 June. As often in the recent past, this was the occasion for a phenomenal race. Komen did 13:01.38 yet had to be content with fifth. Hissou won in a fast 12:50.80 from Philip Mosima (12:53.72), Kiptanui (12:54.85) and Tom Nyariki (12:59.19), all of Kenya. Komen rounded into top form at Stockholm on 8 July when he lowered the Kenyan record to 12:51.60 and drove Bob Kennedy, second, to a new US record of 12.58.75. The Kenyan found further reason to pity his poor show at the Trials when, barely two weeks before the Games, he lowered the world's best for 2 miles to 8:03.54 at Lappeenranta, Finland, on 14 July.

Atlanta offered warm weather conditions, more suitable for sprinting than for distance running. A very hard track gave Michael Johnson of USA a helping hand in setting what is still regarded as the greatest of all world records - 19.32 for 200 metres. But the same surface hurt all distance runners, including Gebrselassie, who said after the 10,000 metre final: "It was like running on a road. It was very difficult to run 25 laps on this bad track. I have never been so tired after an important race". Even so, his sufferings were partly caused by a man who proved capable of challenging him in the closing stage as no else (save perhaps Kirui at his best) could have done – Paul Tergat of Kenya.

The fastest qualifier in the 10,000 metres on 26 July was Worku Bikila, who won heat 1 in 27:50.57. Gebrselassie won heat 2 in a leisurely (for him) 28:14.20. The final three days later started at 10.10 pm, yet in warm weather conditions (27° C). After a relatively slow first half (13:55.22) the Kenyans got busy with a series of bursts. However, that was not enough to take the sting out of the impeccable Gebrselassie, who rolled into the lead just before the bell and opened up a gap on Paul Tergat, his only remaining rival, the only one who could make it difficult for him. The Kenyan gamely hung on and actually regained a little near the end, but that was all he could do. Gebrselassie ran the last 400 metres in 57.5 (Tergat 57.9) and the last 200 in 29.1. Once again, the fastest European, Stéphane Franke, finished no better than 9th. Details:

Atlanta, 29 July 1996 – 10,000 metres: 1.Haile Gebrselassie (Eti) 27:07.34, 2.Paul

Tergat (Ken) 27:08.17, 3.Salah Hissou (Mor) 27:24.67, 4.Aloÿs Nizigama (Bur) 27:33.79, 5.Josephat Machuka (Ken) 27:35.08, 6.Paul Koech (Ken) 27:35.19, 7.Khalid Skah (Mor) 27:46.98, 8.Mathias Ntawulikura (Rwa) 27:50.73.

Gebrselassie stayed away from the 5000 metres, saying: "My feet are aching (from bad blisters)". The prospect of three rounds (heats on 31 July, semis on 1 August, final on 3 August) was really too much, under such conditions. Also missing for various reasons were other prominent runners like Komen, Hissou and Kiptanui The decisive race opened with a 69 secs. first lap, after which Tom Nyariki, the latest of Kenya's "young flowers", led for more than 10 laps, only to lose contact when the final battle flared up. Quickest of all in the closing stage was Vénuste Niyongabo of Burundi, not yet 23, who as a 1500 metre runner was known as one of Noureddine Morceli's most serious rivals (he ran the distance in 3:30.09 shortly before the Atlanta Games). He had first tried the 5000 metres in April, with 13:24.20, later improving to 13:03.29. In Atlanta he covered the last 800 metres in 1:54.9 and the last 400 in 54.9. He finally nosed out Paul Bitok and Khalid Boulami to win in 13:07.96. Dieter Baumann was a close fourth. Details:
Atlanta, 3 August 1996 – 5000 metres: 1.Vénuste Niyongabo (Bur) 13:07.96, 2.Paul Bitok (Ken) 13:08.16, 3.Khalid Boulami (Mor) 13:08.37, 4.Dieter Baumann (Ger) 13:08.81, 5.Tom Nyariki (Ken) 13:12.29, 6.Bob Kennedy (USA) 13:12.35, 7.Enrique Molina (Spa) 13:12.91, 8.Brahim Lahlafi (Mor) 13:13.26.

After missing the Games as explained above, Daniel Komen was eager to take revenge. He distilled his wrath in European post-Olympic meets. He delivered his first blow at Monaco on 10 August, where he ran 3000 metres in 7:25.16, missing Morceli's world record by a tantalizing margin, 0.05 sec. His failure was curiously counteracted, statistically speaking, by the magnitude of the race as a whole as four others ducked under 7:30 – Nyariki (7:27.75), Bitok (7:28.41), Tergat (7:28.70) and Kiptanui (7:29.95). Dieter Baumann was only tenth and the world 5000 metre champion of 1993 and '95,

Kirui, barely twelfth.
But the cream of post-Olympic action was once more reserved for the Zurich meet (14 August). "Clou" of the night was the Gebrselassie vs. Komen duel over 5000 metres, with Paul Tergat as dangerous third party. Following his return home from Atlanta, the Ethiopian had celebrated his Olympic victory with .... his wedding ceremony. Apart from that, lack of sufficient training in the last ten days due to bad blisters on his feet caused him to reach Zurich in far from ideal conditions. Komen found himself in the lead after 3000 metres (7:41.28), well ahead of Gebrselassie's pace in his world record race on the same track in 1995. The Ethiopian stayed glued to Komen's shoulder as they remained alone to fight for victory. Most knowledgeable spectators waited for Gebrselassie to unleash his patented finishing kick. But with 200 metres to go it was Komen who turned the trick, running away from his great rival. The fading Gebrselassie was even threatened by Tergat but managed to retain second place. Komen had slowed down just a bit near the end – just enough to miss Gebrselassie's world record by 0.70 sec. Clock-wise this was another great race: 1.Komen 12:45.09, 2.Gebrselassie 12:52.70, 3. Tergat 12:54.72, 4.Khalid Boulami 12:55.76, 5.Bob Kennedy 12:58.21, 6.Ismail Sghyr 12:58.99, 7.Paul Koech 13:00.22.

After such close misses, world records eventually fell as the season was drawing to an end. At the Van Damme Memorial in Brussels (23 August), 24-year-old Salah Hissou of Morocco surprised a lot of poeple by conquering the world record for 10,000 metres with a great 26:38.08 - 5.45 secs. under Gebrselassie's one-year-old mark. The Moroccan did this after staying behind record pace, in the wake of work-horses, for the greater part of the distance. When he took over, a penultimate kilometre in 2:35.53 helped him to reverse the situation. He was only a shade slower in the last kilometre and that sufficed to settle the issue in his ample favour – time 26:38.08. Paul Tergat was no match for the Moroccan yet finished in 26:54.41, a new PB. Details:
Brussels, 23 August 1996 – 10,000 metres: 1.Salah Hissou (Mor) 26:38.08, 2.Paul

Vénuste Niyongabo puts Burundi on the map of world athletics by winning the 5000 metres at the 1996 Olympics in Atlanta. Runner-up is Paul Bitok (Kenya).

Tergat (Ken) 26:54.41, 3.Paul Koech (Ken) 26:56.78, 4.William Kiptum (Ken) 27:18.84, 5.Aloÿs Nizigama (Bur) 27:25.13, 6.Mathias Ntawulikura (Rwa) 27:25.48, 7. Abel Antón (Spa) 28:18.44.

Kilometre fractions:

1000 m	2:38.99	
2000 m	5:20.44	(2:41.45)
3000 m	8.02.62	(2:42.18)
4000 m	10:44.81	(2:42.19)
5000 m	13:25.45	(2:40.64)
6000 m	16.04.70	(2:39.25)
7000 m	18.46.99	(2:42.29)
8000 m	21:26.44	(2:39.45)
9000 m	24:01.97	(2:35.53)
10,000 m	26:38.08	(2:36.11)

Hissou ran the last 400 metres in 61.1.

Salah Hissou (born at Kasba Tadla on 16 January 1972; 1.76 m. / 62 kg.) had his major breakthrough in 1994, with notable successes in cross-country running. His progression:

Year	Age	5000 m	10,000 m
1989	17	14:15.0	-
1990	18	14:05.9	-
1991	19	13:37.40	-
1992	20	13:41.55	28:31.62
1993	21	13:49.5	-
1994	22	13:04.93	27:21.75
1995	23	13:02.25	27:09.30
1996	24	12:50.80	26:38.08

His technical director Aziz Daouda revealed that Hissou had been making plans for his record attempt for a year, ever since his 27:09.30 in 1995, still in Brussels.

Daniel Komen was after Morceli's 3000 metre record (7:25.11 in 1994). As previously related, he missed the target by only 0.05 at Monaco in August. He finally succeeded at Rieti on 1 September. Curiously enough, he said he decided to go for the record right there, after watching Wilson Kipketer, a Kenya-born Dane, run a great 1:41.83 for 800 metres. A Kenyan hare, John Kosgei, set the pace up to nearly 2000 metres, then Komen took over and achieved a final time of 7:20.67 - to this day one of the greatest feats in the annals of distance running. His kilometre fractions: 2:26.5, 2:26.9 and 2:27.3. Komen closed his great season with a 12:52.38 over 5000 metres in the Grand Prix final at Milan (7 September). On that occasion, however, he had another reason to rejoice as he ended up as winner in the Overall Grand Prix series, a success that netted him $200,000.

Komen was first in "Track & Field News" World Ranking in both 3000 and 5000 metres. Over the longer distance he lost his first three races, as previously related, but he made amends by winning the next four with such times as 12:51.60, 12:45.09, 13:02.62 and 12:52.38. Hissou and Niyongabo were second and third respectively, while Gebrselassie with only one outdoor race – his losing effort in Zurich - was for once no better than fifth, but he was ranked no.1 in the 10,000 metres, just on the strength of his Olympic victory.

1997 was another tremendous year in the ever moving picture of distance running. The World Championship races in Athens offered excellent competition yet they tended to pale if compared with the hectic parade of Grand Prix competition. When the year was over the final verdict sounded somewhat contradictory: Gebrselassie went through the season undefeated in both 5000 (5 races) and 10,000 metres (2 races) and set new world records at both distances, yet in a late season meet in Brussels two Kenyans deprived him of both those records (after he had won a 3000 metre race on the same track earlier in the evening).

The great Ethiopian, by then 24, opened his 1997 account with the first sub-13 min. mark indoors over 5000 metres – 12:59.04 in Stockholm on 20 February. The outdoor season got underway with a new event: the inaugural European 10,000 metre challenge race at Bilbao, Spain, on 5 June. Dieter Baumann won from a strong field in 27:21.53. But when the real action began it was Africa all the way through. In his favourite resort at Hengelo on 31 May Gebrselassie broke Daniel Komen's best-on-record mark for 2 miles with 8:01.08. This was a failure in another sense though – had he ducked under 8 minutes he would have won a prize of 1 million dollars !

First to reach the major heights over one of

the classic distances was Daniel Komen at the Golden Gala in Rome (5 June), a meet that already had a reputation as producer of classy 5000 metre marks. For once the weather played havoc with the hopes of the runners, yet cold and rain could not prevent Komen from chalking up a remarkable 12:48.98, only 4-plus secs. off Gebrselassie's world record. In doing so the Kenyan beat Hissou (12:52.39), Sghyr (13:04.52 and Assefa Mezegebu of Ethiopia (13:05.48). Komen confirmed his excellent condition at Bratislava on 10 June, lowering his 1500 metre best to 3:31.29. With his eyes focussed on the forthcoming World Championships in Athens, Komen this time made no mistakes at the Kenya Trials: he qualified easily in 13:23.8.

Also Gebrselassie was running into top form though. He used the classic Oslo meet (4 July) for an all-out attack on Hissou's world record for 10,000 metres. Four pace-makers were enlisted to give him a helping hand but the greater part of the work was done by Worku Bikila, Haile's friend from childhood, who led up to 4500 metres. Then the master took over and went on relentlessly, finally shaving almost 7 seconds off Hissou's mark. The Ethiopian ace ran the second half (13:14.58) faster than the first (13:16.74). Mohammed Mourhit, a Moroccan-born Belgian, was second in 27:17.09. Details: Oslo, 4 July 1997 – 10,000 metres: 1.Haile Gebrselassie (Eti) 26:31.32, 2.Mohammed Mourhit (Bel) 27:17.09, 3.Dominic Kirui (Ken) 27:31.10, 4.Laban Chege Ken) 27:33.28, 5.Domingos Castro (Por) 27:41.75, 6.Khalid Skah (Mor) 27:44.33, 7.Toshinari Takaoka (Jap) 27:53.03, 8.Elijah Korir (Ken) 27:57.94, 9.Todd Williams (USA) 27:58.13; ....DNF: Bikila (Eti).

Kilometre fractions:

1000 m	2:39.6	
2000 m	5:17.3	(2:37.7)
3000 m	7:56.9	(2:39.6)
4000 m	10:36.3	(2:39.4)
5000 m	13:16.74	(2:40.4)
6000 m	15:56.69	(2:39.95)
7000 m	18:37.04	(2:40.35)
8000 m	21:17.60	(2:40.56)
9000 m	23:54.65	(2:37.05)
10,000 m	26:31.32	(2:36.67)

These splits are for Gebrselassie, as reported in "Track & Field News". He ran the last 400 metres in 61.4.

Two sub-4 miles in one race

In the same Oslo meet Komen won a 3000 metre race in 7:30.49. Only three days later at Stockholm he tried the 5000 metres but came out with a lackluster performance (fourth in 13:01.52 in a race won by Tom Nyariki in 12:55.94), probably due to a respiratory virus and a subsequent allergic reaction. Yet his favourite sphere in pre-Worlds engagements was to be found in shorter distances, as he confirmed at Hechtel on 19 July, when he astounded the track world – particularly its non-metric section – with history's first sub-8 minute 2 miles. Helped by his countryman Elijah Maru, who set the pace till 1200 metres, Komen produced a final time of 7:58.61. This came as a result of two subsequent sub-4 minute miles, 3:59.8 and 3:58.8. Coming as it did, forty-three years after Roger

Daniel Komen (Kenya), a talented but inconsistent performer, here winning a 5000 m. race in 12:48.98 (Rome 1997).

Bannister's first sub-4 for the mile, this was for some observers a mind-boggling achievement. In actual fact, it was probably inferior to Komen's 7:20.67 for 3000 metres at Rieti in 1996. This time, however, there was no 1-million dollar purse at stake (like in Gebrselassie's attempt at Hengelo two months ago) and the Kenyan, though almost two and a half seconds faster than the Ethiopian, had to be content with a $50,000 bonus .....

At the World Championships in Athens the two leading aces chose different paths. True to his favourite strategy, Gebrselassie was content with yet another 10,000 metre crown. In the final (6 August) Paul Tergat was again his toughest rival but finally had to succumb by just over one second. As it generally happens in championship races, in which hares cannot be enlisted (officially at least), the first half (13:59.5) was much slower than the second (13:25.1). His final time, 27:24.58 was of course less impressive than his 1:57.0 for the last 800 or his 55.87 for the last 400. Tergat was faster in the last 400 metres (55.2) but actually slower in the last 200 (27.5 vs. Gebrselassie's 27.3). Details: Athens, 6 August 1997 – 10,000 metres: 1.Haile Gebrselassie (Eti) 27:24.58, 2.Paul Tergat (Ken) 27:25.62, 3.Salah Hissou (Mor) 27:28.67, 4.Paul Koech (Ken) 27:30.39, 5.Assefa Mezegebu (Eti) 27:32.48, 6.Domingos Castro (Por) 27:36.52, 7.Habte Jifar (Eti) 28:00.29, 8.Julio Rey (Spa) 28:07.06.

The 5000 metre final (10 August) was featured by a slow pace in the first two kilometres. The 3000 metre mark was reached in 8:05.15, with Tom Nyariki in the lead, followed by Daniel Komen. But right there and then the latter injected an astounding 56.8 lap which, not surprisingly, took him well clear of the field. He closed with four more laps in the 60.0-to-62.5 range and that amply sufficed to earn him gold well ahead of Khalid Boulami of Morocco and Tom Nyariki. The winner covered the last 2000 metres in a great 5:01.6. Yet his final time was a quasi-ordinary 13:07.38. After the race he said: "This meeting is very different, and much harder, than the Grand Prix....... Now I have two days of rest before I face Gebrselassie in the 5000 metres in Zurich. I am still working on a plan to beat him".

Details:
Athens, 10 August 1997 – 5000 metres: 1.Daniel Komen (Ken) 13:07.38, 2.Khalid Boulami (Mor) 13:09.34, 3.Tom Nyariki (Ken) 13:11.09, 4.Ismail Sghyr (Mor) 13:17.45, 5.Dieter Baumann (Ger) 13:17.64, 6.Bob Kennedy (USA) 13:19.45, 7.El Hassan Lahssini (Mor) 13:20.52, 8.Enrique Molina (Spa) 13:24.54.

A night for the ages

The Zurich meet, 1997 version, offered a memorable night. In the space of 70 minutes the Letzigrund crowd was treated to three new world records! First, 7:59.08 by Wilson Boit Kipketer of Kenya in the steeplechase, then 1:41.24 by Wilson Kipketer of Denmark in the 800 metres and finally 12:41.86 by Gebrselassie in the 5000. The eagerly awaited clash between the Ethiopian and ultra-fresh world champion Daniel Komen, with Paul Tergat as "troisième larron", was truly fantastic. Pace-setters were Noureddine Béhar of Morocco till 1200 metres, then Martin Keino of Kenya till just before 3000 metres. The trio Komen-Gebrselassie-Tergat, in that order, took over at that stage (7:38.07). With two laps to go Tergat lost contact. Komen led at the bell but midway down the last backstretch, as a commentator put it, "the lightning struck": Gebrselassie sprinted in his best manner and his Kenyan rival could not respond. The crowd went wild as the Ethiopian went home in world record time – 12:41.86, i.e. 2.53 secs. under his previous mark. His superb finishing speed was reflected in the following figures: last 400 metres in 54.2, last 200 in 26.6, last 100 in 13.2. Komen's last lap was 58.4. Dieter Baumann, fifth, set a new German and European record of 12:54.70. Said the winner: "I must thank the Kenyan runners for setting a perfect pace". Quite predictably, Komen viewed things from a different angle: "I tried my best but you could see there was no help with the pace from the record holder". Details: Zurich, 13 August 1997 - 5000 metres: 1.Haile Gebrselassie (Eti) 12:41.86, 2.Daniel Komen (Ken) 12:44.90, 3.Paul Tergat (Ken) 12:49.87, 4.Khalid Boulami (Mor) 12:53.41, 5.Dieter Baumann (Ger) 12:54.70, 6.Paul Koech (Ken) 12:56.29,

7.David Chelule (Ken) 13:02.52, 8.Tom Nyariki (Ken) 13:04.41.

Kilometre fractions:

1000 m	2:34.6	
2000 m	5:06.6	(2:32.0)
3000 m	7:38.2	(2:31.6)
4000 m	10:13.2	(2:35.0)
5000 m	12:41.86	(2:28.7)

These were Gebrselassie's splits.

Who could have imagined that none of the three world records set in Zurich would last more than 11 days? And specifically Gebrselassie's record only 9 days? Yet that is what happened. Daniel Komen, vulnerable as he apparently was in head-to-head sprints, nonetheless confirmed his enormous potential nine days later in Brussels, when he bettered Gebrselassie's fresh record by over 2 seconds. That was the meet in which the Ethiopian lost not one but two world records! He was content with a new PB of 7:26.02 in the 3000 metre race (7:26.02) early in the afternoon. Then things began to happen: within one hour, first Komen in the 5000 metres, then Tergat in the 10,000 deprived him of his belongings. At the shorter distance Komen was aided by his countrymen Elijah Maru and Martin Keino, who carried him to 3000 metres in 7:37.3. He did the rest in his own metronomic style with 2:31.21 in each of the last two kilometres! But then the whole race was a masterpiece of pace judgment, with all kilometre fractions in the narrow range of just over one second! His last lap was 59.3 and his final time 12:39.74. Details:
Brussels, 22 August 1997 – 5000 metres:
1.Daniel Komen (Ken) 12:39.74, 2.Tom Nyariki (Ken) 13:08.78, 3.Ismail Sghyr (Mor) 13:11.75.

Kilometre fractions:

1000 m	2:32.7	
2000 m	5:05.4	(2:32.7)
3000 m	7:37.3	(2:31.9)
4000 m	10:08.53	(2:31.21)
5000 m	12:39.74	(2:31.21)

These are Komen's splits.

At the double distance Paul Tergat also had capable „aids-de-camp" from his own coun-

try – four, no less. When Salah Hissou of Morocco dropped back after 7000 metres, Paul decided that his moment had come. His long legs served him splendidly and he went home in 26:27.85, almost three and a half seconds inside Gebrselassie's record. He had run the second half in 13:09.9. Paul Koech completed Kenya's wonderful night with an excellent 26:36.26 for second, well ahead of Hissou. Details:
Brussels, 22 August 1997 – 10,000 metres:
1.Paul Tergat (Ken) 26:27.85, 2.Paul Koech (Ken) 26:36.26, 3.Salah Hissou (Mor) 27:09.07, 4.Mohammed Mourhit (Bel) 27:23.58, 5.Elijah Korir (Ken) 27:27.87, 6.Joshua Chelanga (Ken) 27:36.62, 7.Khalid Skah (Mor) 27:49.36, 8.Paul Evans (GB) 27:53.35.

Kilometre fractions:

1000 m	2:40.6	
2000 m	5:21.0	(2:40.4)
3000 m	8:00.6	(2:39.6)
4000 m	10:37.2	(2:36.6)
5000 m	13:18.0	(2:40.8)
6000 m	15:58.2	(2:40.2)
7000 m	18:37.8	(2:39.6)
8000 m	21:15.7	(2:37.9)
9000 m	23:52.1	(2:36.4)
10,000 m	26:27.85	(2:35.75)

These are Tergat's splits, released by A.Lennart Julin (ATFS/Sweden) as per video analysis.

Notwithstanding these (indirect) blows, Gebrselassie had a peerless season. He closed with a fine 5000 metre victory in 12:55.14 at Berlin on 26 August, beating Koech, Nyariki and Baumann. He went through the season undefeated, with four races at 3000 metres, five at 5000 and two at 10,000 and was no.1 in all three events in "Track & Field News" World Ranking.

Gebrselassie's Best Year

1998 offered no global (Olympic/World) championship. That was probably not the last reason why the ever cautious

Gebrselassie decided to go out early on the record breaking trail. In the space of two weeks in June he recaptured the two records he had lost in Brussels the year before, chalking up marks of 26:22.75 for 10,000 metres and then 12:39.36 for 5000 – records that are still unmatched at the time of writing, almost four years later. He failed only in his attempt to crack Daniel Komen's 3000 metre record. As usual, the Ethiopian ace favoured quality over quantity: he ran no more than 11 races in the distance department – six at 3000 metres, four at 5000 and one at 10,000. With no defeats, as usual.

The Gebrselassie vs. Komen feud was first renewed indoors, but merely on an indirect clock-wise confrontation. The former started with 7:26.15 for 3000 metres at Karlsruhe on 25 January, a new world indoor best. But his rival was quick to respond: 7:24.90 at Budapest on 6 February, with 1500 metre halves in 3:44.8 and 3:40.1. This was followed by another record performance at Stockholm only 13 days later, when the indefatigable Kenyan posted a 12:51.48 for 5000 metres, thus depriving his arch rival of yet another (1-year-old) belonging. The indoor account was closed in Komen's favour.

Always eager "to impress the clock", Komen opened his outdoor account Down Under with 7:58.91 for 2 miles (Sydney, 28 February), missing his own best-on-record mark by merely 0.30. Except that this time he needed only one sub-4 to do it, his halves being 4:01.44 and 3:57.47.

Then came Gebrselassie with two superlative "glory days" in June. He started on his "home" track at Hengelo on 1 June with a great 26:22.75 for the '10' - 5.10 secs. under Paul Tergat's listed record. The weather looked bad in the early hours of the day but it turned for the better by racing time. After availing himself of three team-mates of good quality, who kept the pace alive and hot, Haile was on his own only in the last 4 kilometres. After experiencing a minor crisis between 6000 and 7000 metres, he closed in brilliant style. It was his fourth world record at Hengelo over the last five years. Twenty thousand spectators assembled at the Fanny-Blankers-Koen Stadium cheered the irrepressible "Mr. Hengelo", as he was called

over there. Details:
Hengelo, 1 June 1998 – 10,000 metres: 1.Haile Gebrselassie (Eti) 26:22.75, 2.Habte Jifar Eti) 27:29.97, 3.Girma Tola (Eti) 27:32.02, 4.Philip Kemei (Ken) 27:34.51, 5.Aloÿs Nizigama (Bur) 27:35.74, 6.Miroslav Vanko (Svk) 28:01.84.

Kilometre fractions:

1000 m	2:35.4	
2000 m	5:16.0	(2 :40.6)
3000 m	7:53.03	(2 :37.0)
4000 m	10:31.3	(2 :38.3)
5000 m	13:11.7	(2 :40.4)
6000 m	15:51.1	(2 :39.4)
7000 m	18:32.45	(2 :41.4)
8000 m	21:12.92	(2 :40.5)
9000 m	23:51.53	(2 :38.6)
10,000 m	26:22.75	(2 :31.2)

These are Gebrselassie's splits. He ran the last 400 metres in 58.1.

Twelve days later Gebrselassie administered another blow to his Kenyan rivals. This time his target was Komen's 5000 metre record (12:39.74) and the venue of the meet was one of the "lieux sacrés" of distance running – Helsinki. Once again, a team of hares was there to set the stage for the champion. As it often happens, they barely lasted half the race. After six laps Gebrselassie decided to take command of the operations. He had to, because at that stage he was down vis-à-vis Komen's pace. He ran the last 2000 metres in a superb 5:00.1. A strong last lap (56.77) won the day for him – by merely 0.38 sec. Details:
Helsinki, 13 June 1998 – 5000 metres: 1.Haile Gebrselassie (Eti) 12:39.36, 2.Luke Kipkosgei (Ken) 13.07.06, 3.Daniel Gachara (Ken) 13:07.27, 4.James Kimutai Kosgei (Ken) 13:17.49.

Kilometre fractions:

1000 m 2:34.8
2000 m 5:06.4 (2:31.6)
3000 m 7:39.3 (2:32.9)
4000 m 10:12.1 (2:32.8)
5000 m 12:39.36 (2:27.3)

This was to remain Gebrselassie's last world

record outdoors. Here is a recapitulation of his wonderful series:

Hengelo,
4 June 1994   5000 m.   12:56.96
Kerkrade,
28 May 1995   2 miles   8:07.46 *
Hengelo,
5 June 1995   10,000 m.   26:43.53
Zurich,
16 August 1995   5000 m.   12:44.39
Hengelo,
31 May 1997   2 miles   8:01.08 *
Oslo,
4 July 1997   10,000 m.   26:31.32
Zurich,
13 August 1997   5000 m.   12:41.86
Hengelo,
1 June 1998   10,000 m.   26:22.75
Helsinki,
13 June 1998   5000 m.   12 :39.36

* best-on-record performance at distance no longer recognized by the IAAF.

Between 1996 and 1999 he also amassed 6 world indoor records at distances ranging from 2000 to 5000 metres. In terms of quantity, Gebrselassie's status as a record-breaker would tend to pale if compared with those of Nurmi, Zátopek and Clarke. Apart from the fact that it is not always fair to compare human deeds that occurred in different epochs, it must be remembered that nowadays international competition on a world-wide scale is much more intense than it ever was. This may well explain why 5000/10,000 doubles in global (Olympic/World) championships are an absolute rarity nowadays – the last one dates from 1980 (Miruts Yifter at the Moscow Olympics). The demand in terms of endurance-to-speed is tremendous in this day and age. Suffice it to say that Gebrselassie can point to a PB of 3:31.76 over 1500 metres indoors (1998), incidentally the second best time on record in the annals of indoor competition – as well as 3:33.73 outdoors (1999). And that in the spring of 2002 he ran a marathon in 2 hr 06:35 (in his first try as a senior). His magnitude as a runner seems to be well reflected in such figures.

The rest of Gebrselassie's 1998 season was almost anti-climactic. In the big Zurich meet

(12 August) he won the 5000 metres in 12:54.08. In his wake four runners ducked under 13 minutes: Luke Kipkosgei (12:57.90), Assefa Mezegebu (12:58.31), Paul Tergat (12:58.74) and Million Wolde (12:59.39). Then came a half-hearted attempt to crack Komen's 3000 metre record, on 28 August in Brussels, but on a cold evening Gebrselassie had to be content with 7:25.09, the second best time on record. As for Komen, he suffered an unexpected defeat over 5000 metres in the same Brussels meet as he was outsprinted by Assefa Mezegebu of Ethiopia – 12:54.82 to 12:53.84.

Komen closed on a fairly high note, with 5000 metre victories in the World Cup at Johannesburg (altitude, 1753 m.) in 13:46.57 and in the Commonwealth Games at Kuala Lumpur in 13:22.57. Quite interesting, in the same meet, was the victory of Simon Maina in the 10,000 metres. His time, 28:10.00, was remarkable in view of the difficult weather conditions, hot and humid. Maina, a 20-year-old Kenyan, had a PB of 27:21.14, made in Japan (where he lived) earlier in the year. In the Grand Prix final in Moscow Komen's arch rival

Paul Tergat (Kenya), one of the greatest distance runners of recent years.

167

Gebrselassie won the 3000 metres in 7:50.00. Most regrettably, the two never met throughout such a long season ... Yet the superiority of the Ethiopian was unquestionable. Once again, "Track & Field News" ranked him no.1 in 3000, 5000 and 10,000 metres.

Family Race

In 1998 the most invincible of present-day distance runners, Haile Gebrselassie, became the subject of a film bearing the title "Endurance". The American troupe that made it was in Asela, the native place of the Ethiopian champion, for several months. His entire family provided the cast. As he said to Hannah Wallace: "My nephew plays me when I was a child; my cousin is my father as a young man; my sister plays my mother and my father plays himself. Everyone did very well. The movie starts in 1980 when as a boy I heard about the famous Ethiopian runner Miruts Yifter's wins at the Moscow Olympics". In the Amharic language Haile Gebrselassie means "Strength of the Holy Trinity". That was actually the name of the last Emperor (Negus) of Ethiopia, minus Gebre" (holy).

Early in 1999 Gebrselassie collected what is to this day his last world record: 12:50.38 for 5000 metres in an indoor meet at Birmingham on 14 February, a remarkable achievement on a 200-metre track. Throughout his journey – 25 laps - he was reportedly incensed by 600 wild cheering Ethiopians "bussed from London, courtesy of an Ethiopian restaurant owner".
The World Indoor Championships at Maebashi, Japan, found Haile as sharp as ever, in spite of the fact that he got there just in time, after a 40-hour air trip from Addis Abeba, where he had visited his wife and infant son. Japanese officials gave him a helping hand by doing away with the 3000 metre heats in favour of a straight final. On 5 March he won the 3000 metres in 7:53.57 after a furious battle with Paul Bitok (7:53.79) .Two days later he took the 1500

in 3:33.77, beating Laban Rotich of Kenya (3:33.98), one of the world's best at that distance. He pocketed $100,000 for his two victories. Added to his previous feats, that was enough to stamp him as one of the greatest indoor runners of all time.
As often in the recent past, his rivals had cause for laughter only when he was not there. It happened on 9 June in Milan, where Daniel Komen was beaten by Salah Hissou in a fast 5000 metre race – 12:55.18 to 12:52.53. A day after that Gebrselassie was in Helsinki, where he again failed in an attempt to break Komen's tough 3000 metre record, doing no better than 7:26.03. The tireless Ethiopian went on to set a Bislett track record for 5000 metres: 12:53.92 (Oslo, 30 June). The season's fastest 10,000 metre mark before the Worlds belonged to Habte Jifar with 27:06.45 (Hengelo, 30 May). The last important pre-Seville test was at Zurich on 11 August, and Gebrselassie won a 5000 metre race as he pleased in 12:49.64 from Hissou (12:53.45) and Benjamin Limo of Kenya (12:55.86). That was to remain the year's fastest time.
The Worlds were held at Seville, with temperatures rising consistently to 35° C. and over. Hence, far from ideal conditions for distance runners. The 10,000 metre race, contested in a straight final (32 entries), was not expected to yield fast times. The first half took 14:17.17. The other half was certainly faster (13:40.10), yet the decisive battle flared up with just over a lap to go. Gebrselassie and Tergat were again the chief characters in the play: although trying all he knew with a sizzling 55.1 last lap, the Kenyan had to give way to his formidable rival, who answered with 54.4 and won by a little more than a second. Ethiopians also took third, fourth and sixth! This was Gebrselassie's fourth straight world title at this distance. Details:
Seville, 24 August 1999 – 10,000 metres: 1.Haile Gebrselassie (Eti) 27:57.27, 2.Paul Tergat (Ken) 27:58.56, 3.Assefa Mezegebu (Eti) 27:59.15, 4.Girma Tola (Eti) 28:02.08, 5.Antonio Pinto (Por) 28:03.42, 6.Habte Jifar (Eti) 28:08.82, 7.Benjamin Maiyo (Ken) 28:14.98, 8.Kamiel Maase (Hol) 28:15.58.
As it was to be expected, Gebrselassie stayed away from the 5000 metres. Here Daniel

Komen experienced a bitter defeat. In the final (28 August) he took the lead four laps from home but soon found that conditions would not allow him to go all out in his usual way. In the penultimate lap he lost contact, just when Hissou, Lahlafi and Mourhit – all Moroccan-born, even though the last one was by then a Belgian citizen – engaged the decisive battle and Benjamin Limo followed at a close distance. Limo was actually the fastest of the four in the last lap (55.0) and caught all but Hissou (56.0) who held on to the end. Komen was a dejected fifth. Details: Seville, 28 August 1999 – 5000 metres: 1.Salah Hissou (Mor) 12:58.13, 2.Benjamin Limo (Ken) 12:58.72, 3.Mohammed Mourhit (Bel) 12:58.80, 4.Brahim Lahlafi (Mor) 12:59.09, 5.Daniel Komen (Ken) 13:04.71, 6.Fita Bayissa (Eti) 13:13.86, 7.Hailu Mekonnen (Eti) 13:18.97, 8.Million Wolde (Eti) 13:20.81.

Of course it should be remembered that earlier in the month both Hissou and Benjamin Limo had been flatly beaten by Gebrselassie in Zurich ....

The most surprising late season note was provided by Charles Kamathi, a 21-year-old Kenyan police constable whose only previous races outside his home country were two victorious efforts in India at 3000 (7:56.56) and 5000 metres (13:45.91). His 10,000 metre best at high altitude was just inside 29 minutes. On 3 September in Brussels he "exploded" with a nifty 26:51.49, beating Mohammed Mourhit (26:52.30) and Paul Koech (27:10.38). Said the winner: "Disappointed that I didn't get to measure myself against world record holder Haile Gebrselassie".

As for Mourhit (born at Khourigba on 10 October 1970; 1.64 m. / 55 kg.), he was a Belgian citizen since July 1997. Therefore his time of 26:52.30 represented a new European record. The previous one was quite fresh: 27:12.47 by António Pinto of Portugal earlier in 1999.

The final act of the Golden League (Berlin, 7 September) saw the Kenyans on top as Benjamin Limo won the 5000 metres in 12:59.54 from Richard Limo (12:59.75) and Sammy Kipketer (12:59.90). Komen was only fourth (13:00.69) and the newly crowned world champion Salah Hissou sixth (13:01.07).

Once again, Gebrselassie was no.1 in "Track & Field News" World Ranking - in three events. He did all this with 11 races: seven at 3000, three at 5000 and one at 10,000 metres. And no defeats, as usual. Kamathi, whose best time was over one minute faster than Gebrselassie's, was ranked fourth. Said the compilers about the Ethiopian: "Given the conditions during his "unrabbited" World Championship win in the heat of Seville, compared to the professionally paced, balmy weathered Kamathi race in Brussels, there was little doubt as to which of the performances was best".

A new star emerged in the early stages of 2000 – Algeria's Ali Saidi Sief (born at Constantine on 15 March 1978; 1.80 m. / 68 kg.), whose pre-2000 best at 5000 metres was no better than 13:39.5. He was until then at his best in the 1500 metres (3:30.91 in 1999). Early in the Olympic year he served a warning of things to come in a 3000 metre race at Saint-Denis (23 June), beating Daniel Komen as he pleased – 7:27.67 to 7:31.47. Exactly a week later, at the Golden Gala in Rome, the 22-year-old Algerian won a classy 5000 metres in 12:50.86 from Sammy Kipketer (12:54.07)

Salah Hissou (Morocco), winner of the 5000 metres at the 1999 World Championships in Seville.

Million Wolde (Ethiopia), left, beating Ali Saidi Sief (Algeria) in the 5000 metres at the 2000 Olympics in Sydney.

and Paul Tergat (12:55.18). Kipketer, not yet 19, had been doing very well since 1999 (12:58.10).

As usual, the Kenyan Championships at Nairobi in July were to serve as Trial meet for the Olympics. The real sensation was John Korir, still a junior, who won the 10,000 metres in 27:48.42, fastest ever at high altitude (1000 m. or higher). The 5000 metres was a race of upsets: Julius Gitachi won in 13:24.4 from Richard Limo and Tergat. New star Kipketer was only fourth and Benjamin Limo fifth and so they did not make the Olympic team. Nor did Komen and Ismael Kirui, who were eliminated in the heats. These races (both on 22 July) were watched by a crowd estimated at 15,000.

Sammy Kipketer found partial consolation in subsequent European meets. In Oslo (28 July) he won a good 5000 in 12:55.03, beating his older countryman Mark Bett (12:55.63). The winner was still hopeful: "If I can continue without injuries, I have a good hope for the 5000 metres in Sydney". But his hopes were dashed by officials of the Kenya AAA, who confirmed that they intended to respect the results of the Trials. Haile Gebrselassie was by then sparing nervous energies for the Olympic test, scheduled for late September in Australia. He won three 5000 metre races with times in the 13-plus region, then improved to 12:57.95 in Zurich (11 August), beating Tergat (12:58.21) and Kipketer (12:58.63) in a close finish. In the meantime Ali Saidi Sief was collecting new credentials. The African Championships at Algers were once more depleted by the absence of many leading athletes then busy on the European circuit. Local matador Saidi Sief won the 5000 metres unopposed in 13:26.86. He showed a lot more at Monaco on 18 August, when he won a classy 3000 metre race in 7:25.02, third best ever at that non-Olympic distance. In so doing he beat the likes of Mourhit, Komen and Lahlafi.

The Brussels meet (25 August) yielded the fastest times of 2000, even though people like Gebrselassie and Saidi Sief were not there. Brahim Lahlafi of Morocco won a hotly contested 5000 in 12:49.28, a new national record. Mohammed Mourhit of Belgium, second, set a new European record of 12:49.71. Komen, far from his best condition, was third (13:01.78). Poor Kipketer finished a disappointing ninth. Paul Tergat won the 10,000 metres in 27:03.87 from Felix Limo (27:04.54). The latter race was featured by a first half much faster than the second: 13:18.98 vs. 13:44.89.

The Sydney Olympics – second to be held in the Southern Hemisphere, after Melbourne 1956 – came after the end of the European circus, yet the dates were more comfortable than those allowed to their predecessors forty-four years earlier (late November). The 10,000 metres (two rounds) came first and offered a fascinating duel. Gebrselassie's counterpart was once again Paul Tergat of Kenya, who had been playing second fiddle to the Ethiopian in four global (Olympic/World) tests between 1995 and '99. The Kenyan tried to turn the tables on his "bête noire" and at one time it looked as if he may at last succeed ... The Ethiopian had been considered a doubtful starter due to an Achilles tendon injury, but at the last moment he decided to try. Aloÿs Nizigama of Burundi and Patrick Ivuti of Kenya alternated in the lead and the former reached 5000 metres in 13:45.8. With less than 7 laps remaining John Korir, holder of the fastest time ever run at altitude, took over. Approaching the bell, five men were still in contention – Korir, Gebrselassie, Tergat, Mezegebu and Ivuti. In the final lap, Tergat made his break with 250 metres to go, with Gebrselassie in his wake. The long-legged Kenyan – at 1.82 m. eighteen centimetres taller than his Ethiopian rival – held a narrow lead till 50 metres to go, when Gebrselassie drew even. What followed was the most dramatic struggle ever seen in a long distance event, save perhaps for the Kolehmainen vs. Bouin classic in the 5000 metres of the Stockholm Olympics, back in 1912. As they approached the line, Tergat appeared to tie up a little bit and Gebrselassie dipped past to win by 0.09 sec. - a smaller margin than that of Maurice Green of USA (0.12 sec.) in winning the 100 metres in the same meet. Gebrselassie's second half (13:32.1) was much faster than the first (13:46.1). He ran the last lap in 56.4, the last 200 in 25.4. Assefa Mezegebu, third, earned Ethiopia another medal. Details:

Sydney, 25 September 2000 – 10,000 metres: 1.Haile Gebrselassie (Eti) 27:18.20, 2.Paul Tergat (Ken) 27:18.29, 3.Assefa Mezegebu (Eti) 27:19.75, 4.Patrick Ivuti (Ken) 27:20.44, 5.John Korir (Ken) 27:24.75, 6.Said Bérioui (Mor) 27:37.83, 7.Toshinari Takaoka (Jap) 27:40.44, 8.Karl Keska (GB) 27:44.09.

As expected, Gebrselassie did not run the 5000 metres. Curiously enough, he can point to just one medal (silver at the 1993 Worlds) in global tests at this distance, no matter if his competitive record and his times clearly stamp him as the no.1 performer of our time. In his absence, Saidi Sief was the favourite of many, thanks to his speed potential. But the Algerian, visibly lacking experience in the 5000 metres, shifted from second to fifth and vice versa for most of the race. Yet he was in the lead coming off the final turn, only to be punished by Million Wolde's closing burst. The Ethiopian ran the last 200 metres in 27.3, the last 100 in 13.8 – as opposed to Saidi Sief's 28.1 and 14.5. Final times were in the 13:30-plus region, ordinary stuff nowadays. It could be said that the supposedly speediest runner had been beaten in the slowest possible race. Details: Sydney, 30 September 2000 – 5000 metres: 1.Million Wolde (Eti) 13:35.49, 2.Ali Saidi Sief (Alg) 13:36.20, 3.Brahim Lahlafi (Mor) 13:36.47, 4.Fita Bayissa (Eti) 13:37.03, 5.David Chelule (Ken) 13:37.13, 6.Dagned Alemu (Eti) 13:37.17, 7.Sergey Lyebed (Ukr) 13:37.80, 8.Jirka Arndt (Ger) 13:38.57.

Million Wolde (born in Addis Abeba on 17 March 1979; 1.75 m. / 59 kg.) was world junior champion in the 5000 metres in 1998 and in the same year he ran the distance in 12:59.39. Officially his fastest 1500 metre time was 3:39.15 (1998), much slower than Saidi Sief's 3:30.82 (2000). Wolde's victory over the Algerian was therefore a surprise. What's more, out of five major 5000 metre races he ran in 2000, the young Ethiopian won just one – the Olympic final! No surprise he was only seventh in "Track & Field News" World Ranking. Gebrselassie, once more undefeated, was no.1 in both 5000 and 10,000 metres. This time he stayed away from the 3000 metres and that allowed Saidi Sief to earn the no.1 spot there, ahead of Daniel Komen.

The Sydney Olympics were a triumph for Ethiopian distance runners: they won 3 of the 6 medals at stake. On the whole, Africans monopolized places 1-to-6 in both 5000 and 10,000 metres.

In November 2000 Gebrselassie underwent surgery on his right Achilles tendon, which had troubled him during the Olympic season. One source described this as "slight surgery", yet he deemed it advisable to stay away from competition for part of 2001, more exactly till the World Championships, scheduled for early August in Edmonton, Canada. Due to his absence or not, it is a fact that the standard of élite runners in 2001 was not very high, particularly in the 5000 metres.

As usual, the indoor season saw little action in the 3000 metres, yet it may be of interest to record a successful inroad by Hicham El Guerrouj of Morocco, the king of milers, who beat quite a few "specialists" in the 3000 of the World Indoor Championships in Lisbon. He won in 7:37.74 from Mohammed Mourhit (7:38.94), while Olympic champion Million Wolde had to be content with fifth.

On 4 May the track of Stanford University at Palo Alto, California, was the theatre of a 10,000 metre race which was to remain the fastest of the year. A little known Kenyan, Abraham Chebii, barely 21, bettered his PR by nearly a minute to win in 27:04.20. In so doing he broke the US All Comers record set by one Gebrselassie at the 1996 Olympics in Atlanta. In his wake two other Kenyans, Benjamin Maiyo (27:07.55) and Luke Kipkosgei (27:12.37). Mebrahtom ("Meb") Keflezighi, fourth, brought the US record to 27:13.98. This last, born at Asmara, Eritrea in 1975 as one of a family of 11 children, applied for US citizenship in 1997, not knowing if his native country of Eritrea would participate in the 2000 Olympics in Sydney. He became a US citizen in 1998 and did compete in the Sydney Games (12th in the 10,000 metres).

However, no one of the Palo Alto heroes was to play a prominent rôle in the spicy part of the 2001 season. Chebii, for example, had to be content with 7th in the Kenyan Championships. The men who were to shine in Edmonton began to appear in the front row in June meets. Olympic bronze medallist Assefa Mezegebu won the 10,000 metres at Hengelo (4 June) after a tight duel with Charles Kamathi. Times, 27:22.30 and 27:22.58. A week later in Athens Sammy Kipketer, not yet 20, won a hotly contested 5000 in 12:59.34 from Benjamin Limo (12:59.60), John Kibowen (12:59.97) and Mezegebu (13:00.86). The Golden Gala in Rome (29 June) provided another close finish: Hailu Mekonnen of Ethiopia won in 12:58.57 from Benjamin Limo (12:59.53) and Kipketer (12:59.94), with Richard Limo fourth (13:00.32) and Kamathi only 10th.

The Kenyan Championships in the high altitude of Nairobi offered excellent times. On 23 June Richard Limo won the 5000 metres in 13:17.2 from Kipketer (13:17.6) and Kibowen (13:19.5), while Benjamin Limo, fourth (13:24.7) failed to qualify for the Worlds. In the 10,000, run on the same day, Kamathi beat defending champion John Korir, 27:47.33 to 27:49.34, with Paul Kosgei third (27:51.87).

Richard Limo, no. 684, winner of the 5000 metres at the 2001 World Championships in Edmonton.

Haile Gebrselassie, now 28, went to the Worlds with no seasonal credentials. He stayed away from running for two months following his operation, then he resumed training, carefully and gradually. Even so, such was the aura of invincibilty surrounding this little great man (no defeat at distances over 1500 metres since 1996) that most prognosticators tipped him as the most likely winner of the 10,000 metres.

At Edmonton the time schedule was strange: heats of the 5000 metres on 6 August, final of the 10,000 on 8 August, final of the 5000 on 10 August. Of course Gebrselassie had his work cut short as he only ran the '10'. Weather conditions were pretty good for distance running (19° C. and humidity 42%). Once again, clock-wise the race seemed just ordinary, yet it offered great competition. It was dormant till 8000-plus metres when the leading pack consisted of 11 men. Gebrselassie was usually second or running alongside the leader. Heading towards the bell, the pace obviously became hotter. Going into the last turn the Ethiopian led as expected and hardly anyone in the crowd would have thought that .... But just around the turn it became evident that he lacked his usual zip. Entering the homestretch Kamathi pulled even, with Mezegebu close. Right there and then Kamathi became the first man in years to run away from the Ethiopian "myth" in a battle down the homestretch. The Kenyan forged ahead, soon followed by Mezegebu. The latter did his utmost for Ethiopia's honour but finally had to settle for second. Gebrselassie was third, in front of his little known compatriot Yibeltal Admassu. A comparison of finishing speeds may be of interest:

	Last 400 m.	200 m.	100 m.
C.Kamathi	55.6	26.4	13.1
A.Mezegebu	56.7	26.8	13.5
H.Gebrselassie	57.0	27.6	14.0

For once, Gebrselassie was beaten at his own game. From the look of things, however, he was not his real self. His teammate Mezegebu pointed to his relative lack of training, and manager Jos Hermens revealed that he ran a high temperature only three days before the race. Gebrselassie himself surprised many a listener when he said: "I'm really in good shape". Surely he was as gracious in defeat as he had always been modest in victory.

Details: Edmonton, 8 August 2001 – 10,000 metres: 1.Charles Kamathi (Ken) 27:53.25, 2.Assefa Mezegebu (Eti) 27:53.97, 3.Haile Gebrselassie (Eti) 27:54.41, 4.Yibeltal Admassu (Eti) 27:55.24, 5.Fabián Roncero (Spa) 27:56.07, 6.José Rios (Spa) 27:56.58, 7.Paul Kosgei (Ken) 27:57.56, 8.John Korir (Ken) 27:58.06.

Even after this, the Kenyans were still eager to avenge their Olympic defeats. A well conceived team tactic appeared to be the answer to the problem in the 5000 metres. Said Richard Limo: "So we sat down and planned how the race would be won". It should be a trick likely to neutralize the finishing speed of Million Wolde and Ali Saidi Sief. Limo and Sammy Kipketer went to work immediately with a 59.0 first lap. Young Kipketer did

Charles Kamathi (Kenya) winning the 10,000 metres at the 2001 World Championships in Edmonton. The invincibility of Haile Gebrselassie, third, came to an end in this race.

most of the work: he led till 3000 metres (7:51.18), after which he slowed down. Then it was Saidi Sief's turn to try and get rid of the rest, but two men , Limo and Wolde, were able to hang on. Early in the last lap the Algerian looked like the most probable winner – until Limo drew level down the last turn and drove away. His last 100 metres, 13.5, was much faster than Saidi Sief's (15.2). Wolde had to be content with third. But shortly afterwards came the news that Saidi Sief had been suspended following a positive test for nandrolone. Consequently, John Kibowen rose to bronze medal status. As far as the long distances were concerned, Kenya and Ethiopia thus tied with three medals each, except that the former supplied the winner in both races - a complete reversal of the Sydney Olympics. Details:

Edmonton, 10 August 2001 – 5000 metres: 1.Richard Limo (Ken) 13:00.77, 2. Million Wolde (Eti) 13:03.47, 3.John Kibowen (Ken) 13:05.20, 4.Alberto Garcia (Spa) 13:05.60, 5.Ismail Sghyr (Fra) 13:07.71, 6.Sammy Kipketer (Ken) 13:08.46, 7.Abiyote Abate (Eti) 13:14.07, 8.Hailu Mekonnen (Eti) 13:20.24. Disqualified: Ali Saidi Sief (Alg) 13:02.16.

Richard Limo (born at Cheptigit on 18 November 1980; 1.67 m. / 53 kg.) progressed from tenth in the Olympics to first in the Worlds, in the space of one year. A member of the great Kalenjin tribe – 10-11 % of Kenya's total population - he set world junior records for 3000 metres (1998) and 2 miles (1999), with 7:36.76 and 8:13.47 respectively. He confirmed his claim to the no.1 position in the 2001 World Ranking when he scored another important victory - in Zurich (17 August), with the year' fastest time, 12:56.72. One had to go back to 1994 to find a slower year leader though …. Runner-up in Zurich was another Kenyan, Mark Bett (12:58.72). Other post-Edmonton meets failed to offer exceptional performances, even considering that Grand Prix meets generally have the 3000 metres as the longest distance. The only world shattering mark occurred in the steeplechase, when Brahim Boulami of Morocco posted a great 7:55.28 in Brussels on 24 August, thus breaking Kenya's long monopoly in the event.

World champions Richard Limo (5000) and Kamathi (10,000) were ranked no.1 in their respective events. Gebrselassie, who never ran the 5000 metres in 2001, was given third place at the longer distance – after six straight "firsts" (1995 through 2000).

" Why don't they break my record?"

Indoor races at 10,000 metres are an absolute rarity. As previously recounted in this book, a record attempt at this distance was made in 1975 by Emiel Puttemans of Belgium, unquestionably one of the greatest indoor "specialists" in the annals of the sport. His time, an excellent 28:12.4 made on a 166.66 metre track at Porte-de-Pantin near Paris, was still unsurpassed at the dawn of 2002. Simply because no one of the great Africans of our time had thought it advisable to negotiate such an exorbitant number of laps. Puttemans himself must have thought: "Why don't they break my record?" Late in 2001 it was revealed that a 10,000 metre race indoors was in the planning. Puttemans himself was said to be an enthusiastic supporter of the idea. Not surprisingly, the project materialized in Belgium. On 10 February 2002 at Gent eight runners lined up at the start of an indoor race over 10,000 metres. The "vehicle" was a 200-metre banked synthetic track, so that the runners had to negotiate "only" 50 laps – instead of 60 as in Puttemans' 1975 attempt. The field included two pace-makers. Only five men finished. Not surprisingly, only the fifth and last failed to better Puttemans' old record. Winner and new record holder was a 25-year-old Kenyan, Mark Bett, in 27:50.29. He was followed by Luke Kipkosgei, also of Kenya (27:50.37), Abderrahim Goumri (27:52.62), Jaouad Gharib (28:02.09) both of Morocco, and the better known Paul Bitok of Kenya (28:20.31). Organizers saw to it that even 6-miles times were taken. First at that stage was Kipkosgei with 27:00.88, this too a world best. In his 1975 race Puttemans was clocked at the English distance in 27:17.6.

WOMEN FROM EARLY WHISPERS TO KAZANKINA AND KRISTIANSEN

10

It is generally assumed by sport historians that women's athletics originated a long, long time ago, though perhaps in forms quite different from those prevalent nowadays. Since the earliest times, however, even illustrious men seemed to have mental reservations about the participation of women in sport. A prejudice that subsisted in modern times as well, especially as regards long distance races, which up to the first half of the 20th century happened to be viewed by several male observers as "unladylike" pastimes. In modern times the earliest references to an athletic activity by women date from the middle of the 17th century, mostly as participants in English fairs and wakes. Yet for incipient forms of the sport as we know it today one had to wait till the 1890's, when early women's meets were held in Ireland, USA and other English speaking countries. In a truly international perspective, however, the real boost came from France, namely from a fervent "suffragette" named Alice Milliat, who in 1917 founded the "Fédération Féminine Sportive de France". Two years later her request to have women events included in the Olympic programme was refused by the IOC. The tenacious French pioneer and her associates went ahead by themselves and decided to organize the first multi-national women's meet. This was held in the Principauté de Monaco from 24 to 31 March 1921 and was essentially an Anglo-French festival. The longest running event on the programme was an 800 metre race which was won by Lucie Bréard of France in 2:30 1/5. Runner-up was Mary Lines of England, the top sprinter of those days! Late in the same year, Madame Milliat and her group founded the "Fédération Sportive Féminine Internationale" (FSFI). The newly born organization held the inaugural Women's World Games at Stade Pershing, Paris, on 20 August 1922. The longest running event was a 1000 metre race, won by said Bréard in 3:12.0. The FSFI held three more editions of the World Games: Göteborg 1926, Prague 1930 and London 1934, in which the longest distance was reduced to 800 metres. The IOC and the IAAF finally abandoned their prejudices and decided to include women's events in the programme of the Olympic Games of 1928 in Amsterdam – merely five events to be sure, with 800 metres as the longest track test. This first experience gave rise to controversies though, partly due to an unwise time schedule which called for heats and final of the 800 metres to be held on consecutive days. Winner of the decisive race was Lina Radke-Batschauer of Germany in 2:16 4/5, a new world record. At the end of the race, several competitors were clearly exhausted. Competent observers valued their condition as "no better no worse" than what sometimes occurred with men under similar circumstances, but "conservatives" within the IAAF thought differently and decided that the 800 metres would no longer appear on the women's Olympic programme. Such an ostracism was abandoned only thirty-two years later ...

Of course, longer distance events like 1500 or 3000 metres - let alone 5000 or 10,000 metres – had to wait longer than that before being accepted at the highest levels. However, Ekkehard zur Megede and Richard Hymans, in their study of the evolution of world best performances, give times of 7:11 2/5 and .... 6:13 1/5 by Elizabeth Atkinson of Great Britain, both in 1921, as the earliest 1-mile records in modern history. The same authorities also give the following as earliest best-on-record marks over longer distances: 1500 metres, 5:54 3/5 by Lucie Cadiès of France in 1918; 3000 metres, 14:44 2/5 Ana Cicanei of Romania in 1927. Even the marathon was explored –

Violet Piercy of Great Britain was timed in 3 hrs 40:22 in a solo time trial on the classic Windsor-to-Chiswick course in 1926.

However, to meet the real "trail blazers" in distance running we must reach the late Sixties. One such performer was Paola Pigni of Italy (born in Milan on 30 December 1945; 1.70 m. / 63 kg.). She was credited with 16:17.4 over 5000 metres at Formia on 11 May 1969. While enroute, she was clocked in 9:42.8 at 3000 metres, another best-on-record mark. Pigni, a keen "explorer" of the sport, excelled over a wide range of distances. Anne O'Brien of Ireland did 38:06.4 for 10,000 metres at Gormanstown on 26 March 1967 – the earliest best-on-record performance at this distance, obliterated by Paola Pigni's 35:30.5 in Milan on 9 May 1970.

Slowly but gradually, prejudices about women were abandoned. In the late Sixties and early Seventies, magazines concerned with distance running gave wide publicity to the theories of Dr. Ernst Van Aaken of Germany, a coach and physician who championed the cause of women's distance running. He actually claimed that women had the ideal physical and mental prerequisites to excel in the long-grind department, also that their mental and physical characteristics are such as to reduce susceptibility to fatigue. He further noted that their lower sweat losses reduced the stress of dehydration and concluded that over the long distances they would come close to men's standards more quickly than in the sprints.

Getting back to Paola Pigni, it should be said that she started as a sprinter (12.9 in the 100 metres and 27.0 in the 200 in 1961, aged 16). She moved up gradually and conquered Italian records for 400 (54.2) and 800 metres (2:07.9), both in 1966. In the two-lap event she reached the semi-finals at the 1968 Olympics in Mexico City. At this distance she was to improve to 2:01.98 in 1975, but her parade event in international competition was the 1500 metres – simply because longer events were not included in the programme of major meets. In 1969 she set a world record for the "metric mile": 4:12.4, but she lost it later in the season when she placed third at the European Championships in 4:12.0 (the winner was Jaroslava Jehlickova of Czechoslovakia in

4:10.7). At the 1972 Olympics in Munich she was clever enough to improve on his PB three times and finally won another bronze medal in 4:02.85, which was to remain her best ever. In 1973 she set a new world record of 4:29.5 for the English mile. In the meantime she had begun to explore longer distances , as previously related. On the last day of 1971 in Rome she won a marathon in 3 hrs 00:47.0.

As far as the Olympic programme was concerned, the 1500 metres was first included in 1972 (Munich), the 3000 in 1984 (Los Angeles) – to be replaced by the 5000 in 1996 (Atlanta). Finally, the 10,000 metres first appeared in 1988 (Seoul).

First to achieve world fame at the longer distances was Lyudmila Bragina of USSR (born at Sverdlovsk on 24 July 1943; 1.65 m. / 57 kg.). In 1972, just before the Munich Olympics, she set world records of 4:06.9 (1500 metres) and 8:53.0 (3000 metres). The latter was history's first sub-9 minute effort: she improved to 8:52.8 in the USA vs USSR dual meet at Durham, North Carolina in 1974, incidentally the first world record officially recognised by the IAAF. In the same year the 3000 metres was included in the programme of the European Championships in Rome and Bragina was upset by Nina Holmén of Finland, who beat the Russian – 8:55.2 to 8:56.2. The winner ran the last 400 metres in 62.2.

Another trail blazer was Grete Andersen of Norway (born in Oslo on 1 October 1953; 1.72 m. / 54 kg.), who in 1975 in Oslo shaved 6.2 secs. off Bragina's 3000 metre record with 8:46.6. Only three days later she married her coach, Jack Waitz. Endowed with great endurance but not equally strong in hectic finishes, this dedicated Norwegian runner suffered – just like Pigni - as a result of the late inclusion of long distance events in the IAAF programme. However - in 1974, after she placed third in the 1500 metres at the European Championships in Rome, somebody asked her if she didn't perhaps contemplate to move up to the 3000 metres. She simply replied: "I have tried that distance already and I think it's too long ..." Be it as it may, she was quick to change her mind: as related above, only a year later she reached a new milestone in the 3000 metres.

In 1976 Andersen-Waitz and Bragina continued to battle for the world record, even though the 3000 metres was not yet part of the Olympic programme. The Norwegian lowered it to 8:45.4 at Oslo on 21 June, with kilometre fractions in 2:55.7, 2:54.8 and 2:54.9. Clearly she had by then become an efficient "racing car", with a great sense of pace judgement. However, Bragina had a superior potential in terms of basic speed, and she showed just that when she put the 3000 metre record out of sight with 8:27.2 at College Park, Maryland in August of the same year. She covered the last kilometre in 2:47.2.

Andersen-Waitz eventually found her ideal "home" not in the 3000 metres but in .... the marathon. She really made history at this distance, up to the day when she ran it in 2 hr 25:28.7 in London in 1983. Her series of 9 victories in the New York marathon – the last one in 1988, when she was 35 – made her a legendary figure in the annals of the event. Her onetime reluctance to even contemplate the 3000 metres as a possible experiment was long forgotten!

The first major titles in women's long distance running were awarded in 1980, when the IAAF conceived the idea of holding an avant-première of the World Championships (to be inaugurated in 1983) just for 3000 and 10,000 metres. This was at Sittard, Holland on 15/16 August. On the first day Kath Binns of Great Britain won the 10,000 in 32:57.17 with nearly 1 minute to spare vis-à-vis the runner-up. The next day Birgit Friedmann of Germany won the 3000 metres in 8:48.05. These races were devalued by the absence of the leading USSR runners, who were to take 8 of the top 10 places in the World Year List for 3000 metres at the end of the season!

The Eighties eventually saw the definitive coming of age of women's long distance events, up to and including 10,000 metres. In 1981 the first official world records accepted by the IAAF were as follows:
5000 metres – 15:14.51 by Paula Fudge (GB) at Knarvik, Norway on 13 September 1981
10,000 metres – 32:17.20 by Yelena Sipatova (USSR) in Moscow on 19 September 1981

From then on record attempts obviously became more and more frequent. 1982 saw a complete re-writing of the record book. Anne Audain of New Zealand, 27, got the ball rolling with 15:13.22 for the 5000 metres at Auckland on 17 March. She won the 3000 metres in 8:45.53 at the Commonwealth Games later in the year.

The summer months of 1982 had an American as the chief character in the play: Mary Decker (born at Flemington, New Jersey, on 4 August 1958; 1.68 m. / 49 kg.), who was to have a long, glorious and troubled career. She showed great precocity and in 1973, aged 15, she amazed the track world with such times as 2:02.43 (800 metres) and 4:25.7 (1500). The former was in the triangular meet Germany-USA-Switzerland in Munich and Baby-Decker was third, one second behind the winner, Hildegard Falck of Germany, then holder of the world record! Her further development was delayed by a long chain of injuries, some of which required surgery. In later years she was deeply involved in athletics even family-wise: her first husband, Ron Tabb, was a distance runner; her second, Richard Slaney of Great Britain, was a discus thrower. In a way, this helped her find the courage to fight back in the face of adversity. In the long run she did herself justice and in 1982 she set two world records for the long distances, both at Eugene, Oregon, the Mecca of American Track & Field: 15:08.26 for 5000 metres on 5 June and 31:35.3 for 10,000 metres on 16 July.

In the meantime, USSR remained the hotbed of distance running, at least in terms of "depth". In the summer of 1982, namely at Kiev on 25 July, Svyetlana Ulmasova succeeded Bragina as holder of the world record for 3000 metres with a time of 8:26.78. Amazingly enough, this came as a result of very uneven pace, with kilometre fractions in 3:04.4, 2:37.4 and 2:45.0. Ulmasova (née Glukharyeva at Novo Balakhly on 4 February 1953; 1.61 m. / 53 kg.) had been crowned European champion in 1978, when the 3000 metres first appeared on the programme of a major title meet. In 1982 she successfully defended her title in Athens and in doing so she honoured her fresh world record at that distance. She won in 8:30.28

Tatyana Kazankina (USSR) at the 1980 Olympics in Moscow. A great middle distance runner, she explored longer distances in the latter part of her career and in 1984 set a new world record for the 3000 metres: 8:22.62.

from Maricica Puica of Romania (8:33.33) and Yelena Sipatova of USSR (8:34.06).

1983 was the year of the inaugural World Championships, held in Helsinki. Longest distance on the women's programme was, of course, the 3000 metres. Before that important rendezvous, however, there had been a new world record for 10,000 metres – this was at Krasnodar on 29 May, when Lyudmila Baranova bettered Decker's recent mark with 31:35.01, beating another Russian, Olga Krentser (31:35.61) in a close finish. The new record-woman, 33, was not selected for the World Championships though.

Mary Decker reached the apex of her career in Helsinki. By then 25, she decided to vie

for a double – 3000/1500 metres. This implied , counting heats and finals, a total of four races in the space of six days. On 8 August Ulmasova won heat 1 of the 3000 metres in 8:46.65, while Tatyana Kazankina took heat 2 from Mary Decker as both were timed in 8:44.72. The final two days later promised a nice feud involving these three women. But Brigitte Kraus of Germany managed to interfere more than somewhat. Decker decided to set the pace but did so without spreading herself thin: 1000 metres in 2:51.0 and 2000 in 5:48.2 (second kilometre in 2:57.2). Having bided her time, the American was still full of running when the decisive battle flared up. Going round the last turn, first Ulmasova and then Kazankina tried to forge ahead but Mary held on. Kazankina drew level with the American with 50 metres to go but Decker was not to be denied and went on to win. In the last stretch of land Kraus came closing fast and nipped Kazankina for second. World record holder Ulmasova had to be content with fourth. Decker covered the last 400 metres in 60.8 and the last 200 in 28.9. Details:

Helsinki, 10 August 1983 – 3000 metres: 1.Mary Decker (USA) 8:34.62, 2.Brigitte Kraus (Ger) 8:35.11, 3.Tatyana Kazankina (USSR) 8:35.13, 4.Svyetlana Ulmasova (USSR) 8:35.55, 5.Wendy Sly (GB) 8:37.06, 6.Agnese Possamai (Ita) 8:37.96.

On 12 August Decker won a heat of the 1500 metres in 4:07.47 and two days later she annexed her second world title after regaining the lead barely 10 metres from the tape. She won in 4:00.90. Her toughest rival was Zamira Zaytseva of USSR, who overstrode and fell with 5 metres to go, rolling across the line in second place (4:01.19). Decker sped the last 300 metres in 44.2.

Before the end of the season there emerged from the inexhaustible USSR reservoir another fine runner, Raisa Sadreydinova, who on 7 September at Odessa lowered the world's 10,000 metre record to 31:27.58, winning from Olga Krentser-Bondarenko (31:38.64) and Tatyana Pozdnyakova (31:48.94).

Among up-and-coming runners of those days one must count Zola Budd of South Africa, a country then barred from international competition on account of its Apartheid policies.

A reserved, shy, light-footed girl, she seemed to have a great talent for running. In the Olympic year 1984 she lowered the world record for 5000 metres to 15:01.83 during a meet at Stellenbosch on 5 January. For the above-mentioned reason this mark was not ratified by the IAAF. Zola Budd (born at Bloemfontein on 26 May 1966; 1.61 m. / 43 kg.) had made the headlines before turning 18. Of course the fact that she was not eligible for international competition dismayed all true sportsmen. However, her father was still a British citizen and on 6 April 1984 this enabled her to obtain the citizenship of that country. The operation was supported by the Conservative government then in power, but it was frowned upon by H.M.'s opposition and more so by political enemies of South Africa in other countries. As a result, Budd did not have an easy life when she settled in Britain to prepare for the Olympic Games in Los Angeles. Just before flying to England she had run the 3000 metres in 8:37.5. At the British Olympic Trials she won over the same distance in 8:40.22.

While this was going on, the USSR cohort kept going strong. On 24 June in Kiev Olga Krentser-Bondarenko shaved nearly 14 seconds off Sadreydinova's 10,000 metre record with 31:13.78. In her wake five other runners ducked under 32 minutes, as follows: 2.Galina Zakharova 31:15.00, 3.Zhanna Tursunova 31:53.53, 4.Lyubov Konyukhova 31:56.01, 5.Anna Domoratskaya 31:56.02, 6. Raisa Smyekhnova 31:59.0.

In the meantime Grete Waitz of Norway had found a worthy heiress in Ingrid Kristiansen (née Christensen at Trondheim on 21 March 1956; 1.69 m. / 58 kg.). As a youth the latter practised cross-country skiing with considerable success, while cultivating almost simultaneously her growing love for running. As time went on she explored all distances ranging from 800 metres to the marathon. She held the Norwegian 800 metre record with 2:09.7 (1981) but in due course she became especially prominent as a marathon runner – to the point of setting best-on-record marks for the distance, up to a final 2 hrs 21:06 (1985). On the track she accounted for the first sub-15 min. mark over 5000 metres – 14:58.89 in Oslo on 28 June 1984. Her devotion to the sport was such

that in 1983 she won a marathon in Houston barely five months after giving birth to a child. She opted for this distance at the 1984 Olympics in Los Angeles.

The Games were held in the Californian city for the second time, after those of 1932. The Memorial Coliseum had been refurbished for the occasion and conditions were well-nigh ideal. Except that the vicious game of political boycotts, as mentioned in the men's section, kept away USSR and allied countries, all except Romania. This obviously cast a giant shadow over the Games and the women's distance events were heavily affected. The 3000 metres was included in the Olympic programme for the first time. In the preliminary round (8 August) Maricica Puica of Romania accounted for the fastest time, 8:43.32. Zola Budd in the colours of Great Britain was third in the same heat and qualified easily. Other heats were won by Decker (8:44.38) and Brigitte Kraus (8:57.53). The final (10 August) was devalued by a dramatic incident. Decker and Budd were active as pace-setters and led the pack at 1000 metres (2:50.5). Early in the second half of the race they were involved in a collision. Budd was leading and Decker repeatedly challenged her on the inside. The two bumped a first time, then bumped again. The American fell, sprawled on the infield grass. She tried to get up but pain in her left hip made things difficult for her. When the field passed her, America's sweetheart was out of it and eventually dropped out. Budd regained her balance but was visibly upset. She probably lost her concentration when she saw Mary lying on the ground. Wendy Sly of Great Britain and Puica were unaffected - even though the latter had to hurdle over Decker's legs - and jumped into the lead. Budd tried to fight back and was again in the lead at 2000 metres (5:44.1), but her effort was short-lived and she lost contact irreparably. With 250 metres to go, Puica passed Sly and built up a massive lead. The Romanian, then 34, thus won the race of her life, covering the last 200 metres in 31.8 – as opposed to Sly's 35.1. Budd finished a dejected seventh. Brigitte Kraus had dropped out soon after 2000 metres due to a leg injury. Details:
Los Angeles, 10 August 1984 – 3000 metres: 1.Maricica Puica (Rom) 8:35.96,

2.Wendy Sly (GB) 8:39.47, 3.Lynn Williams (Can) 8:42.14, 4.Cindy Bremser (USA) 8:42.78 ...... 7.Zola Budd (GB) 8:48.80 ...... DNF: Mary Decker (USA).

The timetables for 1500 and 3000 metres were perversely intertwined. Winner at the shorter distance was Gabriella Dorio of Italy (4:03.25) and Puica, running her fourth race in just as many days, finished a brilliant third. This brave runner (née Luca in Bucharest on 29 July 1950; 1.68 m. / 55 kg.) was by then a veteran who could point to notable performances in several important races. Married to her coach, Ion Puica, she had lost the greater part of the 1983 season due to an injury.

The Los Angeles Games also saw the inaugural women's marathon in the annals of the quadrennial meet. This is still remembered as one of the greatest races ever. Joan Benoit of USA won in 2 hr 24:52 from the likes of Grete Waitz, Rosa Mota of Portugal and Ingrid Kristiansen. A classy field, if ever there was one, since all four were to occupy a choice place among pioneers of the event.

The Russians predictably used post-Olympic meets in Europe to "straighten things out". Tatyana Kazankina won a 3000 metre race in 8:33.01 during a festival of Communist bloc countries – as someone noted, this time was almost 3 seconds faster than Puica's winning effort in the Olympics .... But the best was yet to come: ten days later, Kazankina tried again and brought the world record to 8:22.62. This was in Leningrad on 26 August, and she had kilometre fractions of 2:47.5, 2:49.0 and 2:46.1. The runner-up, Galina Zakharova, did 8:36.19.

Grete Waitz (Norway), centre, competing in a "mixed" marathon race.

Tatyana Kazankina (born at Petrovsk on 17 December 1951; 1.62 m. / 48 kg.), married Kovalenko, had a remarkable record as a middle distance ace. In 1976 she scored a rare 800/1500 metre double at the Montreal Olympics. Four years later, in Moscow, she successfully defended her 1500 metre title. She had several world records to be proud of: 1:54.94 for 800 metres in the Olympic final at Montreal; 3:56.0 (1976), 3:55.0 and a magnificent 3:52.47 (both in 1980). The birth of two children, in 1978 and 1982 respectively, obviously caused pauses but she was at it again as soon as she could.

Sad interlude

Tatyana Kazankina, a sweet and genuine woman from the Saratov region, is remembered as one of the greatest figures in the annals of the middle distances. After conquering all there was to conquer in the 800/1500 metre department, she turned her attention to the 3000 and in 1984 she reached new milestones there too, lowering the world record to 8:22.62. All this when she was 33 and the mother of two children. A week after that wondrous achievement. which was to remain unsurpassed for nine years, she made the headlines again, alas for a decidedly different reason. It happened on 4 September 1984 in Paris, when she tried a new distance, 5000 metres. She won handily in 15:23.12. After the race she was invited to submit to a doping test – but she refused. There was talk of misunderstandings between her and the USSR Athletics federation, but the IAAF was obviously faithful to its rules, under which any such refusal is to be punished and Kazankina was therefore suspended from track activities for 18 months. A sad interlude, no doubt. The ghost of doping in its many forms has accompanied distance runners too, from time to time. There is a PS anyhow: late in 1986 Kazankina, then 35, made a comeback on the road and managed to place fifth in the IAAF World Championship at 15 kilometres.

The lull before the (Chinese) storm

The first noteworthy performance of 1985 came from the indefatigable Ingrid Kristiansen – history's first sub-31 min. mark over 10,000 metres. Venue, the classic Bislett Stadium in Oslo, i.e. in Ingrid's backyard. After following Ria van Landeghem of Belgium, the Norwegian took the lead at 2400 metres and did the rest in fine style, with a final time of 30:59.42. In fact, the second half (15:24.88) was faster than the first (15:34.54). Details:
Oslo, 27 July 1985 – 10,000 metres:
1.Ingrid Kristiansen (Nor) 30:59.42, 2.Aurora Cunha (Por) 31:35.45, 3.Lynn Jennings (USA) 32:03.37.

Kilometre fractions:

1000 m.	3:13.29	
2000 m	6:18.37	(3:05.08)
3000 m.	9:22.32	(3:03.95)
4000 m.	12:27.49	(3:05.17)
5000 m.	15:34.54	(3:07.05)
6000 m.	18:41.53	(3:06.99)
7000 m.	21:47.55	(3:06.02)
8000 m.	24:54.04	(3:06.49)
9000 m.	28:00.76	(3:06.72)
10,000 m.	30:59.42	(2:58.66)

Kristiansen attributed her success, at least in part, to the stellar example of her compatriot and predecessor Grete Waitz. But she also credited her youthful experience in cross-country skiing for giving her the taste of solitary efforts. In this respect she was a trail blazer, resembling the case of Ron Clarke among men. With a difference though: in the Eighties competition in women's distance running was still relatively "soft". Zola Budd probably came from the same mould, mentally at least, in the sense that she too was eager to discover new worlds. She partly made amends for her unhappy Olympic experience by succeeding Kristiansen as holder of the world record for 5000 metres. And she did so in a head-to-head confrontation with the Norwegian at London's Crystal Palace. The two cooperated in setting the pace in the first two kilometres, then the 19-

year-old girl from Bloemfontein (altitude 1426 m.), who used to run barefooted, piled up a sizable lead, which was nearly 10 seconds at the end. Her time was 14:48.07. Kristiansen was badly beaten, yet finished inside her former record. Details:

London, 26 August 1985 – 5000 metres: 1.Zola Budd (SA/GB) 14:48.07, 2.Ingrid Kristiansen (Nor) 14:57.43, 3.Lorraine Moller (NZ) 15:35.75.

Kilometre fractions:

1000 m.	2:53.68	
2000 m.	5:48.99	(2:55.31)
3000 m.	8:50.44	(3:01.45)
4000 m.	11:52.12	(3:01.68)
5000 m.	14:48.07	(2:55.95)

Budd ran the last 400 metres in 68.1.

Mary Decker also overcame the trauma of her Olympic experience and achieved important results at both 1500 and 3000 metres, exactly as she had done at the 1983 Worlds. She lowered the world record for the mile to 4:16.71 (Zurich, 21 August), beating Maricica Puica (4:17.33) and Budd (4:17.57). She also had the year's fastest time at 3000 metres – 8:25.83 (Rome, 7 September). Here again she confined Puica (8:27.83) and Budd (8:28.83) to the rank of ladies-in-waiting.

The three queens of 1985 – Decker, Budd and Kristiansen – bypassed the World Cup, held at Canberra early in October. Aurora Cunha (Eur/Por) won the 10,000 metres in 32:07.50 (5 October) and Ulrike Bruns of the GDR took the 3000 in 9:14.65 (6 October).

In the summer of 1986 Ingrid Kristiansen returned to her favourite venue, Bislett Stadium in Oslo, and literally "massacred" her 1-year-old world record for 10,000 metres with a scintillating 30:13.74 – nearly 46 seconds under her previous mark! This prowess brought back memories of Ron Clarke's historic 27:39.4 at the same distance in the same stadium back in 1965. The Norwegian runner was aided by Lesley Welch of USA till 2800 metres, then she took over and again managed to run a second half (15:02.41) faster than the first (15:11.33). Her final time, 30:13.74, was in the neighbourhood of Paavo Nurmi's one-time "estate"...... Aurora Cunha, a good runner from Portugal, was again second, same as

Tatyana Samolenko (USSR) winning the 3000 metres at the 1987 World Championships in Rome from Maricica Puica (Romania). Four days later the Russian won the 1500 as well.

in the 1985 race. Details:

Oslo, 5 July 1986 – 10,000 metres: 1.Ingrid Kristiansen (Nor) 30:13.74, 2.Aurora Cunha (Por) 31:29.41, 3.Erika Vereb (Hun) 32:19.86, 4.Ria van Landeghem (Bel) 32:29.73.

Kilometre fractions:

1000 m.	3:01.15	
2000 m.	6:05.23	(3:04.08)
3000 m.	9:10.01	(3:04.78)
4000 m.	12:11.24	(3:01.23)
5000 m.	15:11.33	(3:00.09)
6000 m.	18:11.47	(3:00.14)
7000 m.	21:12.40	(3:00.93)
8000 m.	24:16.01	(3:03.61)
9000 m.	27:18.30	(3:02.29)
10,000 m.	30:13.74	(2:55.44)

Kristiansen ran the last 400 metres in 67.8.

1986 was also the year of the Commonwealth Games and the European Championships. The former, held in Edinburgh, were boycotted by no less than 32 countries, as a protest for the British Government's refusal to impose heavy economic sanctions on South Africa, still loyal to its Apartheid policies. Most of the absent teams were from Africa, Asia and the Caribbean area. Under such circumstances the Edinburgh festival in general and the long distance events in particular were heavily devalued. On 27 July Lynn Williams of Canada won the 3000 metres in 8:54.29 from Debbie Bowker of Canada (8:54.83). The following day Liz Lynch of Scotland took the 10,000 metres 31:41.42 from Anne Audain of New Zealand (31:53.31). As it will be seen later, Miss Lynch was to achieve world fame as Mrs. McColgan.

Shortly before the Europeans Ingrid Kristiansen was chasing records again, this time in Stockholm. Her target was Zola Budd's 5000 metre record (14:48.07). Her attempt was crowned by great success as she cut almost 11 seconds off Zola's mark. A Dutch hare, Elly van Hulst, led for 2200 metres, then Kristiansen took command and concluded with a final kilometre almost as fast as the first. Details:

Stockholm, 5 August 1986 – 5000 metres:
1. Ingrid Kristiansen (Nor) 14:37.33,
2. Dorthe Rasmussen (Den) 16:02.20.

Kilometre fractions:

1000 m.	2:52.9	
2000 m.	5:48.0	(2:55.1)
3000 m.	8:45.44	(2:57.5)
4000 m.	11:43.9	(2:58.4)
5000 m.	14:37.33	(2:53.5)

Kristiansen ran the last 400 metres in 67.2, the last 200 in 32.5.

Ingrid Kristiansen (Norwey), a great pioneer in women's long distance running.

Taking into account her above-mentioned marathon best (2 hr 21:06 in 1985), it is clear that the Norwegian deserves a prominent rôle among the pioneers of women's distance running.

At the European Championships in Stuttgart the 3000 metres came first (28 August). Kristiansen, who a couple of weeks earlier in Zurich had won a race at that distance in 8:34.10, decided to stay away, mainly to concentrate on the '10'. This was probably a wise decision after all, because the field at the shorter distance included some very tough competitors. Olga Bondarenko of USSR uncorked a 64.1 last lap to vanquish Olympic champion Maricica Puica. Zola Budd, never at her best in hectic finishes, had to be content with fourth. Details:

Stuttgart, 28 August 1986 – 3000 metres: 1.Olga Bondarenko (USSR) 8:33.99, 2.Maricica Puica (Rom) 8:35.92, 3.Yvonne Murray (GB) 8:37.15, 4.Zola Budd (GB) 8:38.20, 5.Tatyana Samolenko (USSR) 8:40.35.

The 10,000 metres, included in the programme for the first time and held two days later, turned out to be a one-woman's-show. Kristiansen really won as she pleased. Olga Bondarenko, running her third race in the space of four days, was left well over half a minute behind, yet became the second woman to duck under 31 minutes. Details:

Stuttgart, 30 August 1986 – 10,000 metres: 1.Ingrid Kristiansen (Nor) 30:23.25, 2.Olga Bondarenko (USSR) 30:57.21, 3.Ulrike Bruns (GDR) 31:19.76, 4.Aurora Cunha (Por) 31:39.35, 5.Svyetlana Guskova (USSR) 31:42.43.

Kristiansen '86 – a near perfect season

In "Track & Field News" World Ranking for 1986 Ingrid Kristiansen came dangerously close to scoring a grand slam, unique in its kind – being no.1 in four events. She was ranked first in 3000, 5000 and 10,000 metres and second (to her "inspirer" Grete Waitz) in the marathon. The last one was a very difficult decision. The two Norwegians had never met on a marathon course during the year and the ranking was simply based on their best times: 2 hr 24:54 for Waitz in London, 2 hr 24:55 for Kristiansen in Boston. Commented the magazine: " .... a mere 1-second advantage. Yet Kristiansen had a better back-up race. What to do? No matter which way we went, we knew that we'd get stacks of letters saying it was the wrong way. Our final analysis was that New York ended up as the year's major confrontation, and since Waitz won that one, she had title no.6. Her previous leaderships came in 1978-79-80 and in 1982-83". Shaky judgements apart (how can one equate different marathon courses?), it is interesting to note that Kristiansen went through the season without a loss at distances ranging from 3000 metres to the marathon. She ran the 3000 four times, 5000, 10,000 and marathon twice each.

The World Championships in Rome were of course the dominant test of 1987. Fortunately this meet was graced with the presence of all leading athletes, which was a major consolation for those who had suffered the evil effects of Olympic boycotts. Kristiansen was not the outstanding figure, even though she won at her favourite distance, the 10,000 metres. Such a rank should be given to Tatyana Samolenko of USSR (née Khamitova at Orenburg on 12 August 1961; 1.66 m. / 57 kg.), a teacher who had been doing well at shorter distances, up to 3:59.45 in the 1500 and 53.5 in the 400, both in 1986. In the same year she ran the 3000 in 8:36.00. Given such a basic speed, she loomed as a dangerous prospect. She went to Rome with a plan in mind – win both 1500 and 3000 metres and thereby emulate Mary Decker's feat in 1983. At Stadio Olimpico the 3000 came first. Wendy Sly of Britain had the fastest qualifying time, 8:44.79, while Samolenko and Puica came through without any trouble. Olga Bondarenko also qualified easily, but at the last moment she opted for the 10,000 metres, which was to be contested in two rounds, perversely intertwined with those of the shorter race. (It is to be noted that before coming to Rome Bondarenko had won the USSR 3000 metre title in 8:53.92, beating Samolenko, among others). The 3000 metre final was on a hot, humid evening.

Samolenko relied on her finish to win from Puica, then 37. Details:

Rome, 1 September 1987 – 3000 metres: 1.Tatyana Samolenko (USSR) 8:38.73, 2.Maricica Puica (Rom) 8:39.45, 3.Ulrike Bruns (GDR) 8:40.30, 4.Cornelia Bürki (Swi) 8:40.31, 5.Yelena Romanova (USSR) 8:41.33, 6.Elly Van Hulst (Hol) 8:42.56.

Samolenko was not afraid of "doubles", a problem by then affecting even male runners. Two days after the 3000 metre final she lined up for the prelims of the 1500 and qualified easily. Another two days later (5 September) she annexed the title for that distance, after emerging the winner (3:58.56) in a close finish. Third in this race was Sandra Gasser of Switzerland, who later lost her medal for drugs abuse.

In the prelims of the 10,000 metres, Kristiansen was content to qualify with a slow (for her) 33:10.37. In the final (4 September), after a funeral first lap (77.8) the Norwegian deemed it advisable to inject a second lap in 68.4, which was enough to dis-courage her rivals who lost contact immediately. Yet what followed was a difficult solo effort, given weather conditions (hot and humid). Kristiansen had to slow down towards the end, yet she managed to preserve a safe lead. Yelena Zhupiyova of USSR closed faster than anyone else and took second, after covering the last lap in 61.5 – as opposed to Kristiansen's 72.4. The second half (15:44.34) was considerably slower than the first (15:21.51). Maybe some of her rivals repented not having followed the Norwegian in the initial stage .... After the race Kristiansen revealed that prior to the Worlds she had lost three and a half weeks of training due to an injury. Her only workouts were in the pool and on a stationary bicycle. "I am very happy to have won this title – she said – because a month ago I wasn't certain I would be able to start here". Details:

Rome, 4 September 1987 – 10,000 metres: 1.Ingrid Kristiansen (Nor) 31:05.85, 2. Yelena Zhupiyova (USSR) 31:09.40, 3.Kathrin Ullrich (GDR) 31:11.34, 4.Olga

Bondarenko (USSR) 31:18.38, 5.Liz Lynch (GB) 31:19.82, 6.Lynn Jennings (USA) 31:45.43.

In 1988 the Olympic Games were held in Asia for the second time. Twenty-four years after the Tokyo edition, Seoul took the charge of organizing the festival. For once, the boycotting trend was reduced to a minimum, compared to the dramas of 1980 and 1984. All the best distance runners of the distaff side were on hand. Travel brochures labelled South Korea as "The Land of the Morning Calm". As it turned out, such a slogan could just as well apply to the afternoons of athletics because the crowd followed the proceedings in a religious silence, interrupted only on occasion by more or less loud cheers.

Samolenko was again shooting for a 1500/3000 metre double but met strong competition over both distances, mostly from a sturdy Romanian, Paula Ivan. The feud between them ended in a draw. In the prelims of the 3000 metres (23 September) Ivan won her heat in 8:43.10, while Samolenko was content to qualify in fifth place. The other heat was won by Yelena Romanova of USSR in 8:48.47. In the final two days later the early leaders were Mary Decker-Slaney, nursing a bad leg, Vicki Huber (USA) and Paula Ivan. In the decisive stage, Ivan and Samolenko remained alone to fight it out for gold. The strong Russian settled the issue in her favour with a 59.4 last lap and a 28.6 in the last 200 metres. Her time, 8:26.53, was the third fastest ever. Details:

Seoul, 25 September 1988 - 1.Tatyana Samolenko (USSR) 8:26.53, 2.Paula Ivan (Rom) 8:27.15, 3.Yvonne Murray (GB) 8:29.02, 4.Yelena Romanova (USSR) 8:30.45, 5.Natalya Artyomova (USSR) 8:31.67, 6.Vicki Huber (USA) 8:37.25.

On 1 October Paula Ivan evened the count in the 1500 metres, simply by applying the same tactic that had carried Samolenko to victory in the 3000, i.e. forcing the pace from the beginning. Her rivals were soon left behind and no one of them ever had the ghost of a chance. The 25-year-old Romanian won in 3:53.96, second best time ever, leaving her nearest rivals nearly seven seconds behind! And Samolenko was only third (4:00.30).

In the 10,000 metres Olga Bondarenko avenged her defeat of the year before in Rome. It must be said, however, that she was indirectly helped by an incident that befell world record holder Ingrid Kristiansen, who had to drop out after 2000 metres due to an injured right foot. As the game of life has it ("the show must go on"), after the "master" stepped out, the other runners went on with renewed vigour. Bondarenko used a 31.2 last 200 to nail victory over Liz Lynch-McColgan, a feather weight from Great Britain. Details:

Seoul, 30 September 1988 - 10,000 metres: 1.Olga Bondarenko (USSR) 31:05.21, 2.Liz Lynch-McColgan (GB) 31:08.44, 3.Yelena Zhupiyova (USSR) 31:19.82, 4.Kathrin Ullrich (GDR) 31:29.27, 5.Francie Larrieu-Smith (USA) 31:35.52, 6.Lynn Jennings (USA) 31:39.93.

It should be noted that the marks of Seoul winners in both 3000 and 10,000 metres were the fastest of the year.

1989, same as the two preceding years, was to go down in history without a single world record in the 3000/5000/10,000 metre area. This "abstinence" was to continue for three more years, giving rise to speculations. Some critics ventured the opinion that doping tests had become more efficient. As a matter of fact, in the spring of 1989 the IAAF introduced random tests which could be conducted anytime anywhere, even on training camps.

Dominating the 1989 scene were the European Cup at Gateshead and the World Cup at Barcelona, team competitions in which scores were everybody's main concern. Paula Ivan, for example, ran the 3000 metres for Romania at Gateshead and the 1500 as a member of the Europe team at Barcelona. In the former (5 August) she won easily in 8:38.48 from Yvonne Murray of Great Britain (8:44.34). Still at Gateshead (6 August) Kathrin Ullrich of the GDR won the 10,000 as she pleased in 32:17.88 from Viorica Ghican of Romania (32:41.34).

In the 10,000 metres of the World Cup (9 September) Kristiansen led for 9800 metres only to be outshone in the closing stage by Ullrich's devastating kick (last 200 in 28.5). The East German won in 31:33.92, with the Norwegian second (31:42.01) and Natalya

Mary Decker (USA), no. 492, winning the 3000 metres at the inaugural World Championships in Helsinki, 1983, from Brigitte Kraus (Germany), left, and Tatyana Kazankina, no.451.

Sorokivskaya of USSR third (32:15.53). The following day Yvonne Murray won a good 3000 in 8:44.32, quite comfortably from Tatyana Pozdnyakova of USSR (8:49.42) and PattiSue Plumer of USA (8:54.33).

Two more 1989 performances, favoured by clement Scandinavian evenings, are worth a mention: 30:48.51 for 10,000 metres by Kristiansen (Oslo, 1 July) and 14:59.01 for 5000 by Ullrich (Stockholm, 3 July).

1990 offered a richer programme, with the Commonwealth Games in January/February at Auckland and the European Championships at Split, Yugoslavia, in late August. The former were blessed with a record number of entries. Angela Chalmers of Canada scored an upset victory in the 3000 metres (28 January) , beating two better known Scotswomen, Yvonne Murray and Liz Lynch-McColgan. They finished in that order – times 8:38.38, 8:39.46 and 8:47.66. In the 10,000 metres (2 February) the light-footed McColgan won almost as she pleased in 32:23.56.

Yvonne Murray managed to peak twice during that long season and in August she won the European 3000 metre title at Split, at the end of a heated battle with Yelena Romanova of USSR. The Scotswoman had to produce three final 200-metre fractions of 30.5, 29.7 and 31.8 to win the game. Details:

Split, 29 August 1990 – 3000 metres: 1.Yvonne Murray (GB) 8:43.06, 2.Yelena Romanova (USSR) 8:43.68, 3.Roberta Brunet (Ita) 8:46.19, 4.Lyubov Kremlyova (USSR) 8:46.94, 5.Margareta Keszeg (Rom) 8:48.04, 6.Päivi Tikkanen (Fin) 8:50.26.

Romanova, a 27-year-old student from Volgograd, had better luck in the 10,000 metres two days later. At the end of a strange race (first half in 16:10.6, second half in 15:36.3), the Russian outsprinted Kathrin Ullrich with a 31.2 last 200. Details:

Split, 31 August 1990 - 10,000 metres: 1.Yelena Romanova (USSR) 31:46.83, 2.Kathrin Ullrich (GDR) 31:47.70, 3.Annette Sergent (Fra) 31:51.68, 4.Midde Hamrin (Swe) 31:58.25, 5.Nadia Dandolo (Ita) 32:02.37, 6.Nadyezhda Gallianova (USSR) 32:03.07.

A fine performance by Liz McColgan highlighted the early part of the 1991 season: 30:57.07 for 10,000 metres at Hengelo on 25 June. This lithe Briton (née Lynch at Dundee on 24 May 1964; 1.68 m. / 45 kg.) was already a well-known runner in 1987 when she married steeplechaser Peter McColgan, having won the 10,000 metres at the Commonwealth Games the previous year. The feather-weight type of runner, she was sporting a peculiar coiffure. In November 1990 she gave birth to a daughter, after which she made a surprisingly fast recovery to place second in the World Cross-Country Championships barely four months later.

The outstanding figure in the 3000 metres was once again Tatyana Samolenko, who in the meantime had married walker Viktor Dorovskikh. She and McColgan turned out to be the top performers at the World Championships in Tokyo. Incidentally, these opened a three-year streak of consecutive "global" meets, the first in track history - Worlds '91, Olympics '92 and Worlds '93.

Samolenko-Dorovskikh again tried for a double - 3000/1500 metres. Same as in the Seoul Olympics, she hit gold at the longer distance but had to be content with a lesser metal (this time, silver) in the 1500. The fastest time in the 3000 metre heats (24 August) was 8:46.56 by Susan Sirma of Kenya. The shocking event of the final two days later materialized in the last lap when Yvonne Murray, then in the leading pack with Romanova, Samolenko and Sirma, suddenly lost contact and eventually faded to 10th. The Russian duo finally had the upper hand and Samolenko used a 30.3 last 200 to vanquish her teammate. Sirma, a 25-year-old Kenyan who had been living in Japan and then in Britain, took third with a new national record. Said the 30-year-old winner: "My choice now is whether I want another baby or if I want to try to run in next year's Olympics. Training is very difficult and tiring". Details:

Tokyo, 26 August 1991 – 3000 metres: 1.Tatyana Samolenko-Dorovskikh (USSR) 8:35.82, 2. Yelena Romanova (USSR) 8:36.06, 3.Susan Sirma (Ken) 8:39.41, 4.Päivi Tikkanen (Fin) 8:41.30, 5.Margareta Keszeg (Rom) 8:42.02, 6.Roberta Brunet (Ita) 8:42.64.

The 10,000 metres introduced a new trend: for the first time in high-level competition there were signs of a forthcoming ... Chinese danger. Wang Xiuting, 26, and the lesser known Zhong Huandi, 24, both won medals, were it only in the wake of a scintillating Liz McColgan. Wang, to be sure, had been a finalist in the 1987 Worlds and in the 1988 Olympics (8th and 7th respectively). The two Chinese women shunted Kathrin Ullrich to fourth. The Tokyo race was run under unfavourable weather conditions (high humidity) and McColgan had the courage to take command of the operations, grabbing a solo lead just before 3000 metres. After a first half in 15:34.2, she managed to run the second in 15:40.1. Visibly tired, she walked home with more than 20 seconds to spare vis-à-vis her nearest pursuer, Zhong Huandi. Ingrid Kristiansen lost contact early and had to be content with seventh. Details:

Tokyo, 30 August 1991 – 10,000 metres: 1.Liz McColgan (GB) 31:14.31, 2.Zhong Huandi (Chi) 31:35.08, 3.Wang Xiuting (Chi) 31:35.99, 4.Kathrin Ullrich (Ger) 31:38.96, 5.Lynn Jennings (USA) 31:54.44, 6.Uta Pippig (Ger) 31:55.68.

South African athletes were still banned from international competition, luckily for the last time. In 1992 the event all true sportsmen had been looking for finally materialized: the return of that country in the Olympic family. This came as a result of the fact that South Africa had by then abandoned its Apartheid policies. In this respect it must be recorded that sport – in this case, "Athletics South Africa" – had acted as trail blazer in promoting multi-racial competitions, several years before the government of that country decided to change its policies.

One to derive immediate benefit from the new situation was Elana Meyer, a 25-year-old South African who late in 1991 had run the 3000 metres in 8:32.00, the world's fastest time for that year. In doing so she beat Zola Budd (8:35.72), who had by then returned to her native country and married Mike Pieterse.

Stirred at the prospect of being able to compete in the Barcelona Olympics, Meyer rounded into form early. On 6 March 1992 at Bellville she ran 5000 metres in 14:44.15, the second fastest time on record, next to Kristiansen's world mark. Then she decided to run the 10,000 in the Olympics.

The 3000 metres came first on the Olympic time-table. Marie-Pierre Duros of France accounted for the fastest time in the heats (31 July) - 8:42.32. This turned out to be faster than the winner's time in the final, but poor Duros paid a price for her untimely effort and actually did not finish. The decisive race (2 August) offered yet another chapter of the feud between Tatyana Dorovskikh and Yelena Romanova. Following the dismantling of USSR, athletes from that vast country now represented their respective republics but were momentarily allowed to compete as a United Team, a compromise that was to last only for the duration of the Games. Dorovskikh had solved her dilemma by remaining faithful to athletics for at least one

Zola Budd (South Africa) at the 1986 Weltklasse meet in Zurich.

Elana Meyer (South Africa), left, and Derartu Tulu (Ethiopia) in the 10,000 metres at the 1992 Olympics in Barcelona. The latter, barely 20, won and the South African was second.

more year. But in Barcelona Romanova had the last word: at the end of a quasi-dormant race, she turned the tables on her arch rival with a nifty 28.6 in the last 200 metres. Details:

Barcelona, 2 August 1992 – 3000 metres: 1.Yelena Romanova (EUN/Rus) 8:46.04, 2.Tatyana Dorovskikh (EUN/Ukr) 8:46.85, 3.Angela Chalmers-Espinoza (Canada) 8:47.22, 4. Sonia O'Sullivan (Ire) 8:47.41, 5. PattiSue Plumer (USA) 8:48.29, 6.Yelena Kopitova (EUN/Rus) 8:49.55.

The results of the 10,000 metres provided further proof that the athletics world was growing fast. Four continents – Africa, Europe, North America and Asia - were represented among the top ten of the final. In the heats (1 August), the fastest time was posted by Derartu Tulu of Ethiopia, barely 20, with 31:55.67, who finished ahead of Elana Meyer. The other heat went to Helen Kimaiyo (Kenia) in 31:58.63, with McColgan an easy third. The final followed six days later and old Europe had to bow to the emerging forces of Africa, luckily impersonated by both black (Tulu) and white (Meyer). The latter set the pace for the greater part of the race but near the end she had to surrender to the precocious Tulu, who exhibited a finishing speed reminiscent of Miruts Yifter's closing bursts. She ran the last 400 metres in 65.9, as opposed to Meyer's 71.7. The top four were rewarded with new national and/or area records. Details:

Barcelona, 7 August 1992 – 10,000 metres: 1.Derartu Tulu (Eti) 31:06.02, 2.Elana Meyer (SA) 31:11.75, 3.Lynn Jennings (USA) 31:19.89, 4.Zhong Huandi (Chi) 31:21.08, 5.Liz McColgan (GB) 31:26.11, 6.Wang Xiuting (Chi) 31:28.06.

Derartu Tulu (born in the Arusi province on 21 March 1972; 1.55 m./ 44 kg.) had achieved international prominence by placing second in the 1991 World Cross-Country Championships at 19. At the summer Worlds the same year she was 8th in the 10,000 metres, after staying with the leaders till the 7th kilometre. A shepherdess in her youth, she now had an employment as prison administrator in Addis Abeba. She was the first black woman from Africa to win an Olympic title. Her progression:

Year	Age	3000 m.	5000 m.	10,000 m.
1990	18	9:11.21	-	32:56.26
1991	19	9:01.04	15:21.29	31:45.95
1992	20	9:01.12	15:36.5	31:06.02

On 8 August the indefatigable Tatyana Dorovskikh competed in the 1500 metre final but for once failed to make the podium. She was 4th (3:57.92) and victory went to Hassiba Boulmerka of Algeria (3:55.30).

Another sign of things to come was offered by the World Junior Championships in Seoul. On 19 September Wang Junxia of China won the 10,000 metres in 32:29.90. The following day another Chinese, Zhang Linli, took the 3000 metres in 8:46.86. The former in particular was to become a headline stealer within a few months. The World Cup, held at Habana in late September, fully confirmed young Tulu's talent. In difficult weather conditions she won, on consecutive days, first the 10,000 metres in 33:38.97, then the 3000 in 9:05.89. In the latter she ran the last lap in 59.8.

THE MARCH OF PROGRESS. CHINESE HIGH-WATER MARKS IN 1993 AND '97

In 1993 the new Chinese wave reached high-water marks. In the Liaoning Province, in the northern part of that huge country, there was a coach whose devotion to the sport bordered on fanaticism. He worked with a group of young women, subjecting them to a training regimen possibly without parallel in terms of quality and quantity. This man, Ma Junren, had carefully studied training methods from various parts of the world but also other subtleties such as the running movements of certain animals. In the early Nineties his seeds turned out to be conspicuous, yet the athletics world was certainly not prepared for the kind of record figures that were to come out of China in 1993. Especially outstanding was the leap forward made by Wang Junxia (born at Jiapigou, a village in the Jilin province, on 9 January 1973; 1.60 m./ 45 kg.). According to a story which appeared in "China Sports" magazine, "as a little girl she was small, thin and weak. But she was not what she seemed ... rather like the ugly duckling who turned out to be not a duck at all, but a beautiful swan". At school she revealed high intellective qualities though. Her physical education teacher, Miao Zhigong, soon discovered that she had great qualities as a runner. These were fully brought to bear when she joined Ma Junren's squad in 1991. Gradually growing workloads transformed her from a lithe young girl into a solid and mature athlete. Her early progression:

Year	Age	1500 m.	3000 m.	10,000 m.
1991	18	4:17.18	-	-
1992	19	-	8:55.50	32:29.90

I have already referred to her victory in the 10,000 metres at the 1992 World Junior Championships. In 1993 she and her teammates made the headlines very soon. On 4 April the 20-year-old Wang won a marathon at Tianjin in 2 hr 24:07 - a time that was to remain the world's best for 1993 ! In her wake three other girls also showed a marvellous condition: Qu Yunxia 2 hr 24:32, Zhang Linli 2 hr 24:42, Zhang Lirong 2 hr 24:52. The better known Zhong Huandi was 5th in 2 hr 25:36. Western observers began to doubt the length of the course ..... But that was only the beginning. At the Chinese Championships, held at Jinan, the winner of that amazing marathon showed brilliance in track events too, with victories in the 10,000 metres in 31:08.42 (2 June) and in the 3000 in 8:27.68 (6 June). Second in the latter race was Qu Yunxia (8:29.30). This girl (born in the Liaoning Province on 25 December 1972; 1.70 m./ 58 kg.) had emerged before her rival, showing preference for the shorter distances. In the 1500 metres she started with 4:11.36 in 1989 and progressed till 3:57.08 in 1992, when she also did 8:58.58 in the 3000.

Notwithstanding these thunderbolts, most European critics remained sceptical and looked forward to seeing the Chinese at the forthcoming World Championships in Stuttgart. At Gottlieb-Daimler-Stadion doubts vanished rather quickly: the girls from China annexed five of the six medals at stake in the distance events – no more, since they had only five entries altogether! I may add that they also provided the winner in the 1500 metres, when Liu Dong outclassed Sonia O'Sullivan of Ireland and Olympic champion Hassiba Boulmerka with an easy 4:00.50.

It became apparent from the very first round of the 3000 metres (14 August) that the so-called "Ma's Army" really meant business, just to use a Western expression. The fastest times were made by Zhang Linli (8:48.85) and Qu Yunxia (8:49.20). In the final (16 August) the Chinese always had things under control. Sonia O'Sullivan, undefeated, was considered as the no.1 European. She soon realized, however, that she was confronted with a most arduous task. The strategy of progressive acceleration - splendidly illustrated by Lasse Viren in the Seventies – was applied in a most diligent and effective manner by Ma's girls. The winner, Qu Yunxia, ran the first kilometre in 2:59.2, the second in 2:50.3 and the third in a brisk 2:39.2, with the nice surplus of a 59.5 last lap. That amply sufficed to vanquish the pride of Europe. Zhang Linli and Zhang Lirong shunted O'Sullivan to fourth. Details:

Stuttgart, 16 August 1993 – 3000 metres: 1.Qu Yunxia (Chi) 8:28.71, 2. Zhang Linli (Chi) 8:29.25, 3.Zhang Lirong (Chi) 8:31.95, 4.Sonia O'Sullivan (Ire) 8:33.38 5.Alison Wyeth (GB) 8:38.42, 6.Yelena Romanova (Rus) 8:39.69, 7.Paula Radcliffe (GB) 8:40.40.

Qu Yunxia (China) lowered the world's 1500 m. record to a great 3:50.46 during the Chinese "Revolution" of 1993.

The three medal winners from China had an age aggregate barely exceeding 60 years! After such a prologue, the 10,000 metres seemed a safe bet for China, since most European observers now had little or no doubt about the endurance potential of the girls from the Far East. More so in view of the fact that two dangerous prospects like Derartu Tulu and Liz McColgan were not in the field on account of injuries. The heats (19 August) were won by a .....15-year.-old Kenyan, Sally Barsosio (32:27.99) and Anne Marie Letko of USA (32:26.22). The two Chinese entries, Wang Junxia and Zhong Huandi, qualified with ease. In the final the duo from the East had no problems. Wang was head and shoulders above the rest: she ran the first half in 15:43.38 and the second in 15:05.92. Her last kilometre was the fastest of all – 2:43.3. She covered the last 400 metres in 61.0. Zhong Huandi was a distant second. The race was partly ruined by hideous incidents, chiefly caused by the inexperienced Barsosio, a teen-ager full of talent but too quick in using her elbows. Her conduct led Elana Meyer to retire – a decision she later considered too hasty. Barsosio was originally disqualified for obstructing other runners but later reinstated because officials had issued no second warning. The young Kenyan thus won a bronze medal at the unripe (?) age of 15 years 153 days!

Stuttgart, 21 August 1993 – 10,000 metres: 1.Wang Junxia (Chi) 30:49.30, 2.Zhong Huandi (Chi) 31:12.55, 3.Selina Barsosio (Ken) 31:15.38, 4.Tegla Loroupe (Ken) 31:29.91, 5.Lynn Jennings (USA) 31:30.53, 6.Maria Conceição Ferreira (Por) 31:30.60..... DNF: Elana Meyer (SA).

Wang Junxia: 3 world records in one race

It should be noted that coach Ma Junren had entered each of his protégées in only one event – no more. A wise decision, no doubt, considering their lack of experience in international competition. That most if not all of them had several seconds tucked up their sleeves was just as obvious. The athletics world was served confirmation of this pretty soon. Next on the agenda of Ma's girls was a meet to which they attached the utmost importance: China's National Games to be held in Beijing in the first half of September. World records for 3000 and 10,000 metres were in the books since 1984 and 1986 respectively and knowledgeable observers felt that they were likely to fall anytime – but the margin of improvement registered in Beijing by not one but several girls was such as to astound the track world. Suffice it to say that Kazankina's 3000 metre record was bettered in the space of two days by five different runners! This infernal carrousel began with the 10,000 metres. Wang Junxia literally annihilated Ingrid Kristiansen's world record (30:13.74 in 1986) – by nearly 42 seconds, with a great 29:31.78. Although this was the only record that could be credited to her, it may be of interest to note that she actually bettered two more - with the slight advantage of a "flying" start, that's true. Details:

1) She covered the last 3000 metres in 8:17.7est. (at that stage she was behind Zhong Huandi) i.e. well under Kazankina's world record (8:22.62 in 1984) for that distance!

2) She ran the second half of the race in 14:26est. (at that stage she was trailing Zhong Huandi, who was timed in 15:05.69), i.e. well below Kristiansen's world record for 5000 metres (14:37.33 in 1986).

Wang was helped up to 7000 metres by Zhong Huandi, who was herself rewarded with a time just inside the previous record. Details:
Beijing, 8 September 1993: 10,000 metres: 1.Wang Junxia 29:31.78, 2.Zhong Huandi 30:13.37, 3.Zhang Lirong 31:09.25, 4.Ma Liyan 31:10.46, 5.Zhang Linli 31:16.28 , 6.Liu Jianying 31:23.92, 7.Wei Li 31:28.83, 8.Wang Yongmei 31:31.54.

Kilometre fractions:

1000 m.	2:54.70	
2000 m.	5:56.52	(3:01.82)
3000 m.	8:59.14	(3:02.62)
4000 m.	12:02.73	(3:03.59)
5000 m.	15:05.69	(3:02.96)
6000 m.	18:10.03	(3:04.34)
7000 m.	21:14.31	(3:04.28)
8000 m.	23:59.88	(2:45.57)
9000 m.	26:44.80	(2:44.92)
10,000 m.	29:31.78	(2:46.98)

On 11 September Tatyana Kazankina lost the record many observers regarded as her best ever – 3:52.47 for 1500 metres (1980). Qu Yunxia ran the distance in 3:50.46, which would have been a world record in the male ranks up to 1930! Wang Junxia was second in 3:51.92, also under the previous record, and Zhang Linli was 3 rd in 3:57.46. The 3000 metres, with heats and final on consecutive days, came next, and that was the Chinese festival at its best. Kazankina's world record (8:22.62) was bettered again and again. Details:
Beijing, 12 September 1993 – 3000 metres (Heat 1): 1.Zhang Linli 8:22.06, 2.Zhang Lirong 8:22.44, 3.Zhang Huandi 8:47.39.

Kilometre fractions:

1000 m.	2:45.85	
2000 m.	5:35.16	(2:49.31)
3000 m.	8:22.06	(2:46.90)

Beijing, 12 September 1993 – 3000 metres (Heat 2): 1.Wang Junxia 8:12.19, 2.Qu Yunxia 8:12.27, 3.Ma Liyan 8:19.78, 4.Wei Li 8:47.96.

Kilometre fractions:

1000 m.	2:43.61	
2000 m.	5:29.43	(2:45.82)
3000 m.	8:12.19	(2:42.76)

Time for recovery was very short, yet the next day in the final ......
Beijing, 13 September 1993 - 3000 metres (Final): 1.Wang Junxia 8:06.11, 2.Qu Yunxia 8:12.18, 3.Zhang Linli 8:16.50, 4.Ma Liyan 8:21.26, 5.Zhang Lirong 8:21.84, 6.Wei Li 8:39.74. 7.Zhong Huandi 8:41.67.

Kilometre fractions:

1000 m.	2:41.98	
2000 m.	5:29.65	(2:47.67)
3000 m.	8:06.11	(2:36.46)

The two outstanding characters in the play, Wang Junxia and Qu Yunxia, had an "infernal" week. Counting heats and finals, Qu ran six races in just as many consecutive days: in

Wang Junxia (China) winning the 10.000 m. at the 1993 World Championships. Later in the same year she lowered the world record to a superb 29:31.78.

the 800 metre final, on 9 September, she was second to Liu Dong, 1:56.24 to 1:55.54; Wang ran five races in six days. What really amazed observers was that Ma's girls, who exhibited impasssible faces even under strain, could do just as well in the 800 metres as in the marathon. Once again, suspicions arose among die-hard critics, who found it hard to believe that even the toughest training regimen (sometimes up to 40 kilometres per day) could yield such an endurance. An article in "Track & Field News" bore the following sub-title: "China, the most populous nation on earth, has been aroused in a track & field sense; the question is: what's the secret behind the arousal?" There was talk of various performance-enhancing products – from a caterpillar fungus used as a drink to soft-shell turtle soups. Dr. Enrico Arcelli, an Italian sports physician who knows a thing or two about China, had this to say in the magazine "Correre" (running): "It's altogether possible that the Chinese may use a substance derived from herbs deeply rooted in their traditional medicine. Such a substance may not only produce a performance-enhancing effect but also act as an anti-stress medium likely to speed up recovery from physical exertion and thereby preserve from stress injuries, the plague of so many athletes in the Western world".

Europe was the great loser at the end of 1993. No medals at the World Championships, it was also deprived of world records at both 3000 and 10,000 metres. Even Sonia O'Sullivan, the Irish woman who was often a dominant figure in European Grand Prix meets, had been unable to keep pace with the Chinese advance. As a meager consolation she could point to a world's seasonal best of 14:45.92 in the 5000 metres. Without forgetting, of course, that Wang had done much better in the second half of her extraordinary '10' at Beijing. Incidentally, Wang's mark (29:31.78) was just a little more than one minute slower than the Chinese male record (28:24.85).

Ma's Thorny Road

No coach of modern times has been sung and praised but also criticized and even vituperated like Ma Junren. However, everybody seems to agree at least on one point: the boom of women's distance runners in China - first in 1993 and again in 1997 - was chiefly if not entirely his merit. Even in his own country, Ma has been valued from different angles, as it became apparent from a series of articles published in "China Sports" magazine early in 1994. This "Iron Man" was born at Qinjia Village, Shenyang, in the Liaoning province, on 28 October 1944, as the third of eight children in a family of poor farmers. His life was described in the above-mentioned articles by Deng Xuezheng as "A Thorny Path to Success". Ma went through harsh experiences first as a hard working teenager, then as a soldier. In 1968 he lost his mother, who committed suicide by jumping into a well. In 1971 he became a PE instructor at a middle school in Ansham, some 20 Km. away from home. Then he began to coach young girls, some of whom went on to distinguish themselves at the national level. Ma is described as a busy man, "with his mind never at rest except in a dreamless sleep". He really put his protégées to hard work, so much in fact that a colleague of his ridiculed his training methods as "helping the shoots grow by pulling them upwards". Authoritarian and at times cocky, he was known for his uncompromising ways. Each year he took his pupils on five or six trips to a training centre at high altitude, where he subjected them to an intense mixture of speed work and aerobic training. His pupils spent the better part of the year away from home, training up to 300 Km. per week. No wonder Wang, Qu and the rest could do just as well in the middle distances as in the marathon. Except that there was little room left for their private life. But then Ma himself was ready to sacrifice anything for his mission. Indeed "he felt sorry for having taken little care of his family, for being neither a good husband to his wife nor a good father to his two children, nor a good son to his old father". But, as the writer went on to say, "there is a soft side to Ma's character. For the sake of his pupils he is ready to sacrifice anything he is entitled to - rest, health and even domestic joys".

1994 offered an entirely different picture. To add to the Chinese dilemma, Ma's girls had an indifferent season. Wang Junxia did no better than 8:50.79 in the 3000 metres and 30:50.34 in the 10,000. Qu Yunxia was content with 4:00.34 in the 1500 metres.

The first notable mark of the year was Sonia O'Sullivan's new European record for 3000 metres. This Irish woman (born at Cobh on 28 November 1969; 1.73 m. / 53 kg.) grew up athletically speaking while in USA. Up to and including 1993 she had been pretty close to the top of the world, but the news from China had surprised her more than somewhat and she was clearly among the Doubting Thomases .... As a logical consequence of this, her target during a 3000 metre race in London on 15 July was confined to Kazankina's European record . She broke it with 8:21.64 (kilometre fractions 2:48.0, 2:49.6 and 2:44.1). Yvonne Murray was second in 8:29.60. This duo played a dominant rôle in this event at the European Championships in Helsinki. Athletes from the onetime USSR, now representing their own republics, were having problems in adapting to the new situation. Tatyana Dorovskikh had fallen the victim of a doping test in June 1993 and was now under suspension. O'Sullivan thus won as she pleased in Helsinki. Details:

Helsinki, 10 August 1994 – 3000 metres: 1:Sonia O'Sullivan (Ire) 8:31.84, 2.Yvonne Murray (GB) 8:36.48, 3.Gabriela Szabó (Rom) 8:40.08, 4.Olga Churbanova (Rus) 8:40.48, 5.Lyudmila Borisova (Rus) 8:41.71, 6.Alison Wyeth (GB) 8:45.76.

The 10,000 metre field was excellent, though obviously far from 1993 Chinese standards. Fernanda Ribeiro of Portugal, 25, offered a good display of progressive acceleration, with halves in 15:49.79 and 15:18.96 and a final time of 31:08.75. In winning this title she fulfilled a long-time promise, considering that she had been setting age records since she was 13. Her compatriot Maria Conceição Ferreira, 32, also had a comethrough performance in taking second. Details:

Helsinki, 13 August 1994 – 10,000 metres: 1.Fernanda Ribeiro (Por) 31:08.75, 2.Maria Conceição Ferreira (Por) 31:32.82, 3.Daria Nauer (Swi) 31:35.96, 4.Kathrin Wessel (Ger) 31:38.75, 5.Cristina Misaros (Rom) 31:41.03, 6.Maria Guida (Ita) 31:42.14.

The Commonwealth Games, held later in August at Victoria, British Columbia, Canada, had the finals of distance events on consecutive days, which obviously made doubling almost impossible. Local heroine Angela Chalmers, of Sioux Indian descent on her mother's side, successfully defended her 3000 metre title on 23 August, winning easily in 8:32.17. Yvonne Murray beat Elena Meyer in the 10,000 the following day, times 31:56.97 and 32:06.02 respectively.

The World Cup, held at Crystal Palace, London, was an anti-climax, coming as it did at the end of a busy season. It was at any rate the right occasion for Elana Meyer to finally

Sonia O'Sullivan (Ireland), one of the greatest distance runners of recent years.

achieve her first major success. After leading practically from start to finish, the South African won the 10,000 metres in 30:52.51, ahead of European champion Fernanda Ribeiro (31:04.25). Third went to Wei Li of China (32:37.94), who had placed no higher than 7th in Wang's record shattering race at Beijing in 1993. This was on 10 September. The next day Yvonne Murray won the 3000 metres in 8:56.81.

The so-called Ma's Army was not in the news, if one excepts a good 30:50.34 in the 10,000 metres by Wang Junxia at the Asian Games, held at Hiroshima early in October. In the same meet Qu Yunxia scored an 800/1500 double (1:59.85 and 4:12.48). News from China hinted to divergent opinions within Ma's clan and to his own ill health.

1995 saw a further evaporation of Chinese might. The girls who had made world shattering news two years before stayed away from the World Championships in Göteborg. The dubious reasons for this sabbatical obviously added new fuel to the scepticism of some Western observers. The only good marks to come out of China during the year were a 14:45.90 for 5000 metres by 18-year-old Jiang Bo (Nanjing, 24 October) and 31:23.24 for 10,000 metres by Wang Junxia (Changchun, 7 September).

Fernanda Ribeiro of Portugal was the dominant figure on the European scene. She accounted for the only world record of the year as she chalked up a 14:36.45 for 5000 metres at Hechtel on 22 July. This solid performer (born at Penafiel on 23 June 1969; 1.61 m. / 48 kg.) had won European titles indoors and out in 1994. At Hechtel she rose to new heights, beating Meyer and McColgan by impressive margins. Details:

Hechtel, 22 July 1995 – 5000 metres: 1.Fernanda Ribeiro (Por) 14:36.45, 2.Elana Meyer (SA) 14:44.05, 3.Liz McColgan (GB) 14:59.56.

Kilometre fractions:

1000 m.	2:57.0	
2000 m.	5:51.0	(2:54.0)
3000 m.	8:50.0	(2:59.0)
4000 m.	11:46.0	(2:56.0)
5000 m.	14:36.45	(2:50.45)

In the World Championships, held in Göteborg, the 5000 metres replaced the 3000 – a decisive step in bringing the women's programme on a par with that of the other sex. Ribeiro attempted the 5000/10,000 double and came fairly close to succeeding in this arduous venture (four races within a week, counting heats and finals). At the longer distance she won from Olympic champion Derartu Tulu in a race characterized by a crescendo (first half in 15:46.89, second half in 15:18.10), but in the 5000 metre final three days later she had to bow to Sonia O'Sullivan's superior speed in the closing stage (last 400 metres in 61.5, last 200 in 28.8). Details:

Göteborg, 9 August 1995 - 10,000 metres: 1.Fernanda Ribeiro (Por) 31:04.99, 2.Derartu Tulu (Eti) 31:08.10, 3.Tegla Loroupe (Ken) 31:17.66, 4.Maria Guida (Ita) 31:27.82, 5.Elana Meyer (SA) 31:36.96, 6.Liz McColgan (GB) 31:40.14.

Göteborg, 12 August 1995 – 5000 metres: 1.Sonia O'Sullivan (Ire) 14:46.47, 2.Fernanda Ribeiro (Por) 14:48.54, 3.Zohra Ouaziz (Mor) 14:53.77, 4.Gabriela Szabó (Rom) 14:56.57, 5.Paula Radcliffe (GB) 14:57.02, 6.Marya Pantyukhova (Rus) 15:01.23.

O'Sullivan beat Ribeiro again in Berlin on 1 September, still over 5000 metres: 14:41.40 to 14:45.10. The Irish runner had a very brilliant season at this distance, with 6 wins in just as many races. About her beginnings, Noel Henry, noted Irish historian of women's athletics, relates that "she joined her local club when she was 12 years of age, not so much because she was mad about running, more because of the social possibilities – she was thinking of parties, discos, and the like." Once in the club, however, she lost little time in becoming involved in cross-country running. And she did so with notable success. Before she turned 18, scholarship offers from USA began to pour in. She decided to attend Villanova University, Pennsylvania, where she studied accountancy but also did a lot of running, indoors and out. In the 1992 Olympics at Barcelona, aged 23, she was fourth in the 3000 metres. Her subsequent achievements have been related already.

In the 1996 Olympics in Atlanta the 5000 metres were to replace the 3000 – as in the Worlds of the previous year. Wang Junxia was contemplating a comeback. She had left the Ma Junren group, reportedly because of problems arising from a hip injury, but probably because she could no longer put up with the excessive training regimen prevalent in the group. Consequently, she started her Olympic preparation under a new coach. It soon became apparent that she contemplated a 5000/10,000 metre double - at the Chinese National Championships, held at Nanjing, she made a good rehearsal, winning the 5000 metres on 5 May in 14:51.87, a new Chinese record, and the 10,000 on 8 May in 31:11.59, after doing 31:01.76 in a heat the previous day. Europeans seemed ready for the challenge though. Particularly Fernanda Ribeiro, who was involved in a hot 5000 metre duel with an up and coming Romanian at Oslo on 5 July. The girl in question was Gabriela Szabó, not yet 21, who gave the experienced Fernanda a

good race for her money, succumbing by a narrow margin - 14:41.12 to 14:41.07. Unlike Wang, however, Ribeiro had decided to concentrate on only one event, the 10,000 metres, for the Games. This was to prove a wise decision: hot weather conditions in Atlanta and a very hard track seemed hardly conducive to repeated efforts over the long distances. The Olympic time-table did not make things easier – 5000 m. heats on 26 July, 10,000 m. heats on 27 July, 5000 m. final on 28 July and 10,000 m. final on 2 Aug. Wang took things easy in her heat of the 5000 and qualified without any trouble. The fastest time in this round was 15:07.01 by Pauline Konga, a relatively little known Kenyan. Wang was even more conservative the next day, qualifying for the 10,000 metre final with an indifferent 32:36.53. Here the fastest qualifier was Derartu Tulu with 31:35.90.

The final of the 5000 metres - third race in just as many days for Wang - was partly ruined by a sad happening: in the third kilometre Sonia O'Sullivan dropped back and finally retired, claiming "a medical problem". In this connection it must be recorded that her father, John, showed great dignity and good measure in replying to questions from the press: "No one has died – it's only sport. There will be another day." After a relatively calm journey up to 4000 metres, Wang injected a 67.5 lap and opened up a gap. Pauline Konga was stronger than others in trying to resist but to no avail. By then sure of victory, the Chinese slowed down to 71.1 in the last lap (as opposed to Konga's 69.8), obviously saving herself for the 10,000 metre final. She won in 14:59.88. Details: Atlanta, 28 July 1996 – 5000 metres: 1.Wang Junxia (Chi) 14:59.88, 2.Pauline Konga (Ken) 15:03.49, 3.Roberta Brunet (Ita) 15:07.52, 4.Michiko Shimizu (Jap) 15:09.05, 5.Paula Radcliffe (GB) 15:13.11, 6.Yelena Romanova (Rus) 15:14.09. ..... DNF: Sonia O'Sullivan (Ire).

Five days elapsed before the 10,000 metre final – that seemed to be ample space for recovery, especially for Wang Junxia, who had passed unscathed through harder labours in 1993. Yet she did not make it – maybe the hard track that ruined runners' legs was responsible, at least in part, for her failure. Fernanda Ribeiro did the rest. The

Liz McColgan (GB) in the final of the 1995 European Cup at Lille.

Portuguese was active in setting the pace on occasion, and with one kilometre to go she led a tiny group with Wang and two Ethiopians, Gete Wami and Derartu Tulu. The world record holder from China launched her attack just before the bell. But Ribeiro held on grimly. Entering the homestretch she saw a gap inside Wang and decided to take a risk, choosing the inside path. She shot ahead to win by nearly a second. It is always dangerous to compare marks made under different conditions, yet one could hold the view that Wang Junxia 1996 version was not the same irresistible athlete that had shocked the athletics world in 1993 and brought the 10,000 metre record to 29:31.78. Ribeiro ran the last 400 metres in 63.6, to Wang's 64.3. The Chinese thus lost her invincibility at this distance: her debut was in 1992 and she had won 13 consecutive finals.

Details:
Atlanta, 2 August 1996 – 10,000 metres:
1.Fernanda Ribeiro (Por) 31:01.63, 2.Wang Junxia (Chi) 31:02.58, 3.Gete Wami (Eti) 31:06.65, 4.Derartu Tulu (Eti) 31:10.46, 5.Masako Chiba (Jap) 31:20.62, 6.Tegla Loroupe (Ken) 31:23.22.

1997 was to be the year of the World Championships in Athens but these were finally overshadowed, clock-wise at least, by a lot of stunning performances made at China's National Games, held at Shanghai in the second half of October. Same as in 1993, but with one exception: the Chinese girls who shocked the world in the fall of that year had previously won medals galore at the Worlds in Stuttgart, whereas those of the 1997 vintage had previously stayed away from the Athens gala.

In European circles the dominant figure of 1997 was a little, light-footed Romanian of Hungarian descent, Gabriela Szabó (born at Bistrita on 14 November 1975; 1.58 m. / 42 kg.). A precocious talent from the beginning, she was second in the 3000 metres at the 1992 World Junior Championships, aged 17, and won that event at the 1994 edition of the same meet. In the senior ranks she made a promising debut at the 1995 World Championships: fourth in the 5000 metres. She had a splendid season in 1997. On 4 July in Oslo she won the 5000 metres in 14:42.43. She decided to compete at that dis-

tance at the Worlds: on a particularly hot day (28° C.) she ran a wise race, exhibiting for the first time what was to become her trademark - a very strong finish. By negotiating the last lap in 61.7 and the last 200 in 31.5 she overcame the resistance of Italy's Roberta Brunet to win by a narrow margin in 14:57.68. Olympic champion Ribeiro was only third. It must be said, however, that the Portuguese had previously competed in the 10,000, held four days earlier. At this distance she was upset by Sally Barsosio of Kenya. As previously related, the latter had first made the news at the unripe age of 15, causing havoc at the 1993 Worlds with her inconsiderate maneuvers; and again at the 1996 Olympics, where Wang Junxia remonstrated with her and later said: "I don't understand how a country (Kenya) can let such an athlete compete without any consideration of sportsman-

Sally Barsosio (Kenya) winning the 10,000 metres at the 1997 World Championships in Athens.

ship". But in Athens Barsosio showed that she could outrun the best in the world: after a first half in 16:12.9 she ran the second in 15:20.0 and won in 31:32.92, leaving Ribeiro over 6 seconds behind. Barsosio's last three laps were 67.9, 69.5 and 70.3. Details:

Athens, 5 August 1997 – 10,000 metres: 1. Sally Barsosio (Ken) 31:32.92, 2. Fernanda Ribeiro (Por) 31:39.15, 3. Masako Chiba (Jap) 31:41.93, 4. Birhane Adere (Eti) 31:48.95, 5. Ren Xiujuan (Chi) 31:50.63, 6. Tegla Loroupe (Ken) 32:00.93.

Athens, 9 August 1997 – 5000 metres: 1. Gabriela Szabó (Rom) 14:57.68, 2. Roberta Brunet (Ita) 14:58.29, 3. Fernanda Ribeiro (Por) 14:58.85, 4. Paula Radcliffe (GB) 15:01.74, 5. Lynda Cheromei (Ken) 15:07.88, 6. Liu Jianying (Chi) 15:10.64.

Another Chinese Earthquake

China's representatives passed almost unnoticed in Athens. But the track world soon discovered that for some reason they had left at home their best "cards". Once again, the explosion occurred during the National Games, held at Shanghai in October. It so happened, for example, that Liu Jianying, 6th in the 5000 metres at the Worlds, was only 8th in the same event at Shanghai, and Yang Siju, 7th in the 10,000 at the Worlds, was only 9th in that event at Shanghai ! The girls who had not come to Athens were, for the most part, members of Ma Junren's newest "army". This time the chief actors in the play were two 20-year-old novices: Jiang Bo (born at Wafangdian, Liaoning province, on 13 March 1977) and Dong Yanmei (born at Xuengdong, Liaoning province on 16 December 1977; 1.66 m. / 51 kg.). Here, in chronological order, is a summary of their labours during the Shanghai festival:

But then these Herculean labours were only a "hors-d'oeuvre" for Dong. Three days after her last race at Shanghai she was in Dalian where she won ..... a marathon in 2 hr 28:09 ! As for Wang Junxia, apparently she stayed away from the Shanghai meet.

Details of the two world record races:
Shanghai, 21 October 1997 – 5000 metres (Heat 1): 1.Dong Yanmei 14:31.27, 2.Jiang Bo 14:31.30, 3.Liu Shixiang 14:32.33, 4. Wang Dongmei 15:09.32, 5.Yang Siju 15:11.79.

Kilometre fractions:

1000 m.	2:55.0	
2000 m.	5:43.0	(2:48.0)
3000 m.	8:43.0	(3:00.0)
4000 m.	11:45.0	(3:02.0)
5000 m.	14:31.27	(2:46.27)

Shanghai, 23 October 1997 – 5000 metres (final): 1.Jiang Bo 14:28.09, 2.Dong Yanmei 14:29.82, 3.Liu Shixiang 14:38.14, 4.Yin Lili 14:39.96, 5.Dong Zhaoxia 14:47.20, 6.Wang Dongmei 14:48.45, 7.Song Liqing 15:06.43, 8.Liu Jianying 15:06.73.

Kilometre fractions:

1000 m.	2:53.4	
2000 m.	5:46.0	(2:52.6)
3000 m.	8:41.1	(2:55.1)
4000 m.	11:40.6	(2:59.5)
5000 m.	14:28.09	(2:47.49)

Of course it should be remembered that back in 1993 Wang Junxia ran a faster 5000 (14:26est) in the second half of her record race in the 10,000 metres.

The heats on 21 October were so hard that quite a few runners were unable to duplicate their best form in the final. Among these was

		Jiang Bo	Dong Yanmei
17 October	1500 m. (heats)	3:57.27 (2nd)	3:55.82 (4th)
18 October	1500 m. (final)	3:50.98 (1st)	3:55.07 (6th)
19 October	10,000 m.	-	30:38.09 (1st)
21 October	5000 m. (heats)	14:31.30 (2nd)	14:31.27 (1st)
23 October	5000 m. (final)	14:28.09 (1st)	14:29.82 (2nd)

the famous Qu Yunxia, who did 15:04.36 in heat 2 (won by Yin Lili in 14:41.47) but faded to 15:26.89 and 10th in the final. A similar case: Song Liqing did 14:45.71 in heat 2 but was only 7th with a much slower time in the final – no surprise after all as she was said to be only 17! But then the above-mentioned Yin Lili, 18, did 14:41.47 in heat 2 and improved to 14:39.96 in the final.

Here is something more about the two main figures. Jiang Bo emerged in 1995 with a world junior record of 14:45.90. On that occasion she upset none other than the famous Wang Junxia, who was second in 14:53.08. In the same year Jiang, then 18, also ran a marathon in 2 hr 32:18.

Dong Yanmei had pre-1997 PB's of 15:11.80 and 32:04.42 (both in 1995, hence at 18) and 2 hr 34:52 in the marathon (1996).

To add to the Chinese dilemma, in 1998 the two heroines of the previous year went to USA to compete in the Goodwill Games at Uniondale, New York but came out of that venture with indifferent, not to say alarming, results. Dong Yanmei was fourth in the 5000 metres in 16:00.56 in a race won by Olga Yegorova of Russia (15:53.05) and third in the 10,000 in 32:59.85 in a race won by Tegla Loroupe of Kenya (32:15.44). In the same races, Jiang Bo was ninth both times (16:17.32 and 35:43.13 respectively).

In 1998 Europeans had an intense season, as usual, with O'Sullivan, Ribeiro and Szabó well ahead of the rest. The Portuguese offered an acute very early, in the European Challenge race over 10,000 metres at Lisbon on 4 April - 30:48.06, which was to remain the fastest time of the year. Szabó ran a creditable 8:24.31 for 3000 metres in Paris on 29 July, moving to 8th in the All-Time list.

Another notable development occurred in the marathon: Tegla Loroupe of Kenya, good but not exceptional in track events, reached greater heights as a marathon runner, succeeding Ingrid Kristiansen as owner of the best-on-record time with a scintillating 2 hr 20.47 at Rotterdam on 19 April. Later in the season she chalked up another best ever mark by covering 18,340 kilometres in an hour.

As far as track events were concerned the big laurels of 1998 belonged to Sonia O'Sullivan. She went to Budapest for the European Championships fully determined to erase memories of her disasters in the 5000 metres at the 1996 Olympics (did not finish) and the 1997 Worlds (eliminated in a heat). On 19 August she lined up at the start of the 10,000 metres – reportedly the first time she ever raced over such a distance on the track. With 150 metres to go she swept past Olympic champion Fernanda Ribeiro to win by a comfortable margin in 31:29.33. A swift 28.1 for the last 200 did it for her. Four days later she faced Gabriela Szabó, a feared kicker, in the 5000 metres. For once the blond Romanian was beaten at her own game as a 28.6 for the last 200 sealed the issue in favour of the Irish woman, no matter

Gabriela Szabó (Romania), whose terrific finish earned her quite a few victories in the Golden League in 1998/99.

if her final time was an ordinary 15:06.50. As it happens sometimes even in the best families, the two expressed different views when the battle was over. O'Sullivan said: "It was just the perfect race for me when Szabó went to the front so early". The Romanian retorted: "Sonia was lacking in fair play. She made me make all the pace and I expected some cooperation". Details:

Budapest, 19 August 1998 – 10,000 metres: 1.Sonia O'Sullivan (Ire) 31:29.33, 2.Fernanda Ribeiro (Por) 31:32.42, 3.Lidia Simon (Rom) 31:32.64, 4.Olivera Jevtic (Yug) 31:34.26, 5.Paula Radcliffe (GB) 31:36.51, 6.Julia Vaquero (Spa) 31:46.47.

Budapest, 23 August 1998 – 5000 metres: 1.Sonia O'Sullivan (Ire) 15:06.50, 2.Gabriela Szabó (Rom) 15:08.31, 3.Marta Dominguez (Spa) 15:10.54, 4.Olivera Jevtic (Yug) 15:16.61, 5.Annemari Sandell (Fin) 15:20.78, 6.Blandine Bitzner-Ducret (Fra) 15:38.61.

Szabó took partial revenge when she chalked up a year's best of 14:31.48 in Berlin on 1 September. She won from Zahra Ouaziz of Morocco (14:32.08) and Gete Wami of Ethiopia (14:36.08). O'Sullivan was only fourth (14:51.61). With her European record the Romanian rose to no.3 on the All-Time list.

1999 was Gabriela Szabó's vintage season from top to bottom. She went through a total of 13 races (10 at 3000 metres and 3 at 5000) without a loss and reigned supreme in the Grand Prix / Golden League circus, racking up record earnings in the prize-money department. On top of that she won three world titles, two indoors (1500/3000) and one outdoors (5000). According to "Track & Field News", her haul for an undefeated campaign came to just over a million dollars ($1,015,000 to be precise). Not counting her earnings from a shoe factory she was allied with, appearance fees and a bonus from the Romanian government. Most probably an all-time record as far as women distance runners were concerned. Gabriela celebrated by getting married to her coach Zsolt Gyöngyössy in October, shortly before turning 24. She was unanimously voted as "Athlete of the Year". In a clock-wise perspective there were no "Chinese pearls" in her collection. But then the Chinese them-selves had a very obscure season. At the end of the year the best times reported from China were 15:26.32 and 32:10.51, a far cry vis-à-vis the performances of 1993 and '97.

Szabó was particularly brilliant in the 3000 metres, with six sub-8:30 marks and a top effort of 8:25.03 in the Zurich meet (11 August). At the World Championships in Seville she was content with the 5000 metre crown. In the final (27 August) she won from two Africans, Zahra Ouaziz of Morocco and Ayelech Worku of Ethiopia. The petite Romanian covered the last 200 metres in 29.4 to seal victory in 14:41.82. The 10,000 metres, held the previous day, had produced the fastest race of the year as Gete Wami ran the distance in 30:24.56, moving to no.4 in the World All-Time list. This race was featured by uneven halves, the first in 15:25.5 and the second in 14:59.1. Details:

Seville, 26 August 1999 – 10,000 metres: 1.Gete Wami (Eti) 30:24.56, 2.Paula Radcliffe (GB) 30:27.13, 3.Tegla Loroupe (Ken) 30:32.03, 4.Harumi Hiroyama (Jap) 31:26.84, 5.Chiemi Takahashi (Jap) 31:27.62, 6.Merima Hashim (Eti) 31:32.06.

Seville, 27 August 1999 – 5000 metres: 1.Gabriela Szabó (Rom) 14:41.82, 2.Zahra Ouaziz (Mor) 14:43.15, 3.Ayelech Worku (Eti) 14:44.22, 4.Irina Mikitenko (Ger) 14:50.17, 5.Ebru Kavaklioglu (Tur) 14:51.69, 6.Julia Vaquero (Spa) 14:56.00.

Szabó closed her immaculate season with another victory over Zahra Ouaziz over 5000 metres in Berlin on 7 September - 14:40.59 to 14:41.34, the fastest times of the year.

The last year of the 20th century, 2000, supplied no earth shattering performances but plenty of exciting high-level competition, which is what counts most in the eyes of sports loving fans.

Derartu Tulu of Ethiopia had made the headlines with her victory in the 10,000 metres at the 1992 Olympics in Barcelona, when barely 20. After that she had ups and downs due to various reasons such as injuries, plus childbirth in 1998. However, she managed to win a silver medal in the 10,000 at the 1995 Worlds. But it was only in 2000 that she returned to her splendour of eight years before. She started with a victory (her third) in the World Cross Country Championships. By then she had a serious rival in her own country in the person of Gete Wami, only two years her junior and equally petite in physical build, whose honours have been dealt with already. It was Wami who turned in the best performance prior to the Sydney Olympics: at Heusden on 5 August she ran the 5000 metres in 14:30.88, moving to third in the World All Time list. By then Ethiopia was well established as the no.1 country in the domain of women's distance running.

The most notable pre-Olympic result was registered in Berlin on 1 September when Szabó suffered an unexpected defeat in the 5000 metres. She bowed to Leah Malot of Kenya – 14:40.61 to 14:39.83. But Malot, 28, was not selected for the Kenya Olympic team.

In Sydney Gabriela Szabó courageously tried for a double – 5000/1500 metres. Counting prelims and finals, this implied running 5 races in the space of 8 days. The Romanian was her usually reliable self at the shorter distance, which came first. Her most serious rival turned out to be Sonia O'Sulivan. The Irish star had given birth to a daughter in July 1999 yet she was back only three months later when she won a 5-mile race with a world road best for that distance (24:27). In 2000, aged 31, she was better than ever. She too competed in two events in Sydney, 5000 and 10,000 metres, achieving new PB's at both distances – a rare competitive achievement in the Olympics. The battle between her and Szabó in the decisive stage of the 5000 metres was one of the most stirring sights ever in women's athletics – Sonia's long strides vs. Gabriela's mincing but awfully fast steps. The former had an imposing advantage in height - 1.73 to 1.58. Yet, when she challenged the leading Romanian in the homestretch, she could not quite make it. The end found Szabó a mere 0.23 sec. ahead. The winner ran the last 200 metres in 28.6 and the last 100 in 14.6 (as opposed to Sonia's 28.7 and 14.7). Times: 14:40.79 and 14:41.02. Both runners had another fight five days later but on different fronts. Szabó met even harder stuff for her teeth in the 1500 metres and had to be content with third in a tactical race.

O'Sullivan was engaged in a fast 10,000 metre journey and even though she set a new PB (30:53.37) she placed no higher than sixth. Derartu Tulu won in 30:17.49, moving to no.4 in the World All Time list. Ethiopia scored a beautiful 1-2, with Gete Wami outsprinting Fernanda Ribeiro for second. It was easily the greatest distance race ever in Olympic history as no fewer than 8 of the top 12 finishers set new PB's. Once again, Chinese representatives were well outside the limelight. Li Ji, 21, was 7th in the 10,000 metres in 31:06.94, still a PB. Jiang Bo and Dong Yanmei did not show up.

Gete Wami (Ethiopia) winning the 10,000 metres at the 1999 World Championships in Seville.

Details:
Sydney, 25 September 2000 – 5000 metres: 1.Gabriela Szabó (Rom) 14:40.79, 2.Sonia O'Sullivan (Ire) 14:41.02, 3. Gete Wami (Eti) 14:42.23, 4.Ayelech Worku (Eti) 14:42.67, 5.Irina Mikitenko (Ger) 14:43.59, 6.Lydia Cheromei (Ken) 14:47.35.
Sydney, 30 September 2000 – 10,000 metres: 1.Derartu Tulu (Eti) 30:17.49, 2.Gete Wami (Eti) 30:22.48, 3.Fernanda Ribeiro (Por) 30:22.88, 4.Paul Radcliffe (GB) 30:26.97, 5.Tegla Loroupe (Ken) 30:37.26, 6.Sonia O'Sullivan (Ire) 30:53.37.

Fernanda Ribeiro (Portugal) winning the 10,000 metres at the 1995 World Championships in Göteborg.

2001, first year of the new millennium, found track in full swing on a world-wide basis. The growth of the sport was accompanied by problems, old and new, among which doping inevitably had its place. In women's long distance running the year was dominated by the Yegorova case.

Olga Yegorova (born at Novocheboksarsk, Cuvashiya, on 28 March 1972; 1.60 m. / 48 kg.) could be described as a late comer or "Spätzünder" as they say in Germany. Her first known mark dates from 1996, when she was 24 and the mother of a 2-year-old baby – 16:00.07 for 5000 metres. She progressed somewhat slowly but steadily, up to 14:42.91 in 2000, when she finished 8th in this event at the Sydney Olympics. A few days before the 2001 World Championships in Edmonton it was announced that Yegorova had tested positive for EPO (erythropoietin) at a meet in Saint-Denis. Her suspension was subsequently lifted by the IAAF as the correct procedure was not carried out by the French laboratory. In fact, her blood was not tested and the urine analysis alone was not satisfactory in the eyes of IAAF Doping Committee chairman Dr. Arne Ljungqvist.

Yegorova's races in pre-Edmonton weeks were mostly at 3000 metres. After winning the world indoor title in 8:37.48 she won in Rome (8:23.96) and in the above-mentioned meet at Saint-Denis (8:23.75). Among her "victims" on all these occasions was none other than Gabriela Szabó. But the latter was in better form by the time the Worlds rolled around. She competed in the 1500 metres and then in the 5000 - five rounds (prelims + finals) in a week's time. She won the title at the shorter distance in 4:00.57. Before the heats of the 5000 metres Szabó threatened to stay away from that test if Yegorova was to take part – but later changed her mind and entered the race. Inside the stadium, other athletes led by distance runner Paula Radcliffe of Great Britain, displayed a sign reading: "EPO cheats out". There was some booing when Yegorova was introduced to the public before the final – and even when she left the stadium as the winner. Be it as it may, she won in impressive style. It was a strange race and little or nothing happened until 1000 metres from home or just about. At

*Olga Yegorova
(Russia), the
world's best
(and most
controversial)
distance runner
in 2001.*

that stage Dong Yanmei of China, who owned the second best time ever (14:29.82 in 1997), went into the lead. Szabó, running her fifth race in the space of a week, was first of the favourites to lose contact. Yegorova struck with 240 metres to go and from then on she looked unbeatable. Dong faded badly near the end and had to be content with fourth, as Marta Dominguez of Spain and Ayelech Worku of Ethiopia took the remaining medals in that order. Szabó was eighth. Yegorova ran the last lap in 60.49 and the last 200 in 29.04. Her winning time, 15:03.39, was not exceptional though. Her post-race comment was terse: "I am so happy I won. I have been training hard for these championships and it paid off". But she added some spice, saying: "Should I have come in 2nd or 3rd to please the crowd?" Szabó held a different view: "She is not the champion here".

Prior to this there had been a great one-two-three by Ethiopia in the 10,000 metres – the first clean sweep by that country in a global (World-Olympic) competition. Derartu Tulu added a world title to her Olympic golds of 1992 and 2000 for a fantastic record achieved in the space of a decade. Her teammates Berhane Adere and Gete Wami finished close to her, particularly the former, 28, was lost by only 0.04 sec.! The most serious threat to Ethiopia was expected to come from Paula Radcliffe of Great Britain. She did in fact launch her attack with three and a half laps to go but during the last lap the Ethiopians blew past. The Englishwoman missed bronze by merely 0.08 sec. Details: Edmonton, 7 August 2001 - 10,000 metres: 1.Derartu Tulu (Eti) 31:48.81, 2.Berhane Adere (Eti) 31:48.85, 3.Gete Wami (Eti) 31:49.98, 4.Paula Radcliffe (GB) 31:50.06, 5.Mihaela Botezan (Rom) 32:03.46, 6.Lyudmila Petrova (Rus) 32:04.94.
Edmonton, 11 August 2001 – 5000 metres: 1.Olga Yegorova (Rus) 15:03.39, 2.Marta Dominguez (Spa) 15:06.59, 3.Ayelech Worku (Eti) 15:10.17, 4.Dong Yanmei (Chi) 15:10.73, 5.Irina Mikitenko (Ger) 15:13.93, 6.Yelena Zadorozhnaya (Rus) 15:16.15.
Back to Europe, Yegorova more than lived up to her newly earned reputation. In the Zurich meet (17 August) she won a 3000 metre race in 8:23.26. She closed her 2001 account on a high note with a new European 5000 metre record on 31 August in Berlin – 14:29.32, second best ever next to Jiang Bo's world record (14:28.09 in 1997). She won from Gete Wami (14:31.69) and Paula Radcliffe (14:32.44). This came as a result of even pace throughout, with kilometre fractions in 2:55.79, 2:55.35, 2:53.35, 2:54.58 and 2:50.25. With one kilometre to go, with Radcliffe then in the lead, the time was 11:39.07 – faster than Jiang's race at the same stage (11:40.6).

HIGHLIGHTS OF THE 2002 SEASON
(up to the middle of July)

12

This brief summary is being written just before the major title meets of the year, which will unfold between late July and early August in the following sequence: Commonwealth Games (Manchester), African Championships (Tunis) and European Championships (Munich). The international season will virtually close with the World Cup (Madrid) in the second half of September.

MEN

Benjamin Limo, runner-up in the 5000 metres at the 1999 World Championships, used his strong finishing kick to good advantage to master classy fields in the first two meets of the Golden League series. He won with 12:57.50 in Oslo (28 June) and 13:02.34 in Saint-Denis (5 July), beating among others his compatriots Sammy Kipketer, John Kibowen, Paul Bitok and Mark Bett as well as Assefa Mezegebu of Ethiopia and Salah Hissou of Morocco. This last, who had beaten Limo in a hectic finish at the 1999 Worlds, returned to his winning ways at the Golden Gala meet in Rome (12 July) with 12:55.85, the year's fastest time so far. Benjamin Limo was a close second (12:57.24) and the 2001 world champion, Richard Limo, third (12:57.52).

The Stanford University track again proved a nice "vehicle" for up and coming distance men. On 3 May Albert Chepkurui of Kenya, 21, beat a strong 10,000 metre field there in 27:19.79, nosing out Meb Keflezighi of USA (27:20.15). Another relatively little known Kenyan, Zakayo Ngatho, 24, ran the same distance in 27:36.68 at Kobe on 28 April. But then all these marks may be intrinsically inferior to Paul Kosgei's 27:44.14, made in the Kenya Championships at Nairobi on 22 June. This is in fact the fastest time ever recorded at high altitude.

Eternal rivals Haile Gebrselassie and Paul Tergat transferred their feud to the road and really made the headlines in the widely heralded London marathon (14 April). The Ethiopian was making his official debut over the distance (but for an alleged 2:50 at age 15 ...) and Tergat was at his third try. To be sure, the Kenyan was once again second .....but not to his "bête noire", who had to be content with third. Both were baffled in the closing stage by a Moroccan-born American, Khalid Khannouchi, who certainly had more experience than his famous rivals, being in fact the owner of the best-on-record time over the classic distance (2 hr 05:42 at Chicago in 1999). The American won the race - branded by many commentators as the best marathon *ever* - in 2 hr 05:38, thus shaving 4 seconds off his record time. Tergat (2 hr 05:48) and Gebrselassie (2 hr 06:35), second and third respectively, did *extremely* well though and may have more to say at this distance in the near future.

WOMEN

Gabriela Szabó opened her 2002 account on a high note, winning a strong 5000 metre race in 14:46.86 (Oslo, 28 June). Her patented finish helped her to beat Berhane Adere of Ethiopia (14:46.99) by the narrowest of margins. The field also included Edith Masai of Kenya and European record holder Olga Yegorova of Russia, fourth and fifth respectively. Masai, who had made an amazing breakthrough in 2001 at the age of 34, turned the tables on both Adere and Szabó in the Rome meet (12 July), winning in 14:53.77.

The fastest 10,000 metre time of the year so far belongs to Yoko Shibui of Japan: 30:48.89 on the by now famous Stanford track at Palo Alto (3 May), winning from Deena Drossin of USA (30:50.32). New national records both.

Paula Radcliffe of Great Britain, for years one of the world's best distance runners on the track , made a splendid marathon debut in the London classic (14 April) with an astounding winning time - 2 hr 18:56, barely nine seconds off the best-on-record for this distance.

Relaxation + Motivation

Managers - or, as they are officially called, athletes' representatives - play a prominent rôle in the ventures of present-day topclass athletes. Josephus ("Jos") Hermens is in the front-row of this profession. This Nijmegen-born Dutchman, now 52, has under his wings an impressive cohort of athletes from many countries, notably including such distance runners as Gebrselassie, Bayissa, Barmasai, Kirui, Lahlafi, Richard Limo, Hailu Mekonnen and Million Wolde among men and Gabriela Szabó, Wami, Adere and Ouaziz on the distaff side.

Hermens himself can look back to an excellent career as an active athlete. In the Seventies he was among Europe's best distance runners and Europe was then at the top in this department. He was fourth in the 5000 metres at the 1974 Europeans, tenth in the 10,000 at the 1976 Olympics, third in the 10,000 in the 1977 World Cup. And he twice bettered the world 1-hour record with 20,907 km. (1975) and 20,944 km (1976). His experience in so many facets of the sport makes him an authoritative observer.

I recently questioned him about the main differences between topclass distance runners of his generation, mostly European, and those of today, almost exclusively African. "The blending between Interval Training and Endurance Training is well-nigh complete by now - he said - but the stress has shifted from high quantity (I used to average 50-to-60 km. running per day back in the Seventies) to high quality. Generally speaking, African runners, being accustomed to a different rhythm of life, are much more relaxed than their European counterparts. No matter if they have strong motivations: they know that top-level sport can help them to improve their social and economic status. I was brought up in a large family and in this respect I can well understand the problems of some of my African pupils".

Hermens also noted that, "notwithstanding all evolutions, endurance to suffering both in training and competition, remains the main key to success in long distance running."

STATISTICS
MEN

ABBREVIATIONS

e	=	estimated non-winning time
h	=	heat
hc	=	off-scratch in a handicap race
m	=	manual time (during coexistence with automatic timing)
q.m.	=	qualifying mark
T	=	tie (ex-aequo)
u	=	unofficial non-winning time
"	=	timing by photo-electric cell
^	=	made on race track
*	=	made in competition with relay team
+	=	intermediate time in longer race

NB. Year Lists for 3 and 6 miles are limited to athletes who had comparatively better marks at these distances.

ALL TIME WORLD LIST OF BEST PERFORMANCES AS AT THE END OF 1900

3 miles

Sidney	Thomas	GB 868	14:24.0	1)	London	03 Jun	1893
Charles	Willers	GB	14:25.0e	2)	London	03 Jun	1893
George	Crossland	GB 872	14:27 2/5	1)	Crewe	13 Jun	1896
Fred	Bacon	GB 870	14:27 3/5	1)	Edinburgh	21 Jul	1894
James	Kibblewhite	GB 866	14:29 3/5	2)hc	London	31 Aug	1889
	Kibblewhite		14:35.0	1)	London	28 Jun	1890

Professionals:

Peter	Cannon	GB 857	14:19 1/2	1)	Govan	05 May	1888
William	Cummings	GB 858	14:21.0+	1)	Preston	12 Jun	1880
Jack	White	GB 838	14:36.0+	1)	London	11 May	1863

5000 metres

Charles	Bennett	GB 870	15:29 1/5	1)	Paris	22 Jul	1900

6 miles

Sidney	Thomas	GB 868	30:17 4/5+	1)	London	22 Oct	1892
Fred	Bacon	GB 870	30:19 4/5+	1)	London	20 Apr	1895
Walter	George	GB 858	30:21 1/2+	1)	London	28 Jul	1884
Harry	Watkins	GB 872	30:26 e +	2)	London	20 Apr	1895
	George		30:36.0+	1)hc	London	07 Apr	1884
	Thomas		30:40 2/5+	1)	London	06 Apr	1889
James	Kibblewhite	GB 866	30:40 4/5e+	2)	London	06 Apr	1889

Professionals:

Jack	White	GB 838	29:50.0+	1)	London	11 May	1863
William	Lang	GB 838	29:50 1/5e+	2)	London	11 May	1863
William	Jackson	GB 820	30:04.0+	1)	London	31 May	1852
Edward	Mills	GB 841	30:11.0	1)	London	30 Aug	1862
William	Cummings	GB 858	30:18 2/5	1)	London	28 Sep	1885
Harry	Watkins	GB c872	30:21.0+	1)	Rochdale	16 Sep	1899
Lewis	Bennett	USA c830	30:25.0+	1)	Brompton	03 Apr	1863
	George		30:26 4/5	1)	Birmingham	02 Oct	1886
	Bacon		30:28 2/5+	1)	Rochdale	19 Jun	1897

10,000 metres

Walter	George	GB 858	31:40.0+	1)	London	28 Jul	1884

Professional:

William	Cummings	GB 858	31:35.0+	1)	London	28 Sep	1885

WORLD ALL TIME LIST OF BEST PERFORMANCES AS AT THE END OF 1920

3 miles

Jean	Bouin	Fra 888	14:07.2+	1)	Stockholm	10 Jul	1912
Hannes	Kolehmainen	Fin 889	14:07.4+	2)	Stockholm	10 Jul	1912
Alfred	Shrubb	GB 879	14:17 1/5	1)	Abergavenny	27 Aug	1904
	Shrubb		14:17 3/5	1)	London	21 May	1903
	Shrubb		14:22 2/5	1)	Horsham	03 Aug	1903
	Kolehmainen		14:22 3/5	1)hc	New York	17 Aug	1913
Sidney	Thomas	GB 868	14:24.0	1)	London	03 Jun	1893
Charles	Willers	GB	14:25.0e	2)	London	03 Jun	1893
	Shrubb		14:25.0	1)	Chelmsford	19 Jul	1902
Joe	Deakin	GB 879	14:26 4/5	1)hc	London	07 Sep	1907
	Shrubb		14:27 1/5+	1)	Glasgow	13 Jun	1904
Arthur	Robertson	GB 879	14:27 1/5	1)	Windsor	19 Aug	1908

Indoors:

Hannes	Kolehmainen	Fin 889	14:18 1/5	1)	Brooklyn, NY	12 Feb	1913
	Kolehmainen		14:20 4/5	1)hc	Brooklyn, NY	22 Nov	1913

Professionals:

George	McCrae	GB 893	14:18 3/5	1)hc	Powderhall	22 Jun	1918
Peter	Cannon	GB 857	14:19 1/2	1)	Govan	05 May	1888
William	Cummings	GB 858	14:21.0+	1)	Preston	12 Jun	1880

5000 metres

Hannes	Kolehmainen	Fin 889	14:36.6	1)	Stockholm	10 Jul	1912
Jean	Bouin	Fra 888	14:36.7	2)	Stockholm	10 Jul	1912
Charles	Hunter	USA	14:45.0	1)	Pasadena	26 Jun	1920
Eric	Backman	Swe 896	14:51.0	1)	Stockholm	31 Aug	1919
Rudolf	Falk	Swe 898	14:54.3	1)	Stockholm	21 Jul	1919
	Backman		14:55.4	1)hc	Gävle	10 Sep	1919
Joseph	Guillemot	Fra 899	14:55.6	1)	Antwerp	17 Aug	1920
	Backman		14:56.7	2)	Stockholm	21 Jul	1919
John	Zander	Swe 890	14:57.5	1)	Stockholm	17 Aug	1918
	Bouin		14:58.8+ °	1)	Marseille	06 Apr	1913

Alf	Halstvedt	Nor 897	14:59.1	3)	Stockholm	21 Jul	1919
	Zander		14:59.6	1)	Stockholm	19 Aug	1917
Paavo	Nurmi	Fin 897	15:00.0	2)	Antwerp	17 Aug	1920
	Backman		15:00.2	1)hc	Göteborg	08 Aug	1918
	Nurmi		15:00.5	1)	Helsinki	03 Jul	1920
Arthur	Robertson	GB 879	15:01.2	1)	Stockholm	13 Sep	1908
	Backman		15:01.4	1)	Stockholm	22 Sep	1920
	Bouin		15:05.0	1)h5	Stockholm	09 Jul	1912
H.Louis	Scott	USA 891	15:06.4	1)hc	New York	26 May	1912
	Backman		15:07.1	2)	Stockholm	17 Aug	1918

(20 performances by 11 performers)
+° = Time taken at 5040 metres during race at longer distance.

Indoors:

George	Bonhag	USA 882	15:05.8	1)hc	New York	25 Jan	1912

6 miles

Jean	Bouin	Fra 888	29:51.6+	1)	Colombes	16 Nov	1911
Alfred	Shrubb	GB 879	29:59.4+	1)	Glasgow	05 Nov	1904
Sidney	Thomas	GB 868	30:17.8+	1)	London	22 Oct	1892
Fred	Bacon	GB 870	30:19.8+	1)	London	20 Apr	1895
Hannes	Kolehmainen	Fin 889	30:20.4+	1)	New York	01 Nov	1913
	Bouin		30:21.0+	1)	Stockholm	06 Jul	1913
Walter	George	GB 858	30:21.5+	1)	London	28 Jul	1884
Harry	Watkins	GB 872	30:26.+e	2)	London	20 Jul	1895
Arthur	Robertson	GB 879	30:26.0+	1)	Stockholm	14 Sep	1908
	Shrubb		30:33.2+	1)	Northampton	25 Apr	1903
	George		30:36.0+	1)hc	London	07 Apr	1884

Indoors:

Hannes	Kolehmainen	Fin 889	30:24.0+	1)	Buffalo, NY	01 Feb	1913

Professionals:

Jack	White	GB 838	29:50.0+	1)	London	11 May	1863
William	Lang	GB 838	29:50.2+e	2)	London	11 May	1863
William	Jackson	GB 820	30:04.0+	1)	London	01 May	1852
Edward	Mills	GB 841	30:09.0	1)	London	15 Dec	1862
	Mills		30:11.0	1)	London	30 Aug	1862
William	Cummings	GB 858	30:18.4+	1)	London	28 Sep	1885
Harry	Watkins	GB 872	30:21.0+	1)	Rochdale	16 Sep	1899
Lewis	Bennett	USA c830	30:25.0+	1)	Brompton	03 Apr	1863

10,000 metres

Jean	Bouin	Fra 888	30:58.8	1)	Colombes	16 Nov	1911
Alfred	Shrubb	GB 879	31:02.4+	1)	Glasgow	05 Nov	1904
	Bouin		31:12.1+	1)	Stockholm	22 Jun	1913
Eric	Backman	Swe 896	31:13.7	1)	Stockholm	18 Aug	1918
	Backman		31:16.0	1)	Örebro	26 Sep	1920
Hannes	Kolehmainen	Fin 889	31:20.8	1)	Stockholm	08 Jul	1912
	Bouin		31:21.0*	1)	Kristiania	15 Jun	1913
	Bouin		31:21.2+	1)	Marseille	22 Oct	1911
	Backman		31:23.4	1)	Göteborg	13 Aug	1918
	Kolehmainen		31:25.2+e	1)	New York	01 Nov	1913
	Bouin		31:27.2+	1)	Stockholm	06 Jul	1913
	Kolehmainen		31:27.4	1)	Tampere	02 Aug	1914
	Bouin		31:28.4	1)	Copenhagen	11 Jul	1913
Georg	Peterson	Swe 883	31:30.0*	1)	Halmstad	05 Jun	1910

(14 performances by 5 performers)

217

Professional:

Viljam	Kolehmainen	Fin 887	31:19.0	1)	Kuopio	12 Sep	1911

Indoors:

Jean	Vermeulen	Fra 895	31:14.2	1)	Paris	01 Jun	1914

WORLD YEAR LISTS 1921 – 1940

1921

5000 metres

Paavo	Nurmi	Fin 897	14:53.8	1)	Göteborg	22 May
Eric	Backman	Swe 896	15:06.1+	2)	Stockholm	22 Jun
Gustaf	Mattsson	Swe 893	15:18.7	2)	Stockholm	20 Aug
Emanuel	Lundström	Swe 896	15:20.7	3)	Stockholm	20 Aug
Lucien	Duquesne	Fra 00	15:22.3	2)	Stockholm	27 Aug
Karl	Östholm	Swe 898	15:22.7	4)	Stockholm	20 Aug
Primo	Brega	Ita 892	15:22.8	1)	Cagliari	02 Sep
Eino	Rastas	Fin 894	15:24.8	2)	Kotka	20 Aug
Joseph	Guillemot	Fra 899	15:25.6	1)	Colombes	11 Sep
Emil	Bedarff	Ger 896	15:26.7	2)hc	Vienna	08 Sep

Noteworthy 3 mile times:

William	Marsh	GB 897	14:52.0	1)	Cambridge	05 Mar
James	Hatton	GB	14:52.6	2)	Colombes	17 Jul
Evelyn	Montague	GB 00	14:54.0	1)	London	19 Mar

10,000 metres

Paavo	Nurmi	Fin 897	30:40.2	1)	Stockholm	22 Jun
Eric	Backman	Swe 896	31:02.1	2)	Stockholm	22 Jun
Gustaf	Mattsson	Swe 893	32:04.2	1)	Stockholm	28 Aug
Hannes	Kolehmainen	Fin 889	32:06.1	1)	Pori	10 Jul
Louis	Corlet	Fra 897	32:06.4	2)	Stockholm	28 Aug
Teodor	Koskenniemi	Fin 887	32:22.0	1)	Kuopio	14 Aug
Carlo	Speroni	Ita 895	32:31.4	1)	Bologna	20 Sep
Nils	Bergström	Swe 898	32:31.8	1)	Motala	07 Aug
Emanuel	Lundström	Swe 896	32:36.5	1)	Stockholm	21 Aug
Taavetti	Kolehmainen	Fin 885	32:41.0	2)	Kuopio	14 Aug

Noteworthy 6 mile times:

Emanuel	Lundström	Swe 896	30:55.5	1)	Stockholm	21 Sep
Gustaf	Mattsson	Swe 893	30:57.5	2)	Stockholm	21 Sep

1922

5000 metres

Paavo	Nurmi	Fin 897	14:35.3	1)	Stockholm	12 Sep
Eric	Backman	Swe 896	14:58.6	1)hc	Stockholm	21 Sep
Charles	Blewitt	GB 895	15:15.2	1)	Paris	08 Oct
Ernesto	Ambrosini	Ita 894	15:18.8	1)	Busto Arsizio	17 Sep
Eino	Rastas	Fin 894	15:20.8	1)	Helsinki	19 Aug
Primo	Brega	Ita 892	15:21.2	2)	Busto Arsizio	17 Sep

Jón	Kaldal	Ice 896	15:23.0	1)	Copenhagen	06 Aug
Gaston	Heuet	Fra 892	15:23	3)	Paris	08 Oct
Väinö	Sipilä	Fin 897	15:23.5	2)	Helsinki	19 Aug
Nils	Bergström	Swe 898	15:25.0	2)	Stockholm	15 Jul

Indoors:

John	Romig	USA 898	15:24.2	1)	New York	21 Feb

Noteworthy 3 mile times:

Edvin	Wide	Swe 896	14:13.6	1)	Stockholm	27 Sep
Eric	Backman	Swe 896	14:19.7	2)	Stockholm	27 Sep
William	Seagrove	GB 898	14:50.0	1)	Cambridge	11 Mar
Ville	Ritola	Fin 896	14:51.2+	1)	New York	28 Oct
Noel	McInnes	GB 01	14:51.4	1)	Oxford	06 Mar

Indoors:

Earle	Johnson	USA 891	14:37.6	1)	New York	01 Feb
John	Romig	USA 898	14:39.4	1)hc	New York	25 Feb

10,000 metres

Eric	Backman	Swe 896	31:26.0	1)	Copenhagen	25 Jul
Ville	Ritola	Fin 896	31:35 +	1)	New York	28 Oct
Emil	Bedarff	Ger 896	31:56.4	1)hc	Vienna	08 Sep
Eino	Rastas	Fin 894	32:11.5	1)	Helsinki	20 Aug
Väinö	Sipilä	Fin 897	32:15.0	2)	Helsinki	20 Aug
George	Webber	GB	32:21.8	1)	London	29 Jul
Halland	Britton	GB 890	32:22 +	1)	London	30 Sep
Louis	Corlet	Fra 897	32:26.4	1)	Colombes	20 Aug
Yrjö	Jokela	Fin 897	32:27.1	1)	Tampere	20 Aug
Gustaf	Mattsson	Swe 893	32:29.0	1)	Stockholm	05 Aug
Nils	Bergström	Swe 898	32:39.1	2)	Stockholm	17 Jul
Hannes	Kolehmainen	Fin 889	32:43.0	1)	Mikkeli	28 May

Noteworthy 6 mile times:

Ville	Ritola	Fin 896	30:25 +	1)	New York	28 Oct
Halland	Britton	GB 890	31:10.6+	1)	London	30 Sep

1923

5000 metres

Paavo	Nurmi	Fin 897	14:39.9	1)	Stockholm	24 Aug
Edvin	Wide	Swe 896	14:44.1	1)	Stockholm	18 Aug
Ville	Ritola	Fin 896	15:02.8	1)	New York	08 Sep
Eric	Backman	Swe 896	15:04.8	2)	Stockholm	18 Aug
Lucien	Duquesne	Fra 00	15:07.6	1)	Paris	09 Jun
Nils	Eklöf	Swe 04	15:08.0	1)	Stockholm	02 Sep
Joseph	Guillemot	Fra 899	15:14.0	1)	Lyon	20 May
Emil	Bedarff	Ger 896	15:14.2	1)	Frankfurt/M.	17 Aug
Halland	Britton	GB 890	15:15.0	1)	Paris	09 Jun
Eino	Rastas	Fin 894	15:19.0	3)	Göteborg	01 Jul

Indoors:

Joie	Ray	USA 894	14:54.6	1)	New York	07 Mar
Ville	Ritola	Fin 896	14:59.6	2)	New York	07 Mar

Noteworthy 3 mile times:

William	Cotterell	GB	14:40.2	1)	Aldershot	17 Jul
William	Seagrove	GB 898	14:49.6	1)	Cambridge	10 Mar

Indoors:

Ville	Ritola	Fin 896	14:15.8	1)hc	New York	28 Feb
Joie	Ray	USA 894	14:16.0e	2)hc	New York	28 Feb

10,000 metres

Ville	Ritola	Fin 896	31:38 +	1)	New York	27 Oct
Eino	Rastas	Fin 894	31:42.7	1)	Göteborg	02 Jul
Väinö	Sipilä	Fin 897	31:45.3	2)	Göteborg	02 Jul
Paavo	Nurmi	Fin 897	31:51.0	1)hc	Joensuu	09 Sep
Eric	Backman	Swe 896	32:05.0	3)	Göteborg	02 Jul
Eero	Berg	Fin 898	32:19.9	2)	Tampere	10 Sep
Emil	Bedarff	Ger 896	32:26.8	1)	Düsseldorf	19 Sep
Costante	Lussana	Ita 892	32:30.0	1)	Bologna	23 Jun
Yrjö	Jokela	Fin 897	32:33.3	1)	Helsinki	26 Aug
Hannes	Kolehmainen	Fin 889	32:41.6	1)hc	Vaasa	15 Jul

Noteworthy 6 mile time:

Ville	Ritola	Fin 896	30:30.4+	1)	New York	27 Oct

1924

5000 metres

Paavo	Nurmi	Fin 897	14:28.2	1)	Helsinki	19 Jun
Ville	Ritola	Fin 896	14:31.5e	2)	Colombes	10 Jul
Edvin	Wide	Swe 896	14:52.9	1)	Stockholm	31 May
Yrjö	Jokela	Fin 897	15:08.3	1)	Helsinki	16 Aug
John	Romig	USA 898	15:12.4e	4)	Colombes	10 Jul
Väinö	Sipilä	Fin 897	15:14.2	1)	Hamina	30 Aug
Eino	Seppälä	Fin 896	15:15.4	1)	Kotka	29 May
Emil	Bedarff	Ger 896	15:15.8	1)	Copenhagen	22 Jun
Elias	Katz	Fin 01	15:17.2	1)	Lahti	23 Aug
Harold	Phelps	USA 03	15:18.5e	2)	Cambridge, MA	14 Jun

Noteworthy 3 mile times:

Verne	Booth	USA 899	14:35.8	1)	London	19 Jul
Halland	Britton	GB 890	14:39.4	2)	London	19 Jul
George	Webber	GB	14:40.4	3)	London	19 Jul
Joseph	Guillemot	Fra 899	14:45.2	1)	Colombes	28 Sep

Indoors:

Robert	Brown	USA897	14:39e	2)	New York	21 Feb
John	Romig	USA898	14:39e	3)	New York	21 Feb

10,000 metres

Paavo	Nurmi	Fin 897	30:06.1	1)	Kuopio	31 Aug
Ville	Ritola	Fin 896	30:23.2	1)	Colombes	06 Jul
Edvin	Wide	Swe 896	30:55.2e	2)	Colombes	06 Jul
Eero	Berg	Fin 898	31:43.0e	3)	Colombes	06 Jul
Väinö	Sipilä	Fin 897	31:50.2e	4)	Colombes	06 Jul
Yrjö	Jokela	Fin 897	31:51.5	1)	Helsinki	14 Sep

Ernest	Harper	GB 02	31:58 e	5)	Colombes	06 Jul
Axel	Petersen	Den 02	31:59.8	1)	Copenhagen	21 Jul
Carlo	Speroni	Ita 895	32:03.8	1)	Busto Arsizio	11 May
Sven	Thuresson	Swe 00	32:04.1	1)	Stockholm	01 Jun

1925

5000 metres

Edvin	Wide	Swe 896	14:40.4	1)	Stockholm	18 Jun
Paavo	Nurmi	Fin 897	14:50.2	1)	Turku	27 Aug
Yrjö	Jokela	Fin 897	14:54.9	1)	Helsinki	13 Jun
Kalle	Matilainen	Fin 899	14:57.0	1)	Viipuri	15 Aug
Nils	Eklöf	Swe 04	14:57.3	1)	Stockholm	17 Jul
Eero	Berg	Fin 898	15:01.1	2)	Tampere	27 Sep
Joseph	Guillemot	Fra 899	15:03.2	1)	Paris	01 Jun
Ove	Andersen	Fin 899	15:08.8	1)	Berlin	21 Jun
Axel	Petersen	Den 02	15:11.1	1)	Copenhagen	17 Jun
Robert	Marchal	Fra 01	15:12.4	2)	Paris	01 Jun

Indoors:

Ville	Ritola	Fin 896	14:23.2	1)	New York	24 Feb
Paavo	Nurmi	Fin 897	14:38.0	1)	Buffalo, NY	26 Mar

Noteworthy 3 mile times:

Ville	Ritola	Fin 896	13:56.2+	1)	New York	24 Feb

10,000 metres

Paavo	Nurmi	Fin 897	30:40.2	1)	Helsinki	06 Sep
Eric	Stenfeldt	Swe 05	31:27.9	1)	Stockholm	23 Aug
Eero	Berg	Fin 898	31:38.5	2)	Helsinki	06 Sep
Yrjö	Jussila	Fin 00	31:50.6	1)	Turku	13 Sep
Väinö	Sipilä	Fin 897	31:57.0	1)	Tampere	17 May
Robert	Marchal	Fra 01	31:59.4	1)	Colombes	05 Jul
Erkki	Peltonen	Fin 02	32:01.0	2)	Turku	13 Sep
Eino	Rastas	Fin 894	32:02.5	1)	Suonenjoki	23 Aug
Lucien	Dolquès	Fra 05	32:03.8	2)	Stockholm	30 Aug
Yrjö	Jokela	Fin 897	32:04.8	1)	Helsinki	14 Jun

1926

5000 metres

Paavo	Nurmi	Fin 897	14:34.0	1)hc	Vienna	21 Sep
Armas	Kinnunen	Fin 00	14:48.9	2)	Tampere	14 Aug
Edvin	Wide	Swe 896	14:55.3	2)	Turku	23 Jul
Yrjö	Jokela	Fin 897	14:55.5	1)	Helsinki	11 Sep
Kalle	Sarvimäki	Fin 02	14:58.2	2)	Helsinki	11 Sep
Kalle	Matilainen	Fin 899	14:59.1	3)	Tampere	14 Aug
Herbert	Johnston	GB 02	15:00.4	1)	Colombes	25 Jul
Eino	Rastas	Fin 894	15:00.6	4)	Tampere	14 Aug
Joseph	Guillemot	Fra 899	15:00.8	1)	Colombes	26 Sep
Eero	Berg	Fin 898	15:04.9	3)	Turku	23 Jul

Noteworthy 3 mile time:

Jack	Webster	GB 02	14:24.8	1)hc	Rugby	17 Jul

10,000 metres

Paavo	Nurmi	Fin 897	31:12.2	1)	Tampere	15 Aug
Eino	Rastas	Fin 894	31:53.3	2)	Tampere	15 Aug
Manuel	Plaza	Chl 02	31:54.0	1)	Montevideo	16 Apr
Iivari	Rötkö	Fin 893	31:57.4	1)	Helsinki	15 Aug
Toivo	Salmi	Fin 894	31:58.0	2)	Helsinki	15 Aug
Lucien	Dolquès	Fra 05	31:59.6	1)	Colombes	11 Jul
Yrjö	Jokela	Fin 897	31:59.7	1)	Helsinki	12 Sep
Birger	Silén	Swe 00	32:07.8	1)	Stockholm	05 Sep
Ilmari	Posti	Fin 897	32:08.7	3)	Tampere	15 Aug
Eric	Stenfeldt	Swe 05	32:11.3	2)	Stockholm	05 Sep

Noteworthy 6 mile time:

Ville	Ritola	Fin 896	30:55.6+	1)	Yonkers, NY	02 Nov

1927

5000 metres

Nils	Eklöf	Swe 04	14:45.3	1)	Norrköping	06 Aug
Paavo	Nurmi	Fin 897	14:54.4	1)	Turku	20 Aug
Kalle	Matilainen	Fin 899	14:56.4	1)	Kuopio	18 Jun
Ilmari	Posti	Fin 897	15:01.8	1)	Kotka	23 Jul
Lauri	Virtanen	Fin 04	15:02.6	1)	Viipuri	20 Aug
Otto	Kohn	Ger 07	15:03.0	1)	Colombes	21 Aug
Elias	Katz	Fin 01	15:04.2	1)	Berlin	18 Jun
Otto	Petri	Ger 02	15:04.9	1)	Hamburg	11 Jun
Maurice	Norland	Fra 01	15:06.6	2)	Colombes	21 Aug
Armas	Kinnunen	Fin 00	15:08.0	1)	Helsinki	11 Jun

Noteworthy 3 mile times:

Walter	Beavers	GB 03	14:25.8	1)	Stourbridge	07 Jun
Randolph	Rose	NZ 01	14:29.2	1)	Wellington	26 Mar
Herbert	Johnston	GB 02	14:35.4	1)	Cambridge	11 Jun

Indoors:

Ville	Ritola	Fin 896	14:11.0	1)	New York	22 Apr

10,000 metres

Eric	Stenfeldt	Swe 05	31:38.2	1)	Copenhagen	28 Aug
Johan	Badendyck	Nor 02	31:41.7	2)	Copenhagen	28 Aug
Kalle	Matilainen	Fin 899	31:49.2	1)	Oulu	31 Jul
Axel	Petersen	Den 02	31:52.0	3)	Copenhagen	28 Aug
Bror	Öhrn	Swe 05	31:58.6	1)	Stockholm	21 Aug
Bror	Eriksson	Swe 01	31:59.7	3)	Stockholm	21 Aug
Otto	Petri	Ger 02	32:00.8	1)	Berlin	17 Jul
Eino	Rastas	Fin 894	32:02.0	2)	Turku	21 Aug
Kalle	Sarvimäki	Fin 02	32:02.7	3)	Turku	21 Aug
Jalmari	Kaila	Fin 01	32:08.2	1)	Helsinki	18 Jun

Noteworthy 6 mile time:

Ville	Ritola	Fin 896	30:43.4	1)	Lincoln, NE	02 Jul

1928

5000 metres

Ville	Ritola	Fin 896	14:36.2	1)	Helsinki	21 Jun
Eino	Borg (Purje)	Fin 00	14:39.3	2)	Helsinki	21 Jun
Paavo	Nurmi	Fin 897	14:40.0e	2)	Amsterdam	03 Aug
Edvin	Wide	Swe 896	14:41.2e	3)	Amsterdam	03 Aug
Lauri	Virtanen	Fin 04	14:48.3	1)	Turku	18 Aug
Leo	Lermond	USA 06	14:50.0e	4)	Amsterdam	03 Aug
J.Macauley	Smith	USA 05	14:54.4e	2)	Cambridge, MA	07 Jul
David	Abbott	USA 02	14:54.6e	3)	Cambridge, MA	07 Jul
Toivo	Loukola	Fin 02	14:54.9	3)	Helsinki	21 Jun
Ragnar	Magnusson	Swe 01	14:59.6e	5)	Amsterdam	03 Aug

10,000 metres

Paavo	Nurmi	Fin 897	30:18.8	1)	Amsterdam	29 Jul
Ville	Ritola	Fin 896	30:19.4e	2)	Amsterdam	29 Jul
Edvin	Wide	Swe 896	31:00.8e	3)	Amsterdam	29 Jul
Oivo	Loukola	Fin 02	31:20.5	2)	Helsinki	07 Jul
Kalle	Matilainen	Fin 899	31:25.5	3)	Helsinki	07 Jul
Jean-Gunnar	Lindgren	Swe 05	31:26.0e	4)	Amsterdam	29 Jul
Ilmari	Posti	Fin 897	31:27.8	4)	Helsinki	07 Jul
Joie	Ray	USA 894	31:28.4	1)	Cambridge, MA	07 Jul
Arthur	Muggridge	GB 04	31:31.8e	5)	Amsterdam	29 Jul
Ragnar	Magnusson	Swe 01	31:37.2e	6)	Amsterdam	29 Jul

1929

5000 metres

Lauri	Virtanen	Fin 04	14:47.2	1)	Turku	10 Jul
Toivo	Loukola	Fin 02	14:48.7	1)	Viipuri	17 Aug
Karl	Matilainen	Fin 899	14:51.7	2)	Viipuri	17 Aug
Paavo	Nurmi	Fin 897	14:55.4	1)	Colombes	29 Sep
Ragnar	Magnusson	Swe 01	14:57.0	1)	Göteborg	15 Sep
Armas	Toivonen	Fin 899	14:58.5	2)	Göteborg	15 Sep
Albert	Kilp	Ger 03	15:00.0	1)	Bratislava	20 Jul
Volmari	Iso-Hollo	Fin 07	15:00.9	1)	Helsinki	01 Sep
Heikki	Potila	Fin 02	15:01.1	3)	Viipuri	17 Aug
Stanislaw	Petkiewicz	Pol 08	15:02.6	1)	Warsaw	09 Jun

10,000 metres

Toivo	Loukola	Fin 02	31:12.9	1)	Helsinki	08 Sep
Ragnar	Magnusson	Swe 01	31:14.4	2)	Helsinki	08 Sep
Armas	Toivonen	Fin 899	31:23.4	3)	Helsinki	08 Sep
Jean-Gunnar	Lindgren	Swe 05	31:27.3	1)	Borås	22 Sep
Väinö	Sipilä	Fin 897	31:30.2	1)hc	Stettin	06 Aug
Karl	Matilainen	Fin 899	31:45.8	3)	Viipuri	18 Aug
José	Ribas	Arg 899	31:49.4	1)	Buenos Aires	17 Mar
Otto	Petri	Ger 02	31:57.4	1)	Hannover	29 Jun
Emile	Chapuis	Fra 899	32:01.0	1)	Colombes	07 Jul
Eljas	Suoknuuti	Fin 899	32:04.5	4)	Viipuri	18 Aug

Noteworthy 6 mile times:

Paavo	Nurmi	Fin 897	30:35.6	1)hc	New York	02 Jun
Harry	Chauca	USA	30:44.0	1)	Los Angeles	04 May

1930

5000 metres

Paavo	Nurmi	Fin 897	14:40.7	1)	Helsinki	27 Aug
Lauri	Virtanen	Fin 04	14:41.5	2)	Helsinki	27 Aug
Toivo	Loukola	Fin 02	14:48.1	1)	Helsinki	17 Jun
Ragnar	Magnusson	Swe 01	14:49.6	2)	Helsinki	17 Jun
Lauri	Lehtinen	Fin 08	14:49.8	1)	Helsinki	04 Jun
Volmari	Iso-Hollo	Fin 07	14:53.2	1)	Göteborg	07 sep
Janusz	Kusocinski	Pol 07	14:55.6	2)	Warsaw	19 Sep
Erik	Pettersson	Swe 06	14:57.4	2)	Stockholm	10 Jul
Antero	Kössi	Fin 05	14:58.2	3)	Tampere	16 Aug
Armas	Kinnunen	Fin 00	14:58.8	3)	Helsinki	04 Jun

Noteworthy 3 mile time:

Alexander	Hillhouse	Aus 07	14:25.5	1)	Hamilton, Ont	01 Aug

10,000 metres

Paavo	Nurmi	Fin 897	31:04.6	1)	Tampere	17 Aug
Volmari	Iso-Hollo	Fin 07	31:05.3	1)	Helsinki	21 Sep
Toivo	Loukola	Fin 02	31:17.2	2)	Helsinki	21 Sep
Lauri	Virtanen	Fin 04	31:20.1	3)	Helsinki	21 Sep
Giuseppe	Lippi	Ita 04	31:24.2	1)	Bologna	24 Nov
Janusz	Kusocinski	Pol 07	31:39.8	1)	Warsaw	02 Sep
Corrado	Franceschini	Ita 11	31:41.4	2)	Bologna	24 Nov
Birger	Silén	Swe 00	31:45.6	1)	Oslo	30 Aug
Jean-Gunnar	Lindgren	Swe 05	31:46.0	1)	Stockholm	22 Jul
Eric	Stenfeldt	Swe 05	31:47.6	2)	Oslo	30 Aug

Noteworthy 6 mile time:

Paavo	Nurmi	Ita 897	29:36.4	1)hc	London	09 Jun

1931

5000 metres

Lauri	Lehtinen	Fin 08	14:31.7	1)	Helsinki	01 Jul
Volmari	Iso-Hollo	Fin 07	14:36.3	1)	Helsinki	07 Jul
Lauri	Virtanen	Fin 04	14:40.8	3)	Helsinki	15 Aug
Janusz	Kusocinski	Pol 07	14:42.8	1)	Vienna	18 Oct
Paavo	Nurmi	Fin 897	14:47.6	1)	Berlin	01 Oct
Max	Syring	Ger 08	14:49.6	2)	Berlin	01 Oct
Ilmari	Salminen	Fin 02	14:53.3	4)	Helsinki	15 Aug
Friedrich	Schaumburg	Ger 05	14:54.6	3)	Berlin	01 Oct
Thomas	Evenson	GB 10	14:54.8	1)	Cologne	30 Aug
Jack	Winfield	GB 07	14:55.0	2	Cologne	30 Aug

10,000 metres

Paavo	Nurmi	Fin 897	30:50.6	1)	Stockholm	30 Aug
Volmari	Iso-Hollo	Fin 07	30:51.4	2)	Stockholm	30 Aug
José	Ribas	Arg 899	31:18.8	1)	Montevideo	09 May
Juan Carlos	Zabala	Arg 11	31:19.0	1)	Buenos Aires	03 May
Max	Syring	Ger 08	31:26.8	2)	Berlin	13 Sep
Toivo	Loukola	Fin 02	31:35.6	1)	Helsinki	09 Aug
Ragnar	Magnusson	Swe 01	31:38.0	3)	Stockholm	30 Aug

Birger	Silén	Swe 00	31:40.8	4)	Stockholm	30 Aug
Eemil	Kukkonen	Fin 98	31:49.2	1)	Kiuruvesi	28 Jun
Karl	Matilainen	Fin 899	31:51.3	1)	Helsinki	13 Aug

1932

5000 metres

Lauri	Lehtinen	Fin 08	14:16.9	1)	Helsinki	19 Jun
Volmari	Iso-Hollo	Fin 07	14:18.3	2)	Helsinki	19 Jun
Ralph	Hill	USA 08	14:30.0	2)	Los Angeles	05 Aug
Lauri	Virtanen	Fin 04	14:36.8	3)	Helsinki	19 Jun
Janusz	Kusocinski	Pol 07	14:41.8	1)	Warsaw	18 Oct
Jean-Gunnar	Lindgren	Swe 05	14:45.2	1)	Stockholm	10 Jun
Erik	Pettersson	Swe 06	14:48.8	2)	Stockholm	10 Jun
William	Savidan	NZ 02	14:49.6	4)	Los Angeles	05 Aug
Jalmari	Kaila	Fin 01	14:55.0	4)	Helsinki	19 Jun
Juan Carlos	Zabala	Arg 11	14:55.8	1)	Buenos Aires	30 Apr

Noteworthy 3 mile times:

James	Burns	GB 07	14:22.0	1)	Oxford	26 May
Alexander	Hillhouse	Aus 07	14:23.2	1)	Sydney	18 Jan
Walter	Beavers	GB 03	14:23.2	1)	London	02 Jul

10,000 metres

Janusz	Kusocinski	Pol 07	30:11.4	1)	Los Angeles	31 Jul
Volmari	Iso-Hollo	Fin 07	30:12.6	2)	Los Angeles	31 Jul
Lauri	Virtanen	Fin 04	30:35.0	3)	Los Angeles	31 Jul
Paavo	Nurmi	Fin 897	30:40.9	1)	Turku	27 May
William	Savidan	NZ 02	31:09.0	4)	Los Angeles	31 Jul
Max	Syring	Ger 08	31:21.2	1)	Hannover	02 Jul
Tom	McDonough	USA	31:24.0	1)	Cambridge, MA	18 Jun
Juan Carlos	Zabala	Arg 11	31:26.6	1)hc	New York	29 May
Masaji	Kitamoto	Jap 09	31:33.6	1)	Tokyo	28 May
Jean-Gunnar	Lindgren	Swe 05	31:37.0	6)	Los Angeles	31 Jul

Noteworthy 6 mile times:

John	Potts	GB 06	30:23.2	1)	London	01 Jul
Jack	Holden	GB 07	30:26.8	2)	London	01 Jul
Louis	Gregory	USA 05	30:27.4	1)	Bronx, NY	11 Jun
Eino	Pentti	USA 06	30:28.6e	2)	Bronx, NY	11 Jun

1933

5000 metres

Lauri	Lehtinen	Fin 08	14:41.4	1)	Antwerp	25 Jun
Verner	Toivonen	Fin 08	14:41.6	2)	Antwerp	25 Jun
Lauri	Virtanen	Fin 04	14:43.6	1)	Helsinki	27 Aug
Ragnar	Magnusson	Swe 01	14:43.8	1)	Stockholm	26 Aug
Erik	Pettersson	Swe 06	14:44.4	2)	Stockholm	26 Aug
Volmari	Iso-Hollo	Fin 07	14:45.9	1)	Helsinki	14 Jun
Roger	Rochard	Fra 13	14:46.5	2)	Helsinki	27 Aug
Paavo	Nurmi	Fin 897	14:46.6	1)	Oulu	03 Sep
Henry	Nielsen	Den 10	14:54.6	1)	Copenhagen	20 Aug
Roger	Rérolle	Fra 09	14:58.8	1)	Colombes	11 Jun

Noteworthy 3 mile times:

Lauri	Lehtinen	Fin 08	14:09.2	1)	London	08 Jul
Volmari	Iso-Hollo	Fin 07	14:13.4+	1)	Viipuri	20 Jul

10,000 metres

Volmari	Iso-Hollo	Fin 07	30:21.2	1)	Helsinki	21 Sep
Lauri	Lehtinen	Fin 08	30:30.5	1)	Turku	10 Sep
Lauri	Virtanen	Fin 04	30:30.7	2)	Turku	10 Sep
Henry	Nielsen	Den 10	31:13.4	1)	Copenhagen	21 Aug
Ilmari	Salminen	Fin 02	31:29.7	3)	Helsinki	21 Sep
Jean-Gunnar	Lindgren	Swe 05	31:31.7	3)	Turku	10 Sep
Roger	Rérolle	Fra 09	31:32.0	1)	Colombes	15 Jul
Paavo	Nurmi	Fin 897	31:33.0+	1)	Viipuri	24 Sep
Max	Syring	Ger 08	31:38.0	1)	Cologne	12 Aug
Janne	Torikka	Fin 05	31:39.1+	3)	Viipuri	24 Sep

Noteworthy 6 mile time:

Jack	Holden	GB 07	30:32.2	1)	London	07 Jul

Distance 30.42 m. short:

George	Bailey	GB 06	30:08.4+	1)	Sheffield	22 Apr

1934

5000 metres

Roger	Rochard	Fra 13	14:36.8	1)	Turin	09 Sep
Ilmari	Salminen	Fin 02	14:37.8	1)	Helsinki	15 Aug
Lauri	Virtanen	Fin 04	14:38.2	2)	Helsinki	15 Aug
Arvo	Askola	Fin 09	14:39.1	3)	Helsinki	15 Aug
Janusz	Kusocinski	Pol 07	14:40.6	1)	Riga	21 Jul
Gunnar	Höckert	Fin 10	14:41.9	2)	Viipuri	30 Jun
Jean-Gunnar	Lindgren	Swe 05	14:43.6	1)	Stockholm	18 Aug
Roger	Ceballos	Arg 09	14:46.2	1)	Buenos Aires	29 Jun
Lauri	Lehtinen	Fin 08	14:48.4	1)	Copenhagen	16 Sep
Evert	Ek	Swe 07	14:48.6	2)	Stockholm	18 Aug

Indoors:

Joseph	McCluskey	USA 11	14:48.4	1)	Brooklyn, NY	10 Mar

Noteworthy 3 mile time:

Lauri	Lehtinen	Fin 08	14:14.6	1)	Glasgow	04 Aug

10,000 metres

Ilmari	Salminen	Fin 02	31:02.2	1)	Viipuri	01 Jul
Arvo	Askola	Fin 09	31:03.2	2)	Turin	07 Sep
János	Kelen	Hun 11	31:05.8^	-)	Budapest	25 Nov
Lauri	Virtanen	Fin 04	31:06.9	3)	Tampere	29 Jul
Jean-Gunnar	Lindgren	Swe 05	31:18.4	1)	Stockholm	19 Aug
Choshun	Ryu	Jap 12	31:20.2	1)	Tokyo	14 Apr
Tadao	Najima	Jap	31:24.6	2)	Tokyo	14 Apr
Hideo	Tanaka	Jap 09	31:27.0	3)	Tokyo	14 Apr
Henry	Nielsen	Den 10	31:27.4	3)	Turin	07 Sep
Ragnar	Magnusson	Swe01	31:36.6	2)	Stockholm	19 Aug

1935

5000 metres

Lauri	Lehtinen	Fin 08	14:36.8	1)	Kotka	10 Aug
Lauri	Virtanen	Fin 04	14:37.0	2)	Kotka	10 Aug
Taisto	Mäki	Fin 10	14:40.8	1)	Helsinki	25 Jul
Arvo	Askola	Fin 09	14:41.8	3)	Kotka	10 Aug
Ilmari	Salminen	Fin 02	14:41.9	1)	Helsinki	10 Sep
Gunnar	Höckert	Fin 10	14:42.0	2)	Helsinki	10 Sep
Volmari	Iso-Hollo	Fin 07	14:44.4	1)	Copenhagen	15 Sep
Henry	Jonsson (Kälarne)	Swe 12	14:44.6	1)	Stockholm	24 Aug
Erik	Kronberg	Swe 08	14:46.8	2)	Stockholm	24 Aug
Rolf	Hansen	Nor 06	14:48.8	4)	Helsinki	10 Sep

10,000 metres

Ilmari	Salminen	Fin 02	30:38.2	1)	Helsinki	24 Aug
Arvo	Askola	Fin 09	30:38.4	2)	Helsinki	24 Aug
Heinrich	Haag	Ger 10	31:00.7	3)	Helsinki	24 Aug
Kohei	Murakoso	Jap 05	31:07.8	1)	Tokyo	03 Nov
János	Kelen	Hun 11	31:25.8	1)	Stockholm	08 Sep
Erik	Pettersson	Swe 06	31:28.8	2)	Stockholm	08 Sep
Harry	Siefert	Den 10	31:32.2	1)	Copenhagen	19 Aug
Lauri	Virtanen	Fin 04	31:36.2	1)	Tampere	08 Sep
Taisti	Mäki	Fin 10	31:40.4	1)	Düsseldorf	29 Sep
Choshun	Ryu	Jap 12	31:45.2	1)	Tokyo	03 Apr

1936

5000 metres

Gunnar	Höckert	Fin 10	14:22.2	1)	Berlin	07 Aug
Lauri	Lehtinen	Fin 08	14:25.8	2)	Berlin	07 Aug
Henry	Jonsson (Kälarne)	Swe 12	14:29.0	3)	Berlin	07 Aug
Kohei	Murakoso	Jap 05	14:30.0	4)	Berlin	07 Aug
Ilmari	Salminen	Fin 02	14:30.8	2)	Helsinki	12 Jul
Józef	Noji	Pol 09	14:33.4	5)	Berlin	07 Aug
Volmari	Iso-Hollo	Fin 07	14:34.7	1)	Helsinki	14 Sep
Kauko	Pekuri	Fin 12	14:35.4	2)	Helsinki	14 Sep
Syerafim	Znamenskiy	USR 06	14:38.8	1)	Moscow	18 Sep
Miklós	Szabó	Hun 08	14:39.4	1)	Budapest	06 Oct

10,000 metres

Ilmari	Salminen	Fin 02	30:15.4	1)	Berlin	02 Aug
Arvo	Askola	Fin 09	30:15.6	2)	Berlin	02 Aug
Volmari	Iso-Hollo	Fin 07	30:20.2	3)	Berlin	02 Aug
Kohei	Murakoso	Jap 05	30:25.0	4)	Berlin	02 Aug
Max	Syring	Ger 08	30:40.0	1)	Wittenberg	10 Oct
Juan Carlos	Zabala	Arg 11	30:56.2	1)	Stuttgart	21 May
J.Alex	Burns	GB 07	30:58.2	5)	Berlin	02 Aug
Harry	Siefert	Den 10	31:01.8	1)	Copenhagen	16 Jun
Donald	Lash	USA 14	31:06.9	1)	Princeton	03 Jul
Roger	Ceballos	Arg 09	31:21.4	1)	Buenos Aires	08 Nov

Noteworthy 6 mile times:

Józef	Noji	Pol 09	29:43.4	1)	London	10 Jul
J.Alex	Burns	GB 07	29:45.0	2)	London	10 Jul

John	Potts	GB 06	29:47.0	3)	London	10 Jul
William	Eaton	GB 09	29:51.4	1)	Birmingham	13 Apr
Arthur	Penny	GB 07	?	5)	London	10 Jul
Arthur	Furze	GB 03	30:12 e	6)	London	10 Jul

1937

5000 metres

Taisto	Mäki	Fin 10	14:28.8	1)	Viipuri	07 Aug
Arvo	Askola	Fin 09	14:30.0	2)	Viipuri	07 Aug
Lauri	Lehtinen	Fin 08	14:31.1	3)	Viipuri	07 Aug
Tauno	Kurki	Fin 14	14:31.1	4)	Viipuri	07 Aug
Peter	Ward	GB 13	14:31.6	2)	Helsinki	04 Sep
Ilmari	Salminen	Fin 02	14:32.4	1)	Stockholm	05 Aug
Miklós	Szabó	Hun 08	14:33.8	2)	Helsinki	15 Jul
Oiva	Lämsä	Fin 10	14:35.0	2)	Stockholm	05 Aug
Henry	Jonsson (Kälarne)	Swe 12	14:37.2	2)	Stockholm	24 Sep
Bror	Hellström	Swe 14	14:38.0	3)	Stockholm	05 Aug

10,000 metres

Ilmari	Salminen	Fin 02	30:05.5	1)	Kouvola	18 Jul
Lauri	Lehtinen	Fin 08	30:15.0	2)	Kouvola	18 Jul
Arvo	Askola	Fin 09	30:34.2	3)	Kouvola	18 Jul
Kohei	Murakoso	Jap 05	30:39.8	1)	Tokyo	06 Jun
Erkki	Tamila	Fin 11	30:49.4	2)	Viipuri	08 Aug
Giuseppe	Beviacqua	Ita 14	30:59.8	1)	Firenze	24 Oct
Jenö	Szilágyi	Hun 10	31:09.6	1)	Budapest	10 Oct
Oiva	Lämsä	Fin 10	31:11.2	3)	Viipuri	08 Aug
Béla	Németh	Hun 06	31:12.6	1)	Budapest	16 Oct
Max	Syring	Ger 08	31:13.2	1)	Berlin	18 Sep

1938

5000 metres

Taisto	Mäki	Fin 10	14:26.8	1)	Colombes	04 Sep
Kauko	Pekuri	Fin 12	14:27.4	1)	Helsinki	07 Aug
Henry	Jonsson (Kälarne)	Swe 12	14:27.4	2)	Colombes	04 Sep
Ilmari	Salminen	Fin 02	14:28.4	2)	Helsinki	07 Aug
Lauri	Lehtinen	Fin 08	14:30.2	3)	Helsinki	07 Aug
Miklós	Szabó	Hun 08	14:35.6	4)	Helsinki	21 Jun
Harry	Siefert	Den 10	14:36.2	5)	Helsinki	21 Jun
Odd	Rasdal	Nor 11	14:36.7	2)	Copenhagen	10 Jun
Syerafim	Znamenskiy	USR 06	14:39.0	1)	Moscow	01 Sep
Tauno	Kurki	Fin 14	14:40.3	2)	Karhula	12 Jun

Indoors:

| Donald | Lash | USA 14 | 14:39.0 | 1) | New York | 26 Feb |
| Norman | Bright | USA 10 | 14:39.4e | 2) | New York | 26 Feb |

Noteworthy 3 mile times:

| Cecil | Matthews | NZ 14 | 13:59.6 | 1) | Sydney | 05 Feb |
| Peter | Ward | GB 13 | 14:05.6 | 2) | Sydney | 05 Feb |

10,000 metres

Taisto	Mäki	Fin 10	30:02.0	1)	Tampere	29 Sep
Ilmari	Salminen	Fin 02	30:13.4	1)	Helsinki	17 Sep
Kauko	Pekuri	Fin 12	30:14.0	3)	Helsinki	17 Sep
Matti	Laihoranta	Fin 12	30:35.2	4)	Helsinki	17 Sep
Erkki	Tamila	Fin 11	30:42.8	2)	Kouvola	17 Jul
Arvo	Askola	Fin 09	30:48.8	3)	Tampere	29 Sep
Giuseppe	Beviacqua	Ita 14	30:53.2	2)	Colombes	05 Sep
Max	Syring	Ger 08	30:54.2	1)	Stockholm	27 Aug
Eino	Pentti	USA 06	30:54.6	5)	Helsinki	17 Sep
Jenö	Szilágyi	Hun 10	30:56.8	1)	Budapest	15 Aug

1939

5000 metres

Taisto	Mäki	Fin 10	14:08.8	1)	Helsinki	16 Jun
Kauko	Pekuri	Fin 12	14:16.2	2)	Helsinki	16 Jun
Henry	Jonsson (Kälarne)	Swe 12	14:18.8	2)	Stockholm	27 Jul
Tauno	Kurki	Fin 14	14:21.2	3)	Stockholm	15 Sep
Ilmari	Salminen	Fin 02	14:22.0	3)	Helsinki	16 Jun
Jansuz	Kusocinski	Pol 07	14:24.2	1)	Stockholm	16 Jun
Thore	Tillman	Fin 15	14:24.8	2)	Stockholm	16 Jun
Lars	Nilsson	Swe 16	14:26.6	1)	Stockholm	07 Jul
Hermann	Eberlein	Ger 17	14:27.2	1)	Berlin	09 Jul
Friedrich	Shaumburg	Ger 05	14:28.4	2)	Berlin	09 Jul

10,000 metres

Taisto	Mäki	Fin 10	29:52.6	1)	Helsinki	17 Sep
Veikko	Tuominen	Fin 15	30:07.6	1)	Kouvola	06 Aug
Kauko	Pekuti	Fin 12	30:10.6	2)	Kouvola	06 Aug
Ilmari	Salminen	Fin 02	30:10.6	3)	Kouvola	06 Aug
Tauno	Kurki	Fin 14	30:16.0	2)	Helsinki	17 Sep
Thore	Tillman	Swe 15	30:37.6	1)	Oslo	24 Sep
András	Csaplár	Hun 12	30:43.4	1)	Budapest	03 Sep
Syerafim	Znamenskiy	USR 06	30:44.8	1)	Moscow	18 Sep
Georgiy	Znamenskiy	USR 03	30:45.8	2)	Moscow	18 Sep
Matti	Laihoranta	Fin 12	30:47.4	1)	Helsinki	28 Jul
Volmari	Iso-Hollo	Fin 07	30:47.4	3)	Helsinki	28 Aug

1940

5000 metres

Bror	Hellström	Swe 14	14:20.6	1)	Helsinki	01 Aug
Kauko	Pekuri	Fin 12	14:21.2	2)	Helsinki	01 Aug
Veikko	Tuominen	Fin 15	14:22.4	3)	Helsinki	01 Aug
János	Kelen	Hun 11	14:23.0	4)	Helsinki	01 Aug
Matti	A.Järvinen	Fin 10	14:26.8	5)	Helsinki	01 Aug
Taisto	Mäki	Fin 10	14:32.0	2)	Tampere	25 Aug
Greg	Rice	USA 16	14:33.4	1)	Fresno	29 Jun
Max	Syring	Ger 08	14:35.1	1)	Dresden	04 Jul
Otto	Eitel	Ger 09	14:35.9	2)	Dresden	04 Jul
Syerafim	Znamenskiy	URS 06	14:37.0	1)	Moscow	22 Sep

Noteworthy 3 mile times – Indoors:

Greg	Rice	USA 16	13:52.3	1)	New York	31 Mar
Donald	Lash	USA 14	13:55.0	2)	New York	31 Mar
Taisto	Mäki	Fin 10	13:56.8	3)	New York	31 Mar

10,000 metres

Max	Syring	Ger 08	30:06.6	1)	Jena	13 Jul
János	Kelen	Hun 11	30:23.6	1)	Budapest	05 Oct
Giuseppe	Beviacqua	Ita 14	30:27.4	2)	Stuttgart	03 Aug
Jenö	Szilágyi	Hun 10	30:33.8	1)	Budapest	18 Aug
Raúl	Ibarra	Arg 14	30:36.8	1)	Buenos Aires	14 Dec
Veikko	Tuominen	Fin 15	30:37.8	2)	Budapest	22 Sep
Taisto	Mäki	Fin 10	30:39.4	1)	Tampere	26 Aug
Bror	Hellström	Swe 14	30:41.2	1)	Helsinki	08 Sep
Evert	Heinström	Fin 12	30:44.6	4)	Helsinki	08 Sep
Matti	A.Järvinen	Fin 10	30:44.8	1)	Stockholm	08 Sep

ALL TIME WORLD LIST OF BEST PERFORMANCES AS AT THE END OF 1940

3 miles

Taisto	Mäki	Fin 10	13:42.4+	1)	Helsinki	16 Jun	1939
Lauri	Lehtinen	Fin 08	13:50.6+	1)	Helsinki	19 Jun	1932
Volmari	Iso-Hollo	Fin 07	13:50.7+	2)	Helsinki	19 Jun	1932
Kauko	Pekuri	Fin 12	13:58.2+	1)	Helsinki	08 Jun	1939
	Mäki		13:59.4	1)	London	07 Aug	1939
Cecil	Matthews	NZ 14	13:59.6	1)	Sydney	05 Feb	1938

(6 performances by 5 performers)

Indoors:

Greg	Rice	USA 16	13:52.3	1)	New York	31 Mar	1940
Donald	Lash	USA 14	13:55.0	2)	New York	31 Mar	1940
	Rice		13:55.9	1)	New York	24 Feb	1940
Ville	Ritola	Fin 896	13:56.2+	1)	New York	24 Feb	1925
Taisto	Mäki	Fin 10	13:56.8	3)	New York	31 Mar	1940

(5 performances by 4 performers)

5000 metres

Taisto	Mäki	Fin 10	14:08.8	1)	Helsinki	16 Jun	1939
Kauko	Pekuri	Fin 12	14:16.2	2)	Helsinki	16 Jun	1939
Lauri	Lehtinen	Fin 08	14:16.9	1)	Helsinki	19 Jun	1932
	Mäki		14:17.8	1)	Stockholm	27 Jul	1939
Volmari	Iso-Hollo	Fin 07	14:18.3	2)	Helsinki	19 Jun	1932
Henry	Jonsson (Kälarne)	Swe 12	14:18.8	2)	Stockholm	27 Jul	1939
	Pekuri		14:19.4	3)	Stockholm	27 Jul	1939
	Mäki		14:19.8	1)	Stockholm	15 Sep	1939
	Jonsson		14:20.6	2)	Stockholm	15 Sep	1939
Bror	Hellström	Swe14	14:20.6	1)	Helsinki	01 Aug	1940
Tauno	Kurki	Fin 14	14:21.2	3)	Stockholm	15 Sep	1939
	Pekuri		14:21.2	2)	Helsinki	01 Aug	1940
Ilmari	Salminen	Fin 02	14:22.0	3)	Helsinki	16 Jun	1939
Gunnar	Höckert	Fin 10	14:22.2	1)	Berlin	07 Aug	1936
Veikko	Tuominen	Fin 15	14:22.4	3)	Helsinki	01 Aug	1940
János	Kelen	Hun 11	14:23.0	4)	Helsinki	01 Aug	1940

230

Janusz	Kusocinski	Pol 07	14:24.2	1)	Stockholm	16 Jun	1939
Thore	Tillman	Swe 15	14:24.8	2)	Stockholm	16 Jun	1939
	Pekuri		14:25.6	1)	Helsinki	08 Jun	1939
	Lehtinen		14:25.8	2)	Berlin	07 Aug	1936
	Tillman		14:26.0	4)	Stockholm	15 Sep	1939
Lars	Nilsson	Swe 16	14:26.6	1)	Stockholm	07 Jul	1939
	Mäki		14:26.8	1)	Colombes	04 Sep	1938
	Mäki		14:26.8	1)	Helsinki	01 Jun	1939
	Tillman		14:26.8	2)	Stockholm	07 Jul	1939
Matti	A. Järvinen	Fin 10	14:26.8	5)	Helsinki	01 Aug	1940
Hermann	Eberlein	Ger 17	14:27.2	1)	Berlin	09 Jul	1939
	Pekuri		14:27.4	1)	Helsinki	07 Aug	1938
	Jonsson		14:27.4	2)	Colombes	04 Sep	1938
	Nilsson		14:28.0	4)	Stockholm	27 Jul	1939
Paavo	Nurmi	Fin 897	14:28.2	1)	Helsinki	19 Jun	1924
	Salminen		14:28.4	2)	Helsinki	07 Aug	1938
Friedrich	Schaumburg	Ger 05	14:28.4	2)	Berlin	09 Jul	1939
	Mäki		14:28.8	1)	Viipuri	07 Aug	1937
	Jonsson		14:28.8	1)	Helsinki	21 Jun	1938
	Jonsson		14:29.0	3)	Berlin	07 Aug	1936
	Mäki		14:29.0	2)	Helsinki	21 Jun	1938
Max	Syring	Ger 08	14:29.0	1)	Frankfurt/M.	12 Aug	1939
	Pekuri		14:29.2	3)	Colombes	04 Sep	1938
Rolf	Fellersmann	Ger 14	14:29.2	2)	Frankfurt/M.	12 Aug	1939
	Kurki		14:29.4	1)	Kotka	30 Aug	1939
	Pekuri		14:29.5	3)	Helsinki	21 Jun	1938
	Kusocinski		14:29.8	2)	Helsinki	08 Jun	1939
Otto	Eitel	Ger 09	14:29.8	3)	Frankfurt/M.	12 Aug	1939
	Lehtinen		14:30.0	1)	Los Angeles	05 Aug	1932
Ralph	Hill	USA 08	14:30.0	2)	Los Angeles	05 Aug	1932
Kohei	Murakoso	Jap 05	14:30.0	4)	Berlin	07 Aug	1936
Arvo	Askola	Fin 09	14:30.0	2)	Viipuri	07 Aug	1937
	Lehtinen		14:30.2	3)	Helsinki	07 Aug	1938
Veikko	Tuominen	Fin 15	14:30.2	3)	Helsinki	08 Jun	1939
	Höckert		14:30.8	1)	Helsinki	12 Jul	1936
	Salminen		14:30.8	2)	Helsinki	12 Jul	1936

(52 performances by 25 performers)

Indoors:

Ville	Ritola	Fin896	14:23.2	1)	New York	24 Feb	1925

6 miles

Taisto	Mäki	Fin 10	28:55.6+	1)	Helsinki	17 Sep	1939
Paavo	Nurmi	Fin 897	29:07.1+	1)	Kuopio	31 Aug	1924
Ilmari	Salminen	Fin 02	29:08.3+	1)	Kouvola	18 Jul	1937
	Salminen		29:25.4+	1)	Stockholm	07 Sep	1937

(4 performances by 3 performers)

10,000 metres

Taisto	Mäki	Fin 10	29:52.6	1)	Helsinki	17 Sep	1939
	Mäki		30:02.0	1)	Tampere	29 Sep	1938
Ilmari	Salminen	Fin 02	30:05.5	1)	Kouvola	18 Jul	1937
Paavo	Nurmi	Fin 897	30:06.1	1)	Kuopio	31 Aug	1924
Max	Syring	Ger 08	30:06.6	1)	Jena	13 Jul	1940
Veikko	Tuominen	Fin 15	30:07.6	1)	Kouvola	06 Aug	1939
	Mäki		30:09.4	1)	Helsinki	28 Aug	1939
Kauko	Pekuri	Fin 12	30:10.6	2)	Kouvola	06 Aug	1939
	Salminen		30:10.6	3)	Kouvola	06 Aug	1939

Janusz	Kusocinski	Pol 07	30:11.4	1)	Los Angeles	31 Jul	1932
Volmari	Iso-Hollo	Fin 07	30:12.6	2)	Los Angeles	31 Jul	1932
	Salminen		30:13.4	1)	Helsinki	17 Sep	1938
	Mäki		30:13.4	2)	Helsinki	17 Sep	1938
	Pekuri		30:14.0	3)	Helsinki	17 Sep	1938
Lauri	Lehtinen	Fin 08	30:15.0	2)	Kouvola	18 Jul	1937
	Salminen		30:15.4	1)	Berlin	02 Aug	1936
Arvo	Askola	Fin 09	30:15.6	2)	Berlin	02 Aug	1936
Tauno	Kurki	Fin 14	30:16.0	2)	Helsinki	17 Sep	1939
	Pekuri		30:18.2	2)	Tampere	29 Sep	1938
	Nurmi		30:18.8	1)	Amsterdam	29 Jul	1928
Ville	Ritola	Fin 896	30:19.4	2)	Amsterdam	29 Jul	1928
	Salminen		30:19.4	1)	Kouvola	17 Jul	1938
	Iso-Hollo		30:20.2	3)	Berlin	02 Aug	1936
	Nurmi		30:20.9	1)	Tampere	15 Sep	1924
	Iso-Hollo		30:21.2	1)	Helsinki	21 Sep	1933
	Salminen		30:21.4	1)	Stockholm	07 Sep	1937
	Ritola		30:23.2	1)	Colombes	06 Jul	1924
János	Kelen	Hun 11	30:23.6	1)	Budapest	05 Oct	1940
Kohei	Murakoso	Jap 05	30:25.0	4)	Berlin	02 Aug	1936
	Syring		30:25.2	1)	Stuttgart	03 Aug	1940
	Salminen		30:26.2	3)	Helsinki	17 Sep	1939
Giuseppe	Beviacqua	Ita 14	30:27.4	2)	Stuttgart	03 Aug	1940
	Lehtinen		30:30.5	1)	Turku	10 Sep	1933
Lauri	Virtanen	Fin 04	30:30.7	2)	Turku	10 Sep	1933
	Kusocinski		30:31.4	1)	Warsaw	05 Jun	1932
	Nurmi		30:32.2	1)	Lahti	24 Aug	1924
Jenö	Szilágyi	Hun 10	30:33.8	1)	Budapest	18 Aug	1940
	Kelen		30:34.0	2)	Budapest	18 Aug	1940
	Askola		30:34.2	3)	Kouvola	18 Jul	1937
	Virtanen		30:35.0	3)	Los Angeles	31 Jul	1932
Matti	Laihoranta	Fin 12	30:35.2	4)	Helsinki	17 Sep	1938
	Ritola		30:35.4	1)	Helsinki	25 May	1924
	Mäki		30:35.4	1)	Stockholm	28 Jul	1939
	Salminen		30:35.6	2)	Stockholm	28 Jul	1939
Raúl	Ibarra	Arg 14	30:36.8	1)	Buenos Aires	14 Dec	1940
Thore	Tillman	Swe 15	30:37.6	1)	Oslo	24 Sep	1939
	Szilágyi		30:37.8	1)	Budapest	22 Sep	1940
	Tuominen		30:37.8	2)	Budapest	22 Sep	1940
	Kelen		30:37.8	3)	Budapest	22 Sep	1940
	Lehtinen		30:38.0	2)	Stockholm	07 Sep	1937
	Salminen		30:38.2	1)	Helsinki	24 Aug	1935
	Askola		30:38.4	2)	Helsinki	24 Aug	1935
	Mäki		30:39.4	1)	Tampere	26 Aug	1940
	Murakoso		30:39.8	1)	Tokyo	06 Jun	1937

(54 performances by 20 performers)

WORLD YEAR LISTS 1941 – 1960

1941

5000 metres

Bror	Hellström	Swe 14	14:15.8	1)	Stockholm	28 Sep	
Arne	Andersson	Swe 17	14:18.2	2)	Stockholm	28 Sep	
Max	Syring	Ger 08	14:30.5	1)	Wittenberg	06 Jul	
Jenö	Szilágyi	Hun 10	14:35.8	1)	Milan	21 Sep	

András	Csaplár	Hun 12	14:36.0	2)	Milan	21 Sep
Viljo	Heino	Fin 14	14:36.6	1)	Helsinki	11 Jun
Raúl	Ibarra	Arg 14	14:37.0	1)	Buenos Aires	15 Mar
Lars	Nilsson	Swe 16	14:37.0	2)	Stockholm	09 Aug
Giuseppe	Beviacqua	Ita 14	14:37.0	3)	Milan	21 Sep
Hans	Raff	Ger 10	14:39.8	1)	Berlin	19 Jul

Noteworthy 3 mile times:

Lennart	Flodqvist	Swe 18	13:55.0	2)	Stockholm	19 Sep
Lars	Nilsson	Swe 16	13:59.0	3)	Stockholm	19 Sep
Gösta	Pettersson (Tegerholm)	Swe 17	14:04.8	4)	Stockholm	19 Sep
Karl-Erik	Larsson	Swe 17	14:05.4	3)	Stockholm	05 Sep

Indoors:

Greg	Rice	USA16	13:51.0	1)	New York	22 Feb

10,000 metres

András	Csaplár	Hun 12	30:25.6	1)	Göteborg	18 Jul
Gösta	(Karlsson) Östbrink	Swe 15	30:26.6	2)	Göteborg	18 Jul
Thore	Tillman	Swe 15	30:28.0	3)	Göteborg	18 Jul
Giuseppe	Beviacqua	Ita 14	30:33.6	1)	Bologna	29 Jun
Gösta	Pettersson (Tegerholm)	Swe 17	30:34.6	2)	Stockhlm	24 Aug
Raúl	Ibarra	Arg 14	30:45.0	1)	Buenos Aires	03 May
Jenö	Szilágyi	Hun 10	30:46.8	1)	Budapest	10 Aug
Bror	Hellström	Swe 14	30:47.6	1)	Sundbyberg	12 Oct
Anton	Haushofer	Ger 13	30:52.8	2)	Bologna	29 Jun
Béla	Németh	Hun 06	30:56.2	2)	Budapest	12 Oct

1942

5000 metres

Gunder	Hägg	Swe 18	13:58.2	1)	Göteborg	20 Sep
Bror	Hellström	Swe 14	14:25.4	1)	Stockholm	15 Aug
Karl-Erik	Larsson	Swe 17	14:26.0	2)	Stockholm	15 Aug
Gösta	(Karlsson) Östbrink	Swe 15	14:31.0	3)	Stockholm	15 Aug
Giuseppe	Beviacqua	Ita 14	14:31.8	1)hc	Florence	13 Sep
Lars	Nilsson	Swe 16	14:32.2	1)	Stockholm	03 Jul
Thore	Tillman	Swe 15	14:32.8	4)	Stockholm	15 Aug
Gunnar	Bratt	Swe 16	14:34.8	5)	Stockholm	15 Aug
Göte	Hagström	Swe 18	14:36.8	6)	Stockholm	15 Aug
Greg	Rice	USA 16	14:39.7	1)	New York	20 Jun

Noteworthy 3 mile time:

Greg	Rice	USA 16	14:00.0	1)	New York	06 Jun

Indoors:

Greg	Rice	USA 16	13:45.7	1)	New York	28 Feb

10,000 metres

Jenö	Szilágyi	Hun 10	30:09.4	1)	Budapest	14 Oct
Gösta	Pettersson (Tegerholm)	Swe 17	30:19.4	1)	Stockholm	16 Jul
Gösta	(Karlsson) Östbrink	Swe 15	30:20.8	2)	Stockholm	16 Jul
Thore	Tillman	Swe 15	30:21.4	3)	Stockholm	16 Jul
Jean	Lalanne	Fra 14	30:22.8	1)	Bordeaux	11 Oct
Fyeodosiy	Vanin	USR 14	30:35.2	1)	Moscow	06 Sep

Georges	Gaillot	Fra 17	30:36.4	1)	Paris	11 Oct
Giuseppe	Beviacqua	Ita 14	30:54.8	1)	Berlin	02 Aug
Harry	Siefert	Den 10	30:55.4	1)	Copenhagen	24 Aug
Karl	Larsson	Swe 14	30:55.8	4)	Stockholm	16 Jul

1943

5000 metres

Åke	Durkfeldt	Swe 17	14:22.8	1)	Stockholm	02 Jul
Gösta	Jacobsson	Swe 19	14:24.2	1)	Copenhagen	18 Jul
Karl-Erik	Larsson	Swe 17	14:25.6	2)	Stockholm	02 Jul
Gösta	(Karlsson) Östbrink	Swe 15	14:29.4	4)	Stockholm	02 Jul
Viljo	Heino	Fin 14	14:34.6	1)	Helsinki	14 Aug
Evert	Heinström	Fin 12	14:36.8	2)	Helsinki	19 Aug
Sulo	Jousenlahti	Fin 13	14:37.6	3)	Helsinki	19 Aug
Tauno	Kurki	Fin 14	14:37.6	4)	Helsinki	19 Aug
Miklós	Szabó	Hun 08	14:40.2	2)	Stockholm	15 Jul
Bror	Hellström	Swe 14	14:42.8	3)	Stockholm	15 Jul

Noteworthy 3 mile time (indoors):

Greg	Rice	USA 16	13:53.5	1)	New York	27 Feb

10,000 metres

Viljo	Heino	Fin 14	30:15.2	1)	Helsinki	19 Sep
Jenö	Szilágyi	Hun 10	30:16.0	1)	Stockholm	16 Jul
Gösta	Jacobsson	Swe 19	30:17.4	1)	Stockholm	28 Aug
Gösta	(Karlsson) Östbrink	Swe 15	30:18.0	2)	Stockholm	28 Aug
Gösta	Pettersson (Tegerholm)	Swe 17	30:20.8	2)	Stockholm	16 Jul
Harry	Siefert	Den 10	30:26.8	3)	Stockholm	28 Aug
Evert	Heinström	Fin 12	30:39.6	2)	Helsinki	15 Aug
Fred	Eriksson	Swe 14	30:40.8	3)	Stockholm	16 Jul
Fyeodosiy	Vanin	USR 14	30:43.0	1)	Gorkiy	05/09 Sep
Béla	Németh	Hun 06	30:43.8	2)	Budapest	19 Sep

1944

5000 metres

Viljo	Heino	Fin 14	14:09.6	1)	Göteborg	17 Sep
Gösta	Jacobsson	Swe 19	14:19.8	2)	Helsinki	20 Jun
Gunder	Hägg	Swe 18	14:24.4	1)	Helsinki	24 Sep
Raúl	Ibarra	Arg 14	14:24.8	1)	Buenos Aires	01 Jul
Gaston	Reiff	Bel 21	14:27.6	1)	Brussels	23 May
Ernst	Andersson (Rickne)	Swe 20	14:27.6	1)	Stockholm	13 Jul
Karl-Erik	Larsson	Swe 17	14:28.4	2)	Stockholm	13 Jul
Eskil	Wallin	Swe 15	14:31.0	3)	Stockholm	30 Aug
Bertil	Andersson (Albertsson)	Swe 21	14:34.8	4)	Stockholm	13 Jul
Arne	Gustafsson	Swe 19	14:39.6	1)	Stockholm	27 Jul

10,000 metres

Viljo	Heino	Fin 14	29:35.4+	1)	Helsinki	25 Aug
Gösta	Pettersson (Tegerholm)	Swe 17	30:22.6	2)	Helsinki	25 Aug
Thore	Tillman	Swe 15	30:34.4	1)	Malmö	02 Jul
János	Kelen	Hun 11	30:51.6	1)	Budapest	01 Oct
Jenö	Szilágyi	Hun 10	30:52.6	2)	Budapest	01 Oct

234

Béla	Németh	Hun 06	30:52.8	3)	Budapest	01 Oct
Ferenc	Szegedi	Hun 24	31:00.8	4)	Budapest	01 Oct
Kauko	Pekuri	Fin 12	31:01.6	3)	Helsinki	25 Aug
Gustav	Östling	Swe 14	31:02.8	1)	Gävle	20 Jun
Grigoriy	Yermolayev	USR 11	31:11.8	1)	Moscow	08 Sep

+ Went on to cover 10,131.60 Km. in half an hour.

1945

5000 metres

Viljo	Heino	Fin 14	14:17.2	1)	Turku	11 Aug
Åke	Durkfeldt	Swe 17	14:25.6	1)	Stockholm	21 Aug
Gösta	(Karlsson) Östbrink	Swe 15	14:25.8	1)	Stockholm	05 Jul
Taisto	Mäki	Fin 10	14:27.0	2)	Stockholm	05 Jul
Gunder	Hägg	Swe 18	14:29.0	1)	Stockholm	12 Aug
Toivo	Sarkama	Fin 08	14:32.2	2)	Turku	11 Aug
Thore	Tillman	Swe 15	14:33.4	3)	Stockholm	05 Jul
Ernst	Andersson (Rickne)	Swe 20	14:37.8	3)	Stockholm	12 Aug
Lars	Nilsson	Swe 16	14:39.6	4)	Stockholm	12 Aug
Gösta	Jacobsson	Swe 19	14:41.2	1)	Malmö	21 Jul

10,000 metres

Viljo	Heino	Fin 14	30:02.0	1)	Helsinki	02 Sep
Gösta	Jacobsson	Swe 19	30:12.0	1)	Stockholm	12 Jul
Taisto	Mäki	Fin 10	30:12.6	1)	Helsinki	17 Jul
Thore	Tillman	Swe 15	30:15.2	2)	Stockholm	12 Jul
Evert	Heinström	Fin 12	30:36.4	2)	Helsinki	17 Jul
Eskil	Wallin	Swe 15	30:46.0	1)	Stockholm	06 Oct
Gösta	(Karlsson) Östbrink	Swe 15	31:07.0	3)	Söderhamn	01 Jul
Valter	Nyström	Swe 15	31:11.2	4)	Söderhamn	01 Jul
Helge	Perälä	Fin 15	31:14.0	2)	Karhula	16 Sep
Gustav	Östling	Swe 14	31:15.0	5)	Söderhamn	01 Jul

1946

5000 metres

Sydney	Wooderson	GB 14	14:08.6	1)	Oslo	23 Aug
Wim	Slykhuis	Hol 23	14:14.0	2)	Oslo	23 Aug
Viljo	Heino	Fin 14	14:20.4	1)	Tampere	04 Aug
Evert	Nyberg	Swe 25	14:23.2	3)	Oslo	23 Aug
Emil	Zátopek	Cze 22	14:25.8	5)	Oslo	23 Aug
Gaston	Reiff	Bel 21	14:26.1	1)	Brussels	14 Jul
Helge	Perälä	Fin 15	14:27.7	2)	Bergen	28 Aug
Erik	Ahldén	Sze 23	14:30.7	1)	Colombes	06 Oct
Toivo	Sarkama	Fin 08	14:31.6	1)	Helsinki	03 Jul
Åke	Durkfeldt	Swe 17	14:32.2	2)	Stockholm	11 Aug

10,000 metres

Viljo	Heino	Fin 14	29:52.0	1)	Oslo	22 Aug
Helge	Perälä	Fin 15	30:31.4	2)	Oslo	22 Aug
András	Csaplár	Hun 12	30:35.2	3)	Oslo	22 Aug
Sven	Rapp	Swe 20	30:37.6	1)	Uppsala	06 Oct
Thore	Tillman	Swe 15	30:37.8	1)	Helsinki	02 Aug
Matti	A. Järvinen	Fin 10	30:40.8	3)	Helsinki	12 Aug

Bertil	(Andersson)Albertsson	Swe 21	30:51.8	3)	Uppsala	06 Oct
Ellmar	Johansson	Swe 18	30:54.0	4)	Uppsala	06 Oct
Evert	Heinström	Fra 12	30:54.9	4)	Helsinki	12 Aug
Salomon	Könönen	Fin 16	30:55.4	5)	Helsinki	12 Aug

1947

5000 metres

Emil	Zátopek	Cze 22	14:08.2	1)	Prague	25 Jun
Viljo	Heino	Fin 14	14:15.4	2)	Helsinki	30 Jun
Evert	Nyberg	Swe 25	14:24.6	1)	Stockholm	06 Sep
Helge	Perälä	Fin 15	14:25.6	2)	Stockholm	06 Sep
Åke	Durkfeldt	Swe 17	14:26.0	3)	Stockholm	06 Sep
Erik	Ahldén	Swe 23	14:27.2	1)	Stockholm	17 Jul
Bertil	(Andersson)Albertsson	Swe 21	14:30.8	1)	Stockholm	06 Aug
Bertil	Karlsson	Swe 19	14:31.4	2)	Stockholm	06 Aug
Valter	Nyström	Swe 15	14:33.6	3)	Stockholm	06 Aug
Väinö	Koskela	Fin 21	14:34.0	4)	Stockholm	06 Sep

10,000 metres

Viljo	Heino	Fin 14	30:07.4	1)	Copenhagen	29 Jul
Valter	Nyström	Swe 15	30:14.4	1)	Göteborg	31 Jul
Thore	Tillman	Swe 15	30:18.4	2)	Göteborg	31 Jul
Salomon	Könönen	Fin 16	30:27.2	1)	Tampere	18 Aug
Evert	Heinström	Fin 12	30:27.6	2)	Tampere	18 Aug
Bertil	(Andersson)Albertsson	Swe 21	30:29.6	1)	Stockholm	08 Sep
Helge	Perälä	Fin 15	30:32.2	1)	Karhula	21 Sep
Taisto	Mäki	Fin 10	30:34.0	3)	Tampere	18 Aug
Martin	Stokken	Nor 23	30:36.2	1)	Oslo	25 Sep
Fyeodosiy	Vanin	USR 14	30:36.8	1)	Kharkov	05 Sep

1948

5000 metres

Emil	Zátopek	Cze 22	14:10.0	1)	Prague	22 Jun
Erik	Ahldén	Swe 23	14:13.2	1)	Gävle	21 Jul
Gaston	Reiff	Bel 21	14:14.2	1)	Brussels	16 Jun
Bertil	(Andersson)Albertsson	Swe 21	14:20.2	2)	Gävle	21 Jul
Evert	Nyberg	Swe 25	14:26.8	1)	Stockholm	09 Jul
Wim	Slykhuis	Hol 23	14:26.8	3)	London	02 Aug
Ellmar	Johansson	Swe 18	14:27.0	2)	Stockholm	09 Jul
Viljo	Heino	Fin 14	14:27.8	1)	Kouvola	23 Jul
Väinö	Koskela	Fin 21	14:28.0	1)	Turku	04 Jun
Sven-Olof	Borg	Swe 23	14:28.8	3)	Stockholm	09 Jul

10,000 metres

Emil	Zátopek	Cze 22	29:37.0	1)	Prague	17 Jun
Viljo	Heino	Fin 14	30:03.2	1)	Oslo	23 Sep
Bertil	(Andersson)Albertsson	Swe 21	30:05.2	1)	Södertälje	26 Sep
Salomon	Könönen	Fin 16	30:10.8	1)	Helsinki	09 Jul
Evert	Heinström	Fin 12	30:11.0	2)	Helsinki	09 Jul
Helge	Perälä	Fin 15	30:22.6	3)	Helsinki	09 Jul
Martin	Stokken	Nor 23	30:24.4	1)	Oslo	05 Jul
Ellmar	Johansson	Swe 18	30:28.2	2)	Södertälje	26 Sep

Gösta	Jacobsson	Swe 19	30:29.0	2)	Uppsala	04 Jul
Sven	Rapp	Swe 20	30:29.6	3)	Södertälje	26 Sep

1949

5000 metres

Emil	Zátopek	Cze 22	14:10.2	1)	Warsaw	09 May
Väinö	Koskela	Fin 21	14:13.2	2)	Turku	15 Jul
Väinö	Mäkelä	Fin 21	14:20.0	1)	Göteborg	29 Aug
Jacques	Vernier	Fra 23	14:20.6	2)	Göteborg	29 Aug
Bertil	(Andersson)Albertsson	Swe 21	14:23.8	1)	Stockholm	09 Sep
Evert	Nyberg	Swe 25	14:25.4	2)	Stockholm	09 Sep
Alain	Mimoun	Fra 21	14:26.0	2)	Helsinki	17 Sep
Pentti	Salonen	Fin 18	14:27.2	2)	Karhula	20 Aug
Viljo	Heino	Fin 14	14:28.2	3)	Helsinki	01 Jul
Erik	Ahldén	Swe 23	14:29.8	2)	Stockholm	21 Aug

Noteworthy 3 mile times:

John Joe	Barry	Ire 25	13:56.2	1)	Dublin	09 Jun
Fred	Wilt	USA 20	13:58.5	2)	Dublin	09 Jun

10,000 metres

Emil	Zátopek	Cze 22	29:21.2	1)	Ostrava	22 Oct
Viljo	Heino	Fin 14	29:27.2	1)	Kouvola	01 Sep
Alain	Mimoun	Fra 21	29:53.0	1)	Oslo	22 Sep
Martin	Stokken	Nor 23	29:58.0	2)	Oslo	22 Sep
Väinö	Koskela	Fin 21	30:12.0	2)	Stockholm	10 Sep
Severt	Dennolf	Swe 20	30:13.2	3)	Stockholm	10 Sep
Valter	Nyström	Swe 15	30:16.8	4)	Stockholm	10 Sep
Salomon	Könönen	Fin 16	30:20.4	1)	Kotka	26 Jul
Erik	Wredling	Swe 20	30:23.4	5)	Stockholm	10 Sep
Curtis	Stone	USA 22	30:38.4	3)	Oslo	29 Jul

1950

5000 metres

Emil	Zátopek	Cze 22	14:03.0	1)	Brussels	26 Aug
Väinö	Mäkelä	Fin 21	14:20.2	1)	Jyväskylä	12 Aug
Hannu	Posti	Fin 26	14:20.4	2)	Jyväskylä	12 Aug
Herbert	Schade	Ger 22	14:22.8	1)	Hamburg	25 Jun
Väinö	Koskela	Fin 21	14:24.6	3)	Jyväskylä	12 Aug
Alain	Mimoun	Fra 21	14:26.0	2)	Brussels	26 Aug
Bertil	(Andersson)Albertsson	Swe 21	14:26.2	2)	Stockholm	27 Jul
Gaston	Reiff	Bel 21	14:26.2	3)	Brussels	26 Aug
Fred	Wilt	USA 20	14:26.8	1)	Helsinki	29 Jun
Nikifor	Popov	USR 13	14:27.8	1)	Moscow	31 Jul

10,000 metres

Emil	Zátopek	Cze 22	29:02.6	1)	Turku	04 Aug
Ivan	Semyonov	USR 26	30:07.0	1)	Kiev	23 Sep
Fyeodosiy	Vanin	USR 14	30:09.6	2)	Kiev	23 Sep
Herbert	Schade	Ger 22	30:10.6	1)	Wuppertal	07 Oct
Valter	Nyström	Swe 15	30:11.0	1)	Uppsala	01 Oct
Martin	Stokken	Nor 23	30:14.4	1)	Trondheim	10 Sep

Vladimir	Kazantsev	USR 23	30:20.0	3)	Kiev	23 Sep
Alain	Mimoun	Fra 21	30:21.0	2)	Brussels	23 Aug
Nikifor	Popov	USR 13	30:23.8	4)	Kiev	23 Sep
Bertil	(Andersson)Albertsson Swe 21		30:28.6	2)	Stockholm	16 Sep

1951

5000 metres

Gaston	Reiff	Bel 21	14:10.8	1)	Brussels	13 Jun
Emil	Zátopek	Cze 22	14:11.6	1)	Berlin	18 Aug
Herbert	Schade	Ger 22	14:15.4	1)	Stuttgart	02 Sep
Nikifor	Popov	USR 13	14:20.8	1)	Moscow	15 Jun
Bertil	Albertsson	Swe 21	14:20.8	1)	Helsinki	23 Jul
Väinö	Koskela	Fin 21	14:21.6	2)	Helsinki	23 Jul
Hannu	Posti	Fin 26	14:22.6	3)	Helsinki	23 Jul
Alain	Mimoun	Fra 21	14:23.0	2)	Brussels	13 Jun
Martin	Stokken	Nor 23	14:23.8	1)	Oslo	31 Jul
Vladimir	Kazantsev	USR 23	14:24.0	1)	Bucharest	23 Sep

10,000 metres

Emil	Zátopek	Cze 22	29:29.8	1)	Trebic	01 Sep
Herbert	Schade	Ger 22	29:42.2	1)	Wuppertal	29 Sep
Bertil	Albertsson	Swe 21	29:46.0	1)	Uppsala	14 Oct
Martin	Stokken	Nor 23	29:55.0	1)	Trondheim	12 Aug
Alain	Mimoun	Fra 21	30:01.4	1)	Colombes	22 Jul
Väinö	Koskela	Fin 21	30:10.0	1)	Helsinki	24 Jul
Bertil	Karlsson	Swe 19	30:10.0	2)	Helsinki	24 Jul
Valter	Nyström	Swe 15	30:14.4	3)	Helsinki	24 Jul
Gaston	Reiff	Bel 21	30:18.8	1)	Brussels	29 Jul
Vladimir	Kazantsev	USR 23	30:21.8	1)	Minsk	01 Sep

Noteworthy 6 mile time:

| Walter | Hesketh | GB 30 | 29:13.8 | 1) | London | 06 Aug |

1952

5000 metres

Emil	Zátopek	Cze 22	14:06.4	1)	Opava	04 Oct
Herbert	Schade	Ger 22	14:06.6	1)	Nienburg	08 Jun
Alain	Mimoun	Fra 21	14:07.4	2)	Helsinki	24 Jul
Vladimir	Kazantsev	USR 23	14:08.8	1)	Leningrad	02 Jul
Aleksandr	Anufriyev	USR 26	14:12.2	2)	Leningrad	02 Jul
Bertil	Albertsson	Swe 21	14:15.0	1)	Stockholm	24 Aug
Gaston	Reiff	Bel 21	14:15.4	1)	Brussels	24 Sep
Valter	Nyström	Swe 15	14:15.8	2)	Stockholm	24 Aug
Nikifor	Popov	USR 13	14:16.0	2)	Kiev	10 Jun
Åke	Andersson	Swe 25	14:16.0	3)	Stockholm	24 Aug
Helmut	Gude	Ger 25	14:16.0	1)	Berlin	21 Sep

Noteworthy 3 mile time:

| Gordon | Pirie | GB 31 | 13:44.8 | 1) | London | 31 May |

238

10,000 metres

Emil	Zátopek	Cze 22	29:17.0	1)	Helsinki	20 Jul
Valter	Nyström	Swe 15	29:23.8	1)	Düsseldorf	14 Sep
Herbert	Schade	Ger 22	29:24.8	2)	Düsseldorf	14 Sep
Alain	Mimoun	Fra 21	29:29.4	1)	Stockholm	04 Sep
Leksandr	Anufriyev	USR 26	29:31.4	2)	Kiev	12 Jun
Öistein	Saksvik	Nor 25	29:48.4	1)	Copenhagen	29 Aug
Franjo	Mihalic	Yug 21	29:48.6	1)	Zagreb	04 Oct
Gustaf	Jansson	Swe 22	29:51.2	3)	Düsseldorf	14 Sep
Hannu	Posti	Fin 26	29:51.4	4)	Helsinki	20 Jul
Frank	Sando	GB 31	29:51.8	5)	Helsinki	20 Jul

1953

5000 metres

Aleksandr	Anufriyev	USR 26	13:58.8	1)	Moscow	06 Jun
József	Kovács	Hun 26	14:01.2	1)	Budapest	20 Sep
Vladimir	Kuts	USR 27	14:02.2	1)	Moscow	27 Aug
Gordon	Pirie	GB 31	14:02.6	1)	Berlin	29 Aug
Emil	Zátopek	Cze 22	14:03.0	1)	Bucharest	05 Aug
Alain	Mimoun	Fra 21	14:08.4	1)	Brussels	17 Jun
Ilmari	Taipale	Fin 28	14:14.4	1)	Kouvola	11 Jun
Hannu	Posti	Fin 26	14:14.6	2)	Kouvola	11 Jun
Herbert	Schade	Ger 22	14:15.6	3)	Kouvola	11 Jun
Gaston	Reiff	Bel 21	14:15.6	2)	Brussels	17 Jun
Bertil	Albertsson	Swe 21	14:15.6	2)	Stockholm	30 Jul

10,000 metres

Emil	Zátopek	Cze 22	29:01.6	1)	Stará Boleslav	01 Nov
Gordon	Pirie	GB 31	29:17.2	1)	Stockholm	03 Sep
József	Kovács	Hun 26	29:21.2	1)	Bucharest	04 Oct
Aleksandr	Anufriyev	USR 26	29:23.2	1)	Moscow	07 Jun
Vladimir	Kuts	USR 27	29:41.4	2)	Bucharest	09 Aug
Gyula	Pénzes	Hun 26	29:48.6	2)	Bucharest	04 Oct
Hannu	Posti	Fin 26	29:49.8	1)	Helsinki	05 Sep
Lain	Mimoun	Fra 21	29:51.0	2)	Helsinki	05 Sep
Frank	Sando	GB 31	29:56.2	2)	Stockholm	03 Sep
Urho	Julin	Fin 28	30:00.0	1)	Imatra	13 Jul

Noteworthy 6 mile times:

Alain	Mimoun	Fra 21	28:37.6	1)	London	03 Aug
Frank	Sando	GB 31	28:47.2	2)	London	10 Jul
Ian	Binnie	GB 30	28:53.4	3)	London	10 Jul

1954

5000 metres

Vladimir	Kuts	USR 27	13:51.2	1)	Prague	23 Oct
Chris	Chataway	GB 31	13:51.6	1)	London	13 Oct
Emil	Zátopek	Cze 22	13:57.0	1)	Stockholm	03 Sep
József	Kovács	Hun 26	14:08.2	1)	Helsinki	16 Jul
Helmut	Gude	Ger 25	14:10.0	1)	Brussels	16 Jun
Lucien	Hanswyck	Bel 29	14:11.0	2)	Brussels	16 Jun
Sándor	Iharos	Hun 30	14:12.2	1)	Budapest	24 Oct

Sándor	Garay	Hun 20	14:13.4	1)	Budapest	16 May
Ilmari	Taipale	Fin 28	14:13.8	1)	Helsinki	08 Jul
Herbert	Schade	Ger 22	14:14.2	3)	Brussels	16 Jun
Rolf	Haikkola	Fin 27	14:14.2	1)	Helsinki	17 Aug

Noteworthy 3 mile times:

Fred	Green	GB 26	13:32.2	1)	London	10 Jul
Frank	Sando	GB 31	13:37.4	3)	Vancouver	03 Aug

10,000 metres

Emil	Zátopek	Cze 22	28:54.2	1)	Brussels	01 Jun
József	Kovács	Hun 26	29:09.0	1)	Budapest	03 Jul
Vladimir	Kuts	USR 27	29:21.4	1)	Kiev	12 Sep
Frank	Sando	GB 31	29:27.6	3)	Berne	25 Aug
Herbert	Schade	Ger 22	29:30.0	1)	Hamburg	06 Aug
Ken	Norris	GB 31	29:35.4	1)	London	13 Oct
Franjo	Mihalic	Yug 21	29:37.6	1)	Belgrade	25 Jul
Aleksandr	Anufriyev	USR 26	29:44.6	3)	London	13 Oct
Grigoriy	Basalayev	USR 26	29:45.4	1)	Kiev	23 May
Albert	Ivanov	USR 31	29:45.6	2)	Kiev	23 May

Noteworthy 6 mile time:

Peter	Driver	GB 32	28:34.8	1)	London	09 Jul

1955

5000 metres

Sándor	Iharos	Hun 30	13:40.6	1)	Budapest	23 Oct
Vladimir	Kuts	USR 27	13:46.8	1)	Belgrade	18 Sep
László	Tábori	Hun 31	13:53.2	2)	Budapest	23 Oct
Jerzy	Chromik	Pol 31	13:55.2	1)	Warsaw	06 Aug
József	Kovács	Hun 26	13:57.6	3)	Warsaw	06 Aug
Miklós	Szabó II	Hun 28	13:59.0	3)	Budapest	23 Oct
Ernö	Béres	Hun 28	14:01.0	3)	Budapest	20 Aug
Hubert	Berta	Hun 31	14:01.8	5)	Budapest	20 Aug
Ivan	Chernyavskiy	USR 30	14:03.4	1)	Kiev	05 Oct
Gordon	Pirie	GB 31	14:03.8	1)	Prague	14 Sep

Noteworthy 3 mile times:

Chris	Chataway	GB 31	13:23.2	1)	London	30 Jul
Gordon	Pirie	GB 31	13:29.8	1)	Manchester	22 Jun
Frank	Sando	GB 31	13:29.8	1)	Chiswick	25 Jun
Ken	Norris	GB 31	13:29.8	2)	Chiswick	25 Jun
David	Stephens	Aus 28	13:31.8	1)	Melbourne	23 Feb

10,000 metres

Vladimir	Kuts	USR 27	28:59.2	1)	Bucharest	03 Oct
József	Kovács	Hun 26	29:02.6	1)	Bratislava	24 Sep
Aleksandr	Anufriyev	USR 26	29:10.6	1)	Minsk	20 May
Ivan	Chernyavskiy	USR 30	29:14.6	1)	Kiev	02 Oct
Gordon	Pirie	GB 31	29:19.0	1)	London	12 Oct
Ken	Norris	GB 31	29:21.4	2)	London	12 Oct
Jerzy	Chromik	Pol 31	29:23.0	1)	Lodz	25 Oct
Emil	Zátopek	Cze 22	29:25.6	1)	Prague	15 Sep
Miklós	Szabó II	Hun 28	29:28.4	1)	Sofia	06 Nov
Ivan	Ullsperger	Cze 31	29:29.2	1)	Kladno	16 Oct

1956

5000 metres

Gordon	Pirie	GB 31	13:36.8	1)	Bergen	19 Jun
Vladimir	Kuts	USR 27	13:39.6	2)	Bergen	19 Jun
Sándor	Iharos	Hun 30	13:46.6	1)	Stockholm	01 Sep
Jerzy	Chromik	Pol 31	13:51.0	2)	Poznan	07 Jul
Miklós	Szabó II	Hun 28	13:54.4	2)	Stockholm	01 Sep
Derek	Ibbotson	GB 32	13:54.4	3)	Melbourne	28 Nov
Kazimierz	Zimny	Pol 35	13:58.6	1)	Brussels	17 Oct
Velisa	Mugosa	Yug 31	13:58.8	2)	Belgrade	01 Jul
Chris	Chataway	GB 31	13:59.6	1)	Budapest	29 Sep
Allan	Lawrence	Aus 30	14:01.8	1)	Sydney	08 Sep

Noteworthy 3 mile time:

John	Landy	Aus 30	13:27.4	1)	Melbourne	25 Feb

10,000 metres

Vladimir	Kuts	USR 27	28:30.4	1)	Moscow	11 Sep
Sándor	Iharos	Hun 30	28:42.8	1)	Budapest	15 Jul
József	Kovács	Hun 26	28:52.4	2)	Melbourne	23 Nov
Allan	Lawrence	Aus 30	28:53.6	3)	Melbourne	23 Nov
Zdzislaw	Krzyszkowiak	Pol 29	29:05.0e	4)	Melbourne	23 Nov
Jerzy	Chromik	Pol 31	29:10.0	1)	Warsaw	09 Sep
Alain	Mimoun	Fra 21	29:13.4	2)	Warsaw	09 Sep
Gordon	Pirie	GB 31	29:17.2	1)	Croydon	04 Jul
Albert	Thomas	Aus 35	29:21.0	2)	Sydney	01 Sep
Ken	Norris	GB 31	29:21.6e	5)	Melbourne	23 Nov

Noteworthy 6 mile times:

David	Stephens	Aus 28	27:54.0	1)	Melbourne	25 Jan
Ken	Norris	GB 31	28:13.6	1)	London	13 Jul
Frank	Sando	GB 31	28:14.2	2)	London	13 Jul

1957

5000 metres

Vladimir	Kuts	USR 27	13:35.0	1)	Rome	13 Oct
Miklós	Szabó II	Hun 28	13:51.8	1)	Moscow	04 Aug
Friedrich	Janke	GDR 31	13:52.0	2)	Moscow	04 Aug
Alan	Lawrence	Aus 30	13:54.2	3)	Moscow	04 Aug
Pyotr	Bolotnikov	USR 30	13:54.4	4)	Moscow	04 Aug
Zdzislaw	Krzyszkowiak	Pol 29	13:55.8	1)	Cologne	31 Jul
Murray	Halberg	NZ 33	13:56.8	1)	Auckland	09 Feb
George	Knight	GB 33	13:57.6	1)	London	25 Sep
Miroslav	Jurek	Cze 35	13:57.8	5)	Moscow	04 Aug
Gordon	Pirie	GB 31	13:58.6	1)	London	23 Aug

Noteworthy 3 mile times:

Derek	Ibbotson	GB 32	13:20.8	1)	London	13 Jul
Albert	Thomas	Aus 35	13:25.9	1)	Melbourne	08 Dec
Murray	Halberg	NZ 33	13:27.2	1)	Auckland	28 Dec

10,000 metres

George	Knight	GB 33	29:06.4	1)	Warsaw	07 Sep
Pyotr	Bolotnikov	USR 30	29:09.8	1)	Moscow	29 Aug
Vladimir	Kuts	USR 27	29:10.0	2)	Moscow	29 Aug
Allan	Lawrence	Aus 30	29:16.4	2)	Moscow	30 Jul
Nikolay	Pudov	USR 30	29:19.4	3)	Moscow	29 Aug
Yuriy	Zakharov	USR 33	29:19.6	4)	Moscow	29 Aug
Aleksey	Desyatchikov	USR 32	29:20.4	5)	Moscow	29 Aug
Yevgeniy	Zhukov	USR 30	29:20.4	6)	Moscow	29 Aug
Friedrich	Janke	GDR 31	29:21.2	1)	Brno	12 Oct
Ivan	Chernyavskiy	USR 30	29:24.8	7)	Moscow	29 Aug

Noteworthy 6 mile time:

Allan	Lawrence	Aus 30	28:10.4	1)	Auckland	21 Dec

1958

5000 metres

Gordon	Pirie	GB 31	13:51.6	1)	Göteborg	28 Aug
Kazimierz	Zimny	Pol 35	13:52.2	1)	Warsaw	01 Aug
Miroslav	Jurek	Cze 35	13:52.2	2)	Göteborg	28 Aug
Zdzislaw	Krzyszkowiak	Pol 29	13:53.2	1)	Erfurt	25 Sep
Peter	Clark	GB 33	13:53.8	1)	Colombes	13 Sep
Marian	Jochman	Pol 35	13:54.6	2)	Warsaw	01 Aug
Sándor	Iharos	Hun 30	13:57.2	2)	Erfurt	25 Sep
Yevgeniy	Zhukov	USR 30	13:57.8	3)	Göteborg	28 Aug
Pyotr	Bolotnikov	USR 30	13:58.8	1)	Tallinn	19 Jul
Friedrich	Janke	GDR 31	13:59.4	1)	Leipzig	07 Sep

Noteworthy 3 mile times:

Albert	Thomas	Aus 35	13:10.8	1)	Dublin	09 Jul
Murray	Halberg	NZ 33	13:15.0	1)	Cardiff	22 Jul
Stanley	Eldon	GB 36	13:22.4	1)	London	12 Jul
Neville	Scott	NZ 35	13:26.2	3)	Cardiff	22 Jul

10,000 metres

Zdzislaw	Krzyszkowiak	Pol 29	28:56.0	1)	Stockholm	19 Aug
Yevgeniy	Zhukov	USR 30	28:58.6	2)	Stockholm	19 Aug
Nikolay	Pudov	USR 30	29:02.2	3)	Stockholm	19 Aug
Stanley	Eldon	GB 36	29:02.8	4)	Stockholm	19 Aug
Stanislaw	Ożóg	Pol 33	29:03.2	5)	Stockholm	19 Aug
John	Merriman	GB 36	29:03.8	6)	Stockholm	19 Aug
Pyotr	Bolotnikov	USR 30	29:04.4	2)	Moscow	07 Jul
Aleksey	Desyatchikov	USR 32	29:05.4	3)	Moscow	07 Jul
József	Kovács	Hun 26	29:05.6	4)	Moscow	07 Jul
Lembit	Virkus	USR 32	29:06.4	1)	Moscow	25 Aug

1959

5000 metres

Friedrich	Janke	GDR 31	13:42.4	1)	Berlin	05 Sep
Kazimierz	Zimny	Pol 35	13:44.4	2)	Berlin	05 Sep
József	Kovács	Hun 26	13:47.6	1)	Budapest	21 Aug

Stanley	Eldon	GB 36	13:47.8	1)	Turku	15 Sep
Hans	Grodotzki	GDR 36	13:48.4	3)	Berlin	05 Sep
Sándor	Iharos	Hun 30	13:50.8	1)	Ostrava	12 Sep
Matti	Huttunen	Fin 30	13:51.8	1)	Helsinki	23 Jun
Reijo	Höykinpuro	Fin 33	13:52.6	2)	Helsinki	23 Jun
Pyotr	Bolotnikov	USR 30	13:52.8	1)	Moscow	14 Aug
Aleksandr	Artinyuk	USR 34	13:53.0	2)	Moscow	14 Aug

10,000 metres

Pyotr	Bolotnikov	USR 30	29:03.0	1)	Moscow	09 Aug
Hans	Grodotzki	GDR 36	29:08.8	1)	Oslo	17 Jul
Lembit	Virkus	USR 32	29:16.2	2)	Moscow	09 Aug
Gerhard	Hönicke	GDR 30	29:17.6	2)	Oslo	17 Jul
Martin	Hyman	GB 33	29:18.0	1)	Helsinki	13 Sep
Erkki	Rantala	Fin 35	29:21.0	2)	Helsinki	13 Sep
John	Merriman	GB 36	29:24.6	3)	Helsinki	13 Sep
Hubert	Pärnakivi	USR 32	29:25.0	1)	Moscow	05 Jul
József	Kovács	Hun 26	29:25.6	2)	Moscow	05 Jul
Aleksey	Desyatchikov	USR 32	29:26.0	3)	Moscow	05 Jul
Osvaldo	Suárez	Arg 34	29:26.0	1)	Prague	22 Sep

Noteworthy 6 mile times:

Stanley	Eldon	GB 36	28:12.4	1)	London	10 Jul
John	Merriman	GB 36	28:15.8	2)	London	10 Jul
Michael	Bullivant	GB 34	28:16.2	1T)	London	15 Aug

1960

5000 metres

Pyotr	Bolotnikov	USR 30	13:38.1	1)	Kiev	07 Oct
Murray	Halberg	NZ 33	13:43.4	1)	Rome	02 Sep
Hans	Grodotzki	GDR 36	13:44.6	2)	Rome	02 Sep
Kazimierz	Zimny	Pol 35	13:44.8	3)	Rome	02 Sep
Friedrich	Janke	GDR 31	13:46.8	4)	Rome	02 Sep
Zdzislaw	Krzyszkowiak	Pol 29	13:51.6	1)	Tula	25 Jun
Gordon	Pirie	GB 31	13:51.6	1)	London	01 Aug
Jim	Beatty	USA 34	13:51.7	1)	Compton	03 Jun
David	Power	Aus 28	13:51.8	5)	Rome	02 Sep
László	Tábori	Hun 31	13:52.6	1)	London	30 Jul
Aleksey	Desyatchikov	USR 32	13:52.6	2)	Moscow	13 Aug

Notewortht 3 mile times:

Murray	Halberg	NZ 33	13:11.4	1)	Auckland	13 Feb
Bruce	Tulloh	GB 35	13:17.2	1)	Southampton	02 Jul

10,000 metres

Pyotr	Bolotnikov	USR 30	28:18.8	1)	Kiev	15 Oct
Hans	Grodotzki	GDR 36	28:37.0	2)	Rome	08 Sep
David	Power	Aus 28	28:38.2	3)	Rome	08 Sep
Aleksey	Desyatchikov	USR 32	28:39.6	4)	Rome	08 Sep
Murray	Halberg	NZ 33	28:48.0	1)	Auckland	28 Mar
Max	Truex	USA 35	28:50.2	6)	Rome	08 Sep
Zdzislaw	Krzyszkowiak	Pol 29	28:52.4	7)	Rome	08 Sep
John	Merriman	GB 36	28:52.6	8)	Rome	08 Sep
Aleksandr	Artinyuk	USR 35	28:58.0	1)	Moscow	03 Jul
Robert	Bogey	Fra 35	29:01.6	1)	London	30 Jul

243

ALL TIME WORLD LIST OF BEST PERFORMANCES AS AT THE END OF 1960

3 miles

Albert	Thomas	Aus 35	13:10.8	1)	Dublin	09 Jul	1958
Murray	Halberg	NZ 33	13:11.4	1)	Auckland	13 Feb	1960
Sándor	Iharos	Hun 30	13:14.2+	1)	Budapest	23 Oct	1955
	Halberg		13:15.0	1)	Cardiff	12 Jul	1958
Kazimierz	Zimny	Pol 35	13:15.6	1)	London	14 Aug	1959
Bruce	Tulloh	GB 35	13:17.2	1)	Southampton	02 Jul	1960
	Halberg		13:17.4	1)	Auckland	17 Dec	1960
	Thomas		13:20.6	1)	London	02 Aug	1958
Derek	Ibbotson	GB 32	13:20.8	1)	London	13 Jul	1957
Stanley	Eldon	GB 36	13:22.4	1)	London	12 Jul	1958

5000 metres

Vladimir	Kuts	USR 27	13:35.0	1)	Rome	13 Oct	1957
Gordon	Pirie	GB 31	13:36.8	1)	Bergen	19 Jun	1956
	Kuts		13:38.0	1)	Prague	06 Oct	1957
Pyotr	Bolotnikov	USR 30	13:38.1	1)	Kiev	07 Oct	1960
	Kuts		13:39.6	2)	Bergen	19 Jun	1956
	Kuts		13:39.6	1)	Melbourne	28 Nov	1956
Sándor	Iharos	Hun 30	13:40.6	1)	Budapest	23 Oct	1955
	Kuts		13:42.2	1)	Moscow	13 Aug	1956
Friedrich	Janke	GDR 31	13:42.4	1)	Berlin	05 Sep	1959
Murray	Halberg	NZ 33	13:43.4	1)	Rome	02 Sep	1960
Kazimierz	Zimny	Pol 35	13:44.4	2)	Berlin	05 Sep	1959
Hans	Grodotzki	GDR 36	13:44.6	2)	Rome	02 Sep	1960
	Zimny		13:44.8	3)	Rome	02 Sep	1960
	Iharos		13:46.6	1)	Stockholm	01 Sep	1956
	Kuts		13:46.8	1)	Belgrade	18 Sep	1955
	Janke		13:46.8	1)	Oslo	16 Jul	1959
	Janke		13:46.8	4)	Rome	02 Sep	1960
József	Kovács	Hun 26	13:47.6	1)	Budapest	21 Aug	1959
Stanley	Eldon	GB 36	13:47.8	1)	Turku	15 Sep	1959
	Grodotzki		13:48.4	3)	Berlin	05 Sep	1959
	Kuts		13:48.6	1)	Moscow	02 Sep	1957
	Grodotzki		13:49.2	1)	Budapest	25 Jun	1960
	Iharos		13:50.0	1)	Poznan	07 Jul	1956
	Zimny		13:50.2	1)	Rome	11 Oct	1959
	Pirie		13:50.6	2)	Melbourne	28 Nov	1956
	Iharos		13:50.8	1)	Budapest	10 Sep	1955
	Iharos		13:50.8	1)	Ostrava	12 Sep	1959
Jerzy	Chromik	Pol 31	13:51.0	2)	Poznan	07 Jul	1956
	Kuts		13:51.2	1)	Prague	23 Oct	1954
Chris	Chataway	GB 31	13:51.6	1)	London	13 Oct	1954
	Pirie		13:51.6	1)	Göteborg	28 Aug	1958
Zdzislaw	Krzyszkowiak	Pol 29	13:51.6	1)	Tula	25 Jun	1960
	Pirie		13:51.6	1)	London	01 Aug	1960
	Kuts		13:51.7	2)	London	13 Oct	1954
James	Beatty	USA 34	13:51.7	1)	Compton	03 Jun	1960
Miklós	Szabó II	Hun 28	13:51.8	1)	Moscow	04 Aug	1957
Matti	Huttunen	Fin 30	13:51.8	1)	Helsinki	23 Jun	1959
	Krzyszkowiak		13:51.8	1)	Rostock	10 Jul	1960
David	Power	Aus 28	13:51.8	5)	Rome	02 Sep	1960
	Janke		13:52.0	2)	Moscow	04 Aug	1957
	Bolotnikov		13:52.0	1)	Moscow	13 Aug	1960

	Zimny		13:52.2	1)	Warsaw	01 Aug	1958
Miroslav	Jurek	Cze 35	13:52.2	2)	Göteborg	28 Aug	1958
Reijo	Höykinpuro	Fin 33	13:52.6	2)	Helsinki	23 Jun	1959
László	Tábori	Hun 31	13:52.6	1)	London	30 Jul	1960
Aleksey	Desyatchikov	USR 32	13:52.6	2)	Moscow	13 Aug	1960
	Krzyszkowiak		13:52.6	1)	Warsaw	01 Oct	1960
	Zimny		13:52.6	2)	Warsaw	01 Oct	1960
	Bolotnikov		13:52.8	1)	Moscow	14 Aug	1959
	Eldon		13:52.8	1)	Moscow	05 Sep	1959
Nyandika	Maiyoro	Ken 30	13:52.8	6)	Rome	02 Sep	1960

(51 performances by 22 performers)

6 miles

	Iharos	Hun 31	27:43.8+	1)	Budapest	15 Jul	1956
Sándor	Iharos	Hun 31	27:43.8+	1)	Budapest	15 Jul	1956
Murray	Halberg	NZ 33	27:52.2+	1)	Auckland	28 Mar	1960
David	Power	Aus 28	27:52.8	1)	Sydney	19 Jan	1960
David	Stephens	Aus 28	27:54.0	1)	Melbourne	25 Jan	1956
Emil	Zátopek	Cze 22	27:59.2+	1)	Brussels	01 Jun	1954

10,000 metres

	Bolotnikov	USR 30	28:18.8	1)	Kiev	15 Oct	1960
Pyotr	Bolotnikov	USR 30	28:18.8	1)	Kiev	15 Oct	1960
Vladimir	Kuts	USR 27	28:30.4	1)	Moscow	11 Sep	1956
	Bolotnikov		28:32.2	1)	Rome	08 Sep	1960
	Bolotnikov		28:32.4	1)	Krasnodar	29 Sep	1960
Hans	Grodotzki	GDR 36	28:37.0	2)	Rome	08 Sep	1960
David	Power	Aus 28	28:38.2	3)	Rome	08 Sep	1960
Aleksey	Desyatchikov	USR 32	28:39.6	4)	Rome	08 Sep	1960
Sándor	Iharos	Hun 30	28:42.8	1)	Budapest	15 Jul	1956
	Kuts		28:45.6	1)	Melbourne	23 Nov	1956
Murray	Halberg	NZ 33	28:48.0	1)	Auckland	28 Mar	1960
	Halberg		28:48.8	5)	Rome	08 Sep	1960
Max	Truex	USA 35	28:50.2	6)	Rome	08 Sep	1960
József	Kovács	Hun 26	28:52.4	2)	Melbourne	23 Nov	1956
Zdzislaw	Krzyszkowiak	Pol 29	28:52.4	7)	Rome	08 Sep	1960
John	Merriman	GB 36	28:52.6	8)	Rome	08 Sep	1960
Allan	Lawrence	Aus 30	28:53.6	3)	Melbourne	23 Nov	1956
Emil	Zátopek	Cze 22	28:54.2	1)	Brussels	01 Jun	1954
	Krzyszkowiak		28:56.0	1)	Stockholm	19 Aug	1958
	Kuts		28:57.8	1)	Moscow	05 Aug	1956
	Grodotzki		28:57.8	1)	Schweinfurt	17 Jul	1960
	Zátopek		28:58.0	1)	Berne	25 Aug	1954
Aleksandr	Artinyuk	USR 35	28:58.0	1)	Moscow	03 Jul	1960
	Bolotnikov		28:58.2	2)	Moscow	03 Jul	1960
Yegeniy	Zhukov	USR 30	28:58.6	2)	Stockholm	19 Aug	1958
	Kuts		28:59.2	1)	Bucharest	03 Oct	1955
	Kuts		28:59.8	1)	Kiev	22 Jul	1956
	Desyatchikov		29:00.0	1)	Tula	26 Jun	1960
	Kuts		29:01.4	1)	Moscow	30 Jun	1956
	Zátopek		29:01.6	1)	Stará Boleslav	01 Nov	1953
Robert	Bogey	Fra 35	29:01.6	1)	London	30 Jul	1960
	Merriman		29:01.8	2)	London	30 Jul	1960
Nikolay	Pudov	USR 30	29:02.2	3)	Stockholm	19 Aug	1958
	Zátopek		29:02.6	1)	Turku	04 Aug	1950
	Kovács		29:02.6	1)	Bratislava	24 Sep	1955
Stanley	Eldon	GB 36	29:02.8	4)	Stockholm	19 Aug	1958
	Bolotnikov		29:03.0	1)	Moscow	09 Aug	1959
Stanislaw	Ozóg	Pol 33	29:03.2	5)	Stockholm	19 Aug	1958
	Kovács		29:03.4	3)	Moscow	03 Jul	1960
	Merriman		29:03.8	6)	Stockholm	19 Aug	1958

	Zhukov		29:03.8	4)	Moscow	03 Jul	1960
	Zhukov		29:04.4	1)	Moscow	07 Jul	1958
	Bolotnikov		29:04.4	2)	Moscow	07 Jul	1958
Martin	Hyman	GB 33	29:04.8	9)	Rome	08 Sep	1960
	Krzyszkowiak		29:05.0e	4)	Melbourne	23 Nov	1956
	Desyatchikov		29:05.4	3)	Moscow	07 Jul	1958
	Kovács		29:05.6	4)	Moscow	07 Jul	1958
	Kuts		29:06.2	1)	Lvov	26 Aug	1955
George	Knight	GB 33	29:06.4	1)	Warsaw	07 Sep	1957
Lembit	Virkus	USR 32	29:06.4	1)	Moscow	25 Aug	1958
	Bolotnikov		29:06.8	1)	Tbilisi	28 Oct	1958
	Bolotnikov		29:06.8	1)	Odessa	15 Sep	1959

(51 performances by 22 performer)

WORLD YEAR LISTS 1961-1980

1961

5000 metres

Murray	Halberg	NZ 33	13:35.2	1)	Stockholm	25 Jul
Barry	Magee	NZ 34	13:39.2	2)	Stockholm	25 Jul
Kazimierz	Zimny	Pol 35	13:49.6	1)	Solingen	06 Jul
Sándor	Iharos	Hun 30	13:51.8	1)	Budapest	08 Sep
Horst	Flosbach	Ger 36	13:52.4	2)	Solingen	06 Jul
Bruce	Tulloh	GB 35	13:52.8	1)	Budapest	08 Jul
David	Power	Aus 28	13:53.4	3)	Stockholm	25 Jul
Robert	Bogey	Fra 35	13:53.7	1)	Colombes	23 Jul
Pyotr	Bolotnikov	USR 30	13:53.8	1)	Moscow	29 Jul
József	Mácsár	Hun 38	13:55.4	2)	Budapest	08 Sep

Noteworthy 3 mile times:

Bruce	Tulloh	GB 35	13:12.0	1)	Southampton	17 Aug
Gordon	Pirie	GB 31	13:16.4	1)	London	21 Jul
Max	Truex	USA 35	13:21.0	3)	London	21 Jul

10,000 metres

Barry	Magee	NZ 34	28:50.8	1)	Helsinki	06 Jul
David	Power	Aus 28	28:56.6	2)	Helsinki	06 Jul
John	Merriman	GB 36	29:00.4	1)	London	07 Aug
Basil	Heatley	GB 33	29:01.0	1)	Moscow	02 Jul
Martin	Hyman	GB 33	29:02.0	1)	London	19 Sep
Yuriy	Zakharov	USR 33	29:03.0	2)	Moscow	02 Jul
Pyotr	Bolotnikov	USR 30	29:04.4	1)	Moscow	16 Aug
Boris	Yefimov	USR 35	29:07.2	2)	Moscow	16 Aug
Lembit	Virkus	USR 32	29:07.4	3)	Moscow	02 Jul
Faiz	Khuzin	USR 34	29:08.0	3)	Moscow	16 Aug

Noteworthy 6 mile time:

Martin	Hyman	GB 33	27:54.4	1)	London	22 May

1962

5000 metres

Murray	Halberg	NZ 33	13:38.4	1)	Auckland	17 Feb
Bruce	Kidd	Can 43	13:43.8	1)	Compton	02 Jun
Jim	Beatty	USA 34	13:45.0	1)	Turku	24 Aug

246

Hans	Grodotzki	GDR 36	13:48.2	1)	Turku	11 Jul	
Max	Truex	USA 35	13:49.6	2)	Compton	02 Jun	
Hermann	Buhl	Ger 35	13:50.6	2)	Turku	11 Jul	
Pyotr	Bolotnikov	USR 30	13:50.6	1)	Helsinki	31 Jul	
Kazimierz	Zimny	Pol 35	13:52.8	1)	London	04 Aug	
Bruce	Tulloh	GB 35	13:52.8	2)	London	04 Aug	
Simo	Saloranta	Fin 34	13:53.4	3)	Turku	11 Jul	
Peter	Kubicki	Ger 38	13:53.4	1)h3	Belgrade	13 Sep	

Noteworthy 3 mile times:

Bruce	Tulloh	GB 35	13:16.0	1)	London	14 Jul
Derek	Ibbotson	GB 32	13:21.6	2)	London	19 Jun
Albert	Thomas	Aus 35	13:21.6	1)	Melbourne	21 Oct
Max	Truex	USA 35	13:22.2+	2)	Compton	02 Jun

10,000 metres

Pyotr	Bolotnikov	USR 30	28:18.2	1)	Moscow	11 Aug
Hans	Grodotzki	GDR 36	28:49.4	1)	Potsdam	30 Jun
Mamo	Wolde	Eti 32	28:55.6	1)	Berlin	09 Jun
Abebe	Bikila	Eti 33	29:00.8	2)	Berlin	09 Jun
Bruce	Tulloh	GB 35	29:01.4	1)	Oslo	03 Jul
Friedrich	Janke	GDR 31	29:01.6	2)	Belgrade	12 Sep
Roy	Fowler	GB 34	29:02.0	3)	Belgrade	12 Sep
Martin	Hyman	GB 33	29:02.0	4)	Belgrade	12 Sep
Robert	Bogey	Fra 35	29:02.6	5)	Belgrade	12 Sep
Leonid	Ivanov	USR 37	29:04.8	6)	Belgrade	12 Sep

Noteworthy 6 mile times:

Roy	Fowler	GB 34	27:49.8	1)	London	13 Jul
Michael	Bullivant	GB 34	27:49.8	2)	London	13 Jul
Martin	Hyman	GB 33	27:52.0	3)	London	13 Jul
Melvyn	Batty	GB 40	27:56.6	4)	London	13 Jul
Bruce	Tulloh	GB 35	27:57.4	1)	London	11 Jun
Robert	Vagg	Aus 40	28:01.8	1)	Melbourne	18 Oct

1963

5000 metres

Murray	Halberg	NZ 33	13:41.2	1)	Manurewa	17 Jan
Gaston	Roelants	Bel 37	13:45.6	1)	Torhout	09 Sep
Siegfried	Herrmann	GDR 32	13:46.2	1)	Bucharest	12 Oct
Yuriy	Tyurin	USR 37	13:48.2	1)	Moscow	15 Aug
Sven-Olof	Larsson	Swe 38	13:49.2	1)	Stockholm	09 Jul
Leonid	Ivanov	USR 37	13:49.2	2)	Moscow	15 Aug
Valentin	Samoilov	USR 37	13:49.4	3)	Moscow	15 Aug
Neville	Scott	NZ 35	13:49.8	2)	Manurewa	14 Jan
Andrei	Barabas	Rom 37	13:49.8	2)	Bucharest	12 Oct
Michel	Bernard	Fra 31	13:50.1	2)	Torhout	09 Sep
Michel	Jazy	Fra 36	13:50.2	1)	Moscow	02 Jul

10,000 metres

Ron	Clarke	Aus 37	28:15.5	1)	Melbourne	18 Dec
Robert	Bogey	Fra 35	28:48.2	1)	Moscow	03 Jul
Leonid	Ivanov	USR 37	28:48.6	2)	Moscow	03 Jul
Don	Taylor	GB 36	28:52.4	1)	London	23 Aug
Basil	Heatley	GB 33	28:55.8	1)	London	13 Sep

Mel	Batty	GB 40	29:01.0	2)	London	13 Sep
Teruo	Funai	Jap 38	29:06.6	1)	Kita-Kyushu	10 Nov
Gaston	Roelants	Bel 37	29:07.2	1)	Pardubice	24 Sep
Kazumi	Watanabe	Jap 35	29:10.4	2)	Kita-Kyushu	10 Nov
David	Power	Aus 28	29:11.0	2)	Sydney	15 Sep

Noteworthy 6 mile times:

Ron	Hill	GB 38	27:49.8	1)	London	12 Jul
Jim	Hogan	Ire 33	27:54.2	2)	London	12 Jul
Ron	Gomez	GB 35	27:59.4	3)	London	12 Jul
Len	Edelen	USA 37	28:00.8	4)	London	12 Jul

1964

5000 metres

Bob	Schul	USA 37	13:38.0	1)	Compton	05 Jun
Pyotr	Bolotnikov	USR 30	13:38.6	1)	Zurich	23 Jun
Ron	Clarke	Aus 37	13:39.0	2)	Zurich	23 Jun
Bill	Baillie	NZ 34	13:40.0	2)	Compton	05 Jun
Ron	Larrieu	USA 37	13:43.0	3)	Compton	05 Jun
Gaston	Roelants	Bel 37	13:43.4	3)	Zurich	23 Jun
Gerry	Lindgren	USA 46	13:44.0	4)	Compton	05 Jun
Kestustis	Orentas	USR 39	13:45.0	1)	Moscow	04 Jul
Mike	Wiggs	GB 38	13:45.6	2)	Moscow	04 Jul
Neville	Scott	NZ 35	13:46.6	2)	Napier	05 Feb

Noteworthy 3 mile time:

| Ron | Clarke | Aus 37 | 13 :07.6 | 1) | Melbourne | 03 Dec |

10,000 metres

Billy	Mills	USA 38	28:24.4	1)	Tokyo	14 Oct
Mohamed	Gammoudi	Tun 38	28:24.8	2)	Tokyo	14 Oct
Ron	Clarke	Aus 37	28:25.8	3)	Tokyo	14 Oct
Mamo	Wolde	Eti 32	28:31.8	4)	Tokyo	14 Oct
Murray	Halberg	NZ 33	28:33.0	2)	Auckland	17 Nov
Pyotr	Bolotnikov	USR 30	28:39.6	1)	Kiev	27 Aug
Nikolay	Dutov	USR 38	28:40.0	2)	Kiev	27 Aug
Leonid	Ivanov	USR 37	28:40.6	3)	Kiev	27 Aug
Anatoly	Skripnik	USR 35	28:41.6	4)	Kiev	27 Aug
Gaston	Roelants	Bel 37	28:41.8	1)	Brussels	29 Aug

Noteworthy 6 mile times:

Mike	Bullivant	GB 34	27:26.4	1)	London	10 Jul
Ron	Hill	GB 38	27:27.0	2)	London	10 Jul
Jim	Hogan	Ire 33	27:35.0	3)	London	10 Jul
Martin	Hyman	GB 33	27:36.0	4)	London	10 Jul
Mike	Freary	GB 38	27:37.6	5)	London	10 Jul

1965

5000 metres

| Kichoge | Keino | Ken 40 | 13:24.2 | 1) | Auckland | 30 Nov |
| Ron | Clarke | Aus 37 | 13:25.7 | 1) | Los Angeles | 04 Jun |

Michel	Jazy	Fra 36	13:27.6	1)	Helsinki	30 Jun
Siegfried	Herrmann	GDR 32	13:30.0	1)	Potsdam	11 Aug
Mike	Wiggs	GB 38	13:33.0	4)	Helsinki	30 Jun
Gaston	Roelants	Bel 37	13:34.8	3)	Stockholm	06 Jul
Thor	Helland	Nor 39	13:37.4	5)	Helsinki	30 Jun
Bengt	Nåjde	Swe 42	13:37.8	6)	Helsinki	30 Jun
Lajos	Mécser	Hun 42	13:40.0	1)	London	14 Aug
Billy	Mills	USA 38	13:41.4	1)	Oslo	15 Jul

Noteworthy 3 mile times:

Ron	Clarke	Aus 37	12:52.4	1)	London	10 Jul
Gerry	Lindgren	USA 46	13:04.4	2)	London	10 Jul
Lajos	Mécser	Hun 42	13:07.6	3)	London	10 Jul
Bob	Schul	USA 37	13:10.4	1)	San Diego	26 Jun
Neville	Scott	NZ 35	13:10.8	2)	San Diego	26 Jun
Ron	Larrieu	USA 37	13:11.4	2)	Toronto	10 Jun

10,000 metres

Ron	Clarke	Aus 37	27:39.4	1)	Oslo	14 Jul
Gaston	Roelants	Bel 37	28:10.6	1)	Oslo	21 Aug
Billy	Mills	USA 38	28:17.6	1)	Augsburg	12 Aug
Nikolay	Dutov	USR 38	28:22.0	1)	Kiev	31 Jul
Leonid	Ivanov	USR 37	28:29.8	2)	Kiev	31 Jul
Lajos	Mécser	Hun 42	28:31.2	2)	Oslo	21 Aug
Lutz	Philipp	Ger 40	28:35.6	2)	Augsburg	12 Aug
Mike	Freary	GB 38	28:37.2	1)	Berlin	04 Sep
Bernard	Maroquin	Fra 39	28:45.2	4)	Oslo	21 Aug
Kazimierz	Zimny	Pol 35	28:46.0	3)	Stuttgart	11 Sep

Noteworthy 6 mile times:

Gerry	Lindgren	USA 46	27:11.6	2)	San Diego	27 Jun
Mohamed	Gammoudi	Tun 38	27:38.2	1)	London	09 Jul
Ron	Hill	GB 38	27:40.8	2)	London	09 Jul
Mike	Bullivant	GB 34	27:43.8	3)	London	09 Jul

1966

5000 metres

Ron	Clarke	Aus 37	13:16.6	1)	Stockholm	05 Jul
Harald	Norpoth	Ger 42	13:24.8	1)	Cologne	07 Sep
Kipchoge	Keino	Ken 40	13:26.6	1)	Berlin	26 Jun
Keisuke	Sawaki	Jap 43	13:36.2	1)	London	22 Jun
Mohamed	Gammoudi	Tun 38	13:36.4	2)	London	22 Jun
Lajos	Mécser	Hun 42	13:36.6	3)	London	22 Jun
John	Coyle	Aus 41	13:37.2	2)	Geelong	18 Jan
Gerry	Lindgren	USA 46	13:38.0	1)	Los Angeles	04 Jun
Michel	Jazy	Fra 36	13:38.2	1)	Lorient	03 Jun
Henk	Altmann	SA 41	13:39.0	5)	London	22 Jun

Noteworthy 3 mile times:

Gerry	Lindgren	USA 46	12:53.0	1)	Seattle	14 May
Allan	Rushmer	GB 44	13:08.6	3)	Kingston	08 Aug

10,000 metres

Ron	Clarke	Aus 37	27:54.0	1)	Oslo	12 Jul
Jürgen	Haase	GDR 45	28:12.6	1)	Leipzig	25 May

Gaston	Roelants	Bel 37	28:20.8	2)	Oslo	12 Jul
Mike	Freary	GB 38	28:26.0	1)	Stockholm	17 Sep
Lajos	Mécser	Hun 42	28:27.0	2)	Budapest	30 Aug
Leonid	Mikityenko	USR 44	28:32.2	3)	Budapest	30 Aug
Manfred	Letzerich	Ger 42	28:36.8	4)	Budapest	30 Aug
Allan	Rushmer	GB 44	28:37.8	5)	Budapest	30 Aug
Mohamed	Gammoudi	Tun 38	28:40.6	1)	La Coruña	02 Jul
Peter	Kubicki	Ger 38	28:47.8	1)	Berlin	01 Jul

Noteworthy 6 mile times:

Naftali	Temu	Ken 45	27:14.6	1)	Kingston	06 Aug
Mohamed	Gammoudi	Tun 38	27:23.4	1)	London	08 Jul
Bruce	Tulloh	GB 35	27:23.8	2)	London	08 Jul
Lajos	Mécser	Hun 42	27:23.8	3)	London	08 Jul
Roy	Fowler	GB 34	27:24.8	4)	London	08 Jul
Ron	Hill	GB 38	27:26.0	5)	London	08 Jul
Jim	Alder	GB 40	27:30.6	6)	London	08 Jul
Allan	Rushmer	GB 44	27:32.2	7)	London	08 Jul
Mike	Turner	GB 39	27:33.2	8)	London	08 Jul
John	Farrington	GB 42	27:33.8	2)	Melbourne	20 Dec
Mike	Bullivant	GB 34	27:44.0	10)	London	08 Jul

1967

5000 metres

Ron	Clarke	Aus 37	13:18.8	1)	Stockholm	05 Jul
Anatoliy	Makarov	USR 39	13:34.8	1)	Kiev	04 Sep
Leonid	Mikityenko	USR 44	13:36.4	2)	Kiev	04 Sep
Kipchoge	Keino	Ken 40	13:36.8	1)	Los Angeles	09 Jul
Allan	Rushmer	GB 44	13:37.2	1)	London	23 Sep
Mamo	Wolde	Eti 32	13:38.8	2)	Turku	02 Jul
Lajos	Mécser	Hun 42	13:39.0	2)	Berlin	21 Jun
Gennadiy	Khlistov	USR 44	13:39.2	1)	Moscow	03 Aug
Van	Nelson	USA 45	13:39.4	1)	St.Paul, MN	16 May
Nikolay	Sviridov	USR 38	13:39.6	3)	Kiev	04 Sep

Noteworthy 3 mile times:

Lajos	Mécser	Hun 42	13:03.4	2)	London	15 Jul
Ian	McCafferty	GB 44	13:06.4	2)	Dublin	17 Jul
Van	Nelson	USA 45	13:09.2	2)	Toronto	14 Jun
Naftali	Temu	Ken 45	13:09.6	2)	London	28 Aug

10,000 metres

Gaston	Roelants	Bel 37	28:26.6	1)	Oslo	22 Aug
Gennadiy	Khlistov	USR 44	28:27.8	1)	Moscow	30 Jul
Naftali	Temu	Ken 45	28:29.0	1)	Helsinki	29 Jun
Tom	Laris	USA 40	28:33.4	1)	Düsseldorf	17 Aug
Leonid	Mikityenko	USR 44	28:34.8	2)	Moscow	30 Jul
Nikolay	Sviridov	USR 38	28:37.4	3)	Moscow	30 Jul
Jürgen	Haase	GDR 45	28:38.8	2)	Helsinki	29 Jun
Gerry	Lindgren	USA 46	28:40.2	2)	Düsseldorf	17 Aug
Mamo	Wolde	Eti 32	28:41.2	3)	Helsinki	29 Jun
Manfred	Letzerich	Ger 42	28:41.4	1)	London	22 Sep

Noteworthy 6 mile times:

Ron	Clarke	Aus 37	27:21.6	1)	Melbourne	19 Dec
Jürgen	Haase	GDR 45	27:33.2	1)	London	14 Jul
Lajos	Mécser	Hun 42	27:36.0	2)	London	14 Jul
Tim	Johnston	GB 41	27:36.8	1)	Walton	21 Mar

1968

5000 metres

Ron	Clarke	Aus 37	13:27.8	1)	London	02 Sep
Lajos	Mécser	Hun 42	13:29.2	1)	Stockholm	03 Jul
Jean	Wadoux	Fra 42	13:29.6	1)	Paris	13 Jun
Mohamed	Gammoudi	Tun 38	13:30.8	3)	Stockholm	03 Jul
Ahmed	Zammel	Tun 44	13:33.0	4)	Stockholm	03 Jul
Keisuke	Sawaki	Jap 43	13:33.0	5)	Stockholm	03 Jul
Gerry	Lindgren	USA 46	13:33.8	1)	Modesto	25 May
Viktor	Kudinskiy	USR 43	13:34.6	6)	Stockholm	03 Jul
Harald	Norpoth	Ger 42	13:35.2	7)	Stockholm	03 Jul
Kipchoge	Keino	Ken 40	13:35.8	2)	Stockholm	18 Jul

10,000 metres

Ron	Clarke	Aus 37	27:49.4	1)	London	29 Aug
Jürgen	Haase	GDR 45	28:04.4	1)	Leningrad	21 Jul
Kipchoge	Keino	Ken 40	28:06.4	2)	Leningrad	21 Jul
Nikolay	Sviridov	USR 38	28:09.0	3)	Leningrad	21 Jul
Leonid	Mikityenko	USR 44	28:12.4	4)	Leningrad	21 Jul
Evan	Maguire	NZ 42	28:15.4	1)	Auckland	17 Apr
Rex	Maddaford	NZ 47	28:17.8	2)	Auckland	17 Apr
Vyacheslav	Alanov	USR 39	28:23.8	5)	Leningrad	21 Jul
Lutz	Philipp	Ger 40	28:27.2	1)	Kassel	01 Aug
Naftali	Temu	Ken 45	28:27.4	2)	Oslo	11 Jul

Noteworthy 6 mile time:

| Tim | Johnston | GB 41 | 27:22.2 | 1) | London | 12 Jul |

1969

5000 metres

Dick	Taylor	GB 45	13:29.0	1)	London	13 Aug
Jürgen	May	Ger 42	13:33.0	1)	Stockholm	02 Jul
Ron	Clarke	Aus 37	13:33.8	2)	Stockholm	02 Jul
Gaston	Roelants	Bel 37	13:34.6	1)	Cologne	08 Jul
Harald	Norpoth	Ger 42	13:36.0	3)	Stockholm	02 Jul
Ian	Stewart	GB 49	13:36.4	2)	London	13 Aug
Bernd	Diessner	GDR 46	13:36.8	1)	Paris	12 Jun
Ivan	Shopsha	USR 39	13:37.6	1)	Moscow	12 Jun
Werner	Girke	Ger 40	13:37.8	2)	Paris	12 Jun
Rashid	Sharafyetdinov	USR 43	13:37.8	1)	Kiev	20 Aug

10,000 metres

Ron	Clarke	Aus 37	28:03.6	1)	Oslo	08 Jul
Dick	Taylor	GB 45	28:06.6	1)	London	22 Jun
Jürgen	Haase	GDR 45	28:08.2	1)	Moscow	11 Jun
Styepan	Baidyuk	USR 41	28:13.8	2)	Moscow	11 Jun

Gaston	Roelants	Bel 37	28:19.0	1)	Oslo	06 Sep
Dave	Bedford	GB 49	28:24.4	1)	London	19 Apr
René	Jourdan	Fra 43	28:28.0	1)	St. Maur	04 Jun
Vyacheslav	Alanov	USR 39	28:32.8	1)	Odessa	02 Jul
Nikolay	Sviridov	USR 38	28:33.0	2)	Odessa	02 Jul
Mike	Tagg	GB 46	28:33.8	3)	London	22 Jun

Noteworthy 6 mile time:

Jack	Bacheler	USA 43	27:30.0	1)	Des Moines	26 Apr

1970

5000 metres

Ian	Stewart	GB 49	13:22.8	1)	Edinburgh	25 Jul
Ian	McCafferty	GB 44	13:23.4	2)	Edinburgh	25 Jul
Dick	Taylor	GB 45	13:26.2	1)	Edinburgh	13 Jun
Kipchoge	Keino	Ken 40	13:27.6	3)	Edinburgh	25 Jul
Jean	Wadoux	Fra 42	13:28.0	1)	Colombes	08 Jul
Allan	Rushmer	GB 44	13:29.8	4)	Edinburgh	25 Jul
Ron	Clarke	Aus 37	13 :32.4	5)	Edinburgh	25 Jul
Harald	Norpoth	Ger 42	13:34.6	1)	Stuttgart	16 Jul
Mike	Baxter	GB 45	13:35.2	3)	Edinburgh	13 Jun
Kerry	O'Brien	Aus 46	13:37.2	1)	Melbourne	12 Mar

10,000 metres

Dave	Bedford	GB 49	28:06.2	1)	Warsaw	12 Sep
Lachie	Stewart	GB 43	28:11.8	1)	Edinburgh	18 Jul
Ron	Clarke	Aus 37	28:13.4	2)	Edinburgh	18 Jul
Dick	Taylor	GB 45	28:15.4	3)	Edinburgh	18 Jul
Juha	Väätäinen	Fin 41	28:19.6	1)	Oulu	27 Jun
Roger	Matthews	GB 42	28:21.4	4)	Edinburgh	18 Jul
Jürgen	Busch	Ger 42	28:21.8	1)	Berlin	06 Sep
Frank	Shorter	USA 48	28:22.8	1)	Leningrad	23 Jul
Lutz	Philipp	Ger 40	28:23.4	1)	Koblenz	24 Jun
Gaston	Roelants	Bel 37	28:25.4	2)	Koblenz	24 Jun

1971

5000 metres

Dave	Bedford	GB 49	13:22.2	1)	Edinburgh	12 Jun
Emiel	Puttemans	Bel 47	13:24.6	1)	Bonn	11 Sep
Kipchoge	Keino	Ken 40	13:25.8	1)	London	10 Sep
Javier	Alvarez	Spa 43	13:28.4	2)	London	10 Sep
Lasse	Viren	Fin 49	13:29.8	1)	Heinola	22 Aug
Jean	Wadoux	Fra 42	13:30.4	1)	Helsinki	30 Jun
Steve	Prefontaine	USA 51	13:30.4	1)	Berkeley	03 Jul
Dane	Korica	Yug 45	13:31.2	3)	Helsinki	30 Jun
George	Young	USA 37	13:32.2	1)	Bakersfield	15 May
Juha	Väätäinen	Fin 41	13:32.6	1)	Helsinki	14 Aug

Noteworthy 3 mile times:

Steve	Prefontaine	USA 51	12:58.6	1)	Eugene	25 Jun
Steve	Stageberg	USA 47	13:00.4	2)	Eugene	25 Jun
Frank	Shorter	USA 47	13:02.4	3)	Eugene	25 Jun

10,000 metres

Dave	Bedford	GB 49	27:47.0	1)	Portsmouth	10 Jul
Juha	Väätäinen	Fin 41	27:52.8	1)	Helsinki	10 Aug
Jürgen	Haase	GDR 45	27:53.4	2)	Helsinki	10 Aug
Rashid	Sharafyetdinov	USR 43	27:56.4	3)	Helsinki	10 Aug
Dane	Korica	Yug 45	27:58.4	4)	Helsinki	10 Aug
Mariano	Haro	Spa 40	27:59.4	5)	Helsinki	10 Aug
Javier	Alvarez	Spa 43	28:01.4	1)	Munich	03 Sep
Emiel	Puttemans	Bel 47	28:01.4	2)	Munich	03 Sep
Eckhard	Lesse	GDR 48	28:14.0	2)	Erfurt	02 Jun
Mike	Tagg	GB 46	28:14.8	7)	Helsinki	10 Aug

1972

5000 metres

Emiel	Puttemans	Bel 47	13:13.0	1)	Brussels	20 Sep
Lasse	Viren	Fin 49	13:16.4	1)	Helsinki	14 Sep
Dave	Bedford	GB 49	13:17.2	1)	London	14 Jul
Ian	McCafferty	GB 44	13:19.8	2)	London	14 Jul
Gianni	Del Buono	Ita 43	13:22.4	1)	Rome	13 Sep
Steve	Prefontaine	USA 51	13:22.8	1)	Eugene	09 Jul
Ian	Stewart	GB 49	13:24.2	3)	London	14 Jul
Mariano	Haro	Spa 40	13:26.0	4)	London	14 Jul
Javier	Alvarez	Spa 43	13:26.4	1)	Oslo	19 Jul
Mohamed	Gammoudi	Tun 38	13:27.4	2)	Munich	10 Sep

10,000 metres

Lasse	Viren	Fin 49	27:38.4	1)	Munich	03 Sep
Emiel	Puttemans	Bel 47	27:39.6	2)	Munich	03 Sep
Miruts	Yifter	Eti 47	27:41.0	3)	Munich	03 Sep
Mariano	Haro	Spa 40	27:48.2	4)	Munich	03 Sep
Frank	Shorter	USA 47	27:51.4	5)	Munich	03 Sep
Dave	Bedford	GB 49	27:52.4	1)	London	15 Jul
Mohamed	Gammoudi	Tun 38	27:54.8	1)h2	Munich	31 Aug
Gaston	Roelants	Bel 37	28:03.8	1)	Brussels	05 Aug
Rashid	Sharafyetdinov	USR 43	28:05.2	1)	Moscow	18 Jul
Pavel	Andreyev	USR 44	28:07.8	2)	Augsburg	23 Jun

1973

5000 metres

Emiel	Puttemans	Bel 47	13:14.51	1)	Stockholm	07 Aug
Dick	Quax	NZ 48	13:18.33	2)	Stockholm	07 Aug
Harald	Norpoth	Ger 42	13:20.49	1)	Munich	12 Jul
Steve	Prefontaine	USA 51	13:22.4	2)	Helsinki	27 Jun
Paul	Mose	Ken 49	13:23.2	3)	Helsinki	27 Jun
Brendan	Foster	GB 48	13:23.71	1)	London	14 Jul
Dave	Black	GB 52	13:24.6	4)	Helsinki	27 Jun
Lasse	Viren	Fin 49	13:28.0	5)	Helsinki	27 Jun
Pekka	Päivärinta	Fin 49	13:28.51	1)	Helsinki	16 Sep
Dave	Bedford	GB 49	13:28.8	2)	Auckland	19 Dec

10,000 metres

Dave	Bedford	GB 49	27:30.80	1)	London	13 Jul
Dave	Black	GB 52	27:55.50	1)	London	06 Oct
Nikolay	Sviridov	USR 38	27:58.6	1)	Moscow	10 Jul
Pavel	Andreyev	USR 44	27:59.8	2)	Moscow	10 Jul
Vadim	Mochalov	USR 47	28:00.9	3)	Moscow	10 Jul
Tony	Simmons	GB 48	28:01.50	2)	London	06 Oct
Willy	Polleunis	Bel 47	28:07.6	1)	Brussels	14 Sep
Victor	Mora	Col 44	28:08.8	2)	Brussels	14 Sep
Bernard	Ford	GB 52	28:09.95	3)	London	06 Oct
Richard	Juma	Ken 45	28:10.0	1)	Helsinki	18 Jun

1974

5000 metres

Ben	Jipcho	Ken 43	13:14.4	1)	Christchurch	29 Jan
Brendan	Foster	GB 48	13:14.6	2)	Christchurch	29 Jan
Kurt	Kvalheim	Nor 50	13:20.54	1)	Helsinki	26 Jun
Steve	Prefontaine	USA 51	13:21.87	2)	Helsinki	26 Jun
Pal	Geis	USA 53	13:23.38	3)	Helsinki	26 Jun
Dick	Buerkle	USA 47	13:23.4	1)	Oslo	30 Jul
Dave	Black	GB 52	13:23.6	3)	Christchurch	29 Jan
Manfred	Kuschmann	GDR 50	13:23.93	2)	Rome	08 Sep
Lasse	Viren	Fin 49	13:24.57	3)	Rome	08 Sep
Anders	Gärderud	Swe 46	13:25.2	1)	Göteborg	13 Aug

Indoors:

Emiel	Puttemans	Bel 47	13:24.6	1)	Paris	17 Mar

Noteworthy 3 mile times:

Steve	Prefontaine	USA 51	12:51.4	1)	Eugene	08 Jun
Frank	Shorter	USA 47	12:52.0	2)	Eugene	08 Jun

10,000 metres

Steve	Prefontaine	USA 51	27:43.6	1)	Eugene	27 Apr
Richard	Tayler	NZ 48	27:46.4	1)	Christchurch	25 Jan
Dave	Black	GB 52	27:48.6	2)	Christchurch	25 Jan
Richard	Juma	Ken 45	27:57.0	3)	Christchurch	25 Jan
John	Ngeno	Ken 53	28:05.6	1)	Helsinki	27 Jun
Manfred	Kuschmann	GDR 50	28:09.6	1)	Leipzig	04 Jul
Frank	Shorter	USA 47	28:11.03	2)	Stockholm	01 Jul
Karl-Heinz	Leiteritz	GDR 47	28:13.6	2)	Leipzig	04 Jul
Knut	Börö	Nor 48	28:14.6	1)	Oslo	09 Jul
Dave	Bedford	GB 49	28:14.8	4)	Christchurch	25 Jan
Dan	Shaughnessy	Can 44	28:14.8	5)	Christchurch	25 Jan

Noteworthy 6 mile time:

Frank	Shorter	USA 47	27:09.6	1)	Gainesville	18 May

1975

5000 metres

Emiel	Puttemans	Bel 47	13:18.6	1)	Papendal	04 Jun
Rod	Dixon	NZ 50	13:21.6	1)	Oslo	30 Jul

Knut	Börö	Nor 48	13:21.8	2)	Oslo	30 Jul
Jos	Hermens	Hol 50	13:22.4	2)	Papendal	04 Jun
Marty	Liquori	USA 49	13:23.6	2)	Göteborg	12 Aug
Steve	Prefontaine	USA 51	13:23.8	1)	Eugene	29 May
Anders	Gärderud	Swe 46	13:25.0	3)	Göteborg	12 Aug
John	Ngeno	Ken 52	13:26.8	3)	Oslo	30 Jul
Ian	Stewart	GB 49	13:27.00	2)	Stockholm	01 Jul
Enn	Sellik	USR 54	13:27.11	1)	London	25 Aug

10,000 metres

Brendan	Foster	GB 48	27:45.43	1)	London	29 Aug
Frank	Shorter	USA 47	27:45.91	2)	London	29 Aug
Jos	Hermens	Hol 50	27:46.52	3)	London	29 Aug
Dave	Black	GB 52	27:47.66	4)	London	29 Aug
Marc	Smet	Bel 51	27:53.58	5)	London	29 Aug
Tony	Simmons	GB 48	27:53.63	6)	London	29 Aug
Knut	Börö	Nor 48	27:56.2	1)	Oslo	24 Jun
Jim	Brown	GB 52	28:00.62	2)	London	01 Aug
Bernard	Ford	GB 52	28:00.83	7)	London	29 Aug
Bill	Scott	Aus 52	28:00.89	2)	Stockholm	30 Jun

1976

5000 metres

Dick	Quax	NZ 48	13:13.10	1)	Stockholm	05 Jul
Klaus-Peter	Hildenbrand	Ger 52	13:13.69	2)	Stockholm	05 Jul
Enn	Sellik	USR 54	13:17.2	1)	Podolsk	28 Jun
Rod	Dixon	NZ 50	13:17.27	3)	Stockholm	05 Jul
Anders	Gärderud	Swe 46	13:17.59	4)	Stockholm	05 Jul
Bronislaw	Malinowski	Pol 51	13:17.69	5)	Stockholm	05 Jul
Boris	Kuznyetsov	USR 48	13:18.0	2)	Podolsk	28 Jun
Lasse	Orimus	Fin 50	13:18.19	6)	Stockholm	05 Jul
Duncan	McDonald	USA 49	13:19.40	1)	Stockholm	10 Aug
Brendan	Foster	GB 48	13:20.32	1)h3	Montreal	28 Jul

10,000 metres

Lasse	Viren	Fin 49	27:40.38	1)	Montreal	26 Jul
Carlos	Lopes	Por 47	27:42.65	1)	Stockholm	09 Aug
Dick	Quax	NZ 48	27:46.08	2)	Stockholm	09 Aug
Marc	Smet	Bel 51	27:48.50	3)	Stockholm	09 Aug
Garry	Bjorklund	USA 51	27:49.77	4)	Stockholm	09 Aug
Brendan	Foster	GB 48	27:53.70	1)	London	12 Jun
Pekka	Päivärinta	Fin 49	27:54.43	2)	Helsinki	23 Jun
Frank	Shorter	USA 47	27:55.45	1)	Eugene	22 Jun
Franco	Fava	Ita 52	27:55.61	3)	Helsinki	23 Jun
Victor	Mora	Col 44	27:55.72	2)	Munich	29 May

1977

5000 metres

Dick	Quax	NZ 48	13:12.86	1)	Stockholm	05 Jul
Miruts	Yifter	Eti 44	13:13.82	1)	Düsseldorf	04 Sep
Karl	Fleschen	Ger 55	13.13.88	2)	Stockholm	05 Jul
Peter	Weigt	Ger 48	13:14.54	3)	Stockholm	05 Jul

Marty	Liquori	USA 49	13:15.06	2)	Düsseldorf	04 Sep
David	Fitzsimons	Aus 50	13:17.42	3)	Düsseldorf	04 Sep
Manfred	Kuschmann	GDR 50	13:19.51	4)	Stockholm	05 Jul
Suleiman	Nyambui	Tan 53	13:19.59	1)	The Hague	25 Jun
Nick	Rose	GB 51	13:20.35	4)	Düsseldorf	04 Sep
Filbert	Bayi	Tan 53	13:20.72	2)	The Hague	25 Jun

10,000 metres

Samson	Kimobwa	Ken 55	27:30.47	1)	Helsinki	30 Jun
Brendan	Foster	GB 48	27:36.62	1)	London	09 Sep
Henry	Rono	Ken 52	27:37.08	2)	London	09 Sep
Gerard	Tebroke	Hol 49	27:37.63	3)	London	09 Sep
Jos	Hermens	Hol 50	27:41.25	2)	Stockholm	04 Jul
Mike	Musyoki	Ken 56	27:41.92	2)	Helsinki	30 Jun
Dick	Quax	NZ 48	27:41.95	4)	London	09 Sep
Detlef	Uhlemann	Ger 49	27:42.09	3)	Stockholm	04 Jul
Franco	Fava	Ita 52	27:42.65	3)	Helsinki	30 Jun
Ian	Stewart	GB 49	27:43.03	6)	London	09 Sep

1978

5000 metres

Henry	Rono	Ken 52	13:08.4	1)	Berkeley	08 Apr
Ilie	Floroiu	Rom 52	13:15.0	1)	Bucarest	23 Jul
Marty	Liquori	USA 49	13:16.21	1)	Stockholm	04 Jul
Rod	Dixon	NZ 50	13:17.37	2)	Stockholm	04 Jul
Fernando	Mamede	Por 51	13:17.76	3)	Stockholm	04 Jul
Frank	Zimmermann	Ger 55	13:18.20	4)	Stockholm	04 Jul
Markus	Ryffel	Swi 55	13:19.97	2)	Zurich	16 Aug
Venanzio	Ortis	Ita 55	13:20.82	3)	Zurich	16 Aug
Gerard	Tebroke	Hol 49	13:21.68	4)	Zurich	16 Aug
Jos	Hermens	Hol 50	13:21.9 m	1)	Nijmegen	09 Jul

10,000 metres

Henry	Rono	Ken 52	27:22.4	1)	Vienna	11 Jun
Brendan	Foster	GB 48	27:30.3	1)	London	23 Jun
Martti	Vainio	Fin 50	27:30.99	1)	Prague	29 Aug
Venanzio	Ortis	Ita 55	27:31.48	2)	Prague	29 Aug
Aleksandr	Antipov	USR 55	27:31.50	3)	Prague	29 Aug
Dave	Blak	GB 52	27:36.27	5)	Prague	29 Aug
Gerard	Tebroke	Hol 49	27:36.64	6)	Prague	29 Aug
Ilie	Floroiu	Rom 52	27:40.06	7)	Prague	29 Aug
Enn	Sellik	USR 54	27:40.61	8)	Prague	29 Aug
Knut	Kvalheim	Nor 50	27:41.26	9)	Prague	29 Aug

1979

5000 metres

Suleiman	Nyambui	Tan 53	13:12.29	1)	Stockholm	18 Jun
Markus	Ryffel	Swi 55	13:13.32	2)	Stockholm	18 Jun
Valeriy	Abramov	USR 56	13:15.6	1)	Sochi	08 Jun
Aleksandr	Fyedotkin	USR 55	13:17.66	1)	Budapest	10 Jul
Aleksandr	Antipov	USR 55	13:17.9	2)	Sochi	08 Jun
Rod	Dixon	NZ 50	13:18.64	1)	Oslo	05 Jul

Rudy	Chapa	USA 57	13:19.22	1)	Eugene	07 Apr
David	Fitzsimons	Aus 50	13:19.6 m	1)	Göteborg	07 Aug
Henry	Rono	Ken 52	13:19.65	1)	Rieti	21 Jul
Thomas	Wessinhage	Ger 52	13:19.87	2)	Stockholm	03 Jul

10,000 metres

Karl	Fleschen	Ger 55	27:36.8 m	1)	Troisdorf	28 Apr
Craig	Virgin	USA 55	27:39.4	1)	Walnut	17 Jun
Mike	McLeod	GB 52	27:39.76	1)	Brussels	04 Sep
Brendan	Foster	GB 48	27:41.23	2)	Brussels	04 Sep
Léon	Schots	Bel 52	27:41.34	3)	Brussels	04 Sep
Aleksandr	Fyedotkin	USR 55	27:41.89	4)	Brussels	04 Sep
Frank	Zimmermann	Ger 55	27:42.8 m	2)	Troisdorf	28 Apr
Miruts	Yifter	Eti 44	27:44.2	1)	Moscow	21 Jul
Dave	Blak	GB 52	27:46.51	5)	Brussels	04 Sep
Aleksandr	Antipov	USR 55	27:47.4	2)	Moscow	21 Jul

1980

5000 metres

Miruts	Yifter	Eti 44	13:16.38	1)	Bratislava	07 Jun
Mohammed	Kedir	Eti 53	13:17.5	2)	Bratislava	07 Jun
Nat	Muir	GB 58	13:17.9 m	1)	Oslo	15 Jul
Filbert	Bayi	Tan 53	13:18.2 m	2)	Oslo	15 Jul
Suleiman	Nyambui	Tan 53	13:18.6 m	3)	Oslo	15 Jul
Bill	McChesney	USA 59	13:18.6 m	4)	Oslo	15 Jul
Craig	Virgin	USA 55	13:19.1 m	5)	Oslo	15 Jul
Kiprotich	Rono	Ken 58	13:19.24	1)	Stuttgart	12 Jul
Thomas	Wessinghage	Ger 52	13:19.76	1)	Stockholm	08 Jul
Henry	Rono	Ken 52	13:19.8 m	6)	Oslo	15 Jul

10,000 metres

Craig	Virgin	USA 55	27:29.16	1)	Paris	17 Jul
Henry	Rono	Ken 52	27:31.68	1)	Melbourne	06 Feb
Fernando	Mamede	Por 51	27:37.88	2)	Paris	17 Jul
Miruts	Yifter	Eti 44	27:42.69	1)	Moscow	27 Jul
Toshihiko	Seko	Jap 56	27:43.44	1)	Stockholm	07 Jul
Kaarlo	Maaninka	Fin 53	27:44.28	2)	Moscow	27 Jul
Aleksandr	Antipov	USR 55	27:44.58	2)	Stockholm	07 Jul
Mohammed	Kedir	Eti 53	27:44.64	3)	Moscow	27 Jul
Tolossa	Kotu	Eti 52	27:46.47	4)	Moscow	27 Jul
Bill	Scott	Aus 52	27:46.71	2)	Melbourne	06 Feb

ALL TIME WORLD LIST OF BEST PERFORMANCES AS AT THE END OF 1980

5000 metres

Henry	Rono	Ken 52	13:08.4	1)	Berkeley	08 Apr	1978
Suleiman	Nyambui	Tan 53	13:12.29	1)	Stockholm	18 Jun	1979
Dick	Quax	NZ 48	13:12.86	1)	Stockholm	05 Jul	1977
Emiel	Puttemans	Bel 47	13:13.0	1)	Brussels	20 Sep	1972
	Quax		13:13.10	1)	Stockholm	05 Jul	1976
Markus	Ryffel	Swi 55	13:13.32	2)	Stockholm	18 Jun	1979

Klaus-Peter	Hildenbrand	Ger 52	13:13.69	2)	Stockholm	05 Jul	1976
Miruts	Yifter	Eti 44	13:13.82	1)	Düsseldorf	04 Sep	1977
Karl	Fleschen	Ger 55	13:13.88	2)	Stockholm	05 Jul	1977
Ben	Jipcho	Ken 43	13:14.4	1)	Christchurch	29 Jan	1974
	Puttemans		13:14.51	1)	Stockholm	07 Aug	1973
Peter	Weigt	Ger 48	13:14.54	3)	Stockholm	05 Jul	1977
Brendan	Foster	GB 48	13:14.6	2)	Christchurch	29 Jan	1974
Ilie	Floroiu	Rom 52	13:15.0	1)	Bucharest	23 Jul	1978
Marty	Liquori	USA 49	13:15.06	2)	Düsseldorf	04 Sep	1977
	Rono		13:15.5	1)	Rieti	10 Sep	1978
Valeriy	Abramov	USR 56	13:15.6	1)	Sochi	08 Jun	1979
	Liquori		13:16.00	1)	Zurich	24 Aug	1977
	Rono		13:16.12	1)	Zurich	16 Aug	1978
	Liquori		13:16.21	1)	Stockholm	04 Jul	1978
	Puttemans		13:16.28	1)	Zurich	06 Jul	1973
Lasse	Viren	Fin 49	13:16.3	1)	Helsinki	14 Sep	1972
	Yifter		13 :16.38	1)	Bratislava	07 Jun	1980
Ron	Clarke	Aus 37	13:16.6	1)	Stockholm	05 Jul	1966
	Floroiu		13:16.7	2)	Rieti	10 Sep	1978
Enn	Sellik	USR 54	13:17.2	1)	Podolsk	28 Jun	1976
Dave	Bedford	GB 49	13:17.21	1)	London	14 Jul	1972
	Foster		13:17.21	1)	Rome	08 Sep	1974
Rod	Dixon	NZ 50	13:17.27	3)	Stockholm	05 Jul	1976
	Quax		13:17.32	2)	Zurich	24 Aug	1977
	Dixon		13:17.37	2)	Stockholm	04 Jul	1978
David	Fitzsimons	Aus 50	13:17.42	3)	Düsseldorf	04 Sep	1977
Mohamed	Kedir	Eti 54	13:17.5	2)	Bratislava	07 Jun	1980
Anders	Gärderud	Swe 46	13:17.59	4)	Stockholm	05 Jul	1976
Aleksandr	Fyedotkin	USR 55	13:17.66	1)	Budapest	10 Jul	1979
Bronislaw	Malinowski	Pol 51	13:17.69	5)	Stockholm	05 Jul	1976
Fernando	Mamede	Por 51	13:17.76	3)	Stockholm	04 Jul	1978
Aleksandr	Antipov	USR 55	13:17.9	2)	Sochi	08 Jun	1979
Nat	Muir	GB 58	13:17.9 m	1)	Oslo	15 Jul	1980
Boris	Kuznyetsov	USR 47	13:18.0	2)	Podolsk	28 Jun	1976
	Yifter		13:18.12	3)	Zurich	24 Aug	1977
Lasse	Orimus	Fin 50	13:18.19	6)	Stockholm	05 Jul	1976
	Rono		13:18.2	1)	Milan	01 Jul	1978
Filbert	Bayi	Tan 53	13:18.2 m	2)	Oslo	15 Jul	1980
Frank	Zimmermann	Ger 55	13:18.20	4)	Stockholm	04 Jul	1978
	Quax		13:18.33	2)	Stockholm	07 Aug	1973
	Puttemans		13:18.6	1)	Papendal	04 Jun	1975
	Nyambui		13:18.6 m	3)	Oslo	15 Jul	1980
Bill	McChesney	USA 59	13:18.6 m	4)	Oslo	15 Jul	1980
	Dixon		13:18.64	1)	Oslo	05 Jul	1979

(50 performances by 32 performers)

10,000 metres

Henry	Rono	Ken 52	27:22.4	1)	Vienna	11 Jun	1978
Craig	Virgin	USA 55	27:29.16	1)	Paris	17 Jul	1980
Brendan	Foster	GB 48	27:30.3	1)	London	23 Jun	1978
Samson	Kimobwa	Ken 55	27:30.47	1)	Helsinki	30 Jun	1977
Dave	Bedford	GB 49	27:30.80	1)	London	13 Jul	1973
Martti	Vainio	Fin 50	27:30.99	1)	Prague	29 Aug	1978
Venanzio	Ortis	Ita 55	27:31.48	2)	Prague	29 Aug	1978
Aleksandr	Antipov	USR 55	27:31.50	3)	Prague	29 Aug	1978
	Rono		27:31.68	1)	Melbourne	06 Feb	1980
	Foster		27:32.65	4)	Prague	29 Aug	1978
Dave	Black	GB 52	27:36.27	5)	Prague	29 Aug	1978
	Foster		27:36.62	1)	London	09 Sep	1977

Gerard	Tebroke	Hol 49	27:36.64	6)	Prague	29 Aug	1978
Karl	Fleschen	Ger 55	27:36.8 m	1)	Troisdorf	28 Apr	1979
	Rono		27:37.08	2)	London	09 Sep	1977
	Kimobwa		27:37.28	1)	Stockholm	04 Jul	1977
	Tebroke		27:37.63	3)	London	09 Sep	1977
Fernando	Mamede	Por 51	27:37.88	2)	Paris	17 Jul	1980
Lasse	Viren	Fin 49	27:38.35	1)	Munich	03 Sep	1972
	Virgin		27:39.4	1)	Walnut	17 Jun	1979
Emiel	Puttemans	Bel 47	27:39.58	2)	Munich	03 Sep	1972
Mike	McLeod	GB 52	27:39.76	1)	Brussels	04 Sep	1979
Ron	Clarke	Aus 37	27:39.89	1)	Oslo	14 Jul	1965
Ilie	Floroiu	Rom 52	27:40.06	7)	Prague	29 Aug	1978
	Viren		27:40.38	1)	Montreal	26 Jul	1976
Enn	Sellik	USR 54	27:40.61	8)	Prague	29 Aug	1978
Miruts	Yifter	Eti 44	27:40.96	3)	Munich	03 Sep	1972
	Foster		27:41.23	2)	Brussels	04 Sep	1979
Jos	Hermens	Hol 50	27:41.25	2)	Stockholm	04 Jul	1977
Knut	Kvalheim	Nor 50	27:41.26	9)	Prague	29 Aug	1978
Léon	Schots	Bel 52	27:41.34	3)	Brussels	04 Sep	1979
	Tebroke		27:41.5	1)	Bamberg	27 Aug	1977
Aleksandr	Fyedotkin	USR 55	27:41.89	4)	Brussels	04 Sep	1979
Mike	Musyoki	Ken 56	27:41.92	2)	Helsinki	30 Jun	1977
Dick	Quax	NZ 48	27:41.95	4)	London	09 Sep	1977
Detlef	Uhlemann	Ger 49	27:42.09	3)	Stockholm	04 Jul	1977
Carlos	Lopes	Por 47	27:42.65	1)	Stockholm	09 Aug	1976
Franco	Fava	Ita 52	27:42.65	3)	Helsinki	30 Jun	1977
	Yifter		27:42.69	1)	Moscow	27 Jul	1980
Frank	Zimmermann	Ger 55	27:42.8 m	2)	Troisdorf	28 Apr	1979
	Viren		27:42.95	1)	Helsinki	23 Jun	1976
	Hermens		27:43.01	5)	London	09 Sep	1977
Ian	Stewart	GB 49	27:43.03	6)	London	09 Sep	1977
Toshihiko	Seko	Jap 56	27:43.44	1)	Stockholm	07 Jul	1980
Tony	Simmons	GB 48	27:43.59	4)	Helsinki	30 Jun	1977
Steve	Prefontaine	USA 51	27:43.6	1)	Eugene	27 Apr	1974
Bernie	Ford	GB 52	27:43.74	7)	London	09 Sep	1977
	Yifter		27:44.2	1)	Moscow	21 Jul	1979
Kaarlo	Maaninka	Fin 53	27:44.28	2)	Moscow	27 Jul	1980
	Antipov		27:44.58	2)	Stockholm	07 Jul	1980

(50 performances by 35 performers)

WORLD YEAR LISTS 1981-2000

1981

5000 metres

Henry	Rono	Ken 52	13:06.20	1)	Knarvik	13 Sep
Hansjörg	Kunze	GDR 59	13:10.40	1)	Rieti	09 Sep
Valeriy	Abramov	USR 56	13:11.99	2)	Rieti	09 Sep
Thomas	Wessinghage	Ger 52	13:13.47	4)	Rieti	09 Sep
Julian	Goater	GB 53	13:15.59	2)	London	11 Sep
Bill	McChesney	USA 59	13:15.77	1)	Eugene	16 May
Eamonn	Coghlan	Ire 52	13:19.13	1)	Zurich	19 Aug
Venanzio	Ortis	Ita 55	13:19.19	5)	Rieti	09 Sep
Fernanzdo	Mamede	Por 51	13:19.2	1)	Lisbon	26 Apr
Markus	Ryffel	Swi 55	13:19.74	2)	Zurich	19 Aug

10,000 metres

Fernando	Mamede	Por 51	27:27.7	1)	Lisbon	30 May
Werner	Schildhauer	GDR 59	27:38.43	1)	Rome	04 Sep
Mohamed	Kedir	Eti 53	27:39.44	2)	Rome	04 Sep
Alberto	Salazar	USA 58	27:40.69	3)	Rome	04 Sep
Henry	Rono	Ken 52	27:40.78	1)	Brussels	28 Aug
Venanzio	Ortis	Ita 55	27:42.70	4)	Rome	04 Sep
Geoff	Smith	GB 53	27:43.76	1)	Draesden	13 Jun
Martti	Vainio	Fin 50	27:45.50	1)	Oslo	11 Jul
Bill	McChesney	USA 59	27:47.25	2)	Oslo	11 Jul
Julian	Goater	GB 53	27:47.54	2)	Brussels	28 Aug

1982

5000 metres

David	Moorcroft	GB 53	13:00.41	1)	Oslo	07 Jul
Wodajo	Bulti	Eti 57	13:07.29	1)	Rieti	16 Sep
Antonio	Leitao	Por 60	13:07.70	2)	Rieti	16 Sep
Henry	Rono	Ken 52	13:08.97	1)	Stockholm	06 Jul
Peter	Koech	Ken 58	13:09.50	2)	Stockholm	06 Jul
Alberto	Salazar	USA 58	13:11.93	3)	Stockholm	06 Jul
Hansjörg	Kunze	GDR 59	13:12.53	1)	Zurich	18 Aug
Werner	Schildhauer	GDR 59	13:12.54	2)	Zurich	18 Aug
Thomas	Wessinghage	Ger 52	13:12.78	3)	Zurich	18 Aug
Matt	Centrowitz	USA 55	13:12.91	1)	Eugene	05 Jun

10,000 metres

Fernando	Mamede	Por 51	27:22.95	1)	Paris	09 Jul
Carlos	Lopes	Por 47	27:24.39	1)	Oslo	26 Jun
Alberto	Salazar	USA 58	27:25.61	2)	Oslo	26 Jun
Alex	Hagelsteens	Bel 56	27:26.95	3)	Oslo	26 Jun
Henry	Rono	Ken 52	27:28.67	4)	Oslo	26 Jun
Werner	Schildhauer	GDR 59	27:33.66	1)	Jena	29 May
Julian	Goater	GB 53	27:34.58	5)	Oslo	26 Jun
Gabriel	Kamau	Ken 58	27:36.2	1)	Walnut	24 Apr
Mark	Nenow	USA 57	27:36.7	2)	Walnut	24 Apr
Gidamis	Shahanga	Tan 57	27:38.1	3)	Walnut	24 Apr

1983

5000 metres

Fernando	Mamede	Por 51	13:08.54	1)	Tokyo	17 Sep
Antonio	Leitao	Por 60	13:14.13	2)	Rieti	04 Sep
Doug	Padilla	USA 56	13:17.69	1)	Oslo	28 Jun
Antonio	Prieto	Spa 58	13:18.53	3)	Rieti	04 Sep
Thomas	Wessinghage	Ger 52	13:18.86	2)	Oslo	28 Jun
Jim	Spivey	USA 60	13:19.24	3)	Oslo	28 Jun
Markus	Ryffel	Swi 55	13:19.38	3)	Zurich	24 Aug
Jim	Hill	USA 61	13:19.73	4)	Oslo	28 Jun
Martti	Vainio	Fin 50	13:20.07	4)	Zurich	24 Aug
Eamonn	Martin	GB 58	13:20.94	5)	Oslo	28 Jun

Indoors (250 m. track):

Hansjörg	Kunze	GDR 59	13:13.3 m	1)	Senftenberg	20 Feb

10,000 metres

Carlos	Lopes	Por 47	27:23.44	1)	Oslo	09 Jul
Werner	Schildhauer	GDR 59	27:24.95	1)	Jena	28 May
Fernando	Mamede	Por 51	27:25.13	2)	Oslo	09 Jul
Hansjörg	Kunze	GDR 59	27:30.69	2)	Jena	28 May
Nick	Rose	GB 51	27:31.19	3)	Oslo	09 Jul
Alberto	Cova	Ita 58	27:37.59	2)	Lausanne	30 Jun
Steve	Jones	GB 55	27:39.14	4)	Oslo	09 Jul
Antonio	Prieto	Spa 58	27:43.66	3)	Lausanne	30 Jun
Masanari	Shintaku	Jap 57	27:44.5 m	1)	Tokyo	29 Nov
Gidamis	Shahanga	Tan 57	27:46.93	3)h1	Helsinki	07 Aug

1984

5000 metres

Said	Aouita	Mor 59	13:04.78	1)	Florence	13 Jun
Markus	Ryffel	Swi 55	13:07.54	2)	Los Angeles	11 Aug
Antonio	Leitao	Por 60	13:09.20	3)	Los Angeles	11 Aug
Wodajo	Bulti	Eti 57	13:10.08	2)	Florence	13 Jun
Tim	Hutchings	GB 58	13:11.50	4)	Los Angeles	11 Aug
Fernando	Mamede	Por 51	13:12.83	1)	Oslo	28 Jun
Paul	Kipkoech	Ken 62	13:14.40	5)	Los Angeles	11 Aug
Martti	Vainio	Fin 50	13:16.02	2)	Oslo	28 Jun
Carlos	Lopes	Por 47	13:16.38	3)	Oslo	28 Jun
John	Treacy	Ire 57	13:16.81	4)	Oslo	28 Jun

10,000 metres

Fernando	Mamede	Por 51	27:13.81	1)	Stockholm	02 Jul
Carlos	Lopes	Por 47	27:17.48	2)	Stockholm	02 Jul
Hansjörg	Kunze	GDR 59	27:33.10	1)	Potsdam	05 May
Mark	Nenow	USA 57	27:40.56	3)	Stockholm	02 Jul
Martti	Vainio	Fin 50	27:41.75	1)	Florence	13 Jun
Paul	Cummings	USA 53	27:43.7 m	1)	Walnut	28 Apr
Alberto	Salazar	USA 58	27:45.5 m	2)	Walnut	28 Apr
Mike	Musyoki	Ken 56	27:46.0 m	3)	Walnut	28 Apr
Garry	Bjorklund	USA 51	27:46.9 m	4)	Walnut	28 Apr
Tony	Sandoval	USA 54	27:47.0 m	5)	Walnut	28 Apr

1985

5000 metres

Said	Aouita	Mor 59	13:00.40	1)	Oslo	27 Jul
Sydney	Maree	USA 56	13:01.15	2)	Oslo	27 Jul
Alberto	Cova	Ita 58	13:10.06	3)	Oslo	27 Jul
Bruce	Bickford	USA 57	13:13.49	2)	Oslo	27 Jun
Doug	Padilla	USA 56	13:15.44	1)	Helsinki	04 Jul
José Luis	González	Spa 57	13:15.90	3)	Oslo	27 Jun
Markus	Ryffel	Swi 55	13:17.27	2)	Helsinki	04 Jul
Paul	Kipkoech	Ken 63	13:17.64	1)	Seoul	14 Sep
Dietmar	Millonig	Aut 55	13:17.91	4)	Helsinki	04 Jul
Nat	Muir	GB 58	13:18.47	4)	Oslo	27 Jul

10,000 metres

Bruce	Bickford	USA 57	27:37.17	1)	Stockholm	02 Jul
Mark	Nenow	USA 57	27:40.85	2)	Stockholm	02 Jul
Ed	Eyestone	USA 61	27:41.05	1)	Walnut	27 Apr
Fernando	Mamede	Por 51	27:41.09	3)	Stockholm	02 Jul
Toshihiko	Seko	Jap 56	27:42.17	4)	Stockholm	02 Jul
Simeon	Kigen	Ken 61	27:43.9 m	2)	Walnut	27 Apr
Francesco	Panetta	Ita 63	27:44.65	5)	Stockholm	02 Jul
Jesús	Herrera	Mex 62	27:45.0 m	3)	Wanut	27 Apr
Martin	Pitayo	Mex 60	27:45.8 m	4)	Walnut	27 Apr
Alberto	Cova	Ita 58	27:49.36	6)	Stockholm	02 Jul

1986

5000 metres

Said	Aouita	Mor 59	13:00.86	1)	La Coruña	06 Aug
Jack	Buckner	GB 61	13:10.15	1)	Stuttgart	31 Aug
Stefano	Mei	Ita 63	13:11.57	2)	Stuttgart	31 Aug
Tim	Hutchings	GB 58	13:12.88	3)	Stuttgart	31 Aug
Evgeni	Ignatov	Bul 59	13:13.15	4)	Stuttgart	31 Aug
Sydney	Maree	USA 56	13:14.62	3)	Rome	10 Sep
Vincent	Rousseau	Bel 62	13:15.01	4)	Rome	10 Sep
Antonio	Leitao	Por 60	13:15.18	5)	Rome	10 Sep
Pierre	Délèze	Swi 58	13:15.31	1)	Helsinki	07 Jul
Alberto	Cova	Ita 58	13:15.86	1)	Zurich	13 Aug

10,000 metres

Mark	Nenow	USA 57	27:20.56	1)	Brussels	05 Sep
Said	Aouita	Mor 59	27:26.11	1)	Oslo	05 Jul
Hansjörg	Kunze	GDR 59	27:34.68	1)	Jena	31 May
Salvatore	Antibo	Ita 62	27:39.52	3)	Oslo	05 Jul
Paul	Kipkoech	Ken 63	27:43.31	1)	Aachen	30 May
Frank	Heine	GDR 63	27:43.89	2)	Jena	31 May
Stefano	Mei	Ita 63	27:43.97	4)	Oslo	05 Jul
Some	Muge	Ken 59	27:44.53	2)	Aachen	30 May
Martti	Vainio	Fin 50	27:44.57	5)	Oslo	05 Jul
Toshihiko	Seko	Jap 56	27:45.45	6)	Oslo	05 Jul

1987

5000 metres

Said	Aouita	Mor 59	12:58.39	1)	Rome	22 Jul
Jack	Buckner	GB 61	13:10.48	1)	Zurich	19 Aug
José	Luis González	Spa 57	13:12.34	1)	Oslo	04 Jul
José	Manuel Abascal	Spa 58	13:12.49	2)	Oslo	04 Jul
Frank	O'Mara	Ire 60	13:13.02	3)	Oslo	04 Jul
Arturo	Barrios	Mex 63	13:13.52	4)	Oslo	04 Jul
Féthi	Baccouche	Tun 60	13:13.94	5)	Oslo	04 Jul
Pascal	Thiébaut	Fra 59	13:14.60	6)	Oslo	04 Jul
Sydney	Maree	USA 56	13:15.07	7)	Oslo	04 Jul
John	Gregorek	USA 60	13:17.44	8)	Oslo	04 Jul

10,000 metres

Francesco	Panetta	Ita 63	27:26.95	1)	Stockholm	30 Jun
Wodajo	Bulti	Eti 57	27:29.41	1)	Helsinki	02 Jul
Jean-Louis	Prianon	Fra 60	27:34.38	2)	Helsinki	02 Jul
Takeyuki	Nakayama	Jap 59	27:35.33	3)	Helsinki	02 Jul
Paul	Kipkoech	Ken 63	27:38.63	1)	Rome	29 Aug
Hansjörg	Kunze	GDR 59	27:39.60	1)	Potsdam	05 Jun
Xolile	Yawa	SA 62	27:39.65	1)	Port Elizabeth	12 Dec
Martti	Vainio	Fin 50	27:42.65	4)	Helsinki	02 Jul
Haji	Bulbula	Eti 61	27:43.04	5)	Helsinki	02 Jul
Paul	Arpin	Fra 60	27:47.05	6)	Helsinki	02 Jul

1988

5000 metres

John	Ngugi	Ken 62	13:11.70	1)	Seoul	01 Oct
Dieter	Baumann	Ger 65	13:15.52	2)	Seoul	01 Oct
José	Regalo	Por 63	13:15.62	1)	Brussels	19 Aug
Hansjörg	Kunze	GDR 59	13:15.73	3)	Seoul	01 Oct
Sydney	Maree	USA 56	13:15.85	1)	Hengelo	14 Aug
Domingos	Castro	Por 63	13:16.09	4)	Seoul	01 Oct
Salvatore	Antibo	Ita 62	13:16.1 m	1)	Palermo	05 Sep
Yobes	Ondieki	Ken 61	13:17.06	2)	Brussels	19 Aug
John	Doherty	Ire 61	13:17.14	1)	Stockholm	05 Jul
Pascal	Thiébaut	Fra 59	13:17.48	1)	Oslo	02 Jul

10,000 metres

M.Brahim	Boutayeb	Mor 67	27:21.46	1)	Seoul	26 Sep
Eamonn	Martin	GB 58	27:23.06	1)	Oslo	02 Jul
Salvatore	Antibo	Ita 62	27:23.55	2)	Seoul	26 Sep
Arturo	Barrios	Mex 63	27:25.07	3)	Oslo	02 Jul
Kipkemboi	Kimeli	Ken 66	27:25.16	3)	Seoul	26 Sep
Hansjörg	Kunze	GDR 59	27:26.00	4)	Oslo	02 Jul
Francesco	Panetta	Ita 63	27:33.14	1)	Brussels	19 Aug
Jean-Louis	Prianon	Fra 60	27:36.43	4)	Seoul	26 Sep
Paul	Arpino	Fra 60	27:39.36	7)	Seoul	26 Sep
Boniface	Merande	Ken 62	27:40.36	1)	Tokyo	13 May

1989

5000 metres

Yobes	Ondieki	Ken 61	13 :04.24	1)	Oslo	01 Jul
Said	Aouita	Mor 59	13:06.36	1)	Monaco	01 Sep
Arturo	Barrios	Mex 63	13:07.79	1)	London	14 Jul
M.Brahim	Boutayeb	Mor 67	13:12.10	1)	La Coruña	25 Jul
Sydney	Maree	USA 56	13:13.84	1)	Brussels	25 Aug
John	Ngugi	Ken 62	13:14.27	2)	La Coruña	25 Jul
Salvatore	Antibo	Ita 62	13:14.30	1)	Grosseto	10 Aug
Domingos	Castro	Por 63	13:14.41	2)	Brussels	25 Aug
John	Doherty	Ire 61	13:15.09	3)	La Coruña	25 Jul
Dionisio	Castro	Por 63	13:16.90	4)	Brussels	25 Aug

10,000 metres

Arturo	Barrios	Mex 63	27:08.23	1)	Berlin	18 Aug
Salvatore	Antibo	Ita 62	27:16.50	1)	Helsinki	29 Jun
Addis	Abebe	Eti 70	27:17.82	2)	Helsinki	29 Jun
Francesco	Panetta	Ita 63	27:24.16	3)	Helsinki	29 Jun
John	Ngugi	Ken 62	27:28.07	2)	Brussels	25 Aug
Domingos	Castro	Por 63	27:36.00	2)	Stockholm	03 Jul
Kipkemboi	Kimeli	Ken 66	27:38.29	3)	Stockholm	03 Jul
M.Brahim	Boutayeb	Mor 67	27:42.25	3)	Brussels	25 Aug
Mark	Nenow	USA 57	27:42.64	4)	Brussels	25 Aug
Dionisio	Castro	Por 63	27:49.69	4)	Stockholm	03 Jul

1990

5000 metres

Salvatore	Antibo	Ita 62	13:05.59	1)	Bologna	18 Jul
Yobes	Ondieki	Ken 61	13:05.60	1)	Brussels	10 Aug
Mohammed	Issangar	Mor 64	13:08.51	1)	London	20 Jul
Arturo	Barrios	Mex 62	13:08.52	2)	London	20 Jul
Khalid	Skah	Mor 67	13:09.55	1)	Stockholm	02 Jul
John	Ngugi	Ken 62	13:11.14	2)	Brussels	10 Aug
Hammou	Boutayeb	Mor 56	13:11.69	2)	Stockholm	02 Jul
M.Brahim	Boutayeb	Mor 67	13:12.26	1)	Rieti	09 Sep
Dionisio	Castro	Por 63	13:13.59	4)	Zurich	15 Aug
John	Doherty	Ire 61	13:14.17	4)	Stockholm	02 Jul

10,000 metres

Arturo	Barrios	Mex 62	27:18.22	1)	Berlin	17 Aug
John	Ngugi	Ken 62	27:19.15	1)	Koblenz	04 Sep
Salvatore	Antibo	Ita 62	27:25.16	1)	Oslo	14 Jul
Hammou	Boutayeb	Mor 56	27:25.48	2)	Oslo	14 Jul
Khalid	Skah	Mor 67	27:29.27	1)	Brussels	10 Aug
Thierry	Pantel	Fra 64	27:31.16	3)	Oslo	14 Jul
Are	Nakkim	Nor 64	27:32.52	4)	Oslo	14 Jul
Antonio	Orieto	Spa 58	27:37.49	5)	Oslo	14 Jul
Alejandro	Gómez	Spa 67	27:41.30	6)	Oslo	14 Jul
Addis	Abebe	Eti 70	27:42.65	2)	Seattle	25 Jul

1991

5000 metres

Yobes	Ondieki	Ken 61	13:01.82	1)	Zurich	07 Aug
Ibrahim	Kinuthia	Ken 63	13:09.76	1)	Rome	17 Jul
Salvatore	Antobi	Ita 62	13:10.10	2)	Rome	17 Jul
M.Brahim	Boutayeb	Mor 67	13:10.44	3)	Rome	17 Jul
Richard	Chelimo	Ken 72	13:11.76	4)	Rome	17 Jul
Ondoro	Osoro	Ken 67	13:11.77	5)	Rome	17 Jul
Robert	Denmark	GB 68	13:13.01	6)	Rome	17 Jul
Fita	Bayissa	Eti 72	13:16.64	2)	Tokyo	01 Sep
Mikhail	Dasko	Rus 61	13:16.73	1)	Getxo	29 Jun
Dionisio	Castro	Por 63	13:17.25	2)	Getxo	29 Jun

10,000 metres

Richard	Chelimo	Ken 72	27:11.18	1)	Hengelo	25 Jun
John	Ngugi	Ken 62	27:11.62	1)	Brussels	13 Sep
Khalid	Skah	Mor 67	27:23.29	1)	Oslo	06 Jul
Salvatore	Antibo	Ita 62	27:24.55	2)	Oslo	06 Jul
Thomas	Osano	Ken 70	27:28.87	3)	Oslo	06 Jul
Julius	Korir II	Ken 58	27:34.96	1)	Berlin	10 Sep
Moses	Tanui	Ken 65	27:35.89	2)	Berlin	10 Sep
Joseph	Keino	Ken 63	27:36.88	3)	Berlin	10 Sep
Arturo	Barrios	Mex 63	27:37.36	4)	Oslo	06 Jul
Wilson	Omwoyo	Ken 65	27:37.36	4)	Berlin	10 Sep

1992

5000 metres

Moses	Kiptanui	Ken 70	13:00.93	1)	Brussels	28 Aug
Yobes	Ondieki	Ken 61	13:03.58	1)	Lausanne	08 Jul
Paul	Bitok	Ken 70	13:08.89	1)	Oslo	04 Jul
Dieter	Baumann	Ger 65	13:09.03	1)	Seville	06 Jun
Khalid	Skah	Mor 67	13:09.10	2)	Seville	06 Jun
Ian	Hamer	GB 65	13:09.80	1)	Rome	09 Jun
Salvatore	Antibo	Ita 62	13:10.08	2)	Rome	09 Jun
Robert	Denmark	GB 68	13:10.24	3)	Rome	09 Jun
Richard	Chelimo	Ken 72	13:10.46	1)	Monaco	11 Aug
Jack	Buckner	GB 61	13:10.47	4)	Rome	09 Jun

10,000 metres

Fita	Bayissa	Eti 72	27:14.26	1)	Oslo	04 Jul
Richard	Chelimo	Ken 72	27:15.53	2)	Oslo	04 Jul
Antonio	Martins	Fra 63	27:22.78	3)	Oslo	04 Jul
Arturo	Barrios	Mex 63	27:34.60	1)	Berlin	21 Aug
Joseph	Keino	Ken 63	27:35.77	2)	Berlin	21 Aug
Addis	Abebe	Eti 70	27:38.37	4)	Oslo	04 Jul
Martin	Pitayo	Mex 60	27:38.49	5)	Oslo	04 Jul
Domingos	Castro	Por 63	27:39.03	6)	Oslo	04 Jul
Wilson	Omwoyo	Ken 65	27:40.67	2)	Jena	28 May
Francesco	Panetta	Ita 63	27:45.46	2)	Brussels	28 Aug

1993

5000 metres

Ismael	Kirui	Ken 75	13:02.75	1)	Stuttgart	16 Aug
Haile	Gebrselassie	Eti 73	13:03.17	2)	Stuttgart	16 Aug
Khalid	Skah	Mor 67	13:04.67	1)	Zurich	04 Aug
Yobes	Ondieki	Ken 61	13:05.09	2)	Zurich	04 Aug
Richard	Chelimo	Ken 72	13:05.14	3)	Zurich	04 Aug
Fita	Bayissa	Eti 72	13:05.40	3)	Stuttgart	16 Aug
Bikila	Worku	Eti 70	13:06.64	4)	Stuttgart	16 Aug
Francesco	Panetta	Ita 63	13:06.76	6)	Zurich	04 Aug
William	Sigei	Ken 69	13:07.35	2)	Lausanne	07 Jul
Aissa	Belaout	Alg 68	13:08.03	2)	Villeneuve d'Ascq	02 Jul

10,000 metres

Yobes	Ondieki	Ken 61	26:58.38	1)	Oslo	10 Jul
Richard	Chelimo	Ken 72	27:07.91	1)	Stockholm	05 Jul
William	Sigei	Ken 69	27:16.81	2)	Oslo	10 Jul
Khalid	Skah	Mor 67	27:17.74	1)	Brussels	03 Sep
Moses	Tanui	Ken 65	27:18.32	2)	Brussels	03 Sep
Paul	Tergat	Ken 69	27:18.43	3)	Brussels	03 Sep
Vincent	Rousseau	Bel 62	27:23.18	5)	Brussels	03 Sep
Ondoro	Osoro	Ken 67	27:24.24	6)	Brussels	03 Sep
Fita	Bayissa	Eti 72	27:26.90	2)	Durban	24 Jun
Haile	Gebrselassie	Eti 73	27:30.17	3)	Durban	24 Jun

1994

5000 metres

Haile	Gebrselassie	Eti 73	12:56.96	1)	Hengelo	04 Jun
Khalid	Skah	Mor 67	13:00.54	1)	Villeneuve d'Ascq	08 Jul
Bob	Kennedy	USA 70	13:02.93	2)	Oslo	22 Jul
Brahim	Lahlafi	Mor 68	13:03.36	3)	Oslo	22 Jul
Noureddine	Morceli	Alg 70	13:03.85	1)	Zurich	17 Aug
Salah	Hissou	Mor 72	13:04.93	4)	Oslo	22 Jul
William	Sigei	Ken 69	13:06.72	1)	London	15 Jul
Paul	Bitok	Ken 70	13:07.30	2)	London	15 Jul
Simon	Chemoiywo	Ken 69	13:07.57	1)	Monaco	02 Aug
Fita	Bayissa	Eti 72	13:07.70	2)	Zurich	17 Aug

10,000 metres

William	Sigei	Ken 69	26:52.23	1)	Oslo	22 Jul
Haile	Gebrselassie	Eti 73	27:15.00	1)	Lausanne	06 Jul
William	Kiptum	Ken 71	27:17.20	2)	Oslo	22 Jul
Armando	Quintanilla	Mex 68	27:18.59	3)	Oslo	22 Jul
Aloÿs	Nizigama	Bur 66	27:20.51	4)	Oslo	22 Jul
Salah	Hissou	Mor 72	27:21.75	2)	Brussels	19 Aug
Paul	Tergat	Ken 69	27:23.89	4)	Brussels	19 Aug
Ondoro	Osoro	Ken 67	27:28.36	5)	Brussels	19 Aug
Mathias	Ntawulikura	Rwa 64	27:36.15	6)	Brussels	19 Aug
Khalid	Skah	Mor 67	27:38.74	1)	London	09 Sep

1995

5000 metres

Haile	Gebrselassie	Eti 73	12:44.39	1)	Zurich	16 Aug
Moses	Kiptanui	Ken 70	12:55.30	1)	Rome	08 Jun
Daniel	Komen	Ken 76	12:56.15	2)	Rome	08 Jun
Worku	Bikila	Eti 70	12:57.23	3)	Rome	08 Jun
Dieter	Baumann	Ger 65	13:01.72	2)	Zurich	16 Aug
Salah	Hissou	Mor 72	13:02.25	4)	Rome	08 Jun
Ismael	Kirui	Ken 75	13:02.75	3)	Zurich	16 Aug
Shem	Kororia	Ken 72	13:02.80	1)	Stockholm	10 Jul
William	Kalya	Ken 74	13:03.08	2)	Stockholm	10 Jul
Khalid	Boulami	Mor 69	13:03.21	3)	Berlin	01 Sep

10,000 metres

Haile	Gebrselassie	Eti 73	26:43.53	1)	Hengelo	05 Jun
Worku	Bikila	Eti 70	27:06.44	1)	Brussels	25 Aug
Ismael	Kirui	Ken 75	27:06.59	2)	Brussels	25 Aug
Salah	Hissou	Mor 72	27:09.30	3)	Brussels	25 Aug
Josephat	Machuka	Ken 73	27:10.34	4)	Brussels	25 Aug
Paul	Tergat	Ken 69	27:14.08	5)	Brussels	25 Aug
Khalid	Skah	Mor 67	27:14.53	2)	Göteborg	08 Aug
Shem	Kororia	Ken 72	27:18.02	6)	Brussels	25 Aug
Aloÿs	Nizigama	Bur 66	27:20.38	1)	London	07 Jul
Simon	Chemoiywo	Ken 68	27:25.82	1)	Knoxville	06 Apr

1996

5000 metres

Daniel	Komen	Ken 76	12:45.09	1)	Zurich	14 Aug
Salah	Hissou	Mor 72	12:50.80	1)	Rome	05 Jun
Haile	Gebrselassie	Eti 73	12:52.70	2)	Zurich	14 Aug
Philip	Mosima	Ken 77	12:53.72	2)	Rome	05 Jun
Paul	Tergat	Ken 69	12:54.72	3)	Zurich	14 Aug
Moses	Kiptanui	Ken 70	12:54.85	3)	Rome	05 Jun
Khalid	Boulami	Mor 69	12:55.76	4)	Zurich	14 Aug
Bob	Kennedy	USA 70	12:58.21	5)	Zurich	14 Aug
Ismail	Sghyr	Mor 72	12:58.99	6)	Zurich	14 Aug
Tom	Nyariki	Ken 71	12:59.19	4)	Rome	05 Jun

10,000 metres

Salah	Hissou	Mor 72	26:38.08	1)	Brussels	23 Aug
Paul	Tergat	Ken 69	26:54.41	2)	Brussels	23 Aug
Paul	Koech	Ken 69	26:56.78	3)	Brussels	23 Aug
Haile	Gebrselassie	Eti 73	27:07.34	1)	Atlanta	29 Jul
William	Kiptum	Ken 71	27:18.84	4)	Brussels	23 Aug
Aloÿs	Nizigama	Bur 66	27:25.13	5)	Brussels	23 Aug
Mathias	Ntawulikura	Rwa 64	27:25.48	6)	Brussels	23 Aug
Luke	Kipkosgei	Ken 75	27:26.12	1)	Melbourne	25 Nov
Julius	Gitahi	Ken 78	27:28.60	1)	Konosu	05 Oct
Shem	Kororia	Ken 72	27:30.37	1)	Bratislava	29 May

1997

5000 metres

Daniel	Komen	Ken 76	12:39.74	1)	Brussels	22 Aug
Haile	Gebrselassie	Eti 73	12:41.86	1)	Zurich	13 Aug
Paul	Tergat	Ken 69	12:49.87	3)	Zurich	13 Aug
Salah	Hissou	Mor 72	12:52.39	2)	Rome	05 Jun
Khalid	Boulami	Mor 69	12:53.41	4)	Zurich	13 Aug
Dieter	Baumann	Ger 65	12:54.70	5)	Zurich	13 Aug
Tom	Nyariki	Ken 71	12:55.94	1)	Stockholm	07 Jul
Paul	Koech	Ken 69	12:56.29	6)	Zurich	13 Aug
Ismail	Sghyr	Mor 72	13:00.62	3)	Stockholm	07 Jul
David	Chelule	Ken 77	13:02.52	7)	Zurich	13 Aug

10,000 metres

Paul	Tergat	Ken 69	26:27.85	1)	Brussels	22 Aug
Haile	Gebrselassie	Eti 73	26:31.32	1)	Oslo	04 Jul
Paul	Koech	Ken 69	26:36.26	2)	Brussels	22 Aug
Salah	Hissou	Mor 72	27:09.07	3)	Brussels	22 Aug
Mohammed	Mourhit	Bel 70	27:17.09	2)	Oslo	04 Jul
Dieter	Baumann	Ger 65	27:21.53	1)	Barakaldo	05 Apr
Assefa	Mezegebu	Eti 78	27:25.01	1)	Hengelo	31 May
Jon	Brown	GB 71	27:27.47	2)	Hengelo	31 May
Elijah	Korir	Ken 78	27:27.87	5)	Brussels	22 Aug
Luke	Kipkosgei	Ken 75	27:29.44	1)	Melbourne	18 Dec

1998

5000 metres

Haile	Gebrselassie	Eti 73	12:39.36	1)	Helsinki	13 Jun
Assefa	Mezegebu	Eti 78	12:53.84	1)	Brussels	28 Aug
Daniel	Komen	Ken 76	12:54.82	2)	Brussels	28 Aug
Luke	Kipkosgei	Ken 75	12:57.32	2)	Berlin	01 Sep
Salah	Hissou	Mor 72	12:57.73	1)	Saint-Denis	04 Jun
Paul	Tergat	Ken 69	12:58.74	4)	Zurich	12 Aug
Million	Wolde	Eti 79	12:59.39	5)	Zurich	12 Aug
Tom	Nyariki	Ken 71	13:00.04	6)	Zurich	12 Aug
Brahim	Lahlafi	Mor 68	13:00.56	4)	Berlin	01 Sep
Khalid	Boulami	Mor 69	13:00.59	2)	Stockholm	05 Aug

Indoors:

Daniel	Komen	Ken 76	12:51.48	1)	Stockholm	19 Feb

10,000 metres

Haile	Gebrselassie	Eti 73	26:22.75	1)	Hengelo	01 Jun
Paul	Tergat	Ken 69	26:46.44	1)	Brussels	28 Aug
Paul	Koech	Ken 69	26:47.89	2)	Brussels	28 Aug
Julius	Gitahi	Ken 78	27:11.17	1)	Kobe	26 Apr
Fabián	Roncero	Spa 70	27:14.44	1)	Lisbon	04 Apr
António	Pinto	Por 66	27:15.76	2)	Lisbon	04 Apr
Jon	Brown	GB 71	27:18.14	4)	Brussels	28 Aug
Mark	Bett	Ken 76	27:18.66	5)	Brussels	28 Aug
Simon	Maina Munyi	Ken 78	27:21.14	2)	Kobe	26 Apr
Luke	Kipkosgei	Ken 75	27:22.54	1)	Melbourne	05 Dec

1999

5000 metres

Haile	Gebrselassie	Eti 73	12:49.64	1)	Zurich	11 Aug
Salah	Hissou	Mor 72	12:52.53	1)	Milan	09 Jun
Daniel	Komen	Ken 76	12:55.16	1)	Rome	07 Jul
Paul	Tergat	Ken 69	12:55.37	2)	Rome	07 Jul
Benjamin	Limo	Ken 74	12:55.86	3)	Zurich	11 Aug
David	Chelule	Ken 77	12:57.79	5)	Rome	07 Jul
Sammy	Kipketer	Ken 81	12:58.10	2)	Oslo	30 Jun
Richard	Limo	Ken 80	12:58.15	6)	Rome	07 Jul
Mohammed	Mourhit	Bel 70	12:58.45	7)	Rome	07 Jul
Brahim	Lahlafi	Mor 68	12:59.09	4)	Seville	28 Aug

10,000 metres

Charles	Kamathi	Ken 78	26:51.49	1)	Brussels	03 Sep
Mohammed	Mourhit	Bel 70	26:52.30	2)	Brussels	03 Sep
Habte	Jifar	Eti 76	27:06.45	1)	Hengelo	30 May
Paul	Tergat	Ken 69	27:10.08	1)	Stockholm	30 Jul
Paul	Koech	Ken 69	27:10.38	3)	Brussels	03 Sep
Ismail	Sghyr	Mor 72	27:12.39	2)	Stockholm	30 Jul
António	Pinto	Por 66	27:12.47	3)	Stockholm	30 Jul
Girma	Tolla	Eti 75	27:13.48	2)	Hengelo	30 May
Julius	Gitahi	Ken 78	27:17.66	3)	Hengelo	30 May
Hassefa	Mezegebu	Eti 78	27:18.28	4)	Hengelo	30 May

2000

5000 metres

Brahim	Lahlafi	Mor 68	12:49.28	1)	Brussels	25 Aug
Mohammed	Mourhit	Bel 70	12:49.71	2)	Brussels	25 Aug
Ali Saidi	Sief	Alg 78	12:50.86	1)	Rome	30 Jun
Sammy	Kipketer	Ken 81	12:54.07	2)	Rome	30 Jun
Paul	Tergat	Ken 69	12:55.18	3)	Rome	30 Jun
Mark	Bett	Ken 76	12:55.63	2)	Oslo	28 Jul
Benjamin	Limo	Ken 74	12:55.82	3)	Oslo	28 Jul
Luke	Kipkosgei	Ken 75	12:56.50	5)	Oslo	28 Jul
Haile	Gebrselassie	Eti 73	12:57.95	1)	Zurich	11 Aug
Richard	Limo	Ken 80	12:58.70	4)	Rome	30 Jun

10,000 metres

Paul	Tergat	Ken 69	27:03.87	1)	Brussels	25 Aug
Felix	Limo	Ken 80	27:04.54	2)	Brussels	25 Aug
Patrick	Ivuti	Ken 78	27:09.79	3)	Brussels	25 Aug
Haile	Gebrselassie	Eti 73	27:18.20	1)	Sydney	25 Sep
Simon	Maina Munyi	Ken 78	27:18.95	1)	Kobe	23 Apr
Assefa	Mezegebu	Eti 78	27:19.75	3)	Sydney	25 Sep
Girma	Tolla	Eti 75	27:20.03	2)	Villeneuve d'Ascq	17 Jun
Evans	Rutto	Ken 78	27:21.32	3)	Villeneuve d'Ascq	17 Jun
José	Rios	Spa 74	27:22.20	1)	Gijón	12 Aug
William	Kalya	Ken 74	27:23.65	4)	Brussels	25 Aug

ALL TIME WORLD LIST OF BEST PERFORMANCES AS AT THE END OF 2000

5000 metres

Haile	Gebrselassie	Eti 73	12:39.36	1)	Helsinki	13 Jun	1998
Daniel	Komen	Ken 76	12:39.74	1)	Brussels	22 Aug	1997
	Gebrselassie		12:41.86	1)	Zurich	13 Aug	1997
	Gebrselassie		12:44.39	1)	Zurich	16 Aug	1995
	Komen		12:44.90	2)	Zurich	13 Aug	1997
	Komen		12:45.09	1)	Zurich	14 Aug	1996
	Komen		12:48.98	1)	Rome	05 Jun	1997
Brahim	Lahlafi	Mor 68	12:49.28	1)	Brussels	25 Aug	2000
	Gebrselassie		12:49.64	1)	Zurich	11 Aug	1999

269

Mohammed	Mourhit	Bel 70	12:49.71	2)	Brussels	25 Aug	2000
Paul	Tergat	Ken 69	12:49.87	3)	Zurich	13 Aug	1997
Salah	Hissou	Mor 72	12:50.80	1)	Rome	05 Jun	1996
Ali Saidi	Sief	Alg 78	12:50.86	1)	Rome	30 Jun	2000
	Komen		12:51.60	1)	Stockholm	08 Jul	1996
	Komen		12:52.38	1)	Milan	07 Sep	1996
	Hissou		12:52.39	2)	Rome	05 Jun	1997
	Hissou		12:52.53	2)	Milan	09 Jun	1999
	Gebrselassie		12:52.70	2)	Zurich	14 Aug	1996
	Gebrselassie		12:53.19	1)	Berlin	01 Sep	1995
Khalid	Boulami	Mor 69	12:53.41	4)	Zurich	13 Aug	1997
	Hissou		12:53.45	2)	Zurich	11 Aug	1999
Philip	Mosima	Ken 77	12:53.72	2)	Rome	05 Jun	1996
Assefa	Mezegebu	Eti 78	12:53.84	1)	Brussels	28 Aug	1998
	Gebrselassie		12:53.92	1)	Oslo	30 Jun	1999
Sammy	Kipketer	Ken 81	12:54.07	2)	Rome	30 Jun	2000
	Gebrselassie		12:54.08	1)	Zurich	12 Aug	1998
	Gebrselassie		12:54.60	1)	Nuremberg	13 Jun	1997
Dieter	Baumann	Ger 65	12:54.70	5)	Zurich	13 Aug	1997
	Tergat		12:54.72	3)	Zurich	14 Aug	1996
	Komen		12:54.82	2)	Brussels	28 Aug	1998
	Hissou		12:54.83	2)	Milan	07 Sep	1996
Moses	Kiptanui	Ken 70	12:54.85	3)	Rome	05 Jun	1996
	Kipketer		12:55.03	1)	Oslo	28 Jul	2000
	Gebrselassie		12:55.14	1)	Berlin	26 Aug	1997
	Komen		12:55.16	1)	Rome	07 Jul	1999
	Komen		12:55.18	2)	Milan	09 Jun	1999
	Tergat		12:55.18	3)	Rome	30 Jun	2000
	Kiptanui		12:55.30	1)	Rome	08 Jun	1995
	Tergat		12:55.37	2)	Rome	07 Jul	1999
	Hissou		12:55.39	3)	Rome	07 Jul	1999
Mark	Bett	Ken 76	12:55.63	2)	Oslo	28 Jul	2000
	Boulami		12:55.76	4)	Zurich	14 Aug	1996
Benjamin	Limo	Ken 74	12:55.82	3)	Oslo	28 Jul	2000
	B.Limo		12:55.86	3)	Zurich	11 Aug	1999
	Hissou		12:55.93	1)	Paris	28 Jun	1996
Thomas	Nyariki	Ken 71	12:55.94	1)	Stockholm	07 Jul	1997
	Komen		12:56.15	2)	Rome	08 Jun	1995
	Lahlafi		12:56.18	4)	Oslo	28 Jul	2000
Paul	Koech	Ken 69	12:56.29	6)	Zurich	13 Aug	1997
Luke	Kipkosgei	Ken 75	12:56.50	5)	Oslo	28 Jul	2000

(50 performances by 18 performers)

Indoors:

Haile	Gebrselassie	Eti 73	12:50.38	1)	Birmingham	14 Feb	1999
Daniel	Komen	Ken 76	12:51.48	1)	Stockholm	19 Feb	1998

10,000 metres

Haile	Gebrselassie	Eti 73	26:22.75	1)	Hengelo	01 Jun	1998
Paul	Tergat	Ken 69	26:27.85	1)	Brussels	22 Aug	1997
	Gebrselassie		26:31.32	1)	Oslo	04 Jul	1997
Paul	Koech	Ken 69	26:36.26	2)	Brussels	22 Aug	1997
Salah	Hissou	Mor 72	26:38.08	1)	Brussels	23 Aug	1996
	Gebrselassie		26:43.53	1)	Hengelo	05 Jun	1995
	Tergat		26:46.44	1)	Brussels	28 Aug	1998
	P.Koech		26:47.89	2)	Brussels	28 Aug	1998
Charles	Kamathi	Ken 78	26:51.49	1)	Brussels	03 Sep	1999
William	Sigei	Ken 69	26:52.23	1)	Oslo	22 Jul	1994
Mohammed	Mourhit	Bel 70	26:52.30	2)	Brussels	03 Sep	1999

270

	Tergat		26:54.41	2)	Brussels	23 Aug	1996
	P.Koech		26:56.78	3)	Brussels	23 Aug	1996
Yobes	Ondieki	Ken61	26:58.38	1)	Oslo	10 Jul	1993
	Tergat		27:03.87	1)	Brussels	25 Aug	2000
Felix	Limo	Ken 80	27:04.54	2)	Brussels	25 Aug	2000
Worku	Bikila	Eti 68	27:06.44	1)	Brussels	25 Aug	1995
Habte	Jifar	Eti 76	27:06.45	1)	Hengelo	30 May	1999
Ismael	Kirui	Ken 75	27:06.59	2)	Brussels	25 Aug	1995
	Gebrselassie		27:07.34	1)	Atlanta	29 Jul	1996
Richard	Chelimo	Ken 72	27:07.91	1)	Stockholm	05 Jul	1993
	Tergat		27:08.17	2)	Atlanta	29 Jul	1996
Arturo	Barrios	Mex 62	27:08.23	1)	Berlin	18 Aug	1989
	Hissou		27:09.07	3)	Brussels	22 Aug	1997
	Hissou		27:09.30	3)	Brussels	25 Aug	1995
Patrick	Ivuti	Ken 78	27:09.79	3)	Brussels	25 Aug	2000
	Tergat		27:10.08	1)	Stockholm	30 Jul	1999
Josephat	Machuka	Ken 73	27:10.34	4)	Brussels	25 Aug	1995
	P.Koech		27:10.38	3)	Brussels	03 Sep	1999
Julius	Gitahi	Ken 78	27:11.17	1)	Kobe	26 Apr	1998
	Chelimo		27:11.18	1)	Hengelo	25 Jun	1991
John	Ngugi	Ken 62	27:11.62	1)	Brussels	13 Sep	1991
Ismail	Sghyr	Mor 72	27:12.39	2)	Stockholm	30 Jul	1999
António	Pinto	Por 66	27:12.47	3)	Stockholm	30 Jul	1999
	Gebrselassie		27:12.95	1)	Göteborg	08 Aug	1995
Girma	Tolla	Eti 75	27:13.48	2)	Hengelo	30 May	1999
Fernando	Mamede	Por 51	27:13.81	1)	Stockholm	02 Jul	1984
	Tergat		27:14.08	5)	Brussels	25 Aug	1995
Fita	Bayissa	Eti 72	27:14.26	1)	Oslo	04 Jul	1992
Fabián	Roncero	Spa 70	27:14.44	1)	Lisbon	04 Apr	1998
Khalid	Skah	Mor 67	27:14.53	2)	Göteborg	08 Aug	1995
	Tergat		27:14.70	3)	Göteborg	08 Aug	1995
	Gebrselassie		27:15.00	1)	Lausanne	06 Jul	1994
	Chelimo		27:15.53	2)	Oslo	04 Jul	1992
	Pinto		27:15.76	2)	Lisbon	04 Apr	1998
Salvatore	Antibo	Ita 62	27:16.50	1)	Helsinki	29 Jun	1989
	Sigei		27:16.81	2)	Oslo	10 Jul	1993
	Mourhit		27:17.09	2)	Oslo	04 Jul	1997
William	Kiptum	Ken71	27:17.20	2)	Oslo	22 Jul	1994
Carlos	Lopes	Por47	27:17.48	2)	Stockholm	02 Jul	1984

(50 performances by 28 performers)

2001

5000 metres

Richard	Limo	Ken 80	12:56.72	1)	Zurich	17 Aug	
Hailu	Mekonnen	Eti 80	12:58.57	1)	Rome	29 Jun	
Mark	Bett	Ken 76	12:58.72	2)	Zurich	17 Aug	
Sammy	Kipketer	Ken 81	12:59.34	1)	Athens	11 Jun	
Benjamin	Limo	Ken 74	12:59.53	2)	Rome	29 Jun	
John	Kibowen	Ken 69	12:59.97	3)	Athens	11 Jun	
Paul	Bitok	Ken 70	13:00.10	1)	Oslo	13 Jul	
Abiyote	Abate	Eti 80	13:00.36	5)	Rome	29 Jun	
Assefa	Mezegebu	Eti 78	13:00.86	4)	Athens	11 Jun	
Ismail	Sghyr	Fra 72	13:01.64	6)	Rome	29 Jun	

All Time List: no additional performance (q.m. 12:56.50).

271

10,000 metres

Abraham	Chebii	Ken 79	27:04.20	1)	Stanford	04 May
Benjamin	Maiyo	Ken 78	27:07.55	2)	Stanford	04 May
Luke	Kipkosgei	Ken 75	27:12.37	3)	Stanford	04 May
Mebrahtom	Keflezighi	USA 75	27:13.98	4)	Stanford	04 May
Assefa	Mezegebu	Eti 78	27:22.30	1)	Hengelo	04 Jun
Charles	Kamathi	Ken 78	27:22.58	2)	Hengelo	04 Jun
Girma	Tolla	Eti 75	27:22.84	3)	Hengelo	04 Jun
Mark	Bett	Ken 76	27:24.68	1)	Brussels	24 Aug
Richard	Limo	Ken 80	27:25.27	4)	Hengelo	04 Jun
Robert	Kipchumba	Ken 84	27:25.55	2)	Brussels	24 Aug

All Time List: no additional performance (q.m. 27:17.48).

STATISTICS
WOMEN

3000 metres

Lyudmila	Bragina	USR 43	8:27.12	1)	College Park	07 Aug	1976
Grete	Waitz	Nor 53	8:32.1m	1)	Oslo	27 Jun	1978
Svyetlana	Ulmasova	USR 53	8:33.16	1)	Prague	29 Aug	1978
Natalia	Marasescu	Rom 52	8:33.53	2)	Prague	29 Aug	1978
	Waitz		8:34.33	3)	Prague	29 Aug	1978
	Waitz		8:36.8m	1)	Oslo	02 Aug	1977
	Maresescu		8:37.62	1)	Aarhus	05 Jul	1978
	Waitz		8:37.8m	1)	Oslo	03 Aug	1978
Maricica	Puica	Rom 50	8:40.94	4)	Prague	29 Aug	1978
	Waitz		8:41.6m	1)	Steinkjer	11 Aug	1978

(10 performances by 5 performers)

5000 metres

Best performance of all time as at the end of 1978:

Kathy	Mills	USA 58	15:35.52	1)	Knoxville	26 May	1978

Made in mixed race (with men):

Loa	Olafsson	Den 58	15:08.8m	-)	Sölleröd	30 May	1978

10.000 metres

Best performance of all time as at the end of 1978:

Natalia	Marasescu	Rom 52	32:43.2m	1)	Baia Felix	22 Jan	1978

Made in mixed race (with men):

Loa	Olafsson	Den 58	31:45.4m	-)	Copenhagen	06 Apr	1978

WORLD YEAR LISTS 1979 - 2000

1979

3000 metres

Grete	Waitz	Nor 53	8:31.75	1)	Oslo	17 Jul
Svyetlana	Ulmasova	USR 53	8:36.32	1)	Montreal	25 Aug
Lyubov	Smolka	USR 52	8:41.3	1)	Kaunas	11 Aug
Faina	Krasnova	USR 57	8:41.6	2)	Kaunas	11 Aug
Yelena	Sipatova	USR 55	8:44.1	3)	Kaunas	11 Aug

5000 metres

Jan	Merrill	USA 56	15:33.8	1)	Durham	19 May

10.000 metres

Mary	Shea	USA 60	32:52.5	1)	Walnut	15 Jun

1980

3000 metres

Yelena	Sipatova	USR 55	8:33.53	1)	Moscow	12 Jul
Tatyana	Sychova	USR 57	8:33.9	2)	Moscow	12 Jul
Faina	Krasnova	USR 57	8:34.0	3)	Moscow	12 Jul
Lyubov	Smolka	USR 52	8:36.0	4)	Moscow	12 Jul
Tatyana	Pozdnyakova	USR 56	8:37.6	1)	Donyetsk	06 Sep

5000 metres

Jan	Merrill	USA 56	15:30.6	1)	Stanford	22 Mar

10.000 metres

Kathy	Binns	GB 58	32:57.2	1)	Sittard	15 Aug

1981

3000 metres

Maricica	Puica	Rom 50	8:34.30	1)	Bucharest	12 Jul
Tatyana	Pozdnyakova	USR 56	8:34.80	1)	Leningrad	11 Jul
Alla	Yushina	USR 58	8:38.34	2)	Leningrad	11 Jul
Olga	Dvirna	USR 53	8:44.6	1)	Sochi	30 May
Grete	Waitz	Nor 53	8:44.64	1)	Basel	08 Jun

5000 metres

Paula	Fudge	GB 52	15:14.51	1)	Knarvik	13 Sep

10.000 metres

Yelena	Sipatova	USR 55	32:17.19	1)	Moscow	19 Sep

1982

3000 meters

Svyetlana	Ulmasova	USR 53	8:26.78	1)	Kiev	25 Jul
Svyetlana	Guskova	USR 59	8:29.36	2)	Kiev	25 Jul
Mary	Decker-Tabb	USA 58	8:29.71	1)	Oslo	07 Jul
Maricica	Puica	Rom 50	8:31.67	1)	Bucharest	14 Aug
Galina	Zakharova	USR 56	8:33.40	3)	Kiev	25 Jul
Yelena	Sipatova	USR 55	8:34.06	3)	Athens	09 Sep
Tatyana	Pozdnyakova	USR 55	8:35.31	5)	Kiev	25 Jul
Alla	Libutina	USR 53	8:35.74	6)	Kiev	25 Jul
Olga	Dvirna	USR 53	8:36.40	1)	Sochi	30 May
Tatyana	Kazankina	USR 51	8:36.54	2)	Sochi	30 May

5000 metres

Mary	Decker-Tabb	USA 58	15:08.26	1)	Eugene	05 Jun
Grete	Waitz	Nor 53	15:08.80	1)	Oslo	26 Jun
Irina	Bondarchuk	USR 52	15:12.62	1)	Moscow	11 Jun

10.000 metres

Mary	Decker-Tabb	USA 58	31:35.3	1)	Eugene	16 Jul
Anna	Domoratskaya	USR 53	31:48.23	1)	Kiev	27 Jul
Raisa	Sadreydinova	USR 52	31:55.02	2)	Kiev	27 Jul
Galina	Zakharova	USR 56	31:57.0	1)	Chelyabinsk	03 Sep
Lyudmila	Baranova	USR 50	32:04.88	3)	Kiev	27 Jul

1983

3000 metres

Tatyana	Kazankina	USR 51	8:32.08	1)	Leningrad	27 Jul
Alla	Yushina	USR 58	8:34.02	2)	Leningrad	27 Jul
Galina	Zakharova	USR 56	8:34.60	3)	Leningrad	27 Jul
Mary	Decker	USA 58	8:34.62	1)	Helsinki	10 Aug
Svyetlan	Guskova	USR 59	8:35.06	4)	Leningrad	27 Jul
Brigitte	Kraus	Ger 56	8:35.11	2)	Helsinki	10 Aug
Svyetlana	Ulmasova	USR 53	8:35.55	4)	Helsinki	10 Aug
Wendy	Sly	GB 59	8:37.06	5)	Helsinki	10 Aug
Tatyana	Pozdnyakova	USR 56	8:37.32	5)	Leningrad	27 Jul
Olga	Dvirna	USR 53	8:37.40	6)	Leningrad	27 Jul

5000 metres

Zola	Budd	USA 66	15:10.65	1)	Port Elizabeth	17 Oct
Anna	Domoratskaya	USR 53	15:19.0	1)	Kiev	30 Sep
Anne	Audain	NZ 55	15:27.22	1)	Auckland	02 Mar

10.000 metres

Raisa	Sadreydinova	USR 52	31:27.58	1)	Odessa	07 Sep
Lyudmila	Baranova	USR 50	31:35.01	1)	Krasnodar	29 May
Olga	Krentser	USR 60	31:35.61	2)	Krasnodar	29 May
Tatyana	Pozdnyakova	USR 55	31:48.94	3)	Odessa	07 Sep
Lyudmila	Matveyeva	USR 57	31:51.80	4)	Odessa	07 Sep

1984

3000 metres

Tatyana	Kazankina	USR 51	8:22.62	1)	Leningrad	26 Aug
Svyetlana	Guskova	USR 59	8:29.59	1)	Moscow	06 Aug
Tatyana	Pozdnyakova	USR 56	8:32.0	1)	Ryazan	11 Aug
Maricica	Puica	Rom 50	8:33.57	1)	Bucharest	10 Jul
Mary	Decker	USA 58	8:34.91	1)	Los Angeles	23 Jun
Olga	Bondarenko	USR 60	8:36.20	2)	Sochi	09 Jun
Ulrike	Bruns	GDR 53	8:36.38	1)	Berlin	20 Jul
Galina	Zakharova	USR 56	8:37.07	1)	Donyetsk	08 Sep
Zola	Budd	SA 66	8:37.5	1)	Stellenbosch	29 Feb
Alla	Yushina	USR 58	8:37.76	2)	Berlin	20 Jul

5000 metres

Ingrid	Kristiansen	Nor 56	14:58.89	1)	Oslo	28 Jun
Zola	Budd	SA 66	15:01.83	1)	Stellenbosch	05 Jan
Aurora	Cunha	Por 59	15:09.97	2)	Oslo	28 Jun

275

10.000 metres

Olga	Bondarenko	USR 60	31:13.78	1)	Kiev	24 Jun
Galina	Zakharova	USR 56	31:15.00	2)	Kiev	24 Jun
Zhanna	Tursunova	USR 57	31:53.53	3)	Kiev	24 Jun
Lyubov	Konyukhova	USR 56	31:56.01	4)	Kiev	24 Jun
Anna	Domoratskaya	USR 53	31:56.02	5)	Kiev	24 Jun

1985

3000 metres

Mary	Decker-Slaney	USA 58	8:25.83	1)	Rome	07 Sep
Maricica	Puica	Rom 50	8:27.83	2)	Rome	07 Sep
Zola	Budd	SA 66	8:28.83	3)	Rome	07 Sep
Zamira	Zaytseva	USR 53	8:35.74	2)	Moscow	17 Aug
Ulrike	Bruns	GDR 53	8:36.51	3)	Moscow	17 Aug
Lynn	Williams	Can 60	8:37.38	3)	Cologne	25 Aug
Yelena	Zhupiyova	USR 60	8:31.1	1)	Kharkov	11 Aug
Cornelia	Bürki	Swi 53	8:38.71	2)	London	20 Jul
Ingrid	Kristiansen	Nor 56	8:40.34	3)	London	20 Jul
Olga	Bondarenko	USR 60	8:42.19	1)	Leningrad	04 Aug

5000 metres

Zola	Budd	SA 66	14:48.07	1)	London	26 Aug
Natalya	Artyomova	USR 63	14:54.08	1)	Podolsk	09 Sep
Olga	Bondarenko	USR 60	14:55.76	2)	Podolsk	09 Sep

10.000 metres

Ingrid	Kristiansen	Nor 56	30:59.42	1)	Oslo	27 Jul
Olga	Bondarenko	USR 60	31:25.18	1)	Moscow	09 Jun
Aurora	Cunha	Por 59	31:35.45	2)	Oslo	27 Jul
Svyetlana	Guskova	USR 59	31:57.80	2)	Moscow	09 Jun
Lynn	Jennings	USA 60	32:03.37	3)	Oslo	27 Jul
Lisa	Martin	Aus 60	32:17.86	4)	Oslo	27 Jul
Francie	Larrieu	USA 52	32:18.29	1)	Indianapolis	14 Jun
Mary	Knisely	USA 59	32:19.93	2)	Canberra	05 Oct
Yelena	Zhupiyova	USR 60	32:25.37	1)	Donyetsk	27 Aug
Yelizavyeta	Bradu	USR 54	32:25.62	3)	Moscow	09 Jun

1986

3000 metres

Olga	Bondarenko	USR 60	8:33.99	1)	Stuttgart	28 Aug
Ingrid	Kristiansen	Nor 56	8:34.10	1)	Zurich	13 Aug
Zola	Budd	SA 66	8:34.43	1)	Belfast	30 Jun
Maricica	Puica	Rom 50	8:35.92	2)	Stuttgart	28 Aug
Tatyana	Samolenko	USR 61	8:36.00	1)	Tallinn	22 Jun
Doina	Melinte	Rom 56	8:37.11	1)	Bucharest	15 Jun
Yvonne	Murray	GB 64	8:37.15	3)	Stuttgart	28 Aug
Mariana	Stanescu	Rom 64	8:38.83	1)	Moscow	06 Jul
Svyetlana	Ulmasova	USR 53	8:39.19	2)	Moscow	06 Jul
Regina	Chistyakova	USR 61	8:39.25	3)	Moscow	06 Jul

5000 metres

Ingrid	Kristiansen	Nor 56	14:37.33	1)	Stockholm	05 Aug
Svyetlana	Guskova	USR 59	15:02.12	1)	Tallinn	21 Jun
Olga	Bondarenko	USR 60	15:03.51	1)	Moscow	08 Jul

276

10.000 metres

Ingrid	Kristiansen	Nor 56	30:13.74	1)	Oslo	05 Jul
Olga	Bondarenko	USR 60	30:57.21	2)	Stuttgart	30 Aug
Ulrike	Bruns	GDR 53	31:19.76	3)	Stuttgart	30 Aug
Aurora	Cunha	Por 59	31:29.41	2)	Oslo	05 Jul
Elizabeth	Lynch	GB 64	31:41.42	1)	Edinburgh	28 Jul
Svyetlana	Guskova	USR 59	31:42.43	5)	Stuttgart	30 Aug
Yelena	Zhupiyova	USR 60	31:42.99	6)	Stuttgart	30 Aug
Anne	Audain	NZ 55	31:53.31	2)	Edinburgh	28 Jul
Karolina	Szabó	Hun 61	31:55.93	8)	Stuttgart	30 Aug
Angela	Tooby	GB 60	31:56.59	9)	Stuttgart	30 Aug

1987

3000 metres

Ulrike	Burns	GDR 53	8:38.1	1)	Potsdam	14 Jun
Yelena	Zhupiyova	USR 60	8:38.5	1)	Moscow	15 Aug
Tatyana	Samolenko	USR 61	8:38.73	1)	Rome	01 Sep
Paula	Ivan	Rom 63	8:39.28	1)	Bucharest	14 Jun
Maricica	Puica	Rom 50	8:39.45	2)	Rome	01 Sep
Elizabeth	Lynch	GB 64	8:39.85	1)	Nice	13 Jul
Cornelia	Bürki	Swi 53	8:40.31	4)	Rome	01 Sep
Yelena	Romanova	USR 63	8:41.15	1)	Brussels	11 Sep
Yvonne	Murray	GB 64	8:42.07	1)	Lausanne	15 Aug
Elena	Fidatov (Rom)	Rom 60	8:42.16	2)	Bucharest	14 Jun

5000 metres

Elizabeth	Lynch	GB 64	15:01.08	1)	Oslo	05 Aug
Angela	Tooby	GB 60	15:13.22	2)	Oslo	05 Aug
Ingrid	Kristiansen	Nor 56	15:19.76	1)	Oslo	04 Jul

10,000 metres

Ingrid	Kristiansen	Nor 56	31:05.85	1)	Rome	04 Sep
Yelena	Zhupiyova	USR 60	31:09.40	2)	Rome	04 Sep
Kathrin	Ullrich	GDR 67	31:11.34	3)	Rome	04 Sep
Olga	Bondarenko	USR 60	31:18.38	4)	Rome	04 Sep
Elizabeth	Lynch	GB 64	31:19.82	5)	Rome	04 Sep
Wang	Xiuting	Chi 65	31:27.00	1)	Guangzhou	29 Nov
Hou	Juhua	Chi 67	31:27.99	2)	Guangzhou	29 Nov
Wang	Qinghuan	Chi 65	31:44.73	3)	Guangzhou	29 Nov
Lynn	Jennings	USA 60	31:45.43	6)	Rome	04 Sep
M.Albertina	Machado	Por 61	31:46.61	7)	Rome	04 Sep

1988

3000 metres

Tatzana	Samolenko	USR 61	8:26.53	1)	Seoul	25 Sep
Paula	Ivan	Rom 63	8:27.15	2)	Seoul	25 Sep
Zvonne	Murray	GB 64	8:29.02	3)	Seoul	25 Sep
Yelena	Romanova	USR 63	8:30.45	4)	Seoul	25 Sep
Natalya	Artzomova	USR 63	8:31.67	5)	Seoul	25 Sep
Elly van	Hulst	Hol 59	8:33.97	1)	Zurich	17 Aug
Mary	Decker-Slaney	USA 58	8:34.69	2)	Zurich	17 Aug
Vicki	Huber	USA 67	8:37.25	6)	Seoul	25 Sep
Lynn	Williams	USA 60	8:37.30	3)	Zurich	17 Aug
Wendy	Sly	GB 59	8:37.70	7)	Seoul	25 Sep

5000 metres

Elizabeth	Lynch-McColgan	GB 64	15:03.29	1)	Berlin	26 Aug
Ingrid	Kristiansen	Nor 56	15:10.89	2)	Berlin	26 Aug
Olga	Bondarenko	USR 60	15:11.16	1)	Moscow	05 Sep

10,000 metres

Olga	Bondarenko	USR 60	31:05.21	1)	Seoul	30 Sep
Elizabeth	Lynch-McColgan	GB 64	31:06.99	1)	Oslo	02 Jul
Yelena	Zhupiyova	USR 60	31:19.82	3)	Seoul	30 Sep
Kathrin	Ullrich	GDR 67	31:26.79	1)	Potsdam	08 Jun
Ingrid	Kristiansen	Nor 56	31:31.37	2)	Oslo	02 Jul
Francie	Larrieu-Smith	USA 52	31:35.52	5)	Seoul	30 Sep
Lyudmila	Matveyeva	USR 57	31:38.02	1)	Kiev	02 Aug
Lynn	Jennings	USA 60	31:39.93	6)	Seoul	30 Sep
Wang	Xiuting	Chi 65	31:40.23	7)	Seoul	30 Sep
Yekaterina	Khramenkova	USR 56	31:42.02	4)	Kiev	02 Aug

1989

3000 metres

Paula	Ivan	Rom 63	8:38.48	1)	Gateshead	05 Aug
Yvonne	Murray	GB 64	8:38.51	1)	Nice	10 Jul
Marie	Pierre Duros	Fra 67	8:38.97	2)	Nice	10 Jul
Elly van	Hulst	Hol 59	8:40.85	1)	Zurich	16 Aug
PattiSue	Plumer	USA 62	8:42.12	1)	Lausanne	27 Jul
Viorica	Ghican	Rom 65	8:42.61	2)	Pitesti	25 Jun
Päivi	Tikkanen	Fin 60	8:43.50	1)	Tampere	29 Aug
Margareta	Keszeg	Rom 65	8:44.33	4)	Nice	10 Jul
Elizabeth	Lynch McColgan	GB 64	8:44.93	2)	Edinburgh	07 Jul
Iulia	Besliu	Rom 65	8:45.04	3)	Pitesti	25 Jun

5000 metres

Kathrin	Ullrich	GDR 67	14:59.01	1)	Stockholm	03 Jul
PattiSue	Plumer	USA 62	15:00.00	2)	Stockholm	03 Jul
Lynn	Williams	Can 60	15:01.30	3)	Stockholm	03 Jul

10,000 metres

Ingrid	Kristiansen	Nor 56	30:48.51	1)	Oslo	01 Jul
Kathrin	Ullrich	GDR 67	31:33.92	1)	Barcelona	09 Sep
Viorica	Ghican	Rom 65	31:46.43	2)	Duisburg	29 Aug
Iris	Biba	Ger 64	31:52.09	1)	Oslo	01 Jul
Akemi	Matsuno	Jap 68	31:54.0m	1)	Kumamoto	30 Apr
Anne	Audain	NZ 55	32:00.07	1)	Wellington	09 Dec
Maria	Conceição Ferreira	Por 62	32:06.51	1)	Lisbon	05 Jul
Maria	Albertina Dias	Por 65	32:07.95	1)	Maia	18 Jul
Barbara	Moore	NZ 57	32:12.78	2)	Wellington	09 Dec
Miyoko	Asahina	Jap 69	32:14.65	1)	Tokyo	17 Jun

1990

3000 metres

Angela	Chalmers	Can 63	8:38.38	1)	Auckland	28 Jan
Yvonne	Murray	GB 64	8:39.46	2)	Auckland	28 Jan
Elizabeth	Lynch-McColgan	GB 64	8:43.14	1)	Sydney	14 Jan

Yelena	Romanova	USR 63	8:43.68	2)	Split	29 Aug
Patti Sue	Plumer	USA 62	8:44.07	1)	Villeneuve d'Ascq	29 Jun
Nadia	Dandolo	Ita 62	8:44.41	2)	Zurich	15 Aug
Lynn	Jennings	USA 60	8:46.08	2)	Villeneuve d'Ascq	29 Jun
Viorica	Ghican	Rom 65	8:46.13	3)	Zurich	15 Aug
Roberta	Brunet	Ita 65	8:46.19	3)	Split	29 Aug
Ravilya	Kotovich	USR 60	8:46.86	1)	Kiev	05 Jul

5000 metres

Yelena	Romanova	USR 63	15:02.23	1)	Seattle	24 Jul
Lynn	Jennings	USA 60	15:07.92	1)	Stockholm	02 Jul
PattiSue	Plumer	USA 62	15:07.97	2)	Stockholm	02 Jul

10,000 metres

Viorica	Ghican	Rom 65	31:18.18	1)	Helsinki	27 Jun
Uta	Pippig	Ger 65	31:40.92	2)	Helsinki	27 Jun
Maria	Conceição Ferreira	Por 62	31:45.75	1)	Kapfenberg	23 Jun
Yelena	Romanova	USR 63	31:46.83	1)	Split	31 Aug
Kathrin	Ullrich	GDR 67	31:47.70	2)	Split	31 Aug
Zhong	Huandi	Chi 67	31:50.98	1)	Beijing	27 Sep
Annette	Sergent	Fra 62	31:51.68	3)	Split	31 Aug
Wang	Xiuting	Chi 65	31:52.18	2)	Beijing	27 Sep
Kerstin	Pressler	Ger 62	31:55.51	1)	Dortmund	19 Jul
Jill	Hunter	GB 66	31:55.80	3)	Helsinki	27 Jun

1991

3000 metres

Elana	Meyer	SA 66	8:32.00	1)	Durban	29 Apr
Zola	Budd-Pieterse	SA 66	8:35.72	2)	Durban	29 Apr
Tatyana	Samolenko-Dorovskikh	USR 61	8:35.82	1)	Tokyo	26 Aug
Yvonne	Murray	GB 64	8:36.05	1)	Edinburgh	19 Jul
Yelena	Romanova	USR 63	8:36.06	2)	Tokyo	26 Aug
Elizabeth	Lynch-McColgan	GB 64	8:38.23	1)	Nice	15 Jul
Susan	Sirma	Ken 66	8:39.41	3)	Tokyo	26 Aug
Marie-Pierre	Duros	Fra 67	8:40.76	1)	Stockholm	03 Jul
Päivi	Tikkanen	Fin 60	8:41.30	4)	Tokyo	26 Aug
Margareta	Keszeg	Rom 65	8:42.02	5)	Tokyo	26 Aug

5000 metres

Elana	Meyer	SA 66	14:49.35	1)	Cape Town	08 Apr
Kethrin	Ullrich	GDR 67	14:58.71	1)	Berlin	10 Sep
Yelena	Romanova	USR 63	14:59.70	2)	Berlin	10 Sep

10,000 metres

Elizabeth	Lynch-McColgan	GB 64	30:57.07	1)	Hengelo	25 Jun
Kathrin	Ullrich	Ger 67	31:03.62	1)	Frankfurt/M.	30 Jun
Jill	Hunter	GB 66	31:07.88	2)	Frankfurt/M.	30 Jun
Ingrid	Kristiansen	Nor 56	31:20.28	1)	Hechtel	10 Aug
Francie	Larrieu-Smith	USA 52	31:28.92	1)	Austin	04 Apr
Elana	Meyer	SA 66	31:33.46	1)	Cape Town	22 Dec
Zhong	Huandi	Chi 67	31:35.08	2)	Tokyo	30 Aug
Wang	Xiuting	Chi 65	31:35.99	3)	Tokyo	30 Aug
Delilah	Asiago	Ken 72	31:40.56	1)	Tokyo	16 Jun
Derartu	Tulu	Eti 72	31:45.95	1)h2	Tokyo	27 Aug

1992

3000 metres

Yelena	Romanova	Rus 63	8:33.72	1)	Cologne	16 Aug
Yvonne	Murray	GB 64	8:36.63	1)	Edinburgh	19 Jun
Sonia	O'Sullivan	Ire 69	8:37.92	2)	Cologne	16 Aug
Elana	Meyer	SA 66	8:38.45	3)	Cologne	16 Aug
Margareta	Keszeg	Rom 65	8:39.94	1)	Nice	15 Jul
Marie-Pierre	Duros	Fra 67	8:40.38	2)	Nice	15 Jul
PattiSue	Plumer	USA 62	8:40.98	1)	New Orleans	22 Jun
Elizabeth	Lynch-McColgan	GB 64	8:41.07	2)	Edinburgh	19 Jun
Shelly	Steely	USA 62	8:41.28	2)	New Orleans	22 Jun
Annette	Peters	USA 65	8:42.09	3)	Nice	15 Jul

5000 metres

Elana	Meyer	SA 66	14:44.15	1)	Bellville	06 Mar
Sonia	O'Sullivan	Ire 69	14:59.11	2)	Berlin	21 Aug
Elizabeth	Lynch-McColgan	GB 64	15:01.86	1)	Oslo	04 Jul

10,000 metres

Derartu	Tulu	Eti 72	31:06.02	1)	Barcelona	07 Aug
Lisa	Ondieki	Ken 60	31:11.72	1)	Helsinki	30 Jun
Elana	Meyer	SA 66	31:11.75	2)	Barcelona	07 Aug
Maria	Conceição Ferreira	Por 62	31:16.42	2)	Helsinki	30 Jun
Lynn	Jennings	USA 60	31:19.89	3)	Barcelona	07 Aug
Kathrin	Ullrich	Ger 67	31:20.62	1)	Jena	28 May
Zhong	Huandi	Chi 67	31:21.08	4)	Barcelona	07 Aug
Uta	Pippig	Ger 65	31:21.36	2)	Jena	28 May
Elizabeth	Lynch-McColgan	GB 64	31:26.11	5)	Barcelona	07 Aug
Wang	Xiuting	Chi 65	31:28.06	6)	Barcelona	07 Aug

1993

3000 metres

Wang	Junxia	Chi 73	8:06.11	1)	Beijing	13 Sep
Qu	Yunxia	Chi 72	8:12.18	2)	Beijing	13 Sep
Zhang	Linli	Chi 73	8:16.50	3)	Beijing	13 Sep
Ma	Liyan	Chi 68	8:19.78	3)h2	Beijing	12 Sep
Zhang	Lirong	Chi 73	8:21.84	5)	Beijing	13 Sep
Sonia	O'Sullivan	Ire 69	8:28.74	1)	Oslo	10 Jul
Yvonne	Murray	GB 64	8:30.30	2)	Oslo	10 Jul
Elana	Meyer	SA 66	8:32.81	3)	Oslo	10 Jul
Yelena	Romanova	Rus 63	8:35.48	2)	Hengelo	20 Jun
Ma	Ningning	Chi 76	8:36.45	4)	Jinan	06 Jun

5000 metres

Sonia	O'Sullivan	Ire 69	14:45.92	1)	Berlin	27 Aug
Elana	Meyer	SA 66	14:46.41	1)	Hechtel	31 Jul
Annette	Peters	USA 65	14:56.07	2)	Berlin	27 Aug
Maria	Albertina Dias	Por 65	15:05.12	2)	Hechtel	31 Jul
Zhong	Huandi	Chi 67	15:05.69+	1)	Beijing	08 Sep
Wang	Junxia	Chi 73	15:05.8+e	2)	Beijing	08 Sep

10,000 metres

Wang	Junxia	Chi 73	29:31.78	1)	Beijing	08 Sep
Zhong	Huandi	Chi 67	30:13.37	2)	Beijing	08 Sep

Zhang	Lirong	Chi 73	31:09.25	3)	Beijing	08 Sep
Ma	Liyan	Chi 68	31:10.46	4)	Beijing	08 Sep
Sally	Barsosio	Ken 78	31:15.38	3)	Stuttgart	21 Aug
Zhang	Linli	Chi 73	31:16.28	5)	Beijing	08 Sep
Tegla	Loroupe	Ken 71	31:21.20	1)	Warstein	06 Jul
Liu	Jianying	Chi 71	31:23.92	6)	Beijing	08 Sep
Wei	Li	Chi 72	31:28.83	7)	Beijing	08 Sep
Uta	Pippig	Ger 65	31:29.70	1)	Hengelo	20 Jun

1994

3000 metres

Sonia	O'Sullivan	Ire 69	8:21.64	1)	London	15 Jul
Yvonne	Murray	Gb 64	8:29.60	2)	London	15 Jul
Angela	Chalmers	Can 63	8:32.17	1)	Victoria	23 Aug
Gabriela	Szabó	Rom 75	8:40.08	3)	Helsinki	10 Aug
Olga	Churbanova	Rus 64	8:40.48	4)	Helsinki	10 Aug
Yelena	Romanova	Rus 63	8:41.06	1)	St.Peterburg	24 Jul
Lyudmila	Bolrisova	Rus 66	8:41.71	5)	Helsinki	10 ug
Annette	Peters	USA 65	8:41.97	4)	London	15 Jul
Fernanda	Ribeiro	Por 69	8:42.13	2)	St.Peterburg	24 Jul
Robyn	Meagher	Can 67	8:45.59	2)	Victoria	23 Aug

5000 metres

Yelena	Romanova	Rus 63	15:05.94	1)	Stockholm	12 Jul
Sonia	O'Sullivan	Ire 69	15:06.18	1)	Cologne	21 Aug
Fernanda	Ribeiro	Por 69	15:06.91	1)	Tokyo	15 Sep
Catherina	McKiernan	Ire 69	15:09.10	2)	Stockholm	12 Jul
Alison	Wyeth	GB 64	15:10.38	1)	Berlin	30 Aug
Kathrin	Wessel	Ger 67	15:10.84	2)	Berlin	30 Aug
Lyudmila	Borisova	Rus 66	15:13.27	2)	Cologne	21 Aug
Yvonne	Graham	Jam 65	15:13.67	3)	Cologne	21 Aug
Daria	Nauer	Swi 66	15:13.93	4)	Berlin	30 Aug
Nadia	Dandolo	Ita 62	15:14.23	5)	Berlin	30 Aug

10,000 metres

Wang	Junxia	Chi 73	30:50.34	1)	Hiroshima	15 Oct
Elana	Meyer	SA 66	30:52.51	1)	London	10 Sep
Fernanda	Ribeiro	Por 69	31:04.25	2)	London	10 Sep
Catherina	McKiernan	Ire 69	31:19.11	1)	Dublin	12 Jun
Dong	Li	Chi 73	31:31.08	2)	Hiroshima	15 Oct
Maria	Conceição Ferreira	Por 62	31:32.11	1)	Braga	09 Apr
Daria	Nauer	Swi 66	31:35.96	3)	Helsinki	13 Aug
Kathrin	Wessel	Ger 67	31:38.75	4)	Helsinki	13 Aug
Cristina	Misaros	Rom 69	31:41.03	5)	Helsinki	13 Aug
Maria	Guida	Ita 66	31:42.14	6)	Helsinki	13 Aug

1995

3000 metres

Sonia	O'Sullivan	Ire 69	8:27.57	1)	Zurich	16 Aug
Gabriela	Szabó	Rom 75	8:30.03	2)	Zurich	16 Aug
Yvonne	Graham	Jam 65	8:37.07	3)	Zurich	16 Aug
Paula	Radcliffe	GB 73	8:40.82	4)	Zurich	16 Aug

Olga	Churbanova	Rus 65	8:41.42	1)	Rome	08 Jun
Lyudmila	Borisova	Rus 66	8:41.51	5)	Zurich	16 Aug
Fernanda	Ribeiro	Por 69	8:41.99	1)	Lausanne	05 Jul
Yvonne	Murray	GB 64	8:42.82	2)	London	27 Aug
Claudia	Lokar	Ger 64	8:43.11	5)	Monaco	09 Sep
Zahra	Ouaziz	Mor 69	8:43.19	6)	Zurich	16 Aug

5000 metres

Fernanda	Ribeiro	Por 69	14:36.45	1)	Hechtel	22 Jul
Sonia	O'Sullivan	Ire 69	14:41.40	1)	Berlin	01 Sep
Elana	Meyer	SA 66	14:44.05	2)	Hechtel	22 Jul
Jiang	Bo	Chi 77	14:45.90	1)	Nanjing	24 Oct
Paula	Radcliffe	Gb 73	14:49.27	2)	London	07 Jul
Wang	Junxia	Chi 73	14:53.08	2)	Nanjing	24 Oct
Lydia	Cheromei	Ken 77	14:53.44	3)	Berlin	01 Sep
Zahra	Ouaziz	Mor 69	14:53.77	3)	Göteborg	12 Aug
Gabriela	Szabó	Rom 75	14:53.91	1)	Cologne	18 Aug
Yvonne	Murray	GB 64	14:56.94	4)	London	07 Jul

10,000 metres

Fernanda	Ribeiro	Por 69	31:04.99	1)	Göteborg	09 Aug
Derartu	Tulu	Eti 71	31:08.10	2)	Göteborg	09 Aug
Catherina	McKiernan	Ire 69	31:08.41	1)	Villeneuve d'Ascq	17 Jun
Tegla	Loroupe	Ken 73	31:17.66	3)	Göteborg	09 Aug
Wang	Junxia	Chi 73	31:23.24	1)	Changchun	07 Sep
Elana	Meyer	SA 66	31:23.96	1)	Stellenbosch	11 Feb
Maria	Guida	Ita 66	31:27.82	4)	Göteborg	09 Aug
Junko	Kataoka	Jap 70	31:31.12	2)	Mito	07 May
Elizabeth	Lynch-McColgan	GB 64	31:40.14	6)	Göteborg	09 Aug
Hiromi	Suzuki	Jap 68	31:43.41	1	Tokyo	11 Jun

1996

3000 metres

Sonia	O'Sullivan	Ire 69	8:35.42	1)	Nice	10 Jul
Gabriela	Szabó	Rom 75	8:36.07	1)	Monaco	10 Aug
Roberta	Brunet	Ita 65	8:36.12	2)	Monaco	10 Aug
Paula	Radcliffe	GB 73	8:37.07	3)	Monaco	10 Aug
Pauline	Konga	Ken 70	8:37.76	4)	Monaco	10 Aug
Rose	Cheruiyot	Ken 76	8:39.34	5)	Monaco	10 Aug
Julia	Vaquero	Spa 70	8:41.23	2)	Nice	10 Jul

5000 metres

Fernanda	Ribeiro	Por 69	14:41.07	1)	Oslo	05 Jul
Gabriela	Szabó	Rom 75	14:41.12	2)	Oslo	05 Jul
Roberta	Brunet	Ita 65	14:44.50	2)	Cologne	16 Aug
Julia	Vaquero	Spa 70	14:44.95	3)	Oslo	05 Jul
Rose	Cheruiyot	Ken 76	14:46.41	3)	Cologne	16 Aug
Gete	Wami	Eti 74	14:46.45	4)	Cologne	16 Aug
Paula	Radcliffe	GB 73	14:46.76	5)	Cologne	16 Aug
Pauline	Konga	Ken 70	14:47.51	6)	Cologne	16 Aug
Sally	Barsosio	Ken 78	14:47.81	4)	Oslo	05 Jul
Sonia	O'Sullivan	Ire 69	14:48.36	1)	London	12 Jul

10,000 metres

Fernanda	Ribeiro	Por 69	31:01.63	1)	Atlanta	02 Aug
Wang	Junxia	Chi 73	31:01.76	1)h2	Nanjing	07 May
Gete	Wami	Eti 74	31:06.65	3)	Atlanta	02 Aug
Derartu	Tulu	Eti 72	31:10.46	4)	Atlanta	02 Aug
Ren	Xiujuan	Chi 74	31:13.21	2)	Nanjing	08 May
Hiromi	Suzuki	Jap 68	31:19.40	1)	Osaka	09 Jun
Yuko	Kawakami	Jap 75	31:20.19	2)	Osaka	09 Jun
Masako	Chiba	Jap 76	31:20.46	3)	Osaka	09 Jun
Tegla	Loroupe	Ken 73	31:23.22	6)	Atlanta	02 Aug
Julia	Vaquero	Spa 70	31:24.08	1)	Leiria	06 Apr

1997

3000 metres

Gabriela	Szabó	Rom 75	8:27.78	1)	Zurich	13 Aug
Paula	Radcliffe	GB 73	8:35.28	2)	Zurich	13 Aug
Roberta	Brunet	Ita 65	8:35.65	1)	Monaco	16 Aug
Sally	Barsosio	Ken 78	8:35.89	2)	Monaco	16 Aug
Lydia	Cheromei	Ken 77	8:36.11	3)	Zurich	13 Aug
Fernanda	Ribeiro	Por 69	8:37.14	1)	Nice	16 Jul
Anita	Weyermann	Swi 77	8:37.69	6)	Zurich	13 Aug

5000 metres

Jiang	Bo	Chi 77	14:28.09	1)	Shanghai	23 Oct
Dong	Yanmei	Chi 77	14:29.82	2)	Shanghai	23 Oct
Liu	Shixiang	Chi 71	14:32.33	3)h1	Shanghai	21 Oct
Yin	Lili	Chi 79	14:39.96	4)	Shanghai	23 Oct
Gabriela	Szabó	Rom 75	14:42.43	1)	Oslo	04 Jul
Lan	Lixin	Chi 79	14:45.33	2)h2	Shanghai	21 Oct
Paula	Radcliffe	GB 73	14:45.51	2)	Brussels	22 Aug
Song	Liqing	Chi 80	14:45.71	3)h2	Shanghai	21 Oct
Sally	Barsosio	Ken 78	14:46.71	3)	Brussels	22 Aug
Lydia	Cheromei	Ken 77	14:46.72	2)	Berlin	26 Aug

10,000 metres

Dong	Yanmei	Chi 77	30:38.09	1)	Shanghai	19 Oct
Lan	Lixin	Chi 79	30:39.41	2)	Shanghai	19 Oct
Yin	Lili	Chi 79	30:39.98	3)	Shanghai	19 Oct
Dong	Zhaoxia	Chi 74	30:47.22	4)	Shanghai	19 Oct
Wang	Dongmei	Chi 72	30:47.72	5)	Shanghai	19 Oct
Liu	Shixiang	Chi 71	30:55.83	6)	Shanghai	19 Oct
Song	Liqing	Chi 80	31:11.26	7)	Shanghai	19 Oct
Wang	Mingxia	Chi 71	31:12.58	8)	Shanghai	19 Oct
Julia	Vaquero	Spa 70	31:14.51	1)	Barakaldo	05 Apr
Yang	Siju	Chi 73	31:16.39	9)	Shanghai	19 Oct

1998

3000 metres

Gabriela	Szabó	Rom 75	8:24.31	1)	Paris	29 Jul
Zahra	Ouaziz	Mor 69	8:27.26	2)	Paris	29 Jul
Sonia	O'Sullivan	Ire 69	8:28.82	2)	Nice	16 Jul
Gete	Wami	Eti 74	8:29.24	3)	Paris	29 Jul
Jackline	Maranga	Ken 77	8:38.02	4)	Paris	29 Jul
Paula	Radcliffe	GB 73	8:38.84	1)	Sheffield	02 Aug
Regina	Jacobs	USA 63	8:39.56	1)	Edwardsville	25 Jul

283

5000 metres

Gabriela	Szabó	Rom 75	14:31.48	1)	Berlin	01 Sep
Zahra	Ouaziz	Mor 69	14:32.08	2)	Berlin	01 Sep
Gete	Wami	Eti 74	14:36.08	3)	Berlin	01 Sep
Paula	Radcliffe	GB 73	14:51.27	2)	Stockholm	05 Aug
Sonia	O'Sullivan	Ire 69	14:51.61	4)	Berlin	01 Sep
Regina	Jacobs	USA 63	14:52.49	1)	Brunswick	04 Jul
Julia	Vaquero	Spa 70	14:55.91	5)	Berlin	01 Sep
Tegla	Loroupe	Ken 73	14:57.77	6)	Berlin	01 Sep
Marta	Dominguez	Spa 75	14:59.49	3)	Rome	14 Jul
Harumi	Hiroyama	Jap 68	15:03.67	5)	Stockholm	05 Aug

10,000 metres

Fernanda	Ribeiro	Por 69	30:48.06	1)	Lisbon	04 Apr
Paula	Radcliffe	GB 73	30:48.58	2)	Lisbon	04 Apr
Chiemi	Takahashi	Jap 76	31:27.57	1)	Sendai	16 May
Sonia	O'Sullivan	Ire 69	31:29.33	1)	Budapest	19 Aug
Lidia	Simon	Rom 73	31:32.64	3)	Budapest	19 Aug
Olivera	Jevtic	Yug 77	31:34.26	4)	Budapest	19 Aug
Yuko	Kawakami	Jap 75	31:39.35	1)	Naruto	12 Jun
Alla	Zhilyayeva	Rus 69	31:45.02	1)	Moscow	03 Aug
Julia	Vaquero	Spa 70	31:46.47	6)	Budapest	19 Aug
Esther	Wanjiru	Ken 77	31:52.98	1)	Mito	05 May

1999

3000 metres

Gabriela	Szabó	Rom 75	8:25.03	1)	Zurich	11 Aug
Zahra	Ouaziz	Mor 69	8:26.48	2)	Zurich	11 Aug
Paula	Radcliffe	GB 73	8:27.40	3)	Zurich	11 Aug
Gete	Wami	Eti 74	8:29.72	3)	Rome	07 Jul
Maria	Pantukhova	Rus 74	8:30.18	4)	Zurich	11 Aug
Carla	Sacramento	Por 71	8:30.22	2)	Monaco	04 Aug
Fernanda	Ribeiro	Por 69	8:30.66	3)	Monaco	04 Aug
Olga	Yegorova	Rus 72	8:33.02	4)	Oslo	30 Jun

5000 metres

Gabriela	Szabó	Rom 75	14:40.59	1)	Berlin	07 Sep
Zahra	Ouaziz	Mor 69	14:41.34	2)	Berlin	07 Sep
Irina	Mikitenko	Ger 72	14:42.03	3)	Berlin	07 Sep
Paula	Radcliffe	GB 73	14:43.54	2)	London	07 Aug
Ayelech	Worku	Eti 79	14:44.22	3)	Seville	27 Aug
Tegla	Loroupe	Ken 73	14:49.12	4)	Berlin	07 Sep
Ebru	Kavaklioglu	Tur 70	14:51.69	5)	Seville	27 Aug
Fernanda	Ribeiro	Por 69	14:52.59	1)	Stockholm	30 Jul
Berhane	Adere	Eti 73	14:54.88	4)	Hengelo	30 May
Julia	Vaquero	Spa 70	14:56.00	6)	Seville	27 Aug

10,000 metres

Gete	Wami	Eti 74	30:24.56	1)	Seville	26 Aug
Paula	Radcliffe	GB 73	30:27.13	2)	Seville	26 Aug
Tegla	Loroupe	Ken 73	30:32.03	3)	Seville	26 Aug
Harumi	Hiroyama	Jap 68	31:26.84	4)	Seville	26 Aug
Chiemi	Takahashi	Jap 76	31:27.62	5)	Seville	26 Aug
Leah	Malot	Ken 72	31:31.73	1)	Villeneuve d'Ascq	13 Jun
Restituta	Joseph	Tan 71	31:32.02	2)	Villeneuve d'Ascq	13 Jun
Merima	Hashim	Eti 81	31:32.06	6)	Seville	26 Aug
Berhane	Adere	Eti 73	31:32.51	7)	Seville	26 Aug
Merima	Denboba	Eti 74	31:32.63	3)	Villeneuve d'Ascq	13 Jun

3000 metres

Gabriela	Szabó	Rom 75	8:26.35	1)	Zurich	11 Aug	
Sonia	O'Sullivan	Ire 69	8:27.58	2)	Zurich	11 Aug	
Marta	Dominguez	Spa 75	8:28.80	3)	Zurich	11 Aug	
Paula	Radcliffe	GB 73	8:28.85	4)	Zurich	11 Aug	
Lydia	Cheromei	Ken 77	8:29.14	5)	Zurich	11 Aug	
Irina	Mikitenko	Ger 72	8:30.39	6)	Zurich	11 Aug	
Tegla	Loroupe	Ken 73	8:30.95	2)	Monaco	18 Aug	

5000 metres

Gete	Wami	Eti 74	14:30.88	1)	Heusden	05 Aug	
Leah	Malot	Ken 72	14:39.83	1)	Berlin	01 Sep	
Gabriela	Szabó	Rom 75	14:40.61	2)	Berlin	01 Sep	
Sonia	O'Sullivan	Ire 69	14:41.02	2)	Sydney	25 Sep	
Ayelech	Worku	Eti 79	14:41.23	1)	London	05 Aug	
Olga	Yegorova	Rus 72	14:42.91	1)	Stockholm	01 Aug	
Irina	Mikitenko	Ger 72	14:43.59	5)	Sydney	25 Sep	
Paula	Radcliffe	GB 73	14:44.36	2)	London	05 Aug	
Derartu	Tulu	Eti 72	14:44.57	3)	Stockholm	01 Aug	
Regina	Jacobs	USA 63	14:45.35	1)	Sacramento	21 Jul	

10,000 metres

Derartu	Tulu	Eti 72	30:17.49	1)	Sydney	30 Sep	
Gete	Wami	Eti 74	30:22.48	2)	Sydney	30 Sep	
Fernanda	Ribeiro	Por 69	30:22.88	3)	Sydney	30 Sep	
Paula	Radcliffe	GB 73	30:26.97	4)	Sydney	30 Sep	
Tegla	Loroupe	Ken 73	30:37.26	5)	Sydney	30 Sep	
Berhane	Adere	Eti 73	30:51.30	1)	Heusden	05 Aug	
Sonia	O'Sullivan	Ire 69	30:53.37	6)	Sydney	30 Sep	
Leah	Malot	Ken 72	30:57.70	2)	Heusden	05 Aug	
Merima	Hashim	Eti 81	30:59.92	3)	Heusden	05 Aug	
Marlene	Renders	Bel 68	31:03.60	4)	Heusden	05 Aug	

ALL TIME WORLD LIST OF BEST PERFORMANCES AS AT THE END OF 2000

3000 metres

Wang	Junxia	Chi 73	8:06.11	1)	Beijing	13 Sep	1993
Qu	Yunxia	Chi 72	8:12.18	2)	Beijing	13 Sep	1993
Wang	Junxia		8:12.19	1)h2	Beijing	12 Sep	1993
Qu	Yunxia		8:12.27	2)h2	Beijing	12 Sep	1993
Zhang	Linli	Chi 73	8:16.50	3)	Beijing	13 Sep	1993
Ma	Liyan	Chi 68	8:19.78	3)h2	Beijing	12 Sep	1993
Ma	Liyan		8:21.26	4)	Beijing	13 Sep	1993
Sonia	O'Sullivan	Ire 69	8:21.64	1)	London	15 Jul	1994
Zhang	Lirong	Chi 73	8:21.84	5)	Beijing	13 Sep	1993
Zhang	Linli		8:22.06	1)h1	Beijing	12 Sep	1993
Zhang	Lirong		8:22.44	2)h1	Beijing	12 Sep	1993
Tatyana	Kazankina	USR 51	8:22.62	1)	Leningrad	26 Aug	1984
Gabriela	Szabó	Rom 75	8:24.31	1)	Paris	29 Jul	1998
	Szabó		8:25.03	1)	Zurich	11 Aug	1999
	Szabó		8:25.59	1)	Paris	21 Jul	1999
	Szabó		8:25.82	1)	Brussels	03 Sep	1999
Mary	Decker-Slaney	USA 58	8:25.83	1)	Rome	07 Sep	1985
	Szabó		8:26.35	1)	Zurich	11 Aug	2000

Zahra	Ouaziz	Mor 69	8:26.48	2)	Zurich	11 Aug	1999
Tatyana	Samolenko	Ukr 61	8:26.53	1)	Seoul	25 Sep	1988
	Ouaziz		8:26.64	2)	Paris	21 Jul	1999
Svyetlana	Ulmasova	Uzb 53	8:26.78	1)	Kiev	25 Jul	1982
	Ouaziz		8:27.01	2)	Brussels	03 Sep	1999
Lyudmila	Bragina	USR 43	8:27.12	1)	College Park	07 Jul	1976
Paula	Ivan	Rom 63	8:27.15	2)	Seoul	25 Sep	1988
	Szabó		8:27.21	1)	Oslo	30 Jun	1999
	Ouaziz		8:27.26	2)	Paris	29 Jul	1998
Paula	Radcliffe	GB 73	8:27.40	3)	Zurich	11 Aug	1999
	O'Sullivan		8:27.57	1)	Zurich	16 Aug	1995
	O'Sullivan		8:27.58	2)	Zurich	11 Aug	2000

(30 performances by 15 performers)

5000 metres

Jiang	Bo	Chi 77	14:28.09	1)	Shanghai	23 Oct	1997
Dong	Yanmei	Chi 77	14:29.82	2)	Shanghai	23 Oct	1997
Gete	Wami	Eti 74	14:30.88	1)	Heusden	05 Aug	2000
Dong	Yanmei		14:31.27	1)h1	Shanghai	21 Oct	1997
Jiang	Bo		14:31.30	2)h1	Shanghai	21 Oct	1997
Gabriela	Szabó	Rom 75	14:31.48	1)	Berlin	01 Sep	1998
Zahra	Ouaziz	Mor 69	14:32.08	2)	Berlin	01 Sep	1998
Liu	Shixiang	Chi 71	14:32.33	3)h1	Shanghai	21 Oct	1997
	Wami		14:36.08	3)	Berlin	01 Sep	1998
Fernanda	Ribeiro	Por 69	14:36.45	1)	Hechtel	22 Jul	1995
Ingrid	Kristiansen	Nor 56	14:37.33	1)	Stockholm	05 Aug	1986
Liu	Shixiang		14:38.14	3)	Shanghai	23 Oct	1997
Leah	Malot	Ken 72	14:39.83	1)	Berlin	01 Sep	2000
Yin	Lili	Chi 79	14:39.96	4)	Shanghai	23 Oct	1997
	Ouaziz		14:40.19	1)	Stockholm	05 Aug	1998
	Szabó		14:40.59	1)	Berlin	07 Sep	1999
	Szabó		14:40.61	2)	Berlin	01 Sep	2000
	Szabó		14:40.79	1)	Sydney	25 Sep	2000
Sonia	O'Sullivan	Ire 69	14:41.02	2)	Sydney	25 Sep	2000
	Ribeiro		14:41.07	1)	Oslo	05 Jul	1996
	Szabó		14:41.12	2)	Oslo	05 Jul	1996
Ayelech	Worku	Eti 79	14:41.23	1)	London	05 Aug	2000
	Ouaziz		14:41.34	2)	Berlin	07 Sep	1999
	O'Sullivan		14:41.40	1)	Berlin	01 Sep	1995
Yin	Lili		14:41.47	1)h2	Shanghai	21 Oct	1997
	Szabó		14:41.82	1)	Seville	27 Aug	1999
	Ouaziz		14:42.03	1)	London	07 Aug	1999
Irina	Mikitenko	Ger 72	14:42.03	3)	Berlin	07 Sep	1999
	Ouaziz		14:42.11	1)	Saint-Denis	04 Jun	1998
	Wami		14:42.33	3)	Sydney	25 Sep	2000
Olga	Yegorova	Rus 72	14:42.91	1))	Stockholm	01 Aug	2000
	Szabó		14:42.43	1)	Oslo	04 Jul	1997
	Ouaziz		14:43.15	2)	Seville	27 Aug	1999
Paula	Radcliffe	GB 73	14:43.54	2)	London	07 Aug	1999
Elana	Meyer	SA 66	14:44.05	2)	Hechtel	22 Jul	1995
	Szabó		14:44.21	1)	Brussels	22 Aug	1997
	Worku		14:44.22	3)	Seville	27 Aug	1999
	Szabó		14:44.35	1)	Berlin	26 Aug	1997
	Ouaziz		14:44.35	1)	Rome	14 Jul	1998
	Szabó		14:44.42	1)	Cologne	16 Aug	1996
Roberta	Brunet	Ita 65	14:44.50	2)	Cologne	16 Aug	1996
	Wami		14:44.51	2)	Rome	14 Jul	1998
Derartu	Tulu	Eti 72	14:44.57	3)	Stockholm	01 Aug	2000
	Wami		14:44.61	2)	Saint-Denis	04 Jun	1998
Julia	Vaquero	Spa 70	14:44.95	3)	Oslo	05 Jul	1996

	Ribeiro		14:45.10	2)	Berlin	01 Sep	1995
Lan	Lixin	Chi 79	14:45.33	2)h2	Shanghai	21 Oct	1997
Regina	Jacobs	USA 63	14:45.35	1)	Sacramento	21 Jul	2000
	Radcliffe		14:45.51	2)	Brussels	22 Aug	1997
Song	Liqing	Chi 80	14:45.71	3)h2	Shanghai	21 Oct	1997
Jiang	Bo		14:45.90	1)	Nanjing	24 Oct	1995
Tegla	Loroupe	Ken 73	14:45.95	3)	London	05 Aug	2000

(52 performances by 23 performers)

10,000 metres

Wang	Junxia	Chi 73	29:31.78	1)	Beijing	08 Sep	1993
Zhong	Huandi	Chi 67	30:13.37	2)	Beijing	08 Sep	1993
Ingrid	Kristiansen	Nor 56	30:13.74	1)	Oslo	05 Jul	1986
Deartu	Tulu	Eti 72	30:17.49	1)	Sydney	30 Sep	2000
Gete	Wami	Eti 74	30:22.48	2)	Sydney	30 Sep	2000
Fernanda	Ribeiro	Por 69	30:22.88	3)	Sydney	30 Sep	2000
	Kristiansen		30:23.25	1)	Stuttgart	30 Aug	1986
	Wami		30:24.56	1)	Seville	26 Aug	1999
Paula	Radcliffe	GB 73	30:26.97	4)	Sydney	30 Sep	2000
	Radcliffe		30:27.13	2)	Seville	26 Aug	1999
Tegla	Lorouoe	Ken 73	30:32.03	3)	Seville	26 Aug	1999
	Loroupe		30:37.26	5)	Sydney	30 Sep	2000
Dong	Yanmei	Chi 77	30:38.09	1)	Shanghai	19 Oct	1997
Lan	Lixin	Chi 79	30:39.41	2)	Shanghai	19 Oct	1997
Yin	Lili	Chi 79	30:39.98	3)	Shanghai	19 Oct	1997
	Radcliffe		30:40.70	1)	Barakaldo	10 Apr	1999
Dong	Zhaoxia	Chi 74	30:47.22	4)	Shanghai	19 Oct	1997
Wang	Dongmei	Chi 72	30:47.72	5)	Shanghai	19 Oct	1997
	Ribeiro		30:48.06	1)	Lisbon	04 Apr	1998
	Kristiansen		30:48.51	1)	Oslo	01 Jul	1989
	Radcliffe		30:48.58	2)	Lisbon	04 Apr	1998
Wang	Junxia		30:49.30	1)	Stuttgart	21 Aug	1993
Wang	Junxia		30:50.34	1)	Hiroshima	15 Oct	1994
Berhane	Adere	Eti 73	30:51.30	1)	Heusden	05 Aug	2000
Elana	Meyer	SA 66	30:52.51	1)	London	10 Sep	1994
Sonia	O'Sullivan	Ire 69	30:53.37	6)	Sydney	30 Sep	2000
Liu	Shixiang	Chi 71	30:55.83	6)	Shanghai	19 Oct	1997
	Tulu		30:56.4	1)	Gijón	12 Aug	2000
Elizabeth	Lynch-McColgan	GB 64	30:57.07	1)	Hengelo	25 Jun	1991
Olga	Bondarenko	USR 60	30:57.21	2)	Stuttgart	30 Aug	1986
Leah	Malot	Ken 72	30:57.70	2)	Heusden	05 Aug	2000
	Kristiansen		30:59.42	1)	Oslo	27 Jul	1985
Merima	Hashim	Eti 81	30:59.92	3)	Heusden	05 Aug	2000
	Ribeiro		31:01.63	1)	Atlanta	02 Aug	1996
Wang	Junxia		31:01.76	1)h2	Nanjing	07 May	1996
Wang	Junxia		31:02.58	2)	Atlanta	02 Aug	1996
Marleen	Renders	Bel 68	31:03.60	4)	Heusden	05 Aug	2000
Kathrin	Ullrich	Ger 67	31:03.62	1)	Frankfurt/M.	30 Jun	1991
	Ribeiro		31:04.25	2)	London	10 Sep	1994
	Ribeiro		31:04.99	1)	Göteborg	09 Aug	1995
	Bondarenko		31:05.21	1)	Seoul	30 Sep	1988
Maura	Viceconte	Ita 67	31:05.57	5)	Heusden	05 Aug	2000
	Kristiansen		31:05.85	1)	Rome	04 Sep	1987
	Tulu		31:06.02	1)	Barcelona	07 Aug	1992
	Wami		31:06.65	3)	Atlanta	02 Aug	1996
Li	Ji	Chi 79	31:06.94	7)	Sydney	30 Sep	2000
	Lynch-McColgan		31:06.99	1)	Oslo	02 Jul	1988
Jill	Hunter	GB 66	31:07.88	2)	Frankfurt/M.	30 Jun	1991
	Tulu		31:08.10	2)	Göteborg	09 Aug	1995
	Tulu		31:08.27	1)	Brunswick	01 Jul	2000

(50 performances by 26 performers)

2001

3000 metres

Olga	Yegorova	Rus 72	8:23.26	1)	Zurich	17 Aug
Gabriela	Szabó	Rom 75	8:24.19	2)	Zurich	17 Aug
Yelena	Zadorozhnaya	Rus 77	8:25.40	2)	Rome	29 Jun
Tatyana	Tomashova	Rus 75	8:25.56	3)	Rome	29 Jun
Berhane	Adere	Eti 73	8:25.62	3)	Zurich	17 Aug
Paula	Radcliffe	GB 73	8:26.97	5)	Roma	29 Jun
Gete	Wami	Eti 74	8:27.62	4)	Zurich	17 Aug

All Time List: additional performances (q.m. 8:27.58):

Yegorova	8:23.75	1)	Saint-Denis	06 Jul
Yegorova	8:23.96	1)	Rome	29 Jun
Szabó	8:26.44	4)	Rome	29 Jun
Zadorozhnaya	8:26.79	2)	Saint-Denis	06 Jul
Tomashova	8:27.02	3)	Saint-Denis	06 Jul
Szabó	8:27.21	4)	Saint-Denis	06 Jul

5000 metres

Olga	Yegorova	Rus 72	14:29.32	1)	Berlin	31 Aug
Gete	Wami	Eti 74	14:31.69	2)	Berlin	31 Aug
Paula	Radcliffe	GB 73	14:32.44	3)	Berlin	31 Aug
Tatyana	Tomashova	Rus 75	14:39.22	4)	Berlin	31 Aug
Yelena	Zadorozhnaya	Rus 77	14:40.47	1)	Bremen	24 Jun
Edith	Masai	Ken 67	14:45.86	1)	Stockholm	17 Jul
Gabriela	Szabó	Rom 75	14:46.92	2)	Oslo	13 Jul
Rose	Cheruiyot	Ken 76	14:48.97	3)	Oslo	13 Jul
Asmae	Leghzaoui	Mor 76	14:49.32	4)	Oslo	13 Jul
Dong	Yanmei	Chi 77	14:51.58	1)	Guangzhou	23 Nov

All Time List: additional performance (q.m. 14:45.95):

Radcliffe	14:44.21	1)	London	22 Jul

10,000 metres

Paula	Radcliffe	GB 73	30:55.80	1)	Barakaldo	07 Apr
Asmae	Leghzaoui	Mor 76	31:16.94	1)	Tunis	12 Sep
Natalya	Berkut	Ukr 75	31:22.76	1)	Kiev	02 Jul
Susie	Power	Aus 75	31:26.34	1)	Melbourne	06 Dec
Irina	Mikitenko	Ger 72	31:29.55	2)	Barakaldo	07 Apr
Lyudmila	Biktasheva	Rus 74	31:30.6	1)	Tula	08 Jul
Berhane	Adere	Eti 73	31:32.70	1)	Villeneuve d'Ascq	17 Jun
Olivera	Jevtic	Yug 77	31:33.08	2)	Tunis	12 Sep
Ayelech	Worku	Eti 79	31:38.08	2)	Villeneuve d'Ascq	17 Jun
Restituta	Joseph	Tan 71	31:38,18	3)	Villeneuve d'Ascq	17 Jun

All Time List: no additional performance (q.m. 31:08.27).

INDEX MEN
(names mentioned in the written text)

289

Touquet-Daunis, G. (Fra) 17
Treacy, J. (Ire) 114, 118, 129, 131
Truex, M. (USA) 76
Tsuburaya, K. (Jap) 83, 85
Tulloh, B. (GB) 78, 90
Tümmler, B. (Ger) 89, 90
Tuominen, S. (Fin) 96, 101, 102
Tuominen, V. (Fin) 46, 47, 48
Turb, T. (USR) 119

Ukkonen, P. (Fin) 56
Ullsperger, I. (Cze) 68
Ulmala, R. (Fin) 142, 146, 155
Utriainen, M. (Fin) 86

Väätäinen, J. (Fin) 95, 96, 97, 100, 101,
　　　　102, 142
Vainio, M. (Fin) 114, 115, 118, 119, 122,
　　　　123, 124, 125, 128, 129,
　　　　130, 131, 133
Van Aaken, E. (Ger) 178
Van Damme, I. (Bel) 158, 159
Vandewattyne, M. (Bel) 57, 65
Vanin, F. (USR) 50
Vanko, M. (Svk) 166
Verbeeck, B. (Bel) 129
Vermeulen, J. (Fra) 28
Viren, L.A. (Fin) 95, 96, 97, 99, 100, 101,
　　　　102, 103, 105, 106, 107,
　　　　108, 110, 112, 114, 118,
　　　　119, 142, 198
Virgin, C. (USA) 115, 118
Virtanen, L. (Fin) 40, 41, 44, 45, 47
Voigt, E. (GB) 21
Vrábel, M. (Cze) 133
Vuorio, P. (Fin) 97

Wadoux, J. (Fra) 92, 96
Waitz, J. (Nor) 178
Walker, J. (NZ) 128, 129, 131
Warburton, J. (GB) 13
Ward, R. (Aus) 83
Watkins, H. (GB) 17
Watman, M. (GB) 18
Weigt, P. (Ger) 110
Wessinghage, T. (Ger) 115, 120, 122, 124,
　　　　130
Whetton, J. (GB) 149
White, J. (GB) 13, 17
Wide, E. (Swe) 32, 33, 35, 36, 37, 39
Wiggs, M. (GB) 87
Wilhelmsen, T. (Nor) 50
Williams, P. (Can) 141

Williams, T. (USA) 150, 152, 163
Wilson, J. (GB) 30, 31, 65
Wilt, F. (USA) 73
Wolde, Mamo (Eti) 85, 91, 92
Wolde, Million (Eti) 167, 169, 171, 173,
　　　　174, 175, 176, 214
Wooderson, S. (GB) 50, 52

Yefimov, B. (USR) 77
Yifter, M. (Eti) 100, 107, 109, 110, 111,
　　　　112, 115, 118, 119, 120,
　　　　152, 167, 168, 196
Young, G. (USA) 88

Zabala, J.C. (Arg) 45
Zaddem, A. (Tun) 100
Zakharov, Y. (USR) 77
Zamperini, L. (USA) 46
Zander, J. (Swe) 28, 30
Zanta, F. (Cze) 55
Zarcone, L. (Ita) 114
Zátopek, E. (Cze) 9, 49, 52, 53, 54, 55,
　　　　56, 57, 58, 59, 62, 63,
　　　　65, 66, 68, 69, 70, 71,
　　　　72, 73, 75, 79, 108,
　　　　119, 167
Zhukov, Y. (USR) 75, 76
Zimny, K. (Pol) 75, 76, 78
Znamenskiy, G. (USR) 68
Znamenskiy, S. (USR) 68
Zuntar, D. (Yug) 93
Zur Megede, E. (Ger) 177

INDEX WOMEN
(names mentioned in the written text)

BIBLIOGRAPHY

Berendonk, B. "Doping, von der Forschung zum Betrug", Rowohlt Sport, Hamburg 1992.

Clarke, R. "The Unforgiving Minute" (as told to Alan Trengove), Pelham Books, London 1966.

Cumming, J. "Runners and Walkers. A Nineteenth Century Sports Chronicle", Regnery Gateway, Chicago, 1981.

Doherty, K. "Track & Field Omnibook", Tafnews Press, Los Altos, California, 1980.

Espana, R. "Jean Bouin de Marseille", Editions Autres Temps, Marseille 1999.

Haikkola, R. & Vuorio, P. "Lasse Viren, Kullatut Sekunnit", Weilin + Göös, Helsinki 1973.

Hannus, M. "Flying Finns", Tietosanoma, Helsinki 1990.

Hartmann, R. "Schwarzes Gold - auf den Spuren der afrikanischen Läufer", Edition Spiridon, Hilden 1979.

Heidenstrom, P. "Athletes of the Century - 100 Years of New Zealand Track and Field", G.P.Publications Ltd., Wellington, New Zealand, 1992.

Hendershott, J., "Ron Clarke Talks Track", Tafnews Press, Los Altos, California 1972.

Karikko, P. & Koski, M. "Paavo Nurmi", Weilin + Göös, Helsinki 1965.

Kök, N., Magnusson, R., Potts, D.H., Quercetani, R.L.. "Track & Field Performances Through the Years", Volumes 1, 2, 3 and 4, ATFS, Florence/Copenhagen, 1986, '89, '92 and '97.

Laitinen, E. "10,000 m. Results and Statistics", Pikkala 1985.

Phillips, Bob "Honour of Empire, Glory of Sport, The History of Athletics at the Commonwealth Games" , The Parrs Wood Press, Manchester, 2000.

Shearman, M. "Athletics and Football", Longmans, Green and Co., London 1888.

Shrubb, A.A. "Running and Cross-Country Running", Health and Strength, London 1908.

Tanser, T. "Train Hard, Win Easy - the Kenyan Way", Tafnews Press, Mountain View, California, 1997.

Thom, W. "Pedestrianism", Brown and Frost, Aberdeen 1813.

Watman, M. "History of British Athletics", Robert Hale, London 1968.

Webster, F.A.M., "Great Moments in Athletics", Country Life Ltd., London 1947.

Wilt, F., "How They Train", Track & Field News, Los Altos, California 1959.

Zur Megede, E. & Hymans, R., "Progression of World Best Performances and Official IAAF World Records", International Athletic Foundation, Monaco 1995.